# A Land of Milk and Honey?

# A Land of Milk and Honey?
## Making Sense of Aotearoa New Zealand

Edited by Avril Bell, Vivienne Elizabeth,
Tracey McIntosh and Matt Wynyard

AUCKLAND
UNIVERSITY
PRESS

First published 2017

Auckland University Press
University of Auckland
Private Bag 92019
Auckland 1142
New Zealand
www.press.auckland.ac.nz

© The contributors, 2017

ISBN 978 1 86940 862 6

A catalogue record for this book is available from the
National Library of New Zealand

This book is copyright. Apart from fair dealing for the purpose of private study, research, criticism or review, as permitted under the Copyright Act, no part may be reproduced by any process without prior permission of the publisher. The moral rights of the author have been asserted.

Cover photograph by Marti Friedlander, *Mt Eden Normal Primary School, Valley Road*, 1981
Cover design by Gideon Keith, Seven
Typeset by Westchester Publishing Services

This book was printed on FSC® certified paper

Printed in China by Everbest Printing Co. Ltd

This book is dedicated to Emeritus Professor
Ranginui Walker (1932–2016).
His work informed and shaped a nation.
An educator, a scholar and an activist who spoke truth to power.

*Kei te pitau whakarei e Rangi*
*Nā tō uhi ka puta ki te whaiao ngā māharahara o ngai tāua*
*Ko koe rā te whakahua ake o te whakataukī*
*'Ka whawhai tonu tātou mō ake tonu atu'*
*Waiho mā āu pia pono te whawhai e kawe, e moe e te rangatira, e moe*

# Contents

Introduction *Avril Bell* ........ 1

**Part I: Foundations: State and Nation**

1 Plunder in the Promised Land: Māori Land Alienation and the Genesis of Capitalism in Aotearoa New Zealand *Matt Wynyard* ........ 13
2 Rangatiratanga, Kāwanatanga and the Constitution *Ranginui Walker* ........ 26
3 We're All in This Together? Democracy and Politics in Aotearoa New Zealand *Richard Shaw* ........ 43
4 Imagining Aotearoa New Zealand: The Politics of National Imaginings *Avril Bell* ........ 57

**Part II: New Zealand Peoples**

5 Ka Pū Te Ruha, Ka Hao Te Rangatahi: Māori Identities in the Twenty-first Century *Tahu Kukutai and Melinda Webber* ........ 71
6 Pākehā Ethnicity: The Politics of White Privilege *Steve Matthewman* ........ 83
7 Deconstructing the Big Brown Tails/Tales: Pasifika Peoples in Aotearoa New Zealand *Karlo Mila* ........ 95
8 The Asianisation of Aotearoa: Immigration Impacts *Paul Spoonley* ........ 108

**Part III: Social Class and Economic Inequalities**

9 The Land of Me and Money? New Zealand Society under Neoliberalism *Louise Humpage* ........ 121
10 Rich and Poor: Class Division in Aotearoa New Zealand *Bruce Curtis and Marko Galic* ........ 134
11 Poverty in a Land of Plenty: The Poor Will Always Be with Us? *Kellie McNeill* ........ 146

12  Social Mobility in Aotearoa New Zealand in the
    Neoliberal Era: Increasing or Decreasing?
    *Gerry Cotterell*                                                158

**Part IV: Genders and Sexualities**
13  We Still Need Feminism in Aotearoa: The Achievements
    and Unfinished Tasks of the Women's Movement
    *Julia Schuster*                                                 173
14  Homosexuality in Aotearoa New Zealand: Regulation
    and Resistance  *Johanna Schmidt*                                186
15  Man-Up? A Socio-historical Examination of Pākehā and
    Māori Masculinities  *Richard Pringle*                           198
16  Gender Inequalities Are a Thing of the Past. Yeah, Right!
    *Vivienne Elizabeth*                                             212

**Part V: Contemporary Issues and Divides**
17  Ageing Well? Social Support and Inequalities for Older
    New Zealanders  *Ngaire Kerse*                                   227
18  No Promised Land: Domestic Violence, Marginalisation
    and Masculinity  *Vivienne Elizabeth*                            239
19  Locked Up: Incarceration in Aotearoa New Zealand
    *Tracey McIntosh and Bartek Goldmann*                            251
20  The Urban(e) and the Metro-rural in Aotearoa
    *Peter J. Howland*                                               264
21  Clean, Green Aotearoa New Zealand?  *Corrina Tucker*             278

References                                                           291
Contributors                                                         321
Index                                                                325

# Introduction

## Avril Bell

The phrase 'land of milk and honey' originally appeared in the Old Testament, describing the longed-for homeland to Jewish people in exile. It was a utopian image of a homeland of agricultural abundance, promising a good life for all. From this biblical origin, the term has spread widely and been used more broadly to refer to the promise of a good life in a new land. Unsurprisingly then, it has often been used to refer to the promise of New World societies, such as Aotearoa New Zealand, to which settler migrants flocked in the eighteenth and nineteenth centuries. Arguably, it encapsulates the hopes of all migrants, who leave their homes to escape various undesirable realities and in the hope of better lives and futures elsewhere.

    The vision of a land of milk and honey played a powerful part in the mythologies generated by those involved in the colonisation of Aotearoa New Zealand and continued to shape ideas about what it would mean to live in this country throughout much of the twentieth century. In the original usage, the image pointed directly to agricultural abundance, making it particularly appropriate in thinking about Aotearoa New Zealand, where the export economy has always been agriculturally based. In the twenty-first century, milk and honey quite literally play significant roles in the national economy – milk, since dairying became an export leader around the turn of the century, and honey, a much more minor player, but increasingly a valuable export commodity since the identification of its anti-bacterial properties by the Honey Research Unit of the University of Waikato in 1981. If the internet is anything to go by, this phrase is still widely in use in relation to Aotearoa New Zealand. An internet search for 'land of milk and honey' and 'New Zealand' resulted in 41,200 hits (19 April 2016), with migration and agricultural industry websites being prominent, and uncritical, users of this image to describe Aotearoa New Zealand.

But this internet search also uncovered sources that critique the idea that Aotearoa New Zealand lives up to the promise of a land of milk and honey. This collection of essays likewise takes such a critical stance. We invoke this image of the migrants' promised land as a signifier of the failed promises of Aotearoa New Zealand. Our view is that in the twenty-first century it is clear that, for many, the promise is not being fulfilled. Despite how agricultural exporters seek to promote their products and immigration consultants seek to represent this country, there are many signs of the limits of, and problems created by, our agricultural abundance. Environmental issues are very much on the table. Our 'clean, green' image is under the microscope, brought into question especially as the link between the ongoing expansion of dairying and declining water quality is made clear.

There are also significant social problems created by the unequal sharing of economic rewards in our society. Aotearoa New Zealand never offered equal opportunity for all, despite the national mythology of egalitarianism. In recent decades, however, some historical inequalities have been deepened, while others have been lessened, but not overcome. The landscape of inequalities and social divides in our society is a complex one. In particular, thirty years of neoliberal economics and globalising politics have exacerbated already existing inequalities that are differentially experienced by class, ethnicity, gender, sexuality and age, and are also reflected in a number of social problems that are widely recognised to be confronting our society. These social divides and problems are at the heart of this collection.

The editors of this collection have all taught introductory Sociology courses on New Zealand society at the University of Auckland. The idea for the book came about from our desire for an up-to-date collection to act as a reader for our students. We hope also that this book has something to offer to a wider audience of New Zealanders interested in broad overviews of where we have come from, where we are and where we could be headed as a society.

For the collection we approached a number of sociological experts to respond to the image of the land of milk and honey and its inverse – scarcity and inequality – in relation to their various areas of expertise. Given our sociological focus, most of the chapters address the social, economic and cultural inequalities that divide New Zealanders. Some chapters are historical in focus, and many involve an historical dimension, providing a view on how we have come to be where we are today as a society. Each chapter stands alone as the viewpoint of its author(s), based on their research expertise and knowledge base, and no attempt has been made to provide any overall coherence and agreement between them.

Overall, this collection offers various ways of 'making sense' of Aotearoa New Zealand through a sociological lens. The facts of social life don't speak for themselves, but require interpretation. Sociology is particularly concerned with the patterning of social life – with how society's resources and rewards are distributed unevenly to different social groups. Where such uneven patterns are discernible, sociologists argue that the resulting problems are 'public issues' and not just 'personal troubles', in the influential words of American sociologist C. Wright Mills. In other words, what we experience as our personal difficulties – or privileges – are often, in fact, the outcome of large-scale social and historical processes. Rather than being our 'fault' – or evidence of our merit – much of what accounts for our individual social position is the product of forces at work at the societal, or even global, level. Throughout this collection the authors demonstrate how this kind of sociological way of thinking can help us make sense of important features of the society we live in.

## Chapter Overview

The book is divided into sections organised around particular features of New Zealand society. In Part I: Foundations: State and Nation, contributors explore various foundational features of the political and ideological structure that organise social life in Aotearoa New Zealand. We begin the collection with a focus on the historical foundations of Aotearoa New Zealand's agricultural economy in the settler colonial project. Matt Wynyard reminds us that the basis of our capitalist and agricultural economy lies in the alienation of Māori land. Wynyard draws on Marx's theory of primitive accumulation to argue that the systematic dispossession of Māori land in the nineteenth and early twentieth centuries established the preconditions necessary for capitalism in Aotearoa New Zealand and created lasting patterns of inequality between Māori and Pākehā that continue to the present day. This chapter is paired with the next, in which the late Ranginui Walker tracks the evolution of rangatiratanga, as a political response to the arrival of Pākehā, and kāwanatanga, focusing in particular on the history of Te Whakaminenga, the United Tribes of New Zealand, and of the Kīngitanga. Both of these were attempts to unite Māori and to express rangatiratanga that remain relevant today and continue to lay challenges to the nation's developing constitution.

The following two chapters in this part address the themes of democracy and national identity respectively. In his chapter, Richard Shaw explores the state of our democracy, beginning with an overview of the history of political representation and participation of women and Māori in Aotearoa New Zealand as a reminder of how hard-won these democratic rights and freedoms have been, before turning to the current declines in political participation and controversies over political interference in the democratic process in this era of 'dirty politics'. Overall, Shaw argues for the continuing importance of democratic engagement and exhorts us not to take our rights and freedoms for granted. I then focus on some of the key themes involved in the construction of New Zealand national identity, primarily the *politics* of national identity. I consider in particular the ways in which stories of national identity can be exclusionary for some sectors of the population and the ways in which our identification with the nation can be manipulated and exploited by powerful economic and political interests.

Part II: New Zealand Peoples explores some of the issues faced by the diverse ethnic groups that make up our society, and issues we face as a highly culturally diverse society. Tahu Kukutai and Melinda Webber explore continuities and changes in the present patterns and practices of Māori ethnic identification. Kukutai and Webber reflect on the influence that changing socio-cultural contexts have for Māori identifications, particularly in relation to two key institutions – the New Zealand Census of Population and schools. Although whakapapa continues to be an important basis of collectivity and hence identification for Māori, the authors note that what it means to be Māori in the twenty-first century is open to a number of interpretations. Steve Matthewman then takes a critical look at Pākehā through the lens of ethnicity, understood as a system of stratification that bestows advantages and disadvantages, and is linked to a raft of inequalities. Pākehā advantages stem from colonisation, which as I argue elsewhere is better understood as a social structure that continues to have effects rather than an historical event no longer relevant to our present (Bell 2014).

Two of the key 'new settler' groups, Pasifika peoples and Asian New Zealanders, are the focus of the next two chapters. Karlo Mila takes an historical approach to interrogate the socio-economic and discursive positioning of Pasifika peoples in Aotearoa New Zealand. Mila documents the way the economic crises of the 1970s and subsequent structural transformation of the country's economy from the mid-1980s onwards resulted in Pasifika peoples becoming both an economically disadvantaged and racialised minority who are largely blocked from reaping milk and honey. In his chapter, Paul Spoonley provides an overview of the historical changes to Aotearoa New Zealand's ethnic make-up and identifies a number of issues and challenges these changes raise for our society, especially in 'super-diverse' Auckland. Spoonley argues that this rapid cultural diversification creates challenges for the cohesion of New Zealand society, and for our national identity. How biculturalism and multiculturalism are to be coordinated, and what it means to be a 'New Zealander' in this new cultural landscape, are both issues that we face as a society.

In Part III: Social Class and Economic Inequalities, contributors address the present state of significant fractures in the economic fabric of Aotearoa New Zealand in this era of neoliberal economics. This part begins with Louise Humpage's consideration of the impact of neoliberalism on our contemporary society. Humpage begins by defining neoliberalism's predecessor, Keynesianism, and detailing the role it played in post-war Aotearoa New Zealand, before outlining the ideological and political shift towards neoliberalism that took place in Aotearoa New Zealand in the mid-1980s. Humpage also examines the emergence of various alterations and extensions of the neoliberal project embodied in, for example, neoconservative and Third Way strategies of government. Bruce Curtis and Marko Galic then use a Marxist approach to class to identify the class divides of New Zealand society in the neoliberal era. They argue that the divide between the capitalist and working classes remains primary, with the idea of 'middle classness' being an ideological smokescreen that encourages aspiration and entices workers to buy into the capitalist system. However, the logic of neoliberal globalisation has made even middle-class jobs precarious for many, pointing up the essential two-class divide of capitalist economics.

The following two chapters in various ways address the empirical fallout of the neoliberal economy. Kellie McNeill examines poverty in contemporary Aotearoa New Zealand. McNeill considers the structural and historical underpinnings of contemporary poverty and draws attention to the ways in which the experience of poverty is patterned in contemporary Aotearoa New Zealand in terms of social divisions such as age and ethnicity. The issue of social mobility, so crucial to the migrant dream of making good in a new country, is the focus of Gerry Cotterell's chapter. Cotterell defines social mobility before examining the possibilities for social mobility in the post-war Keynesian economy. He then considers the impact of neoliberalism on social mobility, arguing that mobility has become much more difficult for many people in Aotearoa New Zealand since the reforms of the 1980s and 1990s.

In Part IV: Genders and Sexualities, attention turns to the impacts of patriarchy and heteronormativity on gender and sexual difference in Aotearoa New Zealand's history, and on continuing challenges we still face as a society. Julia Schuster charts the history of feminist activism in

Aotearoa New Zealand through an examination of two key issues: women's political participation and male violence against women. While the First, Second and Third Waves of feminist activism have been responsible for some very significant strides towards the achievement of gender justice, Schuster points out that women in Aotearoa New Zealand are still under-represented in formal politics and they still suffer from one of the highest rates of physical and sexual violence in the Western world. Such findings indicate, contrary to the claims of post-feminism, that feminist activism remains necessary if gender justice is to be attained. Johanna Schmidt also brings an historical dimension to her examination of the social and legal regulation of homosexuality. She traces the history of its definition as heterosexuality's deviant other and its legal marginalisation through the 1800s and into the mid-1900s. Paradoxically, the view of homosexuals as deviant individuals created the basis for the rise of the gay liberation movement in the 1960s and 1970s, first in the United States and then in other Western countries like Aotearoa New Zealand. Gay activism in Aotearoa New Zealand has achieved a number of important legal victories, yet Schmidt raises questions about whether its most recent victories – the Civil Union Act in 2004 and the Marriage (Definition of Marriage) Amendment Act in 2013 – are merely indicative of the operation of hegemonic power.

Richard Pringle then explores how power has worked to privilege a particular kind of masculinity that, following Australian sociologist Raewyn Connell, can be described as hegemonic masculinity. Pringle shows that historically this form of masculinity has been aligned with Pākehā men, as reflected in widely shared ideas about who are Aotearoa New Zealand's national heroes. He also shows that Māori masculinity has operated as the marginalised 'other' for Pākehā masculinity, with damaging historical and contemporary consequences for Māori men. Gender inequalities are again the focus of Vivienne Elizabeth's chapter, in which she takes issue with post-feminist contentions that the power of gender has dissipated to such an extent that young women's lives are no longer shaped by it. Through an examination of the contemporary labour market Elizabeth shows that the labour market in Aotearoa New Zealand continues to display marked gender differences and gendered inequalities. In making sense of these and other features of social life that continue to be highly gendered, she argues we need to recognise not only the constraining effects of gender for women but also its capacity to work through our desires to be certain kinds of people and to do certain kinds of things.

The final section of the book, Part V: Contemporary Issues and Divides, addresses a number of key challenges and divisions we face looking forward to the future. Our ageing population is the focus of Ngaire Kerse's chapter. Kerse uses detailed demographic data to identify the ethnic diversity of Aotearoa New Zealand's ageing population and to tease out the issues faced by these different groups in ageing well. Her discussion also points to the challenges and opportunities we face as a society as the proportion of older people greatly increases over coming decades. Problems of violence and crime are the focus of the next two chapters. Vivienne Elizabeth addresses the extensive problem of domestic violence in Aotearoa New Zealand. Elizabeth outlines the social patterning of domestic violence, locating it in structures of power – patriarchy, neoliberal capitalism and colonialism. She argues that these structures establish expectations of dominance and power at home for heterosexual men that are thwarted for some groups of men under the conditions of neoliberal capitalism found in Aotearoa New Zealand. Against this backdrop, violence is used by men who are invested in patriarchal family regimes to restore, albeit often temporarily, their sense of power and control over female partners and children. Tracey McIntosh and Bartek Goldmann then look at changes in the public discourse around, and policy settings relating to, incarceration, arguing that these changes have resulted in the criminalisation of the poor and especially of Māori in a time of declining crime rates. They also point to various alternatives to incarceration that have been introduced, or could be introduced, to reform our criminal justice system.

To conclude the collection we turn again to aspects of New Zealanders' relation to the land. The changing relationships between the urban and the rural in Aotearoa New Zealand are the focus of Peter J. Howland's chapter. Howland uses these relationships to highlight important challenges for our society, ranging from urban gentrification to the development of new 'metro-rural' areas fringing some of our major cities. Corrina

Tucker's focus is also environmental, in this case the environmental consequences of agricultural production. She argues that the 'clean, green' catchphrase is a 'national place myth' that does not reflect the real state of our environment. Tucker identifies food production as the most prominent contributor to our unsustainable ecological footprint, and focuses in particular on the production and consumption of red meat, detailing the interplay of factors that make this environmentally untenable as we grapple with the need to address climate change.

**PART I**

# Foundations

*State and Nation*

CHAPTER 1

# Plunder in the Promised Land

*Māori Land Alienation and the Genesis of Capitalism in Aotearoa New Zealand*

## Matt Wynyard

On 19 November 2014, Prime Minister John Key told Northland's Te Hiku Radio that he believed New Zealand had been 'settled peacefully' by the British in the nineteenth century:

> When we talk about the Treaty and sovereignty and all those matters, you take a step back and say 'well, what was really happening?' In my view New Zealand was one of the very few countries in the world that were settled peacefully. Māori probably acknowledge that settlers had a place to play and bought [*sic*] with them a lot of skills and a lot of capital. (Key 2014)

Here the Prime Minister rehearses what is a widely held – and, for some Pākehā no doubt, comforting – claim: that the historical experience of colonisation in Aotearoa New Zealand was comparatively benign. It is a claim that suggests a past, however, that bears little resemblance to the actual history of the colonisation of Aotearoa: a history of conquest, predation and thievery; a history in which force played a crucial role. Indeed, as Weaver (1999, 18) has argued, the very idea of 'settlement' understates the 'aggressive vigour' that was central to the acquisition of Māori land. Nor is the Prime Minister correct in his assertion that settlers brought with them an abundance of capital. On the contrary, much of the capital necessary to the future wealth of New Zealand was already here, in the form of communally owned Māori land. The British settlers who came to these shores in the nineteenth century were, for the most part, poor people. Many were former peasant farmers, driven from their own homes in Britain and stripped of communally held assets and resources by the self-same processes of enclosure and dispossession that would all but destroy Māori society in the late nineteenth century. Far from unique, the broad experience of colonisation in Aotearoa New Zealand typifies the experience of indigenous peoples around the world as Māori were stripped of their land, and the freedoms, rights and possibilities attached to it, and given no option but to join the cycle of capitalism.

The colonisation of Aotearoa in the nineteenth century followed a particular pattern typical in what Pearson (2001) refers to as 'settler societies'. Settler societies, such as Aotearoa New Zealand, Australia and Canada, are the outcome of a specific form of colonisation in which increasingly large groups of people were encouraged to emigrate and settle permanently in a particular territory. Often the initial interest in these territories was for short-term economic gain through, for example, sealing, whaling and fur-trapping. Only subsequently did the idea of permanent mass settlement begin to crystallise (Pearson 2001, 4–5). As Pearson argues, mass colonisation grew out of more limited patterns of settlement, either as British and settler interests sought to extend direct control over the territory, or as a means to allow Britain to rid itself of a poor and potentially revolutionary surplus population (see also Steven 1989).

These kinds of settler societies, based on permanent and massive colonial settlement, required the ongoing political, economic and cultural subjugation of the indigenous population. Indeed, settler societies are those societies 'in which Europeans have settled and where their descendants have remained politically dominant over the indigenous population'

(Stasiulis and Yuval Davies as cited in Pearson 2001, 5). The colonisation of Aotearoa was all about achieving, extending and maintaining settler dominance over the indigenous Māori population. The alienation of Māori land was one central mechanism of colonisation, along with 'wholesale destruction and killing' (Savage 2010), summary execution, and the suppression of language, culture and spirituality, through which settlers were able to achieve dominance over Māori.

This chapter tells the story of the systematic dispossession of Māori land in the nineteenth and early twentieth centuries, a process that established the preconditions necessary for capitalism in Aotearoa New Zealand and contributed to enduring patterns of inequality between Māori and Pākehā that continue to this day. In telling this story, the chapter makes use of Marx's theory of primitive accumulation. In the closing pages of volume 1 of *Capital*, Marx ([1867] 1976) details the violence that characterises the transition to the capitalist mode of production; and the myriad forms of force, fraud and oppression that establish the conditions necessary to the functioning of capitalist relations. Primitive accumulation describes the process through which various lands and resources hitherto held in common are captured, enclosed and converted into individual private property. The original owners and inhabitants are 'suddenly and forcibly torn' (876) from the land and left with no means of subsistence other than to sell themselves as labour. Marx argues that while capitalism comes into being 'dripping from head to toe, from every pore with blood and dirt' (926), the inherently violent methods of primitive accumulation are often obscured by 'idyllic' accounts of history (874), such as Prime Minister Key's mistaken view that the settlement of Aotearoa New Zealand was peaceful.

In order to tell the story of the genesis of capitalism in Aotearoa New Zealand, I want first to briefly define capitalism as it was revealed through Marx's analysis. Marx understood capitalism as an exploitative relationship between two very different groups of people: the first group being the owners of money and of the means of production and subsistence (i.e., the various tools, farms, factories and raw materials used in production), and the second group being the so-called free workers, those with no means of subsistence other than to sell themselves as labour. There is, Marx ([1867] 1976, 273) argues, nothing natural about this relation: 'Nature does not produce on the one hand owners of money and commodities and on the other hand men possessing nothing but their own labour power. This relation has no basis in natural history, nor does it have a social basis common to all periods of human history.' Rather, Marx contends, this relation had first to be created. Violent methods of primitive accumulation were needed to strip lands and resources away from the many and accrue them in the hands of the few.

For Marx, the basis of the whole process of primitive accumulation is the expropriation of the agricultural producer from the soil. The history of this expropriation 'assumes different aspects in different countries and runs through its various phases in different orders of succession' ([1867] 1976, 876). In chapters 27 and 28 of *Capital*, Marx details the expropriation of the land from the agricultural population in Britain. Here I detail the expropriation of Māori soil in Aotearoa New Zealand, and the processes through which Māori land came to form the basis of a capitalist economy, creating wealth for many settlers and their descendants, and leaving most Māori with nothing to sell but their own labour (for more on class divisions, see Curtis and Galic in this volume).

## Primitive Accumulation Pure and Simple: Cupidity, Conquest, Confiscation

As is typical of settler societies, the initial economic interest in Aotearoa New Zealand was fleeting and lay not in the fat of the land but rather in the fat of the sea. Long before anyone thought of converting communally owned Māori rainforest into pasture for sheep and cattle, sealers and whalers discovered a rich abundance of prey in the waters surrounding these islands. The industrial revolution in Britain fuelled a growing demand for seal and whale oil that was used to light the streets and lubricate factory machinery (Belich 1996, 127). The sealers and whalers who came to Aotearoa in the late eighteenth and early nineteenth centuries did not come as settlers. Rather, the vast majority visited New Zealand only short term, as sojourners, before returning home to Australia, Britain or the United States (see Belich 1996, 127–33). However, a small number of successful whalers such as William Rhodes and Johnny Jones did settle and became increasingly wealthy and prominent (Belich 1996, 133; King 2003, 124). As a result, they were left supremely well placed to prosper once the acquisition of Māori land became a pressing concern. Steven (1989, 27–28) argues that until settlers discovered that pastoral agriculture could yield enormous profits for those who owned the land, it seemed as if peaceful coexistence between settlers and Māori might be possible. As soon as it was discovered that New Zealand's favourable climate allowed for year-round pasture growth, and that wool and meat (and later dairy) could be produced with few resources other than land, settlers wasted no time in contriving ways to separate Māori from their lands (see Wynyard 2016).

Rhodes and Jones were among a small number of wealthy settlers able to exploit a lack of effective Māori resistance in Te Waipounamu (the South Island) and swallow up vast tracts of land into enormous personal estates (see Belich 1996; Eldred-Grigg 1980; King 2003). The introduction of European muskets and diseases had a devastating impact on Māori, reducing both the population and resistance of iwi to colonisation throughout the country. These processes had a particularly devastating impact on Ngāi Tahu (Kāi Tahu), the principle iwi in Te Waipounamu. As Eldred-Grigg (1980, 10) notes, the Māori population of Canterbury fell from around 4000 in 1800 to just 500 in 1840. Further, 'on the Kaikoura coast where 4000 people had been living as late as 1827, despoliation was so complete that by 1857 only 78 Maori survived there. . . . The strength of Ngāi Tahu had been permanently broken. Nothing stood in the way of Pakeha land greed' (10).

Into this vacuum stepped a rapacious few. Rhodes established a vast property empire that stretched from Banks Peninsula to North Otago (Patterson 2012). Jones established himself in Otago and Southland amassing an enormous sub-province of 2 million acres stretching from Waikouaiti to Lake Wanaka, before attempting to purchase the entire South Island, Stewart Island and all adjacent islands for a few hundred pounds (Eldred-Grigg 1980, 10–11). Settler governments subsequently ignored the claims of Rhodes and Jones but this type of land-grabbing nevertheless typified the colonial pattern in Te Waipounamu, where much of the land was snatched up into vast private estates.

Te Tiriti o Waitangi (the Treaty of Waitangi), which gave the British Crown exclusive right to purchase any land Māori were willing to sell and guaranteed Māori the undisturbed possession of any land they wished to retain, should have put an end to settler land-grabbing. This was not the case, however. The European settler population grew dramatically in the middle decades of the nineteenth century, from a little over 2000 in 1840 to just short of 80,000 in 1860 (Statistics New Zealand 2006b, table A 1.1), as more and more would-be settlers left Dickens's Britain for the chance of a new life in this supposed land of milk and honey. For settlers the path to prosperity lay in pastoral farming, which required land; land that Māori in Te Ika-a-Māui (the North Island) were increasingly reluctant to sell or lease to the Crown. Many settlers came to see Māori as an obstacle to their prosperity, and so there was a growing pressure to expropriate Māori land by whatever means necessary (Steven 1989, 28–29; Wynyard 2016).

These tensions came to a head in Taranaki on 17 March 1860 after a junior Te Āti Awa chief, Teira, sold land in Waitara to the Crown against the wishes of the senior chief Wiremu Kingi Te Rangitake. This forced a showdown between a settler government intent on confrontation and Te Āti Awa intent on retaining their ancestral lands. As Belich (1996, 229) puts it, 'War ravaged Taranaki in 1860–1861, and erupted anew in 1863 when [Governor] George Grey . . . invaded the Waikato heartland of the Maori king movement. Warfare continued until 1872, developing into a bewildering series of intersecting conflicts spread over much of the North Island and involving most Maori.'

The New Zealand Wars involved a level of settler ferocity entirely incongruent with the idea of New Zealand as 'settled peacefully' (for a discussion of the Kīngitanga movement, see Walker in this volume). Tony Simpson (1986, 161) argues that settler interests prosecuted the war with a 'ruthless brutality' that shocked even the British Imperial troops called upon to do the settlers' fighting. Eventually these troops, hardened by Britain's imperial adventures elsewhere, 'left the prosecution of the war to the settlers, in disgust at the brutalities the latter were inflicting' (Steven 1989, 29; see also Simpson 1986). Steven (1989, 29) argues that settlers wanted only one thing from Māori, their disappearance altogether, so that their land could be taken and converted into a source of wealth.

As Walker (2004, 129) notes, Māori 'proved a much more formidable military obstacle to the acquisition of land by conquest than anticipated' (see also Walker in this volume). But despite spirited Māori opposition, the better-equipped and more numerous settler forces were able to secure a 'limited but real victory' (Belich [1986] 2015, 200) in the New Zealand Wars. More importantly, in provoking Māori into rebellion, settlers had manufactured a reason to punish Māori, and punish them they did. The key mechanism of punishment was the confiscation of land, facilitated by the 1863 passage of both the Suppression of Rebellion Act and the New Zealand Settlements Act. The former allowed the settler government to punish 'by death, penal servitude or otherwise' (Section II) anyone found to be in rebellion against the Crown, and the latter allowed for the establishment of settlements on any land belonging to Māori in any district where significant numbers had 'entered into combinations and taken up arms ... and are now in open rebellion' (Preamble). The ostensible justification for the Act was the 'protection and security of well-disposed inhabitants of both races' (Preamble). However, the desire for Māori land was palpable in the language of an earlier draft of the legislation, debated in the House of Representatives on 9 November 1863 and reported in both *The Press* and *The New Zealander*, which sought to unlock for settlers 'large tracts of land, lying unoccupied, useless and unproductive' (New Zealand Settlements Bill 1863 Preamble).

These large tracts of land were, of course, far from useless to Māori. But for many settlers, land was 'wrongly idle – wasted – until it yielded wealth' (Weaver 1999, 18). The confiscation of vast tracts of the most fertile land in Waikato, Taranaki and the Eastern Bay of Plenty – sometimes not even from 'rebellious' Māori – certainly enabled future generations of settlers to wrestle wealth from the land. Some 1.2 million acres were taken from Māori in Waikato; 1.28 million were confiscated from Māori in Taranaki; and 738,000 acres were seized by the Crown in Tauranga and the Eastern Bay of Plenty (Ward 1973, 177–8). The impact of confiscation on Māori was devastating, yet not as devastating as what would follow – the legal 'purchase' of Māori land 'at the barrel of the gun' (Walker 2004, 129).

## Theft Made Legal: The Native Land Court

If the primary objective for which the New Zealand Wars had been prosecuted was, as Walker (2004, 135) argues, 'the assertion of sovereignty and the acquisition of land', then a far more successful mechanism for achieving the same ends was the Native Land Court established in 1865. Belich (1996, 258) contends that '[t]his notorious institution was designed to destroy Maori communal land tenure and so both facilitate Pakeha land buying and "detribalise" Maori'. Given the centrality of land to Māori identity as tangata whenua, the forced conversion of communally held land into individual title was 'the most devastating of all the onslaughts the settlers made on Maori as a people' (Steven 1989, 30; see also Walker 2004, 135–6). Similarly, Tony Simpson (1986, 169) claims that the Native Land Court allowed for confiscation with legal countenance: 'It was in its effects one of the most pernicious measures ever enacted by a settler community to get its hands on the estate of the native population.'

There was, as Walker (2004, 136) points out, 'nothing Maori about the Native Land Court since it was designed for Pakeha purposes of freeing up Maori land from collective ownership and making it available to individual settlers'. To this end, the Court granted tenure of Māori land to small numbers of 'owners', usually ten, who, in theory at least, were trustees for wider tribal interests (Belich 1996, 258; Walker 2004, 136). Legally, however, these ten owners were not bound to their wider iwi or hapū and could dispose of the land as they saw fit. With precious few economic opportunities open to Māori at the time, many of those named as owners on certificates of title were tempted into debt. Māori were, Ward (1973, 185–6) notes, confronted by 'a predatory horde of storekeepers, grog sellers, surveyors, lawyers, land agents and money lenders' all seeking to trap them into debt and then use the debt as a lever to force them off their lands (see also Belich 1996; Walker 2004).

The *New Zealand Herald*, a newspaper not renowned for being aligned with Māori interests, was scathing in its assessment of what it saw as the 'scandalous' workings of the Native Land Court:

Time after time has the spectacle been witnessed of large parties of Maoris coming to attend a sitting of the Court. A judge or some indispensable lawyer was not present, and the sitting had to be adjourned for a week or a fortnight. All this time the Maoris were living near a European town; to keep them advances were being made by land buyers, for which advances, as a matter of course enormous interest was being charged . . . the consequence was, that at the end of the Court they had divested themselves of their land, and had spent the whole of the money they had received for it. ('Editorial' 1883, 4)

As far as Belich (1996, 259) is concerned, the actions of the Land Court created a vortex that sucked in enormous tracts of Māori land: 'Between 1861 and 1891 Maori land holdings in the North Island halved from 22 million to 11 million acres or from about 80 per cent to 40 per cent. Less than a sixth of this land was lost to confiscation, the rest to sale.' For Ward (1973, 267), nothing was as damaging to Māori as land-selling: 'It was the sordid and demoralising system of land purchasing, not war and confiscation, that really brought the Maori people low.'

However, the violence of this and other methods of primitive accumulation was obscured, just as Marx ([1867] 1976) contended, by 'tender' and 'idyllic' accounts, such as that offered by the Colonial Secretary and Head of the Native Department, J. C. Richmond (1865, 349) on 24 August 1865 during a parliamentary debate: 'The settler was, quite properly, anxious to extend settlement. Nor could this desire for land be properly called greed. It was not individual wealth he was grasping; he was indulging in the healthy wish for the spread of civilisation.'

A similar apparent concern with the spread of civilisation was central to the land-buying programme of New Zealand's celebrated Liberal Government (1891–1912), a process through which an additional 3.1 million acres of land passed out of Māori hands, and one that has escaped much of the scrutiny that has highlighted the injustices of the earlier forms of dispossession detailed above.

## Dispossession in Disguise: 'Honest Jock' McKenzie and the Liberal Land-buying Programme

The Liberal Government took office in 1891 and remained there for the next 21 years, during which time they earned themselves an enviable reputation as social reformers through, for example, the introduction of women's suffrage (1893) and old-age pensions (1898). The overarching preoccupation of the Liberal administration was, however, land. The Liberals wanted a much denser settling of people on the land. It was, Belich (2001, 44) notes, their panacea for all ills (see also Wynyard 2016). The Liberals' vision proved a popular one among settlers for whom unfarmed land, such as that held communally by Māori, was scandalous (King 2003, 259). Heavily cultivated, closely settled land was, Brooking (1996, 81) argues, seen by most settlers as preferable to rainforest sparsely peopled by Māori, 'because well-tilled fields and villages peopled with families equated to progress and civilisation'. Such a vision was, of course, entirely dependent on the availability of land, and much of that land, even in 1891, remained in Māori hands.

When the Liberals took office they made much of their desire to 'bust up' the so-called Great Estates that were formed by land-grabbers such as Rhodes and Jones in the earlier years of the colony and, indeed, the Liberals had some success in this regard. By the end of their time in office, the Liberals had repurchased 1.3 million acres from estate holders and had settled 22,000 people on repurchased estates (Brooking 1996, 245). The vast majority of settlers were, however, 'placed on land bullied and cajoled from its Maori owners at knockdown prices' (Simpson 1986, 231). As a consequence, Māori lost vast tracts of land, almost as much as had been taken during the confiscations that followed the New Zealand Wars.

John McKenzie, Minister for Lands, was the central figure responsible for the dispossession of Māori land in the Liberal administration. McKenzie had himself witnessed the horrors of land alienation in his native Scotland: at five years old he came face to face with the human cost of the Highland Clearances, a process through which long-settled crofters and tenant farmers were suddenly and forcibly swept from their lands and driven towards Britain's bleak manufacturing towns where they were then 'whipped, branded and tortured by grotesquely terroristic laws into accepting the discipline necessary to the system of wage labour' (Marx [1867] 1976, 899).

In May 1845 McKenzie was taken by his father to visit family in County Sutherland in the Scottish Highlands and on the way back home they stopped at a small Presbyterian church at Croick where McKenzie was greeted by a sight that would never leave him: 'Huddled in the graveyard under a tent-like awning, cold, frightened yet defiant, were some 90 people, including 23 children under ten' (Brooking 1996, 15). These were formerly proud, respectable and long-settled tenant farmers, driven from their lands and into a state of vagrancy by the very same processes of enclosure and dispossession that would, in turn, separate Māori from their lands. Here were people forced to sleep in a graveyard or else face arrest and worse for vagrancy. The idea that people could be driven to such desperation for the want of land coloured every aspect of McKenzie's subsequent career. He devoted his years in the New Zealand Parliament to making land available for those who wished to farm it. As King (2003, 271) notes, however, McKenzie's 'first-hand memories of the Highland clearances did not prevent him from taking every opportunity to part North Island Maori from their land' (see also Wynyard 2016). Brooking (1996, 149) similarly points out that McKenzie's keen sense of social justice had clearly defined limits: it did not stretch to Māori, to 'Asiatics', 'Assyrian hawkers', 'Dalmatians', 'fallen women' or 'loafers'.

Not all members of the Liberal Government were quite so keen to separate Māori from their lands. The Member for the seat of Eastern Māori, James Carroll (Ngāti Kahungunu) urged caution and restraint, and was eventually able to slow the sale of Māori land through his policy of 'Tai-Hoa', or 'Go Slow' (Belich 2001, 200–1; Brooking 1996). Yet this was not before McKenzie had helped effect the purchase of 3.1 million acres of land. As Brooking (1992, 78) notes, the Liberal land-buying programme of the 1890s was the largest of any administration since the wars. Among the mechanisms used by the Liberals to acquire land from Māori was the Native Lands (Validation of Titles) Act of 1892, which empowered judges from the Land Court to investigate disputed land sales and grant new certificates of title. The Act was ostensibly aimed at shielding both Māori and Pākehā from unscrupulous land deals in the past, but in actual fact accelerated the land sales process by vesting full property rights in secure title (Brooking 1996, 137). This was typical of the Liberals' land-buying programme: policies aimed at dispossessing Māori and freeing up land for Pākehā settlement were disguised as acts of benevolent concern and shows of justice (Brooking 1996; Ward 1973; Wynyard 2016).

## Conclusion

While the Liberals' methods of dispossession differed from earlier manifestations of primitive accumulation, the effect on Māori was the same: Māori lost their land and the freedoms, rights and possibilities attached to that land. Māori were deprived of an economic base and alienated from their ancestral homelands. As Walker (2004, 10) notes, by the end of the nineteenth century the outcome of these processes was 'impoverishment of Maori, marginalisation of elders and chiefly authority and a structural relationship of Pakeha dominance and Maori subjection'. Likewise Ward (1973, 305) claims that by the 1890s Māori had 'been subordinated to the settler political and legal system and asked to assume its obligations, while being steadily parted from their lands by processes that favoured speculation and deviousness and hindered Maori farmers'.

Once wrestled from its indigenous owners the vast majority of land was converted, through the burning of native forest, into pasture for sheep and cattle. Land became, and to a very real extent remains, the basis of Aotearoa New Zealand's capitalist economy and the key to the wealth of the nation. Through the mechanisms of primitive accumulation detailed above Māori were largely reduced to members of the labouring class. Ongoing structural inequality and the over-representation of Māori in any manner of negative social statistics from incarceration rates, to unemployment, to poorer physical and mental health is rooted in this violent history of colonisation and the systematic dispossession of Māori land and resources. The inequalities that plague contemporary New Zealand society and that are explored elsewhere in this collection are not accidental; rather, as Poata-Smith (2004, 84) argues, 'exploitation and inequality are essential elements in the realisation of profits for the powerful and privileged actors in New Zealand's capitalist economy'. Or to put it differently, the wealth of contemporary New Zealand society is predicated on the relative impoverishment of the majority of Māori.

CHAPTER 2

# Rangatiratanga, Kāwanatanga and the Constitution

## Ranginui Walker

Māori are the tangata whenua, the indigenous people of the land known today as Aotearoa New Zealand. They connect to the land by whakapapa, the systematic layering of knowledge in a sequential narrative chronicling voyages of discovery, settlement, and naming, claiming and demarcation of tribal territories. The basic socio-political land-holding groups of pre-European Māori society were hapū, independent clans led by rangatira. Rangatira considered themselves first among equals, responsible for the political and economic welfare of the hapū. But as the population increased, competition over resources saw the rise of warfare and the evolution of tribal confederations, so that hapū sometimes acted together as iwi against common enemies.

This chapter provides an overview of the evolution of rangatiratanga as a response to the arrival of Pākehā. New systems of rangatiratanga became necessary to defend hapū lands, autonomy and well-being. While a number of tribal confederations have formed across Aotearoa at different points since Pākehā arrival, this chapter centres on the examples of the United Tribes of New Zealand and the Kīngitanga, or King movement, as two crucial tribal confederations that are still politically significant today (see Cox 1993 for an extensive history of Māori unity movements).

## Emergence of the Māori Nation

As early as 1808, rangatira of the numerous hapū in Taitokerau (Northland) created an assembly known as Te Whakaminenga to regulate trade with Pākehā traders and settlers. In 1828, Kawiti, the rangatira of Ngāti Hine, visited Hongi Hika at Whangaroa to suggest unifying the hapū more formally into a confederation under Hongi. Unfortunately Hongi died and the moment was lost, but the Whakaminenga continued to develop towards becoming the governing body of a unified Māori nation. The Whakaminenga's first tentative step towards nationhood occurred in 1831 when thirteen rangatira assembled at Kerikeri and wrote a petition to King William IV seeking British protection from a potential take-over of their land by the French (Healy, Huygens and Murphy 2012, appendix IV). King William responded to the Whakaminenga by appointing James Busby British Resident in 1833 (Waitangi Tribunal 2014, 118–19).

The Whakaminenga's second step towards nationhood was the selection of the national Flag of the United Tribes. The impounding of a New Zealand (i.e., Māori) ship, *Sir George Murray*, in Sydney for not flying an ensign was a threat to Māori trade. The rangatira wrote again to King William asking for a flag. When the flag arrived it was run up alongside the Union Jack and given a 21-gun salute by HMS *Alligator* – an affirmation of the sovereignty of the Whakaminenga.

The Whakaminenga's third move towards nationhood was to assemble at Waitangi at the instigation of James Busby to sign He Wakaputanga o Te Rangatiratanga o Nu Tirani (the Declaration of Independence of the United Tribes of New Zealand). There were 35 signatories from Taitokerau and as far south as the Hauraki Gulf. The document, signed on 28 October 1835, declared:

- All sovereign power and authority within New Zealand resides exclusively in the hereditary chiefs of tribes who declare they will

- The hereditary chiefs agree to meet in Congress at Waitangi in the autumn of each year to frame laws for the dispensation of justice, preservation of peace and regulation of trade.
- The chiefs agreed to thank the King for acknowledging their flag and, in return for the friendship and protection they give to his subjects who came to trade or settle in New Zealand, they entreated the King to be a parent for the infant state and its protector from external attempts on its independence. (For Declaration text and facsimiles, see Ministry for Culture and Heritage 2016.)

With the signing of He Wakaputanga, the numerous hapū in the Whakaminenga entered into the world of international trade and politics with at least some attributes of statehood. Their independence was recognised by Britain with whom they established a protective relationship for their infant state. They had a name, 'Nu Tirani', for their country. Ships sailed from their harbours under the national flag of the United Tribes (Waitangi Tribunal 2014, 153). The establishment of a tribal congress to make and enforce laws was the only missing element of statehood because, despite the intention to hold an annual congress, rangatira returned home to rule their own tribes as before.

Although Busby was disappointed that the Whakaminenga did not set up an instant government, with himself and the missionary Henry Williams as puppet-masters, the rangatira went about the business of nation-building at their own pace. Over the next four years another ten rangatira signed the Declaration, including the influential Tāmati Wāka Nene, Panakareao, Tirarau, Taonui, Te Hapūku, Pōtatau Te Wherowhero and Te Heuheu. The signing of three ariki – Te Wherowhero of the Tainui Confederation, Te Heuheu of the Tūwharetoa Confederation and Te Hāpuku of the Ngāti Kahungunu Confederation – ranging from Hawke's Bay down to the Wairarapa, spread the mantle of the Declaration over the whole of the North Island (Healy, Huygens and Murphy 2012, 90).

In the meantime, Busby lost faith in the Whakaminenga's ability to form a government to control wrong-doers. In 1837 his pessimistic dispatch to the Colonial Office describing Māori diseases, mortality and exposure to European vices influenced a change in British policy. The Colonial Office replaced Busby with a higher official, Captain William Hobson, who was appointed British Consul (Waitangi Tribunal 2014, 302–3). Hobson arrived at the Bay of Islands on 29 January 1840 with a set of instructions from Lord Normanby of the Colonial Office. Normanby's instructions acknowledged New Zealand's independence as a sovereign state, and instructed Busby to persuade rangatira to sign a treaty surrendering their sovereignty to the British Crown for the benefits of British protection, law and citizenship (Walker 2004, 90).

## Te Tiriti o Waitangi

Under the resulting Tiriti o Waitangi (Treaty of Waitangi) signed by rangatira on 6 February 1840, something less than sovereignty was ceded to the British Crown in the first article of the Māori-language version; that is, the one agreed to by Māori signatories:

> The rangatira of the Confederation and all the rangatira not in the Confederation cede to the Queen of England forever the Kāwanatanga (Governance) of all their lands.

In the second article, rangatira ensured their mana was kept intact:

> The Queen of England guarantees the rangatira, the hapū and all the people of New Zealand the 'tino rangatiratanga' (absolute chieftainship) of their lands, their homes and all their treasured possessions.

Paradoxically that guarantee was circumscribed in the same article by rangatira ceding to the Crown the sole right to purchase their land, thereby denying access to the open market. In the third article:

The Queen guaranteed the safety of all the Māori people of New Zealand and granted them all the rights and privileges of British citizenship. (Author's translation; for Tiriti o Waitangi text, see Ministry for Culture and Heritage 2014b.)

On the basis of the Treaty, Hobson proclaimed sovereignty over the North Island, the South Island and Stewart Island on 21 May 1840 (Healy, Huygens and Murphy 2012, 387). Despite the imprecise translation of 'sovereignty' as 'kāwanatanga' instead of 'mana', the Kāwana (Governor) behaved as if the Crown had sovereignty, while rangatira behaved as if they had never surrendered it.

## Kāwanatanga

In the twenty years after Te Tiriti was signed, rangatira continued to rule their hapū as before. They adapted their political economy by growing crops for the Auckland market and investing in capital goods such as agricultural equipment, flour mills and coastal trading vessels (Walker 2007, 63–66; also Petrie 2006, 120–4). This was a time of prosperity and peaceful coexistence with the Governor and settlers, but it was short-lived. Despite assurances made that Māori lands would be protected, the establishment of a settler government in 1852 and the waning influence of the Colonial Office meant that settler interests in gaining Māori land were given free rein. Governor George Grey went about Empire's business, extinguishing native title to land by 'fair purchase' and flooding the land with settlers. In the face of Governor Grey's aggressive land-buying in the Taranaki, Waikato and Wellington districts, rangatira now had a compelling reason to implement the objective of nation-building proclaimed in He Wakaputanga (the 1835 Declaration of Independence). To transcend tribalism, rangatira in Taranaki developed the political ideology of kotahitanga; that is, of the unification of the tribes as a precondition for the appointment of a king.

The idea of a Māori King as a symbol of national unity was conceived by Wi Tako, Tāmihana te Rauparaha, Matene Te Whiwhi and Wiremu Kingi at Ōtaki in 1853. In 1855 they began preaching kotahitanga among the tribes and, over the next three years, promoters of the King movement toured the country offering the kingship to ariki and high-ranking rangatira in every tribal district (Sinclair 1959, 111–12). All demurred. Ngāti Porou ariki, Te Kani a Takirau, for example, declined, saying his mountain, Hikurangi, was immovable, meaning he had no desire to be king outside his own domain (Grace 1966, 443–5).

## Wiremu Tāmihana

The rangatira who brought three years of tribal kingship discussions to a head was Wiremu Tāmihana of Ngāti Haua, one of the most sagacious leaders of nineteenth-century New Zealand. He established a model Christian village at Peria, south of Matamata. The clusters of whānau houses in the community were surrounded by orchards and fields of wheat, maize, kūmara and potatoes. There was a meeting house, a church, a post office, a flour mill, a school house and a boarding house for a hundred students. There was a code of laws and a rūnanga (council of advisers) to administer justice (Stokes 1990, 516). When Tāmihana realised rangatira had no representation in the first Parliament, set up in 1854, he sought Crown approval for his system of government for Ngāti Haua. Despite section 71 of the New Zealand Constitution Act 1852 having provision for self-governing Māori districts, Tāmihana was rebuffed. He then turned his considerable talents to supporting the King movement.

## Te Wherowhero

In 1856 a candidate for the kingship was identified when the ariki Iwikau Te Heuheu nominated Te Wherowhero for the office. Te Wherowhero belonged to Ngāti Māhuta whose lineages linked him to the commanders of the *Tainui* and the *Arawa* waka. He was a formidable warrior in his own right, who had driven Te Rauparaha out of Kāwhia and put up stout resistance against Ngāpuhi muskets at Mātakitaki in 1822. Te Wherowhero had also refused to sign Te Tiriti, knowing intuitively he was being asked to surrender his mana to the British Crown.

Te Wherowhero's mana was recognised by the colonial governors as well as by Māori. A story that demonstrates this relates to a huge feast Te Wherowhero put on at Remuera in 1844 to honour Governor FitzRoy. It was a conspicuous display of mana. A mock battle of 800 warriors armed with muskets entertained the Governor. A thousand blankets were gifted to visiting rangatira. FitzRoy realised the security of Auckland depended on the goodwill of Te Wherowhero. Two days later FitzRoy staged a reception at Government House with Te Wherowhero as the guest of honour (Jones 1959, 174–5). Governors – Thomas Gore Browne as well as Grey – also often consulted Te Wherowhero on native affairs, and in 1849 Governor Grey persuaded Te Wherowhero to sign an agreement to protect Auckland and to move to Māngere to guard the southern approach to the town.

Te Wherowhero's mana as the most powerful ariki in the land underpinned his nomination as king by Te Heuheu. That nomination was endorsed in 1857 by Ngāti Maniapoto at a meeting named Te Puna Roimata (Well of Tears) (Jones 1959, 206–7). Although Te Wherowhero was reluctant, he capitulated to the will of the assembly. In February 1857 Tāmihana sent a circular notifying the rangatira of Waikato that Ngāti Haua supported Te Wherowhero for the office of king. The protracted tribal discussions were brought to a conclusion at Ngāruawāhia on 2 May 1858 when Pōtatau Te Wherowhero was installed as King. The King's flag, Tapaue, was unfurled and run up the flagpole (Jones 1959, 223). The Kīngitanga also adopted Te Paki o Matariki, incorporating the symbolism of peace and calm associated with the Pleiades, as the King's coat of arms. The motto 'Ko te Mana Motuhake' on the coat of arms signifies the discrete sovereignty of all the tribes under the sheltering mantle of the King (Jones 1959, 231).

Tāmihana set out the objectives of the Kīngitanga. The King would:

- hold mana whenua, the territorial and political authority of those hapū involved
- keep the peace between the tribes

- be joined in concord with the Queen of England with God over them both
- protect tribes from aggression. (Stokes 1990, 517)

King Pōtatau declared Mangatāwhiri as the boundary between himself and the Governor. He envisaged a dual administration, sharing the land in peaceful coexistence with the Crown, and set about establishing his economic base and system of governance. Pōtatau's kingship was supported economically by the fertile lands along the banks of the Waikato and Waipā Rivers. His territory yielded abundant harvests of wheat, maize, potatoes, kūmara and fruit. Pigs were reared and fattened by the thousand. Tainui traders in the Auckland market levied their own taxes to contribute to the King's treasury to help defray the costs of intertribal assemblies (Jones 1959, 166–7). Pōtatau governed with a rūnanga. In 1859 the King's rūnanga promulgated a code of criminal offences (Brookfield 2006, 115). The power to make and enforce law in the King's domain is the hallmark of sovereignty, but unlike the unitary sovereignty of the Crown, the Kīngitanga was a federal system of government where adherent hapū had their own rūnanga and local autonomy.

When Te Wherowhero was crowned King Pōtatau I of the emergent Māori nation, he was no longer welcome in official circles (Oliver 1990, 528). Governor Grey tried to dissuade Pōtatau, saying, 'Let your Kingship be put down.' Pōtatau replied, 'I cannot do that. It is not mine, it belongs to the rangatira of this country' (Jones 1959, 201). When Pōtatau refused to bend to the Governor's will, the British Empire reverted to what empires do: military invasion and conquest; this time, of peaceful Tainui territory.

By the time Grey invaded the Waikato in 1863, Pōtatau was dead, dying after only two years as king. His successor, Matutaera, subsequently known as King Tāwhiao, presided over the most turbulent time in the history of Waikato (Mahuta 1993, 509). Grey issued a proclamation ordering tribes living along the military road pointing south into the King's territory, the Great South Road, to swear an oath of allegiance to the Queen or leave their homes. Most, being related to the Waikato people, left in the middle of winter to rally to the Kīngitanga. Their homes and properties at

Ihumātao, Māngere, Pūkāki, Patumāhoe, Tuakau and Pōkeno were looted by the troops and their horses sold in the Auckland market. Without declaring war, Grey ordered General Cameron to invade Waikato. Cameron's troops crossed the Mangatāwhiri Stream on 12 July 1863 (Parker 2005, 38–39).

The Waikato Tainui defenders were outnumbered and outgunned. Their strategy for such asymmetric warfare was to build lines of defensive redoubts capable of resisting British tactics of artillery bombardment, and to carry out frontal assaults by swift, surprise attacks. Redoubts had no intrinsic value, so after an engagement they were abandoned to the British. These strategies were at odds with those of the British, who were used to pitched battles in open fields being decisive in war, and to the over-running of redoubts leading to surrender. Many significant battles were fought in the Waikato at Meremere, Rangiriri, Rangiaowhia and Ōrākau, with Cameron's army never being able to achieve a decisive victory in the face of Māori strategy (Belich [1986] 2015, 119–76).

After Ōrākau, Kīngitanga supporters from Tauranga returned home and fought a final battle against the British at Gate Pā, a site close to the sea, which allowed the British to utilise even more artillery than in previous battles. With the Pā's defences pulverised the British stormed in, only to find that the Māori defenders remained safe in anti-artillery bunkers dug within the Pā. Cameron's army was routed, with many killed and wounded (Belich [1986] 2015, 178–88). Governor Grey, appalled by the disaster of Gate Pā, decided to make peace. Cameron's campaign, on the other hand, tipped the balance of power away from the Kīngitanga, enabling Governor Grey to confiscate 1.2 million acres of Waikato Tainui lands. Although the Kīngitanga was debilitated, it remained a cohesive force unified by grievance against the Government, and Tāwhiao predicted that in years to come a 'child' would arise to reclaim the confiscated lands (Mahuta 1993, 509).

## The King Country

While the Tauranga Kīngitanga forces had been engaged at Gate Pā, on the other side of the Waikato Rewi Maniapoto and Wiremu Tāmihana had laid down the aukati – the closed boundary – between themselves and the Governor. They informed the British that if their territory was invaded they were ready to fight again (Belich [1986] 2015, 175). Tāwhiao lived within the boundary of the territory known as the King Country, and for years this region was closed to white men under penalty of death.

In 1878, Sir George Grey, then Prime Minister, tried to settle the unquiet peace with the Kīngitanga by offering to recognise Tāwhiao's authority over what was left of the Waikato district. Tāwhiao refused, holding out for the return of the confiscated lands. Tension between the Crown and the Kīngitanga was not alleviated until July 1881 when Tāwhiao made peace with the Government in Alexandra (King 1977, 28). Making peace with the Crown did not signify submission. Even as late as the close of the nineteenth century, the Kīngitanga was still collecting taxes, administering justice and discouraging land sales to the Crown (Brookfield 2006, 114). In 1886 Tāwhiao converted the King's treasury into a bank, for which cheques and banknotes are still extant (Brookfield 2006, 115).

Tāwhiao also continued to struggle for recognition of the mana of the tribes and for restitution of the confiscated lands. In 1884 he led a deputation of rangatira to England. The deputation petitioned the Crown for a Royal Commissioner from England to investigate the injustices carried out in New Zealand. Lord Derby, Secretary of State for the Colonies, met the deputation and exonerated the Crown by referring the petition back to the New Zealand Government. Tāwhiao also sought government approval to establish a Māori Council, but was rebuffed. The Government, committed to controlling and assimilating Māori, again disregarded the provision for self-government in Māori districts under section 71 of the 1852 Constitution. Undeterred by an un-cooperative Government, Tāwhiao established his own Parliament named Te Kauhanganui at Maungakawa in 1895. Before he died, Tāwhiao also established the institution of poukai, feasts where widows and orphans were fed. Poukai served to maintain social cohesion, commitment to the Kīngitanga and settlement of the raupatu (confiscation) claims.

Throughout the twentieth century, iwi and hapū within the Kīngitanga and elsewhere across the country continued to protest and struggle against the injustices of land confiscations and sales they had experienced, asserting their rangatiratanga at every opportunity. Most recently, since the 1980s, the Waitangi Tribunal and Office of Treaty Settlements have led to significant redress for historical injustices, even if the money and land returned remains a small fraction of what was lost. At the same time, Treaty settlements and new political developments have resulted in further evolution of rangatiratanga into the twenty-first century.

## Treaty Settlements and Rangatiratanga

By the era of Treaty settlements, Te Ātairangikaahu was the Kīngitanga leader, crowned Queen on 23 May 1966. It was an inspired choice as she graced the office with dignity and humility. In her first year of office, Te Ātairangikaahu replaced the English title 'Queen' with 'Te Arikinui'. She was now the national figurehead portended by Lord Bledisloe, a monarch above politics, refraining from public comment and leaving that field to her adopted brother Robert Mahuta.

In 1972, Mahuta was appointed director of the Māori Studies Research Centre at Waikato University. The Centre produced the *Tainui Report 1983*, which set the stage for the tribe's raupatu claim to the Waitangi Tribunal. In 1992 the Minister of Treaty Settlements, Doug Graham, introduced direct negotiations to settle claims that were well founded and Mahuta went into negotiations with the Crown. Tainui's position was succinct: 'I riro whenua atu, me hoki whenua mai' (Land was taken, land must be returned). 'Ko te moni te utu mo te hara' (Money is payment for the crime).

In 1993, the Crown ceded the Hopuhopu military base to Waikato Tainui as a down payment on their claim. The land was vested in the Te Wherowhero Trust. On 22 May 1995, Tainui and the Crown signed the Waikato Deed of Settlement, the terms of which were incorporated in the Waikato Raupatu Claims Trust Settlement Act 1995. The Crown apologised for invading Waikato and labelling the people 'rebels'. Waikato Tainui received $170 million in compensation and 3500 acres of Crown land in the settlement.

Tainui Group Holdings (TGH) was established as the commercial arm of the iwi. Initially TGH made a number of high-risk investments, some of which led to a write-off of $42 million in 2000. TGH was then restructured, and directors experienced in business and finance were appointed, leading to a recovery in 2002 (Walker 2004, 304–6). In 2014, TGH assets amounted to $1.1 billion. With a net profit of $70.9 million, a return of 6.7 per cent on assets and a debt-to-assets ratio of 21.3 per cent, the company is soundly based (TGH 2014, 6). The Tainui Raupatu Lands Trust is the charitable arm of the iwi, responsible for distributing funds for social, educational and cultural purposes. Since 2004, the trust has distributed $104.5 million to education, sports, health, marae, kaumātua, poukai, cultural events and community programmes. In 2014, $2.5 million was spent on education, $1.2 million on marae grants and $1.7 million on the Kīngitanga (14).

## Iwi Chairs Forum

The iwi that created the Kīngitanga, and other iwi elsewhere across the country, now have their own rangatiratanga underpinned by tribal trust boards and corporations. These are statutory bodies for managing Treaty-claims settlement funds for beneficiaries. Triennial elections for trustees have become the mechanism for iwi to appoint their leaders. Qualifications, business experience and high achievement are now standard for aspirants to office.

Tribal corporations controlling farming, forestry, fishing, property and business interests are the modern manifestation of rangatiratanga, with considerable business interests both nationally and internationally. With economic power comes political influence. In 2005 the chairs of iwi corporations established the Iwi Chairs Forum (ICF), the latest in a long line of tribal confederations. The ICF appointed Iwi Leaders Groups to enter into talks with the Crown on particular issues including water, climate change, conservation, whānau ora, education, housing, minerals and foreign charter vessels. With the Māori economy estimated at upwards of $37 billion (Nana, Stokes and Molano 2011, 4), the ICF is now an influential lobby group. Meetings at different venues are attended by upwards of a hundred delegates. When the ICF meets annually at Waitangi in February, it invites the Prime Minister for high-level discussions on Māori policy. The Prime Minister acknowledges the mana of the ICF by attending in person with the Deputy Prime Minister and the Minister of Māori Affairs. ICF leaders are direct with the Prime Minister, saying: 'We are interested in investment for the future of our beneficiaries. If you want to sell state assets, talk to us. If you want to engage in public-private partnerships, talk to us.'

While iwi now have considerable and growing economic sovereignty and political influence, the issue of their political sovereignty remains unresolved. In view of these transformations in the Treaty settlement era, there is now a need for a national conversation on Māori sovereignty, kāwanatanga and the Constitution. That conversation is needed because decolonisation remains unfinished business.

## Rangatiratanga and Kāwanatanga: Addressing the New Zealand Constitution

The most recent opening to this constitutional conversation arises from the Ngāpuhi Treaty claim, heard by the Waitangi Tribunal in 2011. Central to the claim was the argument from Ngāpuhi that when their ancestors signed Te Tiriti, they did not cede sovereignty to the Crown (see Healy, Huygens and Murphy 2012). In their report released in 2014, the Waitangi Tribunal concurred, concluding that in signing Te Tiriti:

- rangatira did not cede their sovereignty to the British Crown
- they agreed to a Governor having authority to control British subjects in New Zealand, to keep the peace and protect Māori interests
- the Governor and the rangatira were to be co-equals with different spheres of influence
- rangatira agreed to enter into land transactions with the Crown
- the Crown would protect rangatira from foreign threats and represent them in international affairs. (Waitangi Tribunal 2014, 529)

Those findings by the Tribunal have enormous implications for the history of colonisation, Māori resistance, decolonisation and the issue of where Te Tiriti o Waitangi sits in the New Zealand Constitution. The finding that rangatira did not surrender their sovereignty to the British Crown means that the Declaration of Independence 1835 and Te Tiriti o Waitangi 1840 are the founding documents of kāwanatanga, and the rule of law in New Zealand.

On the Pākehā side also, in recent decades there have been shifts to the view that the Treaty must be given a place in the New Zealand Constitution. Stimulated by the dogged Māori struggle for recognition of their rights under Te Tiriti o Waitangi, during the term of the Fourth Labour Government, the then Hon. Geoffrey Palmer, as Minister of Justice, was the first to respond to the emerging Treaty discourse and jurisprudence from the hearing of Māori claims against the Crown before the Tribunal and the High Court. Judges, lawyers and academics at these hearings couched Treaty discourse in terms of partnership inherent in the 'principles of the Treaty of Waitangi'. This evolutionary process of social change prompted measures to update New Zealand's Constitution. The legal measures taken by the Fourth Labour Government include:

- The Constitution Act 1986 nullified the NZ Constitution Act 1852 so that the laws from the Parliament of the United Kingdom shall cease to have effect as part of New Zealand law. The act sets out the basic elements of the Legislature, Executive and Judiciary as the three branches of government. (McGuinness and White 2011, 96)
- The New Zealand Bill of Rights Act 1990 affirms, protects and promotes fundamental freedoms of the people of New Zealand and recognises Māori as tangata whenua. (McGuinness and White 2011, 101)

However, these Acts are not entrenched, which means they can be altered or rescinded by a simple majority of Parliament at any time. Palmer believes New Zealand should have a written and entrenched constitution, which would mean that certain key statutes that embody the fundamental values of our political system could only be altered by a popular referendum or a 75 per cent majority in the house. He also thinks the Treaty of Waitangi should be entrenched in the constitution (Palmer

2013). As matters stand now, all references to the Treaty in statutes can be repealed by Parliament.

Professor of Law Paul McHugh is even more explicit than Palmer in characterising the Treaty of Waitangi as the 'Māori Magna Carta', the document that sets out the fundamental political rights of hapū and iwi. McHugh argues that any constitution emerging out of New Zealand soil must incorporate the Treaty of Waitangi. The evolving norm arising out of Treaty discourse and jurisprudence is 'tino rangatiratanga' sitting alongside and equal to 'kāwanatanga'. The discourse arising out of Treaty claims supersedes the old fashioned notion of sovereignty as absolute and singular (McHugh 1991, 63–64). Māori, of course, have always understood that to be the case, since the time that the Treaty was signed. It has taken 150 years to convince the Crown signatory to the Treaty that 'kāwanatanga' and 'tino rangatiratanga' are partners in Enterprise New Zealand.

In 2010, the Institute of Policy Studies and the New Zealand Centre for Public Law reiterated the ideas propounded by Palmer and McHugh. Decolonisation means that a new relationship between Māori as tangata whenua and later immigrants must develop, and a framework for a non-colonial form of governance needs to be established. This means repositioning the Treaty of Waitangi as a relationship between equal sovereign powers. Pākehā hegemony is being replaced by a more ethnically diverse power structure. Increased recognition of biculturalism, cultural pluralism and devolution has influenced the way the public sector operates (McLeay 2011, 6–17). These propositions are now taking shape in the composition of Parliament, the bicultural operations of the public service and the behaviour of the government towards iwi in the settlement of claims against the Crown.

The Treaty is in effect a *de facto* but not a *de jure* element in our constitutional arrangements. This ambivalent status prompted the Māori Party to press for a review of the constitution in its coalition agreement with the National Party in 2008. However, the resulting review did not put that ambivalence to rest, opting for the status quo by affirming the Treaty as a foundational document (Constitutional Advisory Panel 2013, 16). Even so, the new thinking of judges, lawyers and intellectuals is cause for optimism in the future. Decolonisation of New Zealand is well advanced.

Māori are now recognised as tangata whenua with a special relationship as kaitiaki, guardians of the natural world. A new relationship is being developed in the spirit of partnership between Māori and the Crown. Power has shifted from Pākehā hegemony towards a more ethnically diversified power structure. The problem arising out of awareness of the significance of Te Tiriti o Waitangi is to determine where it fits in the constitution. The Treaty is not a legal document. It is an historical fact, an agreement between two sovereign nations to coexist in New Zealand for the mutual benefits of trade and development of the county's resources. As McHugh says, the underlying *Grundnorm*, or basis for New Zealand's legal system, has always been one where rangatiratanga sits alongside and is equal to kāwanatanga (McHugh 1991, 64). That being the case, the Crown has to learn to deal with the multiple sovereignties of the Kīngitanga, the ICF and the iwi economic power houses of Waikato Tainui, Ngāi Tahu, Ngāti Whātua and other iwi corporations aspiring to join the billion-dollar club.

## Conclusion

By the nineteenth century, a number of disparate Māori tribes had formed tribal confederations. This natural process of evolution to higher levels of political organisation was accelerated by the advent of European settlement, culminating in the Declaration of Independence 1835, the Treaty of Waitangi 1840 (affirming Māori sovereignty) and the election of a Māori King in 1858. In developing their sovereign right to nationhood, rangatira conformed to McHugh's *Grundnorm* in the Treaty, where rangatiratanga sits alongside and is equal to kāwanatanga. Governor Grey made the serious mistake of not conforming to that *Grundnorm* and neglecting to set up the semi-autonomous Māori districts for which there was provision in section 71 of the New Zealand Constitution Act 1852. Instead, Grey made war on Waikato Tainui, debilitating the Kīngitanga but not conquering it.

With the beginnings of decolonisation in 1984 through Waitangi Tribunal Treaty settlements, the Kīngitanga – as the symbol of Māori nationhood – has recovered status, as have the loose federation of iwi that support the Kīngitanga. There is a need to update New Zealand's constitutional arrangements to accommodate the multiple sovereignties of iwi, the Kīngitanga and the ICF as the political expression of Māori nationalism.

Ngāpuhi, at the instigation of Ngāti Hine, responded to the Waitangi Tribunal finding in November 2014 by convening a hui on sovereignty at Otiria Marae on 30 January 2015. The hui rejected the proposition, made by Jock Brookfield (2006, 11–12), that the Crown's sovereignty was achieved by the revolutionary overthrow of rangatira which with the passage of time became legitimate. However, Brookfield also admits that 'injustice in a legal order is necessarily a deficiency in legitimacy . . . and if not remedied by constitutional and legal means, it may prompt a revolutionary overthrow' (42–43). Ngāpuhi and Ngāti Hine are not advocating revolution. They want a national conversation on Māori sovereignty and recognition of their first-nation status as tangata whenua. Let the conversation begin.

CHAPTER 3

# We're All in This Together?

*Democracy and Politics in Aotearoa New Zealand*

# Richard Shaw

> Out of the dark and from a very long time ago has come a word.
> —John Dunn (2005, 23)

The day after Judd Hall died in a car crash in Greymouth in early 2014 the right-wing blogger Cameron Slater (2014) posted a brief story on the incident under the heading: 'Feral Dies in Greymouth, Did World a Favour'. Taken to task by a reporter from the *Greymouth Star*, Slater retorted: 'It's a tragic situation but where is it written in the rule books that you have to take into account people's feelings?' (Bromley 2014).

Hall was the last of three sons in one family to die: the first had been killed by a drunk driver and the second had died in the Pike River mine explosion. Unsurprisingly, the feelings Slater chose not to take into account ran very high indeed, and may have contributed to thousands of the blogger's personal emails being leaked to investigative journalist Nicky Hager some weeks later. On 13 August 2014 – just before the September general election – Hager published *Dirty Politics*. Amongst its allegations were that Slater and a friend had hacked Labour Party webpages during the 2011 election campaign and downloaded evidence of credit card transactions; that Slater had sought (and gained) favours from the then Minister of Corrections, Judith Collins, in return for working on the Minister's Wikipedia page; and that a political adviser in the Prime Minister's Office had facilitated (in an unusually quick turnaround time) the release of Security Intelligence Service (SIS) documents to Slater who then used them to embarrass the then Leader of the Opposition.[1]

Most people beyond the Wellington 'beltway' simply yawned and went back to what they had been doing previously, and the revelations had little or no bearing on the election. But the tawdry behaviour revealed in *Dirty Politics* matters a great deal. When senior politicians and political parties collude in 'attack politics' the legitimacy of our democratic system is called into question. When that occurs, people's faith in democratic institutions is diminished and they begin to walk away from politics. And at some point, when those institutions are sufficiently undermined, certain people will benefit from the demise of transparency and accountability – and they will not be the marginalised, dispossessed and needy amongst us. British Labour politician David Blunkett (2002, 98–99) did not have New Zealand in mind, but he might as well have when he wrote that politics is

> the only way in which those without wealth and power can exercise any form of influence. I think that political events over recent years have borne out [the] attack on the cynics of both Right and Left who dismiss political activity as irrelevant, boring or unrewarding, [and] who play entirely into the hands of those who already possess power and to whom democracy is a channel for using government for their own ends.

These days we tend to take our democratic rights and freedoms for granted. We do so at our peril, for they are neither inevitable nor permanent; rather, the theme throughout this chapter is that democratic politics is fluid and contested. Using that premise, this chapter sets out one version of the story of democracy and citizenship in Aotearoa New Zealand. It is structured around the struggles of two groups – women and Māori – to secure full citizenship rights.[2]

The chapter begins by defining a series of core concepts. The political journey taken by women and Māori is then set out and, finally, an analysis is offered of the contemporary state of, and challenges confronting, democracy in Aotearoa New Zealand.

## Some Terminology

The chapter focuses on the history of the formal institutions of representative democracy, and specifically on the parliament. Several core concepts will repeatedly pop up. Standard definitions of *democracy* refer to political systems characterised by universal suffrage (i.e., the right to vote); governments chosen by free, regular and competitive elections; and political rights to freedom of speech and association (Stoker 2006, 20). The Gettysburg Address delivered by US President Abraham Lincoln in 1863, and in particular his defence of 'government of the people, by the people, for the people', captures the spirit of this particular understanding of democracy. The specific design of democratic systems varies according to a country's historical and socio-cultural particulars, but the notion that people consent to being governed by others on the basis that they participate in choosing those who govern is central to most contemporary democracies.

The formal term for this model of democracy is *representative democracy*. Once upon a very long time ago, the number of citizens in Athens was sufficiently low – because the category of 'citizen' excluded women, slaves and *metics* (resident aliens) – to enable each citizen to directly participate in the business of governing. The size of most political communities these days is such that Athenian direct democracy is not possible. Instead, citizens delegate their rights to other citizens who are chosen, through an electoral process, to sit in an elected assembly, or parliament, for a specified period of time (three years in our case).

In this way, the institutions of representative government – and, in particular, the bits that are elected – link those who govern with those who are governed. You can see, then, why the question of who gets to vote – and who does not – is so important. You might glimpse, too, how representative government subtly alters Lincoln's words: in practice, what happens in most contemporary democracies is government of the people by *some* of the people. Whether or not government is *for* the people – in the sense that it acts in the interests of all – is a matter for ideological debate.

The terms *democracy* and *citizenship* are not synonyms (although it is difficult to envisage one without some version of the other). Citizenship is associated with membership of a political community (usually a nation-state), and comes with certain legal rights and duties. At different points and places in history, qualification for citizenship has rested on a person's place of birth, social status, gender, wealth, ability to read (sometimes in the language of a colonising nation), income and/or age. At root, therefore, all histories of democracy – including our own – are narratives of the political struggle to determine who counts as a citizen (and who does not), and the specific nature of those citizens' obligations and rights.

The best-known typology of citizenship rights is the three-fold classification proposed by T. H. Marshall ([1950] 1963). For Marshall, a series of *civil citizenship rights* underpin individual freedom, including the rights to free speech, thought, faith and association, the right to own private property and the right to justice. *Social citizenship rights* describe access to the level of economic support (particularly through the welfare state) required to enable a person to 'live the life of a civilized being according to the standards prevailing in the society' (30). Finally, *political citizenship rights* – principally the twin rights to vote and to stand for election to public office – enable a citizen to participate in political life, as someone who votes for the composition of an institution invested with political authority (such as a parliament) and (a right less commonly exercised) as a member of such an institution.

## A Brief History of Democracy and Citizenship in Aotearoa New Zealand

John Dunn (2005, 136) provides a sense of why democracy, despite its flaws, exerts such a powerful appeal for those denied it:

> Until democracy's triumph, [politics] was defined by a layering of exclusions: those without the standing, those without the knowledge or ability, those without a stake in the country, the dependent, foreigners, the unfree or even enslaved, the blatantly untrustworthy or menacing, the criminal, the insane, women, children. Democracy's triumph has been the collapse of one exclusion after another . . . with the collapse of the exclusion of women the most recent, hastiest and most abashed of all.

Dunn's point is that the history of democracy is the story of the incremental inclusion within the political fold of people previously denied the citizenship rights described by Marshall ([1950] 1963). Most of us would consider it outrageous to have groups such as women or Māori (or young people, or New Zealand citizens born in overseas countries) excluded from politics. But it has not always been this way. There is nothing 'natural' about the rolling back of exclusion: the extension of the franchise to hitherto-excluded groups has always to be fought for, and the outcomes of such contests are rarely certain.

In our own country, the paths to inclusion taken by two groups in particular merit closer study. Of the two, the story of women's struggle is probably the better known. One way of recounting it is through Marshall's ([1950] 1963) distinction between having the right to (a) vote and (b) stand for election to public office. It is a significant difference: it is possible to have one but not the other – indeed, some suffragists were ardent supporters of the former (as a means of bringing about the prohibition of alcohol) but opponents of the latter (Atkinson 2003).

The journey to the landmark 1893 legislation that gave all adult women in Aotearoa New Zealand the right to vote began with the New Zealand Constitution Act 1852, which established the institutions of representative government in this country and the means of electing people to them. The right to vote depended on sex, age, nationality and individual possession of property: all male British subjects over the age of 21 could enrol and vote in any electoral district in which they possessed freehold or leasehold property of a minimum value, or lived in rental property attracting a certain rent (Atkinson 2003).[3] Women – along with 'aliens' (such as Chinese), juveniles, lunatics and criminals – could not join the voting club. Neither, by virtue of the individual property test, could the majority of Māori (despite being British subjects), given that Māori land-holdings were largely collectively owned.

Momentum for the right for women to vote gathered across the 1870s and 1880s. Women ratepayers secured the franchise in municipal elections in 1875; adult women could vote in, and contest, elections for school committees and regional education boards from 1877; and between 1878 and 1881 there were at least four unsuccessful attempts to legislate for women's suffrage (Atkinson 2003; Page 1993).

By the end of the 1880s – in part because of the efforts of the New Zealand branch of the (American) Woman's Christian Temperance Union, with Kate Sheppard leading their franchise and legislation wing – women's suffrage had become a major public issue.[4] With the support of sympathetic Members of Parliament (MPs), and following the presentation to Parliament of three successively larger petitions (the last of which, when rolled out on the floor of the House, was over 90 metres long), the Electoral Act was passed on 19 September 1893, granting the right to vote to women (including Māori) aged 21 or over (Atkinson 2003).[5]

So far, so enlightened (at least by international standards of the time). But the fact that women were banned from standing for parliamentary election until the passage of the Women's Parliamentary Rights Act in 1919 should not be brushed over. The removal of the bar on the second of Marshall's tests for full political citizenship was less contentious than the earlier franchise debate had been, but opponents of the Bill (who included some suffrage supporters) were not above arguing that 'women would be "de-sexed" by the hurly-burly of parliamentary politics, [and that] the presence of pretty ladies would distract the attention of weak-willed male legislators from affairs of state' (Atkinson 2003, 132).

It was fully 40 years after women won the vote that Elizabeth McCombs became the first woman elected to Parliament in 1933. In short, behind the self-congratulatory folklore of enlightened social progress that usually accompanies the story of women's suffrage in this country lies a more ambiguous tale.

The corresponding narrative concerning the history of Māori political citizenship rights is even more objectionable. This lesser-known story also begins with the 1852 Act which, while it did not explicitly exclude Māori men, did precisely that in practice through its emphasis on individual property rights.[6] Early opposition to giving Māori men the vote reflected the view that eligibility to vote was a marker of trustworthiness, not a right: something bestowed on those who were fit to exercise it. Māori were considered 'unfit to undertake such an important obligation by virtue of their ignorance of political matters, inability to understand English, questionable loyalty to the Crown, and susceptibility to corruption' (Atkinson 2003, 47). That view was not universally held, and in 1867 Parliament passed the Māori Representation Act. The legislation – initially a temporary measure but extended indefinitely in 1876 – established four Māori seats, elected by Māori men who were at least 21 years old (and who thereby achieved the universal franchise twelve years before non-Māori men, as they had no property-rights criteria to meet).[7]

There are competing interpretations of the motives behind the legislation.[8] A common view has been that the Māori seats were created purely out of pragmatic political interests (Wilson 2003, 1). A key plank of this argument is the assertion that the legislation's architects understood that, over time, the Native Lands Act 1865 would expedite the conversion of unregistered customary title into registered individual title, thus boosting the number of Māori men eligible to vote in general elections. From this position, the 1867 Act was designed to channel a growing political force into a fixed number of seats, thereby limiting Māori electoral power. A related argument is that the Māori seats were created to maintain a balance between North and South Island representation at a time in which the non-Māori population of the South Island far outweighed that of the North. South Island politicians wouldn't countenance more Pākehā seats in the North Island, but could accept three Māori seats (and one in the

South) as long as they were occupied by Māori representatives (see Ward [1974] 1995, 208–9).

A revisionist view, in contrast, sees the Act arising out of 'both a sense of moral obligation to a disenfranchised property-owning people paying substantial taxes, as well as a recognition of the colonists' constitutional obligations under the Treaty of Waitangi' (Wilson 2003, 1; see also McClelland 1997; Orange 1987). Donald McLean, who sponsored the 1867 legislation, is invoked in support of this position. Reprising the rallying cry in the American War of Independence ('No taxation without representation'), McLean argued that Parliament should not be closed to 'a people paying taxes, and [who are] owners of three-fourths of the territory of the North Island' (New Zealand Parliament 1867, 336).

Whatever the motives of those who supported separate representation, the subsequent history of the Māori seats, and of the administration of electoral law in relation to Māori voters generally, is a shoddy one. From 1893, people who were of more than half Māori descent could not vote in 'European'[9] electorates, which did indeed limit their political power to four seats (as perhaps some of those supporting the 1867 Act had hoped); Māori would not get back the right to choose their electorate until 1975 (Wilson 2003). Other examples of how being treated differently has often been to the disadvantage of Māori include: the secret ballot[10] being established for European seats in 1870 but Māori having to vote by show of hand until 1910 and then by declaration (in front of a returning officer and a Māori witness) until 1937; voting in the Māori seats being held the day before voting in European seats between 1919 and 1951; and Māori not being permitted to stand as candidates in European electorates until 1967 (Royal Commission on the Electoral System 1986; Wilson 2003).

A particularly contentious aspect of the 1867 Act was that the number of Māori seats remained fixed at four between 1867 and 1993 regardless of (a) the size of the overall Māori population and the Māori electoral roll, and (b) the number of general seats (which increased from 72 to 99 between 1867 and 1993). Even at their creation the Māori seats were disproportionately large. The average electoral population in each Māori electorate in 1868 was 12,500 people; the equivalent figure across the European seats was 3472. In 1993, when the Electoral Act finally removed the cap on the number of Māori seats, the average voting population of a Māori seat was still twice that of a general seat.

Discussions about Māori parliamentary representation tend to focus on the Māori seats (if for no other reason than that for long stretches of this country's history there would have been no Māori in the House had the seats not existed). Māori MPs have also represented general seats. There have not, however, been terribly many MPs in this last group. Partly this is a legacy of the ban on Māori standing in 'European' seats. It also reflects how difficult it has been since 1967 (when that restriction was lifted) for Māori to gain selection in mainstream parties as candidates in general seats. Between 1967 and 1984, just 23 Māori contested general seats, only three of whom were successful (Sorrenson 1986). To put that figure in perspective: in the six general elections between 1969 and 1984, there were 514 individual contests for general seats. It is unclear how many Māori unsuccessfully sought selection as candidates in those elections, but it *is* clear that when, over a fifteen-year period, only 0.58 per cent of all elected representatives in general seats are Māori, then something is, if not quite rotten, then certainly not quite right in the state of Aotearoa New Zealand.

## The State of Democratic Play Down Under

The preceding discussion demonstrates that the political rights we now assume as given are not only relatively recent but also innately impermanent. The point is all the more relevant given the challenges presently confronting politics in Aotearoa New Zealand. The steady fall in turnout at national elections since the 1980s is typically cited as evidence to this effect. In 2011, turnout slumped to around 72 per cent of all enrolled voters, the lowest level in nearly a century. Three years later nearly 77 per cent of registered electors voted, meaning nearly a quarter of them did not, and a further 252,581 people who were eligible to vote did not even enrol (Electoral Commission of New Zealand 2014). We are far from the heady days of the twentieth century when turnout routinely hovered in the 80–90 per cent range.

The issue is not restricted to any one group. In 2014 only 75 per cent of eligible voters aged 18–24 enrolled and just over 37 per cent of those who did enrol did not vote. Just over 46 per cent of Māori aged 18–24 who enrolled to vote did not do so. Many who are poor and/or unemployed, and members of some (particularly recent) migrant communities, are also drifting towards the democratic margins by not voting. A generation is at risk of being lost to formal institutional politics.

There are many reasons behind people's willingness to walk away from this fundamental act of citizenship. The stale, tired story is that people who do not vote are lazy, apathetic and/or irresponsible, which reduces a complex issue to the supposed and pathologised motivations of individuals. As far as recent migrants are concerned, the issue lies in part in many being acclimatised to differing political cultures. Those least likely to vote are migrants who are socially isolated (through language or employment barriers); young migrants (who, in this respect, are much like other young people); and those from nations without the norms, expectations and habits associated with a culture of democratic participation (Henderson 2013).

Political practitioners are also part of the problem. The introduction of MMP was heralded by some as a new dawn in consensual politics. True, the House is more representative and contains more (and more ideologically diverse) parties, but the gaming aspects of the system still rankle. Chief irritant is the propensity of some parties to strike deals – as the National Party has long done with Peter Dunne in Ōhāriu and with the ACT Party in Epsom – in which a smaller party's candidate is given a free run at a seat (without the major party putting up a candidate) in return for parliamentary support for the major party.

Further, it is usually not that non-voters are disinterested in political *issues*, it is that they are disenchanted with a *form* of politics that is unresponsive to their concerns. It is in this respect that the ethical malaise revealed in *Dirty Politics*, and the lack of public concern about it, is so serious. Hager's story is one of the abuse of political power; the use of attack politics to threaten individuals; the politicisation of public sector agencies, who, in a democracy, are supposed to be politically neutral and not favour any particular party; and failure at the highest levels of Cabinet to accept responsibility for improper conduct on the part of public servants. That many people do not much care about this, or interpret the book as confirmation that this is how all politicians behave (they do not), is of profound concern. *Dirty Politics* is not just about bloggers behaving abysmally, it concerns a high level of contempt in parts of the National Party not only for political opponents but for a democratic system – *our* system – that should be no party's plaything.

There are other consequences of neoliberal orthodoxy that explain why people are walking away from politics. Chief is the primacy given to free markets and to the sovereignty of the individual, which has transformed our conception of what it means to be a citizen. These days we talk about 'consumers' rather than 'citizens', and politics is framed as a series of market-like transactions in which voters are driven by self-interest. Our public concerns as citizens have been shunted aside in favour of economics being seen as central to explaining our individual preferences.

At the heart of this is what Richard Sennett (1977) calls the 'fall of public man [*sic*]'. For the defenders of the Athenian constitution, to be a citizen was to be *public*, to be engaged in public life or that which concerned the lives of all. Increasingly, as the free market triumphs as the dominant means for organising social and economic life, to be a 'citizen' is an individualised and private issue. We no longer just have a market *economy*, we have become a market *society* in which the logic of buying and selling is not restricted to objects alone (Sandel 2012).

Markets, of course, are created by politics: private property rights are both specified and protected by the state. But markets are the antithesis of politics. The reason for governments to use them for public services is to remove questions regarding access to scarce resources from the public realm and to leave these to the supposedly more efficient market. Neoliberal policies, for example, result in cuts to public spending, increasingly leaving individuals and families subject to whichever level of access to health and education they can personally afford. The problem is that, when we do this, we reduce our scope to collectively resolve issues of the distribution of scarce resources through political decision-making. The situation is then further exacerbated by international trade deals and agreements that constrain the power of governments externally, providing even more reasons for voters to consider that politics is futile.

To sum up: the dominance of markets is both a cause of our democratic malaise and, to a degree, an obstacle to its resolution. When the last public service has been marketised there will be no case for politics, because there will be nothing left to decide collectively. There will be no more citizens, only consumers. We will have forgotten what it means to be public. To use the term as it was used in Athens – to describe someone who had withdrawn from public life – we will have become *idiotes*.

## Conclusion: The End Is Not Nigh

As the Blunkett quote near the start of this chapter reminds us, we ignore politics at our peril: in democracies 'wide-spread not-choosing can be a dangerous form of choosing' (Crick 2002, 2). There are consequences of not voting (and of disengaging – or not engaging in the first place – with politics generally). Legal rules will continue to be written, but perhaps without regard to those who opt out. Politicians have strong incentives to listen to those who vote; that's part of the point (and what we expect) of a democratic system in which we vote for our elected representatives. Therefore, over time the substance of governments' policies may fail to reflect the interests of those who have walked away. Young people are already seeing signs of this: superannuation policy tends to privilege the Baby Boomer generation, and tax and other policies are playing a role in the acceleration of house prices that are pricing young people (and those on low incomes) out of first homes and contributing to the emergence of 'Generation Rent' (Eaqub and Eaqub 2015).

There is another important reason for engaging with our democracy. Politics is one way of 'reaching a compromise, and finding ways for those who disagree to rub along together. It is one of the ways we . . . address and potentially patch up the disagreements that characterise our societies without recourse to illegitimate coercion or violence' (Stoker 2006, 2). Politics enables participation in decision-making and helps address (if not always terribly successfully) systemic imbalances in social and economic power.

Four decades of neoliberal orthodoxy have left us facing some stiff democratic challenges, and we have less and less confidence in the capacity of institutions shaped in the nineteenth and twentieth centuries to rise to the challenges of the twenty-first century. Yet crises have played productive roles throughout the history of democracy. One of the reasons liberal democracies survive is because they can accommodate and adapt to challenges. That is one of the lessons to be taken from the political suffrage histories of women and Māori. But it would not do to be complacent about these things. As Split Enz once sang, history never repeats.

## Notes

1   In a subsequent inquiry, the Inspector General of the SIS concluded that the SIS 'had effectively delivered Mr Slater an exclusive story while denying other media the same information' (Young 2014).
2   Inevitably, then, some things must be left aside. The stories of other social groups do not feature here, and understandings of citizenship that extend beyond the right to vote are not covered.
3   One consequence of this was that some men could cast votes in multiple electoral districts; Atkinson (2003, 77) notes that 'some [MPs] cheerfully admitted that they possessed as many as a dozen votes'. The principle of one man, one vote did not apply until the abolition of plural voting in 1889.
4   Sheppard may be the best known of the New Zealand suffragists, but Atkinson (2003, 85) dates the movement to the publication in 1869 of a pamphlet titled 'An Appeal to the Men of New Zealand', in which Nelson woman Mary Ann Muller wonders why women are denied the vote when they possess the same abilities that qualify men for that right.
5   Cooke (1999) recounts that the Premier (Prime Minister) at the time, Richard Seddon, and other senior members of the administration were politically opposed to the Bill, and supported it in the House only on the assumption that it would be vetoed by the Legislative Council (thereby ensuring the appointed upper chamber, rather than the elected House, would be the target of any ensuing public opprobrium). When the Council waved the Bill through, it is said that 'the Prime Minister, in an alcohol-stimulated fury, seized the Leader of the Council by the throat in a parliamentary corridor' (235).
6   An earlier legislative proposal promoted in 1846 would have made literacy in the English language a prerequisite for the franchise (Atkinson 2003). That provision was dropped from the 1852 Act.
7   Māori were not the only group with dedicated parliamentary representation. Two ring-fenced seats for Otago goldminers were already in existence, as was a Pensioners Settlement electorate in Auckland. An electorate for Westland goldminers was also created in 1867 (Atkinson 2003).
8   While most Māori were effectively barred from participation in formal colonial politics until 1867, intense Māori political activity was taking place (and has continued to do so) in other

institutional spaces. Cox (1993) examines the long, vigorous history of Māori political movements from Pai Mārire and Kīngitanga through to the emergence of the Māori Congress near the end of the twentieth century.

9   'European' electorates became 'general' electorates in 1975. Voters of *exactly* half Māori descent (and who knows how that was established) or less could choose to vote in a European or Māori seat.

10  The secret ballot is important to a democratic system to minimise the possibility of voters being coerced to vote a particular way.

CHAPTER 4

# Imagining Aotearoa New Zealand

*The Politics of National Imaginings*

## Avril Bell

Whenever there is an international disaster – an airline crash, a tsunami, an act of terrorism – a major line of reportage locally will centre on any New Zealanders involved. There is a sense of connection between 'us' here at 'home' and these other individuals, personally unknown to us, but whom we somehow feel related to and concerned for. And when the All Blacks, Black Caps or Silver Ferns win an international game, or Peter Jackson releases a new blockbuster movie, 'we' feel a sense of pride at their success, again often despite not knowing any of the individuals concerned or being in any way involved. We feel that their success is also 'our' success in some way. This is the work of national identity, which creates a link between us as individuals and the wider community – and, importantly, between ourselves and the *idea* of the nation, 'New Zealand'. We make this link between by 'scaling up' our identity from the individual to the collective (Taylor and Wetherell 1995, 73). And importantly, this link is not rational, business-like and self-interested, but emotional, kin-like and caring. National identities are powerful and emotional forms of attachment to a cultural community and to a place – a homeland – and they are no less powerful for the ways in which they are often largely invisible to us, so ordinary and everyday that we don't notice them at all.[1]

This kind of powerful, largely taken-for-granted and emotional form of collective identity has a number of dimensions that I will explore here. Although national identities are experienced by many of us as natural, they are very much social and historical – they are social constructs and change in importance and meaning through time and according to context. In this chapter I will identify some of the ways in which national identities work: how our emotional commitments are linked to political projects; how the construction of the national community always involves excluding some and marginalising others; how national unity is constructed through social practices such as sport and through the historical stories we tell ourselves about the nation; and how this sense of unity and community is exploited by politicians and economic interests.

## What Is National Identity and How Is It Constructed?

Benedict Anderson (1991) argues that nations are 'imagined communities'. The sense of belonging to a shared national community is not based on knowing our fellow New Zealanders, but on *imagining* our connection to them. This sense of connection is brought about through media that addresses us as a national audience of both news and advertising; through the education system where we read books written by New Zealanders and set in New Zealand, learn the national anthem and so on; through the address of politicians; and myriad other banal and everyday symbols and practices (Billig 1995). In the media, for example, people, places and events are linked by their simultaneous existence within particular social contexts – there is a flood in Westport and a murder in Hamilton on the same day. Nothing links these events but the date and the idea that they occur within the same nation, New Zealand. And in linking such events – day after day, week after week – the media also constructs the nation as an entity that lives through time, pre-existing the lives of readers and viewers and, we imagine, continuing after we are all long gone. The imagined nation then has a geographical location, a past, present and future, and is comprised of a population of national subjects united by geography and history and by their identification with a shared, common culture. The national community is a mass community, a community usually of millions, and in some cases more than a billion. Inevitably, then, it is a hugely diverse community but one imagined in significant ways as homogeneous and culturally united.

## Feelings and Politics: The Nation and the State

The emotional element of national identity – the welling of feeling at the haka before an All Black game or as the anthem is sung, for example – makes it seem an issue far from politics. National identity is about good feeling, solidarity and community. All this is true, but national identities are also political projects, fostered by states in particular. According to the discourse or rhetoric of nationalism, the state represents the people and governs in *the national interest*. We take it for granted that our Prime Minister is one of 'us', not a foreigner from elsewhere.[2] Looking at the relationship from this perspective, the state serves the nation/people (see Shaw in this volume). But there are also important ways in which the nation serves the state and operates in the interests of political leaders. One of the key arguments I make in this chapter is that we need to be aware of the ways in which political – and economic – interests seek to manipulate and exploit our powerful emotional attachments to the idea of the nation.

National identities construct the nation as singular and unified; the focus is on imagining a community of shared interests, culture and values. In terms of how the nation serves or is used by the state, this construction of social cohesion provides a means to mobilise the community in support of particular political directions or policies. States send armies to war to defend the nation or the national interest by supporting 'our' allies; politicians promote their policies as in the national interest, and appeal to voters at election time by emulating 'ordinary Kiwi' personas. In these and other ways, political leaders seek to draw on the emotional power of national identity to win public consent for their proposals. This also means that there is never one way of imagining the nation. Rather, as Michael Billig argues (1995, 27), there is always a 'battle for hegemony' between competing versions of what characterises the national community and what count as the core national values; there are always dominant and resistant narratives of the nation.³

## Imagining New Zealanders: Inclusions, Exclusions, Centres and Margins

Etienne Balibar (1991, 49) has called national identity a 'fictive ethnicity', effectively created by the state. There is lots of evidence in support of this idea (see Billig 1995, 19–29) and the New Zealand case is no exception. At the time of early colonial contact and settlement, the term 'New Zealanders' referred to Māori. It was only once Pākehā settlement was well established that the white settler population came to refer to *themselves* as New Zealanders and to identify with the idea of a New Zealand nation.⁴ By this stage also the settler state had been centralised out of earlier provincial governments dotted around coastal settlements, and massive swathes of Māori land had been alienated by sales and confiscations, allowing the state to unify the territory with rail and later roading networks. It was only by this point, late in the nineteenth century, that the state could be said to govern the territory on which the imagining of nationhood could develop. Remembering these beginnings of New Zealand national identity also reminds us that it was a colonial project, a means to construct an identity and sense of belonging for the colonising Pākehā (Gibbons 2002).

The standard story since those beginnings is that the hegemonic or dominant version of New Zealand was imagined first in monocultural, Pākehā and masculine terms – the figure of the pioneer, the soldier and the rugby player combining to become the archetypal Kiwi bloke. This then changes from the 1970s onwards as a result of the political activism of Māori requiring a new hegemonic version, so that by the 150-year anniversary of the signing of Te Tiriti o Waitangi (Treaty of Waitangi) in 1990 the national narrative is bicultural, the story of two equal founding peoples, Māori and

Pākehā. The story ends with the question of where we are at now – have we begun to imagine a multicultural nation that includes the many people of other migrant origins that are now part of our community? Are we now a bicultural or multicultural nation? Or can we combine these two forms of imagining in some way (see, e.g., Bartley and Spoonley 2005)?

These questions raise a crucial point about national imaginings – the national people and the citizens of the state (those carrying a local passport or residence rights) do not exactly overlap. National identities can be more or less inclusive than citizenship. Some citizens and residents can be excluded from the imagining of the national community. And some can be more marginal, while others are more central. As a result of the massive population changes since immigration policy was amended in 1986, there is now beginning to be a place for Chinese and other Asian New Zealanders within the national imaginary, but only now, 30 years later and 150 years after the first Chinese settlers came here.

There is a lot of truth to the national standard story. Certainly the image of the 'New Zealander' has been dominated by Pākehā values and concerns – the practical 'Number 8 wire' can-do attitude (and its anti-intellectual downside) harks back to the pioneers who broke in the land, while the friendliness and informality of New Zealanders perhaps bears the trace of what was a strong commitment to egalitarianism or classlessness that lasted for much of the twentieth century, until the inequalities wrought by neoliberal policies made that patently untrue. But even earlier it was a fiction, experienced as true by many migrants from Britain who had far greater opportunities for social mobility here than in the 'mother country', but not true for Māori, Chinese and Pasifika New Zealanders who were largely excluded from the economic opportunities offered to Pākehā.[5] Importantly, these practices of economic exclusion were bolstered and justified by the imagining of a largely white New Zealand, an imagining that supported the white immigration policy that mostly kept Chinese settlers out around the turn of the nineteenth and twentieth centuries and meted out harsh discrimination against those who did manage to migrate (Murphy 2003; see also Spoonley in this volume).

The exclusion of non-white citizens and residents was also political. New Zealand's governments have always been overwhelmingly Pākehā – and male – in make-up until very recently, and even now we have yet to have a Māori, Pasifika or Asian Prime Minister, while we had our first female leader only in the 1990s.[6] The New Zealand state, then, has always embodied Pākehā – and male – interests and, despite its supposed championing of the national interest, it has often thwarted the interests of other sectors of the community throughout its history.

But the standard story is not entirely true as far as Māori go. Māori have always been *symbolically* important to Pākehā imaginings of 'New Zealand', long before the so-called bicultural era.[7] Despite the real, material marginalisation of Māori within New Zealand society, in the national *imaginary* Māori culture and symbolism have always been crucial to marking the distinctiveness of 'New Zealand' as a nation (see Bell 2014, 28–47). Without Māori, Pākehā culture, a colonial settler culture, was just a derivative offshoot of Britain (see also Gibbons 2002). Pākehā gave their children Māori names, wore pounamu (greenstone) jewellery and created a New Zealand literature that based its distinctiveness on the relation with 'Maoriland' (Stafford and Williams 2006).

When facing outwards to the other nations of the world, Pākehā New Zealand has also always pointed to Māori culture to signify the society's unique national identity. In the late nineteenth and early twentieth centuries, for example, efforts to encourage tourism centred on the construction of Rotorua as a spa resort, with the Te Arawa village Whakarewarewa being a crucial part of the attraction, and important overseas visitors were welcomed, then as now, with a modified pōwhiri (e.g., see Werry 2011, 1–43, 90–133).

In some areas of national social life also – certainly rugby – Māori have always had a central role to play. The first international rugby team to leave New Zealand's shores was 'the Natives', a team made up almost entirely of players of Māori descent, which toured Britain in 1888–89. Natives player Tamati (or Tom) Ellison went on to be the first captain of an official national rugby team; wrote one of the early coaching manuals for the game; and introduced the haka, the black jersey and the silver fern as identifiers of the national team. This early Māori involvement has been crucial in shaping the style of New Zealand rugby (see Hokowhitu 2009; Macdonald 2009, 278; Ministry for Culture and Heritage 2014a).

## Constructing National Unity: Sport and War

Sport worldwide is a hugely influential means by which national identities are routinely produced and reproduced. As we watch 'our' national teams, or catch up with the sports news in the papers or on our smartphone apps, we take up the position of national subjects. Watching, and reading about, sports provides an often *daily* practice of nationhood – and especially of masculine nationhood (Billig 1995, 119–27). As Billig (1995, 122) says about sports news, 'There are always sports pages [and now websites and apps], and these are never left empty. Every day, the world over, millions upon millions of men scan these pages, sharing the defeats and victories, feeling at home in this world of [nations]. This routine leisure practice – and the powerful pleasures it offers – is an important, everyday mechanism that builds and rebuilds the sense of connection to the nation as a lived and felt community of commonality and shared allegiances. The traumatic exception of the 1981 Springbok Tour – which split New Zealand in two around competing ways of understanding the relationship between sport, racism and politics – only points to the more usual ways in which sport unites the community. And because our sports addictions are pleasurable, like the emotional attachment to the nation generally, they seem benign. That sense of commonality and unity of purpose is surely a good thing? It certainly has many positive elements to it, but our national attachments can also be a potent means by which we can be influenced by others.

In *Imagined Communities*, Benedict Anderson (1991, 141) asks why people are prepared to die for the nation (as in cases of war). His answer is that soldiers are prepared to fight and die not out of hatred for the enemy so much as love of the nation – it is the positive and powerful attachment to the imagined nation that can motivate, and also provide justification and solace for (otherwise senseless) deaths in war. Building on this idea, Billig (1995, 125) argues that the practice of national allegiance in following (and playing) sports provides a rehearsal for the call to arms that may be activated by the state in time of war: 'Perhaps we – or our sons, nephews, or grandsons – might respond one day, with ready enthusiasm, or with dutiful regret, on hearing that our country needs us to do-or-die. The call will already be familiar; the obligations have been primed; their words have long been installed in the territory of our pleasure.'

In his cultural history of New Zealand national identity, Keith Sinclair (1986, 143) suggests that the connection between sport and war was widely acknowledged in New Zealand in the early twentieth century. Sinclair cites the way soldiers in the Gallipoli campaign talked about the connection in their letters home, as in the following:

> Yes, it thrilled us when practically the whole of the Christchurch Football Club and the Old Boys' Club offered their services. And I thought of that thrill when I saw the remnant afterwards here and at Cape Helles. And when we talked of the race across the red poppy patches near Sedd-ul-Bahr, I pictured the passing rush across 'The Park' in Christchurch, and I thought of the many playing there who might be playing the game of life here with the seashores for trenchlines, rifles and bayonets for weapons, and freedom for the goal. (quoted in Sinclair 1986, 143–4)

This soldier clearly used rugby as a way of interpreting his Gallipoli experience and as a means to appeal to the men still at home to join the 'team' and to play in the (real) 'game of life' – implicitly positioning sports as mere 'practice'. The way this soldier talks about sport in relation to war is one example of the way sporting experience offers both a means to make sense of war and a form of practice for the roles to be carried out in wartime. And this embedded sense of team unity is crucial for the state to draw on when it wants to call for people to go to war. At these times, the call for national unity must override class and ethnic divides, as well as overcome individuals' interest in not risking their own lives in battle.

## Constructing National Unity and Economic Interests

It is not only the state and politicians who appeal to our nationalist allegiances. Corporations routinely do so also, most obviously in advertisements that tell us that 'Kiwi kids' eat Weet-Bix for breakfast, or that McDonald's 'Kiwi Burgers' are what we like to eat. Clearly, even multinational corporations with no national allegiance – who pay few taxes here and take their profits offshore, thereby making little contribution to the national economy – routinely appeal to national identity to sell us their products.

A clear example of the mobilisation of nationalist sentiment in the interests of an American corporate occurred during the industrial dispute in 2010 between the actors' union (Actors Equity) and Warner Brothers over the refusal of the American production company to employ unionised workers in the filming of *The Hobbit* trilogy. This refusal led to the union blacklisting the production. At the time the argument against the union's move was that the standoff between Warner Bros and the union would result in the movies being filmed overseas, 'meaning job losses, destruction of the film industry and a dent to national pride' (Kelly 2012). Public feeling about the dispute was such that on 25 October 2010 protest rallies around the country attracted thousands of people taking an anti-union stance to express their concern at the possibility of the filming going offshore. It was clear that nationalist pride in the accomplishments of director Peter Jackson and his companies was a key driver for these protests.

It later came to light that there was deliberate manipulation of this nationalist feeling in the interests of Warner Bros and the anti-union John Key National Government (Radio New Zealand 2013). The union blacklist of the production had been lifted days before the protest rallies, but this was denied by Warner Bros, Jackson and the Government at the time. Instead the Government exploited this nationalist sentiment to gain public support for a deal by which Warner Bros received a $25 million tax rebate, and industrial law was changed in the interests of the international film industry (Brooks 2010). This example is a clear case of manipulation of nationalist sentiment by representing particular economic and political interests as the interests of us all as a nation.

## Constructing National Unity: Remembering and Forgetting

A key way to construct national unity is through telling ourselves stories about the nation's past. However, such national histories also involve a mix of inclusions and exclusions, or remembering and forgetting. We tend to think of history as the facts of what happened in the past, but all histories select only particular stories to tell and offer interpretations of the facts. In the case of national histories, internal conflicts in the process of creating a nation are typically 'forgotten', marginalised or excluded. History is the 'tale of the victors' (Walter Benjamin quoted in Billig 1995, 71). And, as French philosopher Ernest Renan ([1882] 1990, 11) noted in the 1880s: 'Forgetting, I would go so far as to say historical error, is a crucial factor in the creation of a nation.' Remembering the violence required to forge the nation in the first place can undermine the story of national unity.

This takes me back to the standard story of New Zealand as a bicultural nation with two founding peoples, Māori and Pākehā. In 2014 the Waitangi Tribunal released their report (WAI 1040) on the claim by Ngāpuhi that in signing the Treaty in 1840 their chiefs had no intention to cede sovereignty to the British Crown; in other words, that British sovereignty had never been gained by consent as is now foundational to the nation's bicultural origin story. When asked to respond to this report, Prime Minister Key commented that '[i]n my view New Zealand was one of the very few countries in the world that were settled peacefully' (Key 2014; see also Wynyard and Walker in this volume). In making this comment, John Key was continuing a long-standing Pākehā tradition of forgetting past conflicts to construct national unity. Most significantly in terms of New Zealand history, the nineteenth-century wars between a number of iwi and British and settler soldiers have been repeatedly 'forgotten' in the telling of national history.[8]

One of the most influential forms of this historical amnesia has been in the lack of nineteenth-century New Zealand topics taught to generations of New Zealand school children in secondary school (see Belich 2001, 546; Sheehan 2010; Simon 1992). The history of the New Zealand Wars and other forms of conflict involved in colonial settlement in the nineteenth century continue to be seen as controversial and divisive. James Belich (2001, 546) has called this historical amnesia a 'cultural self-lobotomy', and it is certainly no help in equipping New Zealanders to develop an informed viewpoint on significant political events such as the release of the

WAI 1040 report. At the same time, within the wider society, New Zealand histories are popular, and the Treaty settlement process has brought the history of these conflicts to the fore (Sheehan 2010, 682–3). Recently, there are signs of change in the official amnesia towards these foundational nineteenth-century conflicts. A 2015 petition to Parliament, led by Otorohanga College students, resulted in the Government's announcement in 2016 that a national day of commemoration is to be established. This day will no doubt become an annual focal point for reflection on the heritage of these conflicts, changing the balance of national remembering and forgetting into the future.

## Conclusion

National identity is only one facet of our identities, alongside ethnicity, gender, sexuality, religion, politics, profession and so on. It is less important to some of us and more important to others. However, its very taken-for-grantedness, its barely visible nature for many of us, is a source of its power. Living as we do in large-scale societies where we cannot know each other personally, national identity helps us feel connected to and concerned for our fellow citizens. It is a powerful social 'glue' that binds us together. At the same time, we should always be wary of appeals to our feeling and beliefs as New Zealanders, and think critically about who is being excluded or marginalised by this appeal; who is making the appeal and why; what the political – and/or economic – interests behind it are; and whether these interests are ones we wish to align with.

### Notes

1 There is no space here to consider the nation as a place. The focus of this chapter is on the national *people*, but see Tucker in this volume for a critique of the image of the nation as 'clean and green'.
2 We are not unusual in this respect. The 'birthers', a right-wing faction against US President Barack Obama, hoped to undermine his presidency by erroneously arguing that he was not in fact American-born, and therefore he was ineligible to be President.
3 For example, see McAllister (2012) on resistant indigenous imaginings of national identity.
4 See Bayard and Young (2002) for empirical evidence based on ethnic labelling in Otago newspapers from 1860 to 1995, which clearly shows this shift occurring in the late 1880s.

5 In different but equally significant ways, women were long marginalised, economically and politically (see both Shaw and Elizabeth on gender in this volume).
6 Jenny Shipley became the first female Prime Minister when she replaced Jim Bolger as leader of the National Party in 1997, and Helen Clark was the first woman elected to the position of Prime Minister in 1999.
7 I say 'so-called' because the economic and political marginalisation of many Māori continues even in these recent decades in which we have proclaimed the equality of the two founding peoples. See, for example, Sibley and Liu (2004) and O'Sullivan (2007).
8 See Hilliard (1999) on the omission of this history from the 1940 Centennial Surveys commissioned to mark the centenary of the signing of the Treaty of Waitangi.

**PART II**

# New Zealand Peoples

CHAPTER 5

# Ka Pū Te Ruha, Ka Hao Te Rangatahi

*Māori Identities in the Twenty-first Century*

Tahu Kukutai (Waikato-Maniapoto, Te Aupōuri) and Melinda Webber (Ngāti Whakaue, Ngāti Hau, Ngāti Kahu, Ngāti Hine)

Māori identities in the twenty-first century continue to evolve while retaining vital links with the past. Like indigenous peoples in the colonial settler states of North America and Australia, Māori have shown remarkable resilience in maintaining a distinctive culture and identity in the face of coercive pressures to assimilate. The majority of Māori retain a sense of connection to ancestral iwi and marae, engage in some form of contemporary cultural practice, and see Māori culture as important (Statistics New Zealand 2013a). Māori comprise about 15 per cent of the total population of Aotearoa New Zealand and in some geographical areas the Māori share is as high as half. At the same time, the experience of ongoing forms of colonialism, coupled with demographic transformations and technological innovation, has produced a great deal of cultural and socio-economic diversity within Te Ao Māori (Māori society). This chapter offers a nuanced portrait of the ways Māori peoples adopt diverse cultural expressions to identify themselves, claiming deep connections to elements of traditional Māori identity whilst constantly renewing and reshaping what it means to be Māori in the twenty-first century.

To explore the themes of continuity and change in relation to contemporary Māori identities we draw on the fields of demography, sociology and social psychology. In so doing, we focus on two key contexts where Māori identities are articulated: the national population census and schools. We begin by exploring the dual nature of the census as a site where subjective Māori identities are created and expressed, and where 'objective' data about Māori are collected for the purposes of policy and planning. While Māori experiences with census-taking have at times been fraught, we argue that such data can nevertheless enrich our understanding of collective Māori identities and circumstances (Kukutai 2012).

In the second half of this chapter we consider how schools shape the ways Māori students construct their identities. Schools have long been recognised as a site where students receive and begin to understand messages from society about the value of their ethnic identity. Schools are therefore contexts where we make each other 'ethnic'. Not only are schools central places for forming ethnic identities, but the ways in which teachers and students talk, interact and act in school influences the ways Māori students value and enact their Māori identities in the school context. Furthermore, schools are sites where Māori continue to be subjected to negative expectations that have profound implications for their academic performance (Rubie-Davies, Hattie and Hamilton 2006; Webber 2011).

Social psychology has always suggested that the social groups to which we belong, and the social identities to which we lay claim, help define who we are and thus constitute an essential part of the self (Tajfel 1981). Another fundamental assumption of social identity theory is that people strive to maintain or increase their self-esteem. Māori identity is one type of group identity that influences the self-concept and self-esteem of its members. Whilst Māori identity is only one of the many components that will comprise an individual's sense of self, ethnic identity has been found to be 'consistently positively related[1] to an individual's self-esteem' (Umaña-Taylor 2004, 139). Since self-esteem is determined not only by individual attributes, but also by the collective attributes of the groups with which one identifies, an important question is how Māori cope when they belong to a social group – Māori – that is systemically negatively stereotyped (Mackie and Smith 1998). These socio-emotional aspects of identity development have a significant impact on whether Māori claim, or reject, Māori identity.

## Māori Identities in the National Population Census

The five-yearly Census of Population and Dwellings remains the key source of official data about Māori. Such data are used for a wide range of purposes, from determining electoral boundaries and population-based funding in social spending, to informing policies to enhance Māori cultural and linguistic vitality. Despite appeals to the objective and scientific nature of the census, the context and motivations underpinning census-taking have always been tied to the exercise of power. For indigenous peoples worldwide, the census has often served as an instrument of state control and reflected ideas about racial difference that were (and sometimes still are) used to justify European domination (Anderson 1991). In Aotearoa New Zealand, the interest in counting Māori-European 'halfcastes' in the 1800s and early 1900s was clearly linked to colonial policies of racial amalgamation and government efforts to limit the boundaries of Māori identity and entitlement (Kukutai 2012). Nowadays, the census tends to be seen as a site for group empowerment and recognition rather than control, and receives broad support from iwi and Māori organisations and communities.

Aotearoa New Zealand is one of a small number of countries around the world that asks multiple identity questions in the census. Since 1991 it has been possible to identify as Māori on the basis of ancestry, ethnicity and iwi (tribe). Each of these is conceptually distinct and yields populations that differ in size and composition. As Table 1 shows, the largest and most inclusive grouping is the Māori descent population (ancestry basis).

**Table 1:** Parameters of Māori identity (Statistics New Zealand 2013a).

| | |
|---|---|
| Māori descent | 668,724 |
| Māori ethnic group | 598,602 |
| Iwi affiliated | 545,941 |

In 2013 the question read: 'Are you descended from a Māori (that is, did you have a Māori birth parent, grandparent or great-grandparent, etc)?' Nearly 669,000 individuals ticked the Māori descent box. The number identifying as Māori on the basis of ethnicity – meant as a measure of cultural belonging rather than ancestral heritage – was substantially lower at just under 600,000. Most of the remaining 69,000 Māori descendants identified solely as 'New Zealand European' (in 2013 there was no 'Pākehā' tick-box). That a sizeable number of New Zealanders acknowledge their Māori ancestry but do not feel Māori in a cultural sense may reflect their level of comfort and familiarity with Te Ao Māori in terms of family upbringing and networks, as well as personal choice.

Turning to iwi, just under 536,000 individuals reported at least one iwi affiliation in the 2013 census, representing 83 per cent of the wider Māori descent group (Statistics New Zealand 2013a). This share is surprisingly high when we consider that most Māori live outside of their tribal rohe (boundaries). The migration of Māori from rural heartlands to towns and cities after World War II dramatically changed the Māori social structure. A classic study of urban Māori migrants in the 1950s observed that, for many, 'the tribe was largely an abstract concept' (Metge 1964). The revitalisation of iwi identity, a process that began in the 1970s, reflects a number of factors including Treaty settlement processes which have raised both the public profile of iwi and the incentives for individuals to affiliate, along with shifts in the broader socio-political environment. A significant driver of iwi population growth in the census is the addition of 'new' affiliates who have discovered or reconnected with their whakapapa (genealogy) (Kukutai and Rarere 2013). Waikato and Ngāi Tahu (Kāi Tahu) are instructive examples. Between 1991 and 2013 each iwi increased by 80 and 170 per cent respectively. This growth far exceeds what can be explained by natural increase alone (i.e., more births than deaths). Little is known about whether these patterns of identification carry over into membership registers maintained by iwi themselves. While the census relies entirely on self-report, iwi registers typically require some form of social recognition – such as endorsement by a kaumātua (elder) – and specific details of a whakapapa connection to marae or hapū (sub-tribe). In such contexts, self-identification alone is insufficient to be recognised as an iwi member. Interestingly, in the census, Māori women were more likely than men to identify with an iwi, particularly in middle age (Kukutai and Rarere 2013). Women were also more likely to report having knowledge of their ancestral connections to hapū, awa (river), maunga (mountain) and tupuna (ancestors) (44 per cent of Māori women knew all these, compared to 37 per cent of Māori men) (Statistics New Zealand 2013a).

While most Māori are counted in all three census groupings shown in Table 1, there are stark differences between those who have multiple expressive ties to Te Ao Māori, and those whose only connection is through ancestry (Kukutai 2010). The former are much more likely to speak te reo Māori, to live in areas with a high Māori population share, to be partnered with a Māori and to have a lower socio-economic status. The reasons for this are complex but reflect, among other things, long-standing ethnic inequalities, differences in access to Māori culture and networks, and changes in the 'costs' associated with being Māori.

## Multiple Ethnic Identification

In diverse societies such as Aotearoa New Zealand, there is a general consensus that individuals should be allowed to identify with multiple ethnic groups rather than be forced to choose one. In 2013, the share of the total New Zealand population reporting two or more ethnic groups was 11 per cent, which was double the share recorded in 1991 (5 per cent). Rates of multiple ethnic identification were especially high among Māori and Pacific peoples. Table 2 shows that, for Māori, the likelihood of identifying with two or more ethnic groups declined notably with age. Among tamariki Māori (0–14 years), two-thirds were reported as belonging to at least two ethnic groups, while the share for kaumātua (65-plus years) was

**Table 2:** Single and multiple ethnic identification among Māori by age group (Statistics New Zealand 2013a).

| Ethnic group(s) | Age (Years) | | | | | | Total |
| --- | --- | --- | --- | --- | --- | --- | --- |
| | 0–14 | 15–24 | 25–44 | 45–64 | 65–84 | 85+ | |
| Māori only | 35.0 | 41.8 | 48.2 | 62.7 | 70.5 | 62.7 | 46.5 |
| Māori and European | 48.1 | 47.0 | 45.2 | 34.0 | 27.6 | 35.9 | 43.5 |
| Māori and Pacific | 6.2 | 4.6 | 2.7 | 1.1 | 0.4 | – | 3.8 |
| Māori and Asian | 0.6 | 0.4 | 0.4 | 0.3 | 0.5 | – | 0.4 |
| Māori, European and Pacific | 7.3 | 4.4 | 2.1 | 0.8 | 0.3 | – | 3.9 |
| Māori, European and Asian | 1.4 | 0.8 | 0.6 | 0.4 | 0.2 | – | 0.8 |
| Māori and any other combination | 1.4 | 1.0 | 0.8 | 0.7 | 0.5 | – | 1.0 |
| Total | 100 | 100 | 100 | 100 | 100 | 100 | 100 |

less than one-third. The most common combination by far was Māori and European (43.5 per cent), followed by Māori and Pacific, and Māori, European and Pacific (both nearly 4 per cent). Relatively few Māori identified with an Asian ethnic group.

Why do some Māori identify exclusively as Māori in the census, while others identify with multiple groups? And how do these patterns of identification relate to social relations such as intermarriage and inequality? Māori have a long history of intermarriage with Pākehā, dating back to the early nineteenth century. Most of these unions involved Pākehā men and Māori women, reflecting the dearth of migrant women at the time, as well as gendered and racial norms about sexuality. A study of intermarriage in Auckland in the 1960s found that about two in every five Māori had a Pākehā spouse (Harré 1966). Today intermarriage rates for Māori remain high. In the 2013 census, nearly half of Māori aged between 25 and 44 years were partnered with someone who reported a non-Māori ethnicity (Didham and Callister 2014).

While intermarriage blurs boundaries in a very intimate sense, there is ample evidence that the ethnic labels that people choose, or are designated, are not simply reflections of their parental ethnicities. A 2005 study of birth registrations showed that about 70 per cent of babies born to a Māori-only parent and a European-only parent were identified as both Māori and European (Howard and Didham 2007). The remaining babies were identified as solely Māori, or solely European, with a strong bias towards Māori. Identification decisions are mediated by structural dynamics, personal preferences and experiences, and social context. Structural factors include the ethnic composition of neighbourhoods and networks, the rigidity of status differences between groups, and ethnic politics. Personal influences include family context, lifecycle stage, physical characteristics and socio-economic circumstances. The context in which ethnicity is asked also matters, including how it is asked and by whom, as well as when, where and why (Doyle and Kao 2007; Harris and Sim 2002). In the case of children, it should not be assumed that the decision to identify Māori-European children solely as Māori only reflects the preferences of the Māori parent. Studies suggest that European parents can also play a supportive role in encouraging the intergenerational transmission of Māori identity to their children (Kukutai 2007).

Finally, despite the popular tendency to see ethnicity as a characteristic that is fixed at birth, how people see themselves, and are seen by others, can be fluid. Numerous studies, both in Aotearoa New Zealand and overseas, have shown that how individuals identify themselves, in the census and surveys, can and does change over time and place (Carter et al. 2009; Coope and Piesse 2000; Saperstein and Penner 2014). For Māori, changes in identification usually involve dropping or adding an ethnicity rather than changing groups altogether (e.g., changing from only Māori to only European). The latter does occur but is relatively rare. In the longitudinal Survey of Family, Income and Employment, just over one in five adults who identified solely as Māori in the baseline 2002/2003 survey had changed their ethnic identification within two years (e.g., to Māori and European). For multi-ethnic Māori, the extent of change was much higher, at 57 per cent (Carter et al. 2009). We do not know, of course, whether these changes in identification reflect socially significant changes in how individuals saw themselves or were perceived by others. Checking an ethnic group tick-box on a form provides insights into the expression of identity, but not necessarily the substance in terms of feelings, attitudes, behaviours or lived experiences. To better understand these issues we now look at the context of different expressions of Māori identity in order to inform consideration of how rangatahi Māori (Māori youth) experience and express their identity in the everyday context of schools.

## Emerging Māori Identities

In contemporary Aotearoa, Māori students experience diverse realities and their ethnic identities take various forms in response to the contexts within which they are shaped (Durie 2005). Drawing on Penetito (2011, 29), we assert that 'there are multiple ways of being Māori', none of which are more tuturu (authentic) than the other. Research has shown that the ethnic identities of Māori students can be positively influenced by acquiring and/or maintaining a sense of connection to iwi, hapū and marae, and by engaging in various Māori cultural practices (Hollis 2013; Rata 2012). Nevertheless, there are many Māori who continue to feel disengaged from Māori culture, and as Penetito (2011, 44) has noted, many Māori in this category 'don't know how to join in or how to belong'. Penetito has also stated that disengaged Māori differ in their willingness and ability to access Māori culture, noting that 'they do not know what that is, where to get it if they want it, or even whether it is something worth wanting' (29). For those people of Māori descent who do not consider themselves to be culturally distinct from non-Māori, the social category 'Māori' may not hold much personal significance (Rata 2012). Similarly, there are Māori who consider themselves more affiliated to their iwi or hapū rather than the pan-Māori label. What is clear is that Māori have a plethora of identity options available to them.

For most, if not all of us, our socialisation as racial-ethnic-cultural beings begins early in life within our whānau (family), and much of this socialisation continues during the compulsory years of schooling, from preschool to secondary school, and even further during post-compulsory education, should a person go, and beyond. Māori identity therefore emerges in institutional, cultural and familial contexts; it is neither static nor one-dimensional; and its meanings, as expressed in schools, neighbourhoods, peer groups and whānau, vary across time, space and place. Our focus here is: how and why Māori identity matters to Māori adolescents; and what factors and perceived associated cultural behaviours may impact on their commitment to this ethnic label.

## The Components of Māori Identity

Māori identity, in its broadest sense, is comprised of three key components – race, ethnicity and culture. The three components interact together to give Māori adolescents a sense of individual and collective identity. The first component is race; we cannot avoid the fact that socially constructed *perceptions* of race, and consequently racism, are an everyday occurrence for many Māori adolescents. Notions of race essentialise and stereotype Māori, their social statuses, their social behaviours and their social ranking. In the form of racism, race continues to play an important role in determining how Māori adolescents construe, indeed construct, their Māori identity (Webber 2012).

The second component is ethnicity, which is most closely associated with issues of belonging and membership. Ethnic boundaries operate to determine who is a member, and who is not, by the use of criteria such as language, knowledge of descent, participation in cultural activities and the like (for further discussion of what is meant by ethnicity, see Matthewman in this volume). Therefore, Māori identity is largely dependent on adolescents developing knowledge, and eventual mastery of, component three – culture. Culture dictates the appropriate and inappropriate content of a particular ethnicity; typically knowledge of the language, religion, belief system, art, music, dress and traditions of an ethnic group is designated as the basis of membership in that ethnic group. These elements of culture are part of a 'toolkit', as Swidler (1986) called it, used to create the meaning and way of life seen to be unique to particular ethnic groups. Thus, culture can be seen as the substance of ethnicity and the mechanism by which adolescents might 'demonstrate' their authenticity as group members.

## Positive Māori Identity Development

Developing a positive and strong Māori identity can be complex. Primarily, Māori identity is negotiated, defined and produced through an adolescent's social interactions with others, most importantly their whānau and peers. It is within these interactions that they learn about culture – the behaviours, languages, stories and customs associated with 'being Māori'. However, Māori identity is also influenced by external racial, social, economic and political messages that shape and inform certain identity choices. These components influence the construction of Māori identity, and the meanings Māori adolescents attach to it.

There are a number of key influences on the ways Māori adolescents construct Māori identities (Hollis 2013; Rata 2012; Webber 2011, 2012). The first is their sense of connectedness and belonging to the Māori label. Māori adolescents, across a range of studies, have consistently asserted that Māori identity is associated with knowing what 'being Māori' means, knowing where they come from and knowing what connects them to others as Māori. Hollis's (2013) model of positive Māori youth development identified relationships, involvement in cultural activities, cultural factors (including access to environments to learn about culture and respecting and valuing culture), education/work, health/healthy lifestyles, socio-historical factors (including history, social attitudes towards Māori and Māori youth, community and media) and personal characteristics (such as resilience and having goals/aspirations) as factors contributing towards positive Māori identity development. Hollis's research also argued that key indicators of positive Māori identity development included:

- Collective responsibility – Māori adolescents contributing towards the collective (whānau, community and society) and acknowledging their place amongst these groups.
- Successfully navigating the world – Māori adolescents navigating Māori and non-Māori environments with confidence.
- Cultural efficacy – knowing te reo Māori and tikanga (Māori protocols and traditions); being proud of being Māori and wanting to share that with others.

- Health – Māori students attending to their physical, emotional and intellectual health.
- Personal strengths – individual qualities including confidence, achieving desired goals, personal responsibility and curiosity. (104–5)

Māori adolescents also construct a positive sense of connectedness to their identity as Māori through socialisation messages from their whānau and peers (Webber 2011) and participation in Māori cultural activities (Rata 2012). Arama Rata's (2012) research showed that a school's cultural environment can enhance or constrain Māori identification, which in turn can increase or decrease psychological well-being and engagement in learning. Overall, Rata's results suggested that any school interventions designed to increase Māori adolescents' cultural engagement could consequently enhance their Māori identity, which could then increase their well-being. Māori adolescents who are 'well' are more likely to feel confident in their ability to learn because 'when adolescents . . . develop healthy, positive, and strong racial identities . . . they are freer to focus on the need to achieve' (Ford, Grantham and Moore 2006, 16).

Whānau also play a crucial role in helping Māori adolescents to learn about who they are, and who they are not, by means of socialisation into the cultural aspects of their Māori identity. This form of 'cultural socialisation' can be evidenced in parental practices, including teaching them about their Māori heritage and histories; promoting cultural customs and traditions; and promoting cultural, racial and ethnic pride, either deliberately or implicitly (Webber 2011). Whānau practices like these are likely to promote racial-ethnic pride in Māori adolescents and prepare them to succeed in both their Māori and non-Māori endeavours.

Māori adolescents with salient Māori identity, positive attitudes towards their ethnic group and an awareness of racism are more likely to have the resilience to deal with adversity in the form of racist experiences (Webber 2011). Additionally, the most resilient and tenacious Māori adolescents are those who have a well-developed awareness of the role that racism and discrimination *could* play in their lives. There is clear evidence that having a strong, positive sense of Māori identity may protect Māori adolescents from the negative social and academic impacts of perceived racial-ethnic group barriers or of experiencing interpersonal discrimination and racism based on their ethnic group membership (Webber 2011, 2012).

## Conclusion

'Ka pū te ruha, ka hao te rangatahi' is a well-known Māori proverb which literally means 'Once the old fishing net is worn, it is put aside to make way for the new fishing net'. In the case of this chapter, the old net represents what Māori identity may have signified in the past, while the new net represents the changing and situational nature of Māori identity for younger generations. It refers to the constant remaking of Māori identities to better suit changing contexts, communities and collective needs.

Māori identity in the twenty-first century is a slippery concept. Like other collective or social identities, Māori identity is an overarching category that subsumes others within it. As diverse Māori identities have emerged, a new range of identity expressions – or at least more elastic meanings for old identity expressions – have been required. In examining the parameters of Māori identity, it is clear that there is no absolute, definitive meaning regarding what it means to be Māori. However, the enduring thread that continues to bind Māori together is the ongoing relevance of whakapapa, and a commitment to protecting the collective right to build and maintain salient Māori identities. Who and what constitutes someone as Māori will always be a contested question. Māori peoples in twenty-first-century colonial contexts continue to face many challenges, not least of which is the struggle to retain a distinct identity, beliefs, knowledge and cultural traditions.

### Note

1   A positive relationship implies that when a positive sense of ethnic identity increases, self-esteem also increases.

CHAPTER 6

# Pākehā Ethnicity

*The Politics of White Privilege*

# Steve Matthewman

The novelist Joyce Carol Oates (1999, 189) once wrote: 'Majority populations take themselves for granted as the norm; not accident, still less historical privilege, but "nature" would seem to define us.' Surprisingly, sociology has had little to say about historical privilege and the 'natural' norms of mainstream society. For much of its history the discipline has instead focused on deviance, difference and otherness; in other words, on those who stray from the norm. Its preference has been to gaze down upon the powerless, the minorities and the marginalised, rather than up to those enjoying positions of dominance. Over recent years this has changed, through such developments as the emergence of critical whiteness studies (Delgado and Stefancic 1997). In this chapter I examine this country's majority ethnic population, Pākehā, defined here as New Zealanders of European origin, and consider the privileges that accrue to them.

One of critical whiteness studies' pioneers, Peggy McIntosh (1988), wrote that dominant groups struggle to see their own privilege. She suggests that we should see white privilege 'as an invisible package of unearned assets'

(1) that are regularly used but rarely reflected upon. White people, and their norms and values, are taken as the ideal by which minority groups are judged (and to which they are expected to conform). McIntosh, white herself within a white hegemonic society (the United States), looked at her own life. Things she had previously taken for granted included the abilities to easily hang out with people of her own 'race' most of the time, to rent or buy a house in a desired location without it presenting a problem to her or her new neighbours, to see people of her own ethnicity represented frequently (and positively) in news media and popular culture, to know that most things (education included) will come from her racial perspective (and will validate it), to frequent shops that will sell the things that she likes, to be judged on her own merits rather than as a stereotypical member of her 'race', to deal with authority figures from her 'race', to avoid being the victim of racial profiling, to interact with legal and medical professions that will not racially discriminate against her, and to remain ignorant of persons of colour, their cultures and histories. In short, her advantages are such that she feels welcome in all facets of public life (5–9, 17).

McIntosh also reported reluctance on the part of the majority to close the gaps between disadvantaged groups and themselves. This reluctance sprang from the fear that this would come at the expense of their privileges. A similar situation occurs in New Zealand. Research has shown that Pākehā support the symbolic aspects of Māori culture – things like the inclusion of the Māori version of the national anthem, the use of haka at international sporting events, Waitangi Day celebrations, pōwhiri and the teaching of Māori language – but they remain opposed to anything that challenges the existing structure of economic power. There is widespread opposition to redistribution of material resources, such as Māori ownership of the seabed and foreshore, Māori university scholarships and medical school places, or rates exemptions on Māori land (Sibley, Liu and Khan 2010). McIntosh discusses the systemic advantage of whiteness: it simultaneously confers advantage and offers protection against a large number of social distresses; it provides the opportunity to go through life largely unmarked by ethnicity or race. In contrast, Māori report a different experience of the world, including being on the receiving end of discriminatory practices in the domains of work, housing and healthcare at rates up to ten times those of Pākehā (Harris et al. 2006), running the spectrum from verbal abuse to outright violence, as well as stigmatisation and poorer service provision.

The Treaty Resource Centre (2004) identifies historic and current Pākehā privileges that shape the country's ethnic relations. In the nineteenth and twentieth centuries, Pākehā were able to buy Māori land cheaply; learn and communicate in their own language within educational systems; have the value of their vote increased by the restrictions on the number of Māori parliamentary seats and the (now defunct) prohibition of Māori voting in other electorates (for further discussion, see Shaw in this volume); enjoy full entitlement to unemployment benefits and the old-age pension before Māori could; and access government finance for land development. Some of these privileges have gone, others remain. All of our major sectors (education, healthcare, justice and so on) are structured according to Pākehā values. The Pākehā majority can count upon being free from profiling, surveillance and condemnation on the basis of their ethnicity. Interestingly, when scholars at the University of Auckland's Faculty of Education ran a course in which Polynesian cultural values (both Māori and Pasifika) were dominant, Pākehā students complained about feeling ignorant, peripheral and alienated (Bell 2014, 183). This was a single course in a single degree. They should imagine feeling this way all the time.

## The Sociology of Ethnicity

Thus far we have made reference to skin colour and races. Both form part of everyday discourse. But sociologists prefer to talk about 'ethnicity', which refers to cultural characteristics, rather than 'race', which claims to refer to biological characteristics. The concept of race is problematic. How do you disentangle environmental from genetic factors? Even if you could, would you find biologically distinct populations? Scientists have been unable to. They cannot locate unique races or identify fundamental differences between them. Moreover, race is an identity category that has been put to pernicious uses. Colonial projects, dispossessions, genocides and slavery have been justified on the basis of the racial superiority of the aggressors and the racial inferiority of their victims.

When sociologists speak of ethnicity they are referring to a form of collective identification that is based on selected myths, memories and traditions, and on shared standards and symbols. Membership is conferred through a number of dimensions. Anthony D. Smith (1988, 15–16, 22–31) suggests that those within an ethnic category *typically* share a:

- group name, which separates them from other groups and signifies their 'spirit'
- myth of common ancestry, which bonds the members together
- common history, which gives rise to shared memories and also helps give the group unity
- unique culture, which distinguishes them from non-members. Cultural components include language, religious belief, laws and customs, dress, cuisine, arts and literature
- definite physical territory – a home of their own. This also strengthens notions of community
- collective sense of belonging. Members must identify with each other.

It is important to note that individuals do not have to display all six dimensions in order to 'qualify' for ethnic group membership. There are no strict rules regarding inclusion. For example, it is perfectly possible to be Māori and yet not speak the language.

## Pākehā in Theory and in Practice

Having just detailed a sociological definition of ethnicity, a question comes to the fore: Do Pākehā qualify as an ethnic group? Ethnicity, sociologically understood, speaks to shared memory and history, commonality of customs, language, religion and world view. Yet Pākehā have Scots, Irish, English, Welsh, Croatian, Dutch and other ancestry besides, plus all of the cultural and historical differences that this entails. They may share neither religion nor language nor cuisine, and their histories have often been marked by conflict and warfare. As arguably the foremost theorist of Pākehā ethnicity has said of his own family: 'We were New Zealanders, but Irish New Zealanders. Although statistics may have lumped us among the almost ninety percent of the population descended from the European migration, we did not feel like members of a majority' (King 1985, 29).

Those so lumped now occupy the same terrain and they have the same skin colour. But beyond phenotype (observable traits) and physical location, what do they share? They seem to lack the collective memories and traditions of which Anthony Smith spoke. David Pearson (1989) claims that Pākehā fall short of an actual ethnic group, occupying the more nebulous position of 'ethnic category'. James Urry (1990, 20–21) adds that even then 'it is an empty category as it does not represent an identity but merely means non-Māori'.

In addition to problems in theory there are also problems in practice. Who are Pākehā? Deployment of the term gives us insights into the politics of naming. To begin with, it is unusual for an ethnic group to use a label bestowed by another ethnic group, although not unheard of (Smith 1988, 23). However, in those other cases, it is a minority group adopting the name given them by a majority. In taking on a name provided by a minority group, Pākehā are perhaps unique.

Of course, just who takes on this label yields further insights. Media polls in the early 2000s indicated that at least half of those who qualified as Pākehā eschewed the category ('Editorial' 2001), calling into question the notion of a coherent collective grouping that is conscious of itself. More recently, social scientific research, drawing on a national sample of respondents, shows that New Zealanders of European descent overwhelmingly prefer more depoliticised national identities like 'New Zealander' (49.7 per cent), followed by 'New Zealand European' (24.7 per cent) or 'Kiwi' (13.8 per cent). Preference for 'Pākehā' was a lowly 9.8 per cent (Sibley, Houkamau and Hoverd 2011, 209). Choice of the term was correlated with their replies to a question about something else: feelings towards Māori. Those using 'New Zealander', 'New Zealand European' and 'Kiwi' neither implied nor acknowledged a relationship with Māori. Biculturalism was off the agenda. In contrast, those who self-identified as Pākehā reported positive attitudes towards Māori. The authors concluded that 'the ways in which people name or describe social groups can thus be used . . . to recognize and validate or to mask and exclude peoples and the relationships between them' (Sibley, Houkamau and Hoverd 2011, 214).

We should also note changes in identity politics, the shifting meanings behind being Pākehā. Pākehā and Māori are relational identities. They exist with reference to each other. They are also colonial constructs which came about in the early days of contact. In the 1970s the politicisation of identities accelerated change in settler societies like Australia, Canada, New Zealand and the United States. A 'politics of recognition' emerged (Bell 2014, 140) amongst the majority ethnic group. This politics of recognition acknowledged indigenous peoples, historic injustices wrought by colonisation and the right to redress. Some have explained the emergence of a politics of recognition at this juncture in time as nothing other than an outbreak of white liberal guilt (Rata 2000, 135). But why suddenly feel guilty now? This explanation dismisses history and Māori agency; in particular it ignores a decade of concerted activism involving hīkoi, occupations, protests and intellectual challenges to European supremacy within this country (Awatere 1984). In turn, this local activism was partially inspired by global events, especially the civil rights movement of the 1960s and 1970s in the United States, Black Power and anti-colonial movements.

It is at this precise moment that we see people self-labelling as Pākehā in a different sense: to denote cultural difference, to signal their majority membership status (and the privileges that come with it). Crucially, it was also a way of acknowledging Māori indigeneity. During the 1980s, one claimed Pākehā ethnicity as a mark of respect to Māori, to acknowledge their First Nation status and to recognise the Treaty of Waitangi (O'Connor 1996). Pākehā thus emerged as the necessary 'other' to Māori in a society officially labelled 'bicultural' (Walker 1986). Contemporary Pākehā, then, are a product of the national politics of the 1980s.

A significant new development began in the 1990s: Pākehā calling themselves the 'second indigenous culture' (King 1991), and in the process laying claim to being an ethnic group. As sociologist Paul Spoonley (1991, 56) put it: 'For Pākehā, New Zealand is a young country and we have to create our own traditions, and our own understanding of what it is we are doing and have done. There can't be many cultural groups worldwide who are less tied to a cultural past with so many opportunities.' While the development of a new 'post-colonial' identity can be positive, we should note reservations: first, to be indigenous is to be the traditional occupants of a territory at the point of colonial occupation (United Nations Department of Economic and Social Affairs 2004), which Pākehā were not; and second, this new identity seems to forget settler history and the advantages accruing, both then and now, to the ethnic majority. For Pākehā to say to Māori that 'we are all indigenous' suggests that we are all equal, yet some of us are more equal than others.

## Ethnicity and Inequality: The Myth of Māori Privilege

Ethnicity matters for several reasons. First, it is often a key component of personal identity; how people feel about themselves and their place in the world (for further discussion about ethnic identity and self-esteem, see Kukutai and Webber in this volume). Second, those sharing the same ethnicity are likely to share lifestyles[1] to some extent or another. Anthony D. Smith (1988, 24) reminds us that the origins of the word 'ethnicity' come from the Greek *ethnos*, which signals both living together and being culturally similar. Ethnicity, then, gives us insights into the patterning of social life. Third, members of an ethnic group often share life chances. Simply put, one's ethnicity can have profound impacts upon such things as where you will live, how long you will live and how well you will live. 'Social status hierarchies are literally lethal' (Therborn 2009). Ethnicity, then, is more than individual identity, or shared social activity; it is part of the complex amalgam that determines privilege and deprivation. As such, sociologists recognise it as a fundamental element of social stratification, one of the bases through which systematic inequalities are produced.

Göran Therborn (2009) provides a useful framework for thinking about the causes and consequences of inequality. He argues that there are four mechanisms which create inequalities:

- exclusion: some people are prevented from accessing the good things in life, like good healthcare, schools and jobs
- hierarchical institutions: the social order is constructed with a few at the top and many at the bottom. Those at the top are often reluctant to share their status and privileges with the rest
- exploitation: the 'haves' collectively rip off the 'have-nots'
- distanciation: the idea that some people get ahead and others drop behind, which masks the political and economic decisions that help create inequalities.

Therborn (2009) suggests that through these mechanisms, three types of inequality result: vital inequality, existential inequality, and material or resource inequality. *Vital inequality* relates to quality of health. Evidence suggests that well-being, both physical and mental, is socially shaped. On average, poorer people have worse health and shorter lives, and therefore suffer vital inequality. *Existential inequality* relates to quality of life, the sorts of things one can be and do; the ability to live a life free from prejudice. *Material or resource inequality* includes both social resources, like educational attainment and networks, and financial resources.

We can see how this plays out locally. Statistics New Zealand (2013c) data from the New Zealand Period Life Tables (2010–12) show that '[t]he gap between Māori and non-Māori (which includes Pākehā as well as Pasifika, Asian and others) life expectancy at birth is 7.3 years, in favour of the latter; life expectancy at birth is 76.5 years for Māori women and 83.7 years for non-Māori women; 72.8 years for Māori men and 80.2 years for non-Māori men'. Statistics New Zealand (2013a) data from the 2013 Census show that Māori, when compared to the overall New Zealand population:

- were less likely to have a formal educational qualification (66.7 per cent vs 79.1 per cent)
- had a lower median income ($6,000 less than the national median income of $28,500)
- were less likely to own or part-own a residence (28.2 per cent vs 49.8 per cent).

The Ministry of Social Development's (2010) *Social Report* cited an earlier New Zealand General Social Survey, which found that:

- 16 per cent of Māori had experienced discrimination compared to 8 per cent of Pākehā
- 56 per cent of Māori said when discriminated against it was because of their ethnicity
- 32 per cent of Pākehā said that their experience of discrimination was due to their ethnicity.

The 2010 *Social Report* also noted that:

- 28.3 per cent of Māori were generally very satisfied with life compared to 34.4 per cent of Pākehā
- The Māori unemployment rate was 12.7 per cent compared to the Pākehā rate of 7.8 per cent
- Age-standardised obesity rates were 43 per cent of the Māori population compared to 23 per cent of the non-Māori population
- Age-standardised suicide rates were 16.1 per 100,000 in the Māori population and 9.9 per 100,000 in the non-Māori population.

Avril Bell (2004, 53–54) writes of settler strategies to 'de-authenticate' Māori. Such strategies work to secure white privilege while effacing Māori claims to indigeneity (and vital, existential and material equality). The typical claims are that no full-blooded Māori remain, Māori also colonised (the Moriori) and Māori are immigrants too. An additional strategy is to claim that we are 'awash' in race-based policies which create Māori privilege. These complaints are typically raised by the political right. For example, Dr Don Brash (2004), who was then leader of the opposition National Party, delivered a speech at Orewa which claimed that there are no 'real' Māori left; indeed, no distinct Māori population. He also stated that Māori and Pākehā have very similar income distributions. Finally, history itself was abandoned as a hindrance to progress. Speaking of the

Treaty of Waitangi, he said: 'We cannot allow the loose threads of 19th century law and custom to unravel our attempts at nation-building in the 21st century' (Brash 2004).

This is a routine claim of majority groups in settler societies: that bad things happened in the past, but that the past is now over. The most obvious response to this is that the past powerfully informs the present. As Tracey McIntosh (quoted in Henley 2007) has noted:

> The land issue is the legal, cultural and spiritual focus of almost all Māori grievances today. . . . Many tribes, including mine, never even signed the Treaty, so we just view our land as having been stolen. And above and beyond the Māori's spiritual relationship with their lands, you can make a very strong evidence-based argument for saying that the alienation of our land removed our whole economic base and distorted the whole range of social relationships.

Rather than being an irrelevance, 'this history is so important: for Māori, the injustices of the past have real implications for our present lives. We're still seeing their consequences' (McIntosh quoted in Henley 2007). Drawing on an observation from Patrick Wolfe, Avril Bell (2014, 6) adds that it makes more sense to see colonisation as a structure rather than an (historic) event: 'Structurally, present-day white New Zealanders . . . occupy the positions in our societies that were created by the labour of the early settlers. We still constitute the dominant culture of our societies, and our political and economic institutions are largely governed by people like us.' The majority ethnic group are inheritors of privilege in the broadest sense. Not only are Pākehā inheritors of privilege but Pākehā-dominated institutions, like education, operate to maintain that privilege, for example, through the use teaching resources that are typically written from a Pākehā perspective (Gibbons 2002).

And yet complaints about Māori privilege continue. Such was the topic of a July 2014 speech made by the leader of the ACT Party at the time, Jamie Whyte. Whyte railed against race-based rights, beginning with the Māori electoral roll and Māori parliamentary seats and the existence of a

Māori advisory board for Auckland Council. He has 'forgotten' that originally the seats were established to limit and contain Māori representation (although see Shaw in this volume), and, by extension, advantage Pākehā.[2] Whyte omitted discussion on the first race-based policy in our history: the New Zealand Constitution Act 1852. This made British common law the law of our land, thereby marginalising Māori customary laws and practices (for further discussion, see Walker in this volume). It was fundamental in securing settlers' supremacy, via a system made by them and for them (Durie cited in Borrell and Gregory 2007, 5).

Instead, Whyte condemned 'race-based favouritism' as demonstrated by easier access to university for Māori (his example was admission to law school). Research shows that Māori (and Pasifika) students from low-decile schools are less likely than those from other ethnic groups to go to university, to complete their first year or to continue on with their studies (Madjar et al. 2010). As these students are denied equality of opportunity, what schemes such as lower admission thresholds try to work towards is a greater equality of outcome. The majority of University of Auckland students come from high-decile schools, yet no one rails against years of over-resourcing. As ever, privilege is invisible.

Whyte finished his argument by concluding that the legal 'privileges' Māori have equate to the benefits enjoyed by the French aristocracy prior to the Revolution. He was careful to stress 'legal privilege' as he knew that all of the available social indicators indicate that Māori are not materially privileged. Even setting aside the differences in material privileges (the French aristocracy sat at the top of the social order, owned most of the land and were the nation's wealthiest inhabitants), the comparison with the French aristocracy is still odious. To take but one obvious point of difference: French aristocrats were legally exempt from paying taxes; all Māori are legally obliged to do so. Let us cut to the chase: calls for 'one law for all' and a 'level playing field' are calls to perpetuate the status quo. These current social arrangements systematically advantage some groups over others (as was revealed earlier with official statistics) (Whyte 2014).

## Conclusion

This chapter has looked at Pākehā ethnicity. In considering why ethnicity is important I have focused on the issue of social stratification. This paved the way for a discussion of inequality and of privilege: how it is conferred and denied. In discussing Pākehā ethnicity I suggested that it can only make sense if it is considered in relationship to Māori, Māori activism (demands for recognition and reparation) and British decolonisation (New Zealand has moved away from the 'mother country' but Britain has also moved away from New Zealand). Being Pākehā is being bicultural[3] and being local. Finally, here I claim that it is also necessary to remember that race, or what sociologists prefer to call 'ethnicity', is but one 'identity hook' among many (McIntosh 2001, 145). Thus, who we are cannot be reduced to a single category. We are far too complex for that. Other elements inform our identity, like our age, social class, gender, sexual orientation and nationality. Similarly, ethnicity works as but one 'advantaging system' (McIntosh 1988, 15). Numerous factors contribute to the complex matrix that determines advantage or disadvantage. Often these markers are dismissed. People claim that 'we are all just individuals'. Indeed we are, but sociologists note that we are also social beings enmeshed in networks of mutual dependency. Moreover, privilege and prejudice take no account of individual merit; neither advantage nor discrimination occur because of what we have done; rather, they occur because of what we are seen to be (which links back to our membership of collective groupings like white, black, male, female, gay, straight, etc.). All the more reason, then, to take ethnicity seriously.

### Notes

1. The degree to which those of the same ethnicity share a lifestyle is complicated by other social status hierarchies – like class, gender, sexuality and age – as well differences that arise from locality.
2. While it is true that amendments made in 2012 to the Local Government Act 2002 permit local authorities to constitute Māori wards and constituencies in order to increase representation, very few have. In fact, Māori 'are still chronically under-represented amongst elected councillors' (Hayward 2011, 186).
3. It is important to remember that a bicultural relationship that starts from the vantage point of Māori as indigenous positions Pākehā as just one of a number of tauiwi or 'the rest'.

CHAPTER 7

# Deconstructing the Big Brown Tails/Tales

*Pasifika Peoples in Aotearoa New Zealand*

# Karlo Mila

> ***For Sia Figiel***
> I am the seed of the migrant dream
> the daughter who is supposed to fill the promise
> hope heavy on my shoulders
> I stand on the broken back of physical labour
> knowing the new dawn has been raided
> and milk and honey is linked to obesity and diabetes
> and our hearts are drowning in buckets of povi masima[1]
> —Karlo Mila (2005, 13)

Niu Sila, the land of milk and honey. Niu Sila, the land of opportunity. Niu Sila, the land of education. Niu Sila, the land of good jobs. While Australia is the land of gold, coal, mining and fair weather, no country has been as revered as the promised land of milk and honey by Pacific migrants as Aotearoa New Zealand. And yet, in so many ways, this has not been a migrant dream fully realised, or, as one writer pointed out, it has been 'a dream deferred' (Pearson 1990). This chapter explores the ways in which Pasifika peoples have been positioned and imagined as an ethnic group in Aotearoa New Zealand (for additional analyses of ethnicity in Aotearoa New Zealand, see Matthewman as well as Kukitai and Webber in this volume).

Pasifika peoples made up 7.4 per cent of the New Zealand population (295,941 people) at the 2013 census (Statistics New Zealand 2014b, 16). They are predominantly Samoan (144,138), followed by Cook Islander (61,839), Tongan (60,336), Niuean (23,883), Fijian (14,445), Tokelauan (7176) and Tuvaluan (3,537), as well as a range of much smaller Pacific groups (Statistics New Zealand 2014a). These countries of origin tend to reflect New Zealand's historical colonial relationships in the Pacific.

Pasifika peoples are the third-largest minority ethnic group in New Zealand, after 'Māori' and 'Asian'. A current statistical snapshot of Pasifika peoples tells us that, on average, they live shorter lives and experience a heavier burden of illnesses and health problems compared to others in New Zealand (Statistics New Zealand and Ministry of Pacific Island Affairs 2011). A Pasifika person living in New Zealand is 2.6 times more likely than the average person to be living in hardship (Ministry of Social Development 2009). Pasifika young people are twice as likely to take their own lives, and to experience anxiety and depression (Statistics New Zealand and Ministry of Pacific Island Affairs 2011). The Pasifika unemployment rate almost doubled in the ten years from 2003 to 2013, to 16 per cent, compared with 5.5 per cent for Europeans (Marriot and Sim 2014). An analysis of weekly income shows that Pasifika earn on average $160 less than their Pākehā counterparts (Marriot and Sim 2014). Although education has been a key driver for migration, Pasifika peoples are less likely to be in early childhood education, less likely to pass NCEA, about half as likely as the total population to achieve a level 4 qualification (i.e., a national certificate) or above by the age of 25, and only a third as likely to achieve a bachelor's degree by the same age (Marriot and Sim 2014; Statistics New Zealand and Ministry of Pacific Island Affairs 2010).

It will not take long for these figures to be outdated and updated. However, it is important to understand the enduring aspects of the experiences of Pasifika peoples, and to recognise the implications of being the 'tail' in the national statistics, that is, of significant socio-economic disadvantage and the much poorer health and educational outcomes of Pasifika peoples compared to other citizens of New Zealand. How has this come about? Avtah Brah (2006, 444) writes that 'the manner in which a group comes to be situated and how groups become relationally positioned occurs through a wide variety of discourses, economic processes, state policies and institutional practices, and is critical to its future'.

This chapter interrogates the ways that Pasifika peoples are constituted and positioned as an ethnic minority within Aotearoa New Zealand. I document the ways that structural economic changes have positioned Pasifika peoples in a vulnerable position of socio-economic disadvantage, rather than one in which they reap milk and honey. The chapter also explores the impact on Pasifika peoples of the colonial relationship between the Pacific and New Zealand, and the way that Pasifika peoples are socially constructed and discursively produced as a racialised and visible ethnic minority in New Zealand. This construction leads to the question: Whose interests are served by these representations? In addition, I examine the material, socio-historical and cultural conditions that influence the lives and possibilities of Pacific peoples; and the agency, capital and power available to resist, react and rise.

## Race, Ethnicity and Colonisation

Ethnicity is one of the most significant forces influencing and organising 'individual understandings of reality and the grouping and dividing of peoples in the world today' (Spickard and Burroughs 2000, 1). While the concept of race has been scientifically discredited, ethnicity provides continuing energy to such organising categories: 'People's ethnic identities are often informed and shaped by the ways in which they are racially categorised' (Song 2003, 12).

Pasifika peoples in this country have a history of being racialised, a process that has its roots in a colonial relationship. Examining the socio-historical context of colonisation and migration helps us understand the material and symbolic conditions in which the relationship between Pacifika peoples and other New Zealanders is currently negotiated. Colonial expansion in the Pacific from the late 1700s led to the violent overthrow and forced removal of indigenous sovereignty in multiple Pacific nations, including Aotearoa New Zealand. The might and right of certain countries to conquer and colonise others was legitimised by a racist logic that involved 'ranking peoples in temporal stages, and associating the stages with infancy, adolescence and adulthood', whereby Europeans were the irrefutably superior 'other' (Jolly 2007, 517). To illustrate how deeply this racist logic was entrenched, we can reach back in history to when the New Zealand Administrator in Samoa from 1914 to 1919, Robert Logan, infamously allowed a steamship carrying infected passengers to land in Samoa without quarantine. This led to a pneumonic influenza pandemic killing 7542 Samoans or 20 per cent of the population (Munro 2013). In the midst of this introduced tragedy, the New Zealand Administrator described the grieving Samoan population as being 'like children, they will get over it if they are handled with care. . . . They will later on remember all that has been done for them in the previous four years unless they are spoiled with over consideration' (Meleisea 1987, 122). This is illustrative of simply one colonial encounter in the Pacific. These encounters were characterised by unequal power dynamics, the loss of governance and diminished autonomy of indigenous Pacific peoples over law and decision-making, the extraction of resources and land, and a history of dispossession and possession that marked the beginnings of contemporary ethnic inequalities.

In Aotearoa New Zealand the relationship of domination between Pākehā and Māori, and the dispossession of Māori people and lands forged through war, established the colonial context that pre-dated large-scale Pacific migration to New Zealand. The institutional relationship between Māori and the Crown set the scene for what was possible and probable for Pacific migrants. Article 3 of the dishonoured Treaty of Waitangi provided one of the first statements about citizenship and equality, stating that Māori, as citizens of New Zealand, should have the same rights and privileges as British subjects. If, for Māori, this was understood to extend to the privileges of the same life expectancies, good health, economic security, paid-work opportunities, freedom from incarceration and so on, the Treaty promise that they have parity with British settlers and their descendants has never been fully realised (Durie 2001; Marriot and Sim 2014). Similarly Pasifika peoples, as New Zealand citizens, have not yet experienced the full rights and privileges of equitable citizenship. Although the historical trajectory that brought Pacifika and Māori peoples to their current positioning is very different – an example of a dynamic often glossed as 'roots versus routes' (indigenous vs migrant) (Clifford 1997; Teaiwa 2001) – there are several similarities with regard to current socio-economic, health and educational disadvantage (Marriot and Sim 2014).

The beginnings of mass migration from the Pacific came at a time in the 1960s during which policy towards Māori had shifted from one of assimilation to 'integration'. The shift was stimulated by the 1961 Hunn Report, which officially recognised that the policy of assimilation had not achieved its expected goals (Armitage 1995). This allowed for some continuation of Māori culture and the facilitation of Māori contributions to policy formulation, but also the greater integration of Māori into mainstream Pākehā services (Armitage 1995). Integration came to an end in 1975, when politician Matiu Rata introduced the Treaty of Waitangi Act, signalling a shift to a new era of self-determination, Treaty settlements and increased accommodation by government of Māori interests. With regard to Pacific policy, Fairbairn-Dunlop (2003, 23) explains that the Department of Island Territories (formed as part of the Office of External Affairs in 1919 and then separated off and renamed as the Department of Island Territories in 1943) was abolished in 1968 and amalgamated with Māori Affairs, becoming the Department of Māori and Pacific Island Affairs. In 1974 'Island Affairs' was removed from the mandate of the Department of Māori Affairs, to once again become a concern of the Ministry of Foreign Affairs (Fairbairn-Dunlop 2003). Thus, the timing of the mass migration of Pacific peoples meant that they shared with Māori similar institutional recognition of having distinctive cultural issues and status, rather than simply being subjected to aggressive assimilation policies.

## A Story of Migration

'Migration is largely a response to real and perceived inequalities in socio-economic opportunities, within and between states' (Connell 2006, 60). The opportunities for migration to New Zealand were considered important, especially in a context of relatively 'few opportunities for socioeconomic advancement' in Pacific countries (Lee 2004, 135). Pacific peoples arrived in large numbers in the late 1960s and early 1970s in response to a labour shortage in New Zealand. They were encouraged to migrate by New Zealand, and targeted to fill unskilled and low-skilled jobs in a restricted range of secondary industries (Ongley 1996, 2004).

Lay (1996, 13) writes: 'In most cases these immigrants did the jobs Pākehā New Zealanders no longer wished to do or had been educated beyond: shift work, factory work, assembly line production, processing, cleaning, work involving long hours in unpleasant conditions.' Because of the limited opportunities for permanent entry into New Zealand for most Pacific peoples,[2] many entered as temporary visitors and overstayed their permits (Ongley 1996). It is said that this practice was tolerated by the state and encouraged by employers – as long as there was a need for low-skilled labour in secondary industries (Trlin 1987).

In 1973–74, an oil crisis changed the nature of the global economy and New Zealand faced a recession, during which unemployment rose from 0.1 per cent to 5.6 per cent, and the secondary industries, where the majority of Pasifika workers were concentrated, were hit hardest (Ongley 1996, 20). Jobs, once plentiful, became scarce. One of the responses to this economic downturn, loss of jobs and competition for scarce resources was to 'racialise' workers from the Pacific (Spoonley 1996). The New Zealand Government embarked on an 'overstayers campaign' from 1974 to 1976 in which Pasifika peoples were targeted as illegal immigrants in New Zealand and were seen to be threatening the rights of 'New Zealanders' to jobs (Spoonley 1996). The campaign included policies that identified 'Pacific Islanders' as 'overstayers', leading to the infamous Dawn Raids (Liava'a 1998), which also involved the police stopping and arresting individuals, including Māori, who did not look like 'New Zealanders'. As Lay (1996, 13) says, 'xenophobic feelings were fomented by the National Government during the latter half of that decade and the word "Islander" came to assume a pejorative aspect'.

The recession brought large-scale chain migration to a grinding halt and was followed by a period (1984–92) of intense restructuring and neo-liberal reform that had further significant and negative repercussions for Pasifika peoples (Ongley 1996). Manufacturing industries had relied on tariffs to protect them from competitive imports, and the removal of those tariffs resulted in massive job losses among Māori and Pacific peoples especially (Bedford 1994). Highly concentrated in low-skilled occupations in vulnerable industries, they were particularly susceptible to economic fluctuations and structural reform (Spoonley 1996). Hundreds of thousands of jobs were lost in the primary and secondary sectors. This was paired with growth in the tertiary sector, which required technological, professional and business skills or capital that most Pasifika workers did not have (Ongley 2004).

Within a decade, the unemployment rate of Pasifika peoples rose from 6 per cent to 29 per cent (Ongley 2004). In the late 1980s, Pasifika peoples were more likely to be participating in the labour market than the rest of the population (de Raad and Walton 2007, 8). By the mid-1990s their participation was well below the average and has remained so ever since (de Raad and Walton 2007, 7). In 1986, Pasifika peoples earned a real median income that was 89 per cent of the national real median income (Statistics New Zealand 2002b). By 1991 – only five years later – this had dropped to a ratio of 69 per cent of the national real median income (Statistics New Zealand 2002b). During the early 1990s there were net losses of Pasifika citizens back to Pacific homelands (Bedford 2007, 2).

The chain of events described above shows how Pasifika peoples became positioned in New Zealand society, economically, culturally, socially and symbolically. Pacific migrants were encouraged to come to New Zealand to fill unskilled or semi-skilled jobs in predominantly secondary industries. In competitive markets they occupied devalued positions associated with limited capital. One way of analysing this situation from a sociological perspective points to the role that capitalism and its competitive struggle for scarce resources plays in stimulating racial discrimination against Pacific migrants (Loomis 1990). This perspective argues that capitalism dehumanises migrants as ready-made units of human capital (Miles 1984) who can be dispensed with when demand for their skills is low. Thus, ethnically marked migrant minorities are particularly vulnerable to being targeted as 'surplus to need' and disposed of economically and politically. However, this analysis ignores the history of colonisation and entrenched racism that pre-dates migration of racially marked minorities, and which effectively enables ethnic/racial targeting in the contemporary labour market. To explain the current position of Pasifika peoples in Aotearoa New Zealand we need, therefore, to consider how capitalism, colonialism and racism work together. But before we can do that it is time to think about racism.

## Racism and Pasifika Peoples as an Imagined Community

Ifekwunigwe (1999, 13) describes racism as a process whereby '[b]iology and culture are inaccurately conflated[,] and specific social meanings attached to physical characteristics create politically charged, manufactured[,] hierarchically ranked conceptions of Blackness and Whiteness[,] which in turn govern inter-group relationships'. In a New Zealand context, Pasifika peoples are racially marked and Pasifika embodiment is interpreted differently from context to context (Underhill-Sem 2003). On the rugby field and among the All Blacks, Pasifika male bodies are celebrated. In a crime and punishment context, Pasifika male bodies are associated with racist discourses of violence, rape, gangs, fear and danger. Pasifika peoples thus construct their identities and live their lives at the intersection of positive histories, language and culture, and negative and stereotypical ideas and beliefs produced by the dominant group.

The Human Rights Commission (2012) reported to the United Nations that 'Māori, Pacific and ethnic people do suffer from racism and discrimination in New Zealand', and that Māori and Pasifika peoples are more likely to be economically marginalised and targets of structural discrimination than other people. Of the 10 per cent of New Zealanders who reported feeling discriminated against in the 2008 and 2010 New Zealand General Social Surveys, 6 per cent cited skin colour, race, ethnicity or nationality as the main reason for being discriminated against, with most experiencing this in a public place or their workplace (Statistics New Zealand 2012b). Darity and Nembhard (2000) conducted a multi-country analysis of labour market discrimination that included New Zealand. They observed 'persistent discrimination in all twelve countries studied' and 'institutional racism and cultural discrimination', saying 'those who get the "short stick" continue to face poor prospects for full economic inclusion and justice' (310).

The question must always be asked: Whose interests are served by a particular representation of the Pacific ethnic category? What does it mean to be a Pasifika person growing up in New Zealand, as opposed to a Pākehā? In what ways does the ethnic category of 'Pacific-ness' shut down and close what is possible for young people? To what extent does a body ethnically marked as Pasifika influence trajectories, learning, employment, enjoyment in the world and participation in national life? As Somers (1994, 606) writes, 'all of us come to be who we are (however ephemeral, multiple, and changing) by being located or locating ourselves (usually unconsciously) in social narratives rarely of our own making'. This is essentially a power struggle over how to 'determine, delimit, and define the always open meaning of the present' (Bourdieu 1985, 728).

Given the challenging context of considerable material disadvantage and powerful discourses that stereotype, fix and limit what is possible for people who are identified as belonging to this ethnic group, what are the emancipatory and advantageous options and levers for change available to and for Pasifika peoples? What are the ways of contesting influential racist narratives, of opening up the signifiers of the way this ethnic group is imagined, so that the interests and aspirations of Pasifika peoples are served? How can the material conditions be improved and the entrenched inequalities reduced? There are no easy answers. There is a need to resist the desire to simplify and over-resolve complicated dynamics and provide inadequate policy answers where perhaps there are often only questions that are slowly living themselves out.

## Conclusion

The statistical signs of inequality and significant disadvantage cannot be ignored; they are important because of their implications for many Pacific peoples living here in Aotearoa New Zealand. However, we must ensure that we do not shut down what is possible, or view Pasifika peoples solely as a problem population that requires 'fixing'. In the light of demographic trends for Pasifika peoples – high youth unemployment, disproportionately less economic capital, shrinking opportunities and limited levers for social mobility – the challenge has never been so acute. We must contend with a powerful, persuasive and unsympathetic neoliberal discourse that blames victims for their inability to realise their potential within a system that fundamentally relies on inequalities to sustain it and that protects the interests of those with power and privilege. An empathetic analysis of socio-cultural, discursive and economic conditions that may or may not seed change is critical. The challenge is to find the levers for transformation, to realise advantages and overcome challenges, to work at the personal and political levels, to make an impact in individual and collective ways, to target the macro and the micro.

Similarly important is an agenda of research for resilience, resistance, agency and enabling (Smith 1999). If we are able to recognise sites of influential participation, acknowledge the range of contributions made by Pasifika peoples to New Zealand, and celebrate the realised opportunities within a context of constraints and disadvantage, this will provide important counter-narratives to the dominant discourses, and will provide valuable resources from which subsequent generations can draw to construct empowering identities infused with the sense of entitlement inherent in citizenship.

There is always going to be the tenuous migrant positioning, even for the next generation of Pasifika peoples. On the one hand there is the option of not biting the institutions that feed us and simply seeking a migrant dream of individual economic mobility, following the narrow range of pathways that enable it. On the other, is the option to challenge the state and status quo, to work to open up collective pathways and to consciously choose strategies that enable the benefits of full participation for all. This option requires many of the gifts of sociology, a critical socio-historical and socio-economic analysis, a decolonising agenda, the analytical tools to interrogate and deconstruct dominant discourses, and a commitment to transforming society in order to make it more equitable. Inevitably, of course, it will require more.

### *More than the sum of our parts*
Facts rarely speak for themselves,
with ancestral pride and sociological imagination
let us ask better questions.

Let us not follow the numbers
that make us add up to
not enough.

Even numbers are rarely even.
We find ourselves on odd un-level playing fields
where we have to high jump bar graphs,
pole vault poverty lines,
climb the bell curves
of slippery privilege
to be considered equal.

We always have a way to go.

Some days, the divides in the mind
can be too wide to straddle
especially when widely documented
well-established empirical track-records of failure
are front of mind
for blindfolded professionals and institutions
who find us and forever bind us,
three-legged in every race.

It's easy to get angry
when six-figured salaried head-starts
look back and wave, full of first-place and disdain
for the runners-up, with no idea of the hurdles
or the funny business at the starting gate
or the violent overthrows at the beginning
of a dehumanised race.

With short memories and slow-burning strategies,
national standards, benchmarks, Blueprints, policy docs
search for quick-fire quick-fixes and politicians land low blows
in a game where the gold has gone
to the same people for a long time.

Some days, I have entitlement envy.
But in the cheap seats, still we reach,
still believing in deconstructed dreams
low deciled and deprived, reaching
for the glow we see on the other side.

But we must promise ourselves
that we will never follow the numbers
down the rabbit holes of deficit,
get stuck there in a zero-sum game
finding ourselves adding up to
the sum total of the problem.

Instead we must search for the unseen calculations,
the minuses, the divides, the long distances,
the tiny fractions of proportions left-over,
the skinny pieces on the pie chart plate,
the disproportionate odds ratios
that explain the terrain
where we land disadvantaged feet,

but that never adequately measure our hopes,
energy, effort, offerings, or heartbeats.

With the right information,
let us find the solutions
we already know our people to be,
always so much more
than the sum of our parts.

**Notes**

1. *Povi masima* (Samoan) is a cheap and very fatty form of salted beef, sold in clear plastic buckets in some supermarkets.
2. As New Zealand citizens, Pacific peoples from Niue, Tokelau and the Cook Islands faced no limitations.

CHAPTER 8

# The Asianisation of Aotearoa

*Immigration Impacts*

## Paul Spoonley

As a settler society, New Zealand has been characterised by a particular nation-building project that reflected two things: the fact that the primary colonial agent and arrivals came from the United Kingdom and Ireland; and the desire to create a 'Britain of the South Seas' (Belich 1996). At the core of this was a racial project to ensure that the peopling of the country was largely (and almost exclusively) confined to a particular group of arrivals, with an explicit political and populist framework designed to exclude racialised others, and specifically settlers from Asia.[1] The other key racial 'othering' involved Māori and the marginalisation or replacement of their key cultural identities and practices. This racialised, nation-building project did not change its core elements from the early 1800s through to the 1960s (for more on Pākehā identities, see Matthewman in this volume; for a different take on the nation-building project, see Bell in this volume).

This project and the framework that underpinned it changed dramatically in the 1980s when a reforming Labour Government hollowed out the state in terms of its responsibilities and reach. But while this Government, via neoliberalism, shifted responsibility in core areas of institutional activity from the state to individual citizens, it also simultaneously recognised the rights of tangata whenua (albeit unwittingly at times). It also finally altered the 'white New Zealand' orientation of the nation-building project, and specifically the underpinning immigration framework. This permitted, for the first time, significant migrant flows from Asia to New Zealand, in a distinct counterpoint to the country's colonial history.

By 2000, permanent migrants were increasingly arriving from Asia, and by 2010, inflows were dominated by arrivals from China and India, with the impacts becoming very obvious in Auckland in particular. Asian arrivals had significantly changed the education landscape; Asian food and festivals were now a major part of the leisure landscape; and Asian ethnoburbs (or concentrations of communities from a particular ethnic background) and ethnic precincts (or the co-location of businesses involving owners and operators from the same or similar ethnic backgrounds) had emerged. By the 2013 census, those who self-identified as Asian comprised 11.8 per cent of the national population and 23 per cent of the Auckland population. This complete reversal of a colonial pattern of migration and inclusion/exclusion presents some significant challenges for the construction of 'New Zealandness'; the recognition of minority group rights and the acknowledgement of biculturalism and the political ambitions of Māori; and policy platforms and recognition. The imagined communities (Anderson 1991) of Aotearoa now take on different and contested forms.

## The Sociology of Colonialism and Otherness

New Zealand's colonial trajectory parallels that of certain other white settler societies, notably Canada and Australia (see Wynyard in this volume). This trajectory was dominated by colonial ambitions and controlled by the United Kingdom; displaced an indigenous people and communities; reproduced the values and institutions of the colonial master; and was built on a narrative of nationality which drew upon racial views about the superiority of Europeans, and their institutions (see Rattansi 2005).

In many ways, this colonial trajectory of New Zealand differed little from comparable settler societies (Bell 2014), with some elements that were to become increasingly important in the late twentieth century: a treaty signed in 1840 (soon dismissed) and some interesting concessions (co-option) such as the establishment of four Māori seats in Parliament in the 1880s (see Shaw in this volume). However, these were relatively minor in terms of the overall trajectory of the colonising process, and an orthodox analysis of colonialism is perfectly adequate to explain the sociology of colonial New Zealand.

By the late nineteenth century, natural fertility (births minus deaths) was increasingly responsible for the population growth of New Zealand, so more and more New Zealanders were New Zealand-born. But of those who did arrive from elsewhere, the bulk still came from the United Kingdom; there was no lessening in the national project to populate the country with the preferred 'race'.

> During the inter-war years, the so-called 'British stock' was considered the unquestioned 'race' with which to populate the dominions and create a vaster and more successful British Empire. A social imperialist doctrine of the time saw the dominions as an opportunity for economic development and a means of renewal for a 'British race' polluted by industrial urbanism. (Pickles 2009, 255)

Alongside the settlement of the country, the establishment of the institutions of colonial control, and the replacement of the values and institutions of Māori, there was an explicit project of establishing an exclusive nationalism, targeted specifically (but not only) at Asian arrivals. 'Racialisation' is the construction and articulation of racially defined 'others' in negative ways, as 'problems' and as a threat to dominant groups and nationalities. A group that is racialised is 'assigned a special position in ideological relations (as well as being simultaneously assigned to a specific position in economic and political relations)' (Miles 1982, 168). Chinese miners arrived in New Zealand in the 1860s and by 1871, when there were 2641 Chinese (nearly all men) resident in New Zealand, they represented the largest non-British group. This prompted one of New Zealand's first racially motivated moral panics directed at the 'yellow peril'. New Zealand adopted the policies and legislation of Australia and California, and sought to exclude Asian arrivals and to deny those who had arrived the rights of other residents, settlers and citizens. Between 1879 and 1920, there were 33 Acts which articulated the racialisation of Asians, initially directed at Chinese and then later at Indian arrivals. These ranged from the denial of New Zealand citizenship to Asians (which lasted through to 1951 even if Asians had been born in New Zealand), as well as the denial of normal citizenship rights, such as access to welfare. But there was also a range of minor restrictions and requirements. One Act specified that farmers had to provide separate accommodation for those Chinese who were part of shearing gangs. The 1881 Chinese Immigration Act imposed an excessive arrival tax on Chinese and a limit (according to the tonnage of the ship) on the number of Chinese who could arrive on any given ship. Some of these provisions were altered and made more restrictive by the 1896 Asiatic Restriction Act and others by the 1920 Immigration Restriction Amendment Act (see Spoonley and Bedford 2012).

The exclusive nationalism of New Zealand colonialism had an inward focus – on Māori – and an outward one that targeted all non-British arrivals or residents, particularly Asians. There were some moves to recognise Asians by the First Labour Government both prior to and after World War II. However, it took until the 1950s and, in some cases, the 1960s before the more racist legislative and policy elements were removed. This still did not stop local practices, such as the banning of Chinese from certain public buildings. As late as the 1950s, barbers in Pukekohe refused to cut the hair of Chinese or Indians and the Franklin Federated Farmers were calling for the confiscation of Asian land and the repatriation of Asians (Leckie 1985, 124).

## Internationalising Aotearoa

The neoliberal experiment of the Fourth Labour Government (1984–90) broke the social contract, some elements of which had existed since the 1890s, others since the 1930s. At the core was a hollowing out of the state and the move to private-sector ownership and activity, and an emphasis on making individuals or families/whānau increasingly responsible for meeting their own social needs (such as health and housing) through the private sector. This economic reform was accompanied by two significant departures from the white racialised nationalism of colonial New Zealand. Firstly, there was a new recognition, albeit partial, of Māori as tangata whenua and of the Treaty of Waitangi as part of the legislative and moral foundations of the country. This recognition included limited acknowledgement of Māori self-determination. These changes were not without opposition, disapproval and contestation (Veracini 2008), but there was a noticeable shift in the discursive and constitutional recognition of Māori as what Kymlicka (2007) refers to as 'a national minority' (typically indigenous communities or nations that could lay claim to occupation and cultural identity prior to colonisation).

Secondly, there were significant changes to the white New Zealand immigration framework from 1986. The preferred-country source requirements (primarily a specified preference for migrants from the United Kingdom, although this was extended to other European countries) were dispensed with, and between 1986 and 2000 New Zealand adopted the 'points system' of Canada and Australia in which would-be immigrants are granted points on criteria that have nothing to do with ethnicity, nationality or 'race'. (This is not strictly true as some of the English-language requirements instituted in the 1990s sought to filter out those from non-English-speaking origins.) For the first time, anyone who met the points criteria could apply to come to New Zealand as a settler. And they did. The first major arrival groups from Asia came from Taiwan, Korea and Hong Kong after 1990. Many New Zealanders did not quite realise what the impact of the new immigration policies would be, and there was a reaction.

New Zealand had experienced a major racialised moral panic in the 1970s that was directed at the arrival and presence of Pasifika. It was epitomised in the 'overstayers' campaign, which lasted through the 1970s and continued into the 1980s (Spoonley and Bedford 2012). The arrival of Asians in the 1990s produced another moral panic. The Pat Booth and Yvonne Martin 'Inv-Asian' articles that appeared in Auckland community newspapers in April 1993 marked the beginning of the panic, and eventuated in the establishment of New Zealand First, then primarily an anti-immigrant party. In February 1996 – in preparation for a general election later in the year – the leader of that party, Winston Peters, began a campaign that was directed at immigrants, which was generally understood by the electorate to mean 'Asian immigrants'. New Zealand First's position on Asian immigrants contributed significantly to its winning 20 per cent of the votes.

There were some interesting dimensions to these racialised politics and populism. The points system, which applied to 60 per cent of approvals for permanent residence, targeted those who were well qualified and able to contribute economically to New Zealand. Because of this, the new immigrants (including Asians) were better educated than the average New Zealander and had disposable income that they spent largely in the Auckland housing market and on consumables. These were highly skilled and highly capitalised immigrants; they were also very visible. Together, this visibility and relatively high status socio-economic position fuelled resentment on the part of some other New Zealanders.

In the aftermath of the 1996 general election, a number of restrictive changes were made to New Zealand's immigration policies, and these changes, plus a recession in Asia, saw a significant drop-off in the number of Asians arriving as immigrants. This led to a further re-evaluation and, after 2000, more changes to immigration policy by the Labour-led Government and more positive public views encouraged new migration flows. Since 2000, the number of Asians arriving as both permanent and temporary residents has again increased significantly. This demographic shift has major impacts on New Zealand's ethnic politics and on the nature of its cityscapes, especially in Auckland.

## Twenty-First-Century Super-Diversity

Super-diversity as a concept was first introduced by Steve Vertovec in 2005 and elaborated in a more extensive article two years later (Vertovec 2007). Vertovec sought to highlight three elements: the contemporary impacts of the movement of people and the consequent diversification of populations, which includes not only ethnicity but also other aspects of diversity (gender, age, legal status, religion, languages and transnationalism); the need to 're-tool' sociological theories and methods given the nature of this diversity and the implications for 'inequality, prejudice and segregation'; and finally the need to rethink policy settings and understanding (Meissner and Vertovec 2015, 542–3). The contemporary intensification of diversity and its complexity – for example, the recognition of minority ethnicities and the interlinkage of ethnicity with other social characteristics and systems – has challenged existing conceptual and policy frameworks and approaches. In many ways, New Zealand is at the forefront of these developments, partly because there has been an extensive and ongoing debate about indigenous rights but also because, post-2000, the country has diversified at a very rapid rate, especially in its primate city of Auckland.

By the 2013 census, 40 per cent of Aucklanders – and a quarter of New Zealanders – had been born overseas, and those of Asian ethnicities (whether local- or overseas-born) made up 23 per cent of all Aucklanders (11.8 per cent of New Zealanders). In Auckland, the two dominant groups from Asia are those from China and India, with both numbering well over 100,000. While those who self-identify as being ethnic Chinese (which includes, in itself, very different groups, from those whose ancestors arrived in the late 1800s through to more recently arrived communities from Taiwan, Hong Kong, Singapore and Malaysia as well as immigrants from 'mainland' China) have been the largest group, they are about to be equalled in size by Indians (principally from India but also those from Fiji) as the latter have been the largest group arriving in New Zealand in recent years. The next two largest groups – both about equal size – are Filipinos and Koreans. Then there are ethnic and immigrant groups from many other parts of Asia, including those arriving as refugees. These diverse Asian communities are growing at a very fast rate because of post-Global Financial Crisis inward immigration flows (the highest ever) and are expected to grow to about 28–30 per cent of the Auckland population by the late 2020s, at which point these communities will be equal in size to the Māori population of Aotearoa.

Nationally, super-diversity is largely characterised by the significance of the Māori population (demographically and in terms of unique political status), and the fact that a quarter of New Zealanders have been born in another country. (Notably, the largest group of overseas-born New Zealanders remain those from the United Kingdom.) But in Auckland, the overseas-born make up a much higher proportion (40 per cent) of the normally resident population, and they are more ethnically diverse. In Auckland, Asian communities are much more dominant and have had a significant impact on things such as language use, the ethnic composition of public institutions such as schools, and banal things such as food options and festivals. Auckland is now one of the most super-diverse cities[2] in the Organisation for Economic Co-operation and Development (OECD) and certainly has a very high proportion of residents who identify as Asian compared to most OECD cities outside of Asia. Auckland's super-diversity is distinguished by its location in a settler society, and the resulting significance of Māori culture and politics, and by the rapid shift to the increasingly significant presence of Asian communities and transnational connections with Asia.

The demographic and ethnic changes, and the arrival of super-diversity, have significant impacts for the ethnic politics of Aotearoa. A few of the obvious issues and challenges include:

1. The transformation of urban landscapes through the arrival of new ethnoburbs. An example would be Dominion Road in Auckland where many retail activities are carried out by Asian businesses (primarily Chinese), which advertise using signage displaying Chinese script and which offer a range of products and services especially aimed at an Asian clientele (see Spoonley, Meares and Cain 2015).
2. The arrival of ethnoburbs has led to an increasing concentration of diverse non-hegemonic communities in key institutions. Schools would be a case in point so that while a quarter of Aucklanders might be Asian, in some schools the number can range from 40 to more than 60 per cent. As a result, the Asianisation of Auckland is notable in the demography of the institution, although not necessarily in the staff or the policies.

3. The growth of origin-language communities and minority cultural communities at a size and density that is historically unusual for New Zealand, with the exception of migration from elsewhere in the Pacific from the 1960s to the 1980s. Historic migrant communities from Asia had been relatively small and often geographically isolated (in terms of primarily being located in the gumfields or goldfields). Moreover, these contemporary communities are unlike the traditional immigrant communities (from the United Kingdom and Ireland), especially in terms of individuals being visibly different – and their languages and cultural values are, at times, in sharp contrast to the hegemonic values and institutions of New Zealand. But the growing demographic significance of these immigrants (three-quarters of Asians who are resident in New Zealand have been born in another country) is being increasingly supplemented by New Zealand-born or -raised Asians whose behaviours and values are different again. In the future, these new generations will impact both on origin communities and on New Zealand society and culture more generally.
4. The implications for New Zealand's prolonged debate about what constitutes biculturalism are yet to be addressed. Since the late 1960s, biculturalism has resulted in the limited recognition of the negative effects of colonisation, a new (but partial) constitutional role for the Treaty of Waitangi, and the recognition of the rights of Māori as being distinct from those of other New Zealanders. But the question of what a local multiculturalism might look like alongside this biculturalism is still far from clear. Certainly, some Māori have signalled their concern that multiculturalism might displace biculturalism and the Treaty from its current position (see Walker 1995).
5. The nature of this super-diversity, specifically that in Auckland, recalibrates popular understandings of 'New Zealandness'. For some, it undermines what they see as New Zealand values. Core institutions and shared values are being reshaped by Asian immigrants and their descendants. They are also redefining

the localities and loyalties of identity; immigrant communities maintain households or business in both origin and destination countries. Their links are transnational, and migration is increasingly circular. (This is not particular to Asian communities; the New Zealand diaspora now numbers 800,000.) If earlier social cohesion was a function of Anglo-Irish migration and colonialism, increasingly diverse communities challenge this, raising the question of what it means to be a New Zealander (or Aucklander) in the twenty-first century.

## Conclusion

The arrival and settlement of migrants from various parts of Asia has significantly altered the ethnic composition of Aotearoa and is having a number of effects. The colonial geopolitical connections that New Zealand has had historically with the United Kingdom are being supplemented, even replaced, by connections with the Asia-Pacific region, especially the super-powers of China and India. This has been reflected in cross-border transactions, including the flows of people, both temporary (as students or tourists) or as permanent settlers. In turn, this has changed the ethnic composition of neighbourhoods, schools, retail centres and other public spaces. It has also challenged how New Zealanders understand who they are – what does it mean to be a New Zealander in a culturally diverse country? – and the nation's cultural politics. There remains something of a conceptual and policy gap in terms of rights recognition for these new communities – how should their languages be acknowledged and maintained, for example? And what constitutes an appropriate form of recognition when some effort has been made and remains to be made to create a national space for the culture and identity of Māori?

### Notes

1   The label 'Asian' is a crude label that is not used in the same way in New Zealand as it is in other countries (which itself points to the socially constructed nature of such labels). Firstly, officially (although not in informal discourse) in New Zealand it includes those from the

Indian sub-continent; secondly, it collapses significant cultural, linguistic, religious and regional differences; and thirdly, it includes local- as well as overseas-born Asian residents (the New Zealand European/Pākehā designation has no equivalent for any peoples of Asian descent). At best, 'Asian' is a convenient if inaccurate shorthand.

2  In early 2016, Auckland was ranked the fourth most diverse city in the world.

**PART III**

# Social Class and Economic Inequalities

CHAPTER 9

# The Land of Me and Money?

*New Zealand Society under Neoliberalism*

## Louise Humpage

Neoliberalism constructs us all as self-interested, rational beings in pursuit of material advantage, even as it contributes to growing inequalities and precarious work lives for many citizens. Using employment as an example, this chapter compares neoliberal values and policies with the Keynesian ones they replaced, highlighting how different ideas are used to shape our society. Both Keynesian and neoliberal policies accept capitalism, the economic system where most goods and services are produced by privately owned companies operating for profit (Stanford 2008). But while Keynesian policies aim to *manage* capitalism's negative impacts on all citizens, neoliberal policies *facilitate* capitalism in ways that benefit only a minority of New Zealanders and contribute to increased income inequality and poverty. Public dissatisfaction with such outcomes helps explain modifications to New Zealand's neoliberal agenda since the mid-1990s, but are we too concerned with 'me and money' to consider more radical alternatives?

## 1930s–1970s: Keynesianism Rules

Although the political ideas that dominate each period in history often seem 'second-nature', significant shifts in the economic and social context can challenge and sometimes overturn them. This was the case in the 1930s and 1940s, when public disgruntlement with government responses to the Great Depression and a desire for solidarity after World War II saw the election of social democratic governments in many countries. Social democracy developed as a political and intellectual alternative to both liberalism (which limits the state's role to ensuring that laws to smooth the operation of capitalism are applied in the same way to all individuals) and Marxism (which rejects capitalism and favours socialism, where workers seize control of the means of production from private owners). Social democracy favours democratic elections and the use of a parliamentary Labour Party to incrementally achieve socialist goals. It also accepts individual freedom and capitalism in the short term but works to reduce class inequality by regulating the market (where goods are bought and sold), with the government owning key assets (so all citizens benefit from their profits) and redistributing resources to those most in need (Cheyne, O'Brien and Belgrave 2008; Duncan 2007; Heywood 2012).

These kinds of policy prescriptions became internationally popular following World War II and are often referred to as 'Keynesianism' because they were influenced by John Maynard Keynes's (1936) economic management model. He rejected the dominant neoclassical economic theory, which held that economies would automatically reach 'general equilibrium' when the supply of goods and services equalled demand, meaning all potential economic resources (including wage labour) would be used efficiently. Such ideas had seen governments during the Great Depression *reduce* government spending to combat inflation (prices increasing faster than incomes) without regard to the significant hardship faced by citizens. This was because the *supply* of productive factors was considered the greatest limit on economic production (Duncan 2007; Stanford 2008). Keynes (1936) instead advocated that governments should *increase* spending, going into deficit if necessary, to provide financial assistance to the unemployed and create public works programmes during a recession. These would ensure citizens had sufficient income to maintain *demand* (i.e., to keep purchasing the goods that businesses were producing). He argued this would speed up economic recovery and minimise the risk of inflation, while tight regulation of the financial sector and international capital flows would ensure low-cost credit was available for productive investment (Jessop 2002; Roper 2005).

Keynes (1936) also believed that demand for goods could be sustained through policies of full employment (ensuring all male citizens had a job if they wanted one). To protect jobs, tariffs were placed on imported goods and subsidies were offered to support many local businesses, while government ownership of industries such as railways and electricity generation aimed to ensure their products were available at affordable prices (Duncan 2007). Further, Keynes (1936) regarded the welfare state (a minimum level of institutionalised provisions guaranteeing citizens a basic level of economic and social security) as essential for ensuring a healthy, well-educated and thus productive population (Cheyne, O'Brien and Belgrave 2008).

Castles (1996), however, argues that in the 'social laboratory' of New Zealand and Australia, social security provisions did not need to be as expansive as in Europe because both Australasian countries developed a centralised wage-bargaining system in the late nineteenth century whereby the government, employers and unions negotiated national 'award' wages for various industries. Most male breadwinners – even those in low-skilled, labouring jobs – were thus ensured a decent standard of living for their families. This 'wage earners' welfare state' contributed to New Zealand having smaller differences in wage distributions than most comparable countries during the 1950s and 1960s (Castles 1996).

Nonetheless, New Zealand's First Labour Government (1935–49) developed a welfare state to manage the social and economic risks (such as old age and unemployment) shared by all citizens in a capitalist economy. The 1938 Social Security Act set out key social rights for all citizens (such as social security benefits for widows, orphans and the sick) which enabled living standards to be independent of purely market forces (Duncan 2007; Roper 2005). Universal access to government services aimed to build solidarity (a feeling of unity based on common goals, interests and sympathies) by offering the same services to all citizens, no matter how much they earned. This encouraged trust that services would be available when needed and toleration of the relatively high levels of taxation that such policies required (Dwyer 2004). Although universalism was less fully implemented in New Zealand than in the United Kingdom and Scandinavian countries, such ideas motivated the development of a national education and health system from the 1940s (Duncan 2007).

In the United States, President Richard Nixon's 1971 declaration that he was also now a Keynesian shows how even countries not considered social democratic eventually developed some of the key institutions promoted by the Keynesian model, even if differences in implementation and framing remained (Harvey 2005). The global reach of Keynesian ideas makes the shift to neoliberalism both internationally significant and extremely interesting.

## 1980s and 1990s: Neoliberalism Emerges

Neoliberal advocates, such as Hayek (1944) and Friedman (1962), had long argued for a new or strengthened version of liberalism, whereby individual freedom, market forces and property rights were prioritised above all else (Cheyne, O'Brien and Belgrave 2008; Heywood 2012). But neoliberal ideas did not influence government policy until after the global economic crisis of the 1970s and 1980s, which seemed to provide evidence that Keynesianism was failing and a new model was needed.

In New Zealand, the Fourth Labour Government (1984–90) used a severe financial crisis as a reason to abandon its planned social democratic programme and instead implement neoliberal policies that facilitated capitalism by replicating a 'market model' (by introducing competition and a profit motive) into almost all aspects of society. The Government returned to neoclassical economic theory, arguing that the market offers freely acting individuals the greatest opportunity to pursue their self-interest. This is because 'consumer sovereignty' allows them to offer critical feedback on the price or quality of goods and services (by not buying or using them), and if producers do not respond, they risk going out of business (Stanford 2008).

Influenced by such ideas, macroeconomic policy was refocused on low inflation and reduced public expenditure. With full employment no longer a goal, most financial and trade regulations and controls protecting domestic industries were removed to allow international competition. Many state-owned assets (such as the Post Office and Air New Zealand) were reorganised using a business model ('corporatised') then sold to the highest bidder ('privatised'), often to foreign-owned companies. This minimised state involvement in the economy and introduced competition into the public sector (Roper 2005). Here the Labour Government was also influenced by public choice theory, which applies rational economic models of behaviour to politics, arguing that when only the government delivers a service (i.e., there is no competition), bureaucrats will pursue their own self-interest by seeking more funding to protect or expand their employment, rather than ensuring services are efficient and effective (Cheyne, O'Brien and Belgrave 2008; Duncan 2007).

Overall, these changes benefited New Zealand's wealthiest citizens. While Keynesianism prioritised social rights that ensured the needy had a decent standard of living, neoliberalism focuses on property rights which establish ownership to – and thus the ability to profit from – a particular resource. Thus, business owners benefited from the rapid corporatisation and privatisation that saw many workers lose their jobs, particularly in industries where Māori and Pasifika peoples were predominantly located. This created a surplus of (unemployed) workers willing to take jobs, meaning employers had little incentive to negotiate improved wages and conditions with unions. Many New Zealand businesses initially struggled in the global market with no import tariffs or government subsidies but the Fourth National Government (1990–99) assisted by introducing the 1991 Employment Contracts Act. This enabled employers to lower the cost of producing goods by introducing individually negotiated contracts and restricting even further the ability of workers to negotiate their wages and conditions collectively (Larner 2000). Together, these changes saw strike activity fall to its lowest level since the 1930s and union membership decline from almost 50 to 24 per cent of the total employed labour force between 1990 and 1996. Employers also no longer had to pay penal rates (a higher than normal hourly rate paid for working more than 40 hours per week) and could employ people part time or casually as needed. Thus, workers' average weekly earnings fell at a time when many of the costs formerly borne by the government (e.g., for health and education services) were passed onto 'consumers' through user-pays charges (Roper 2005).

In this context, the real incomes of rich households rose, but incomes fell amongst lower- and middle-income groups. Income inequality (the gap between high- and low-income earners) consequently grew faster in New Zealand than in similarly advanced industrialised countries during the 1980s and 1990s (Rashbrooke 2013a; Roper 2005). Poverty also grew substantially across this period, particularly amongst children and those living in households dependent on social security benefits (Ministry of Social Development 2014). Internationally, neoliberal reforms largely succeeded in 'solving' the problems of the 1970s (inflation and skyrocketing public debt) but were associated with new problems (high levels of private debt, income inequality and child poverty) (Roper 2005).

With social risk reframed as resulting from individual inadequacies not structural factors that governments could influence (Dwyer 2004), unemployment became associated with individuals' poor work habits or attitudes which were thought to be passed on to their children (Mead 1997). By the mid-1990s, these neoconservative beliefs about 'welfare dependency' justified reductions in the generosity of the unemployment benefit and new, mandatory work-search and work-for-dole requirements for the unemployed (Heywood 2012). Sitting in tension with neoliberalism's interest in individual freedom and minimal state intervention, neoconservativism considers it appropriate to intervene in the private lives of 'problem' individuals to encourage a strong work ethic or 'family values' (e.g., having children only within marriage). This contrasts with the Keynesian view that *all* citizens have a right to a basic level of economic and social security, no matter what their circumstances.

Growing concern about neoliberalism's outcomes dominated politics as the twentieth century drew to a close. Public dissatisfaction with neoliberal policies (and politics more generally) contributed to New Zealanders voting to replace First-Past-the-Post with a Mixed-Member Proportional

(MMP) form of political representation in 1993 (Roper 2005). The unexpected coalition of National and New Zealand First in the first MMP Government in 1996 resulted in some policy reversals (notably in superannuation and healthcare). More generally, public dissatisfaction saw National *abandon* some proposed policies (e.g., a voucher system charging tertiary students the full cost of their courses; see Boston 1999). Overall, Roper (2005) views the election of a Labour–Alliance Government in 1999, despite high levels of financial backing for the National and ACT Parties, as evidence of the working class and some sections of the urban middle class becoming more conscious of, and strongly opposed to, the pro-business ideology of neoliberalism.

## 2000s Onwards: Neoliberalism Entrenched

Other governments also faced public dissatisfaction and, as economic conditions improved from the mid-1990s, a variant of neoliberalism emerged. Framed as a middle political space between neoliberalism and social democracy, the Third Way is sometimes said to represent a 'post-neoliberal' era (Brand and Sekler 2009). New Zealand policy history, however, supports the view that the Third Way re-embedded rather than challenged the neoliberal economic agenda (Craig and Porter 2006; Humpage 2015).

The Fifth Labour Government (1999–2008) certainly remained focused on low inflation, not full employment, and free trade instead of the domestic trade protections that were central to Keynesianism. The railways network and Air New Zealand, which had both struggled to make a profit in a competitive market environment, *did* return to government ownership; the top marginal tax rate on income *was* raised to increase the tax burden of the wealthy; and the Employment Relations Act 2000 *did* soften some of National's restrictions on union organisation and bargaining rights (Roper 2005). But Third Way advocates argued that the state-centred approach associated with traditional social democracy was no longer economically or politically feasible, since social democratic parties now needed to attract both traditional working- *and* middle-class votes to win elections (Giddens 1998; Schmidtke 2002).

Both groups had faced rising costs for healthcare and education, so the Fifth Labour Government increased spending in these areas. But it was careful to frame this as a financially sustainable 'social investment' to ensure a supply of the healthy and well-educated workers needed by the twenty-first-century labour market. Third Way governments thus drastically redefined the social democratic commitment to protecting people *from* the market, reframing the government as a facilitator ensuring individuals have opportunities to successfully compete *in* the market – but without the government itself necessarily providing such employment-focused services (Giddens 1998; Schmidtke 2002).

Although individual freedom and individual responsibility remained central, a neocommunitarian focus on 'no rights without responsibilities' also suggested that citizens had responsibilities towards *each other* independent of claims made on government (Giddens 1998, 65). This led to a focus on communities, local governance and partnership-based modes of policy development and programme delivery (Craig and Porter 2006). Nonetheless, critics argue that such attempts to reduce threats to 'social inclusion' (which replaced the social democratic goal of solidarity and, in New Zealand, largely focused on inclusion in paid work) were driven less by genuine political concern about social inequalities and more by an interest in running a market economy more effectively and with fewer crises (Dwyer 2004). In this context, acknowledging public concern about early neoliberal reforms was not so much a political back-step but a way of containing resistance that threatened the neoliberal economic agenda, in order to be able to continue extending that agenda (Craig and Porter 2006).

The Labour-led Government's treatment of work and worklessness illustrates how the government became more neoliberal over time. It initially abandoned National's Community Wage work-for-dole programme and work-testing for sole parents, both driven by neoconservative ideas about welfare dependency. Instead, new Job Seeker Agreements set out a benefit recipient's employment-related responsibilities *and* the education, training and other support government could offer to get the unemployed into work (Roper 2005; St John and Rankin 2009). Regular increases to the minimum wage and the Working for Families package introduced in 2005 also aimed to 'make work pay'. The latter, which included a new In-Work Tax Credit and increases to child-related entitlements for low- and middle-income families with dependent children, is attributed with reducing child poverty between 2004 and 2007, particularly in 'working' households. But its impact was limited by the exclusion of benefit recipients from the In-Work Tax Credit, which continued National's framing of this group as 'undeserving' of assistance (Ministry of Social Development 2014; St John and Rankin 2009). Work-testing requirements and sanctions were strengthened for recipients of the Domestic Purposes, Sickness, and Invalid's benefits as the 2000s progressed; then the 2007 Social Security Amendment Act rewrote the principles behind social security to match the Labour-led Government's policies: it was no longer government's role to support the needy; instead, *work* was framed as the primary source of welfare for all citizens (St John and Rankin 2009).

Although there are differences, the National Government elected in 2008 followed a similar strategy of acknowledging public concern about the negative social outcomes of neoliberal economics to ensure electoral success, while continuing to shift responsibility for such outcomes away from the state and onto individuals and communities. The impact of the Global Financial Crisis (GFC) of 2008–9 was less dramatic in New Zealand than in many parts of the world, but the National Government nonetheless used concerns about public debt and inflation to justify no overall increase in budget spending two years running, significant public sector job cuts, tax cuts and the partial privatisation of several state assets. These policies were driven by neoliberal economic values similar to those promoted in the 1990s (Roper 2011).

However, National's desire to keep middle-class voters happy saw it bolster spending in areas like health and education, and retain some policies not normally associated with neoliberalism. For instance, given that the Fifth Labour Government's Employment Relations Act had not increased the proportion of the population who were union members as feared, National maintained this legislation, along with a new law allowing workers with caring responsibilities to request part-time hours. It also regularly increased the minimum wage. In the immediate wake of the GFC, National even acknowledged that structural factors can affect employment opportunities, offering relatively generous but short-term redundancy and wage supplement packages for individuals temporarily affected by the recession in 2008 and the Canterbury earthquakes in 2010–11 (Roper 2011).

However, over time, the National Government incrementally restricted employee rights, particularly after 2014 (National Party 2014b). The considerably weakened positioned of employees under neoliberalism is illustrated by the global phenomenon known as 'zero-hour contracts', which became the norm in the fast food industry and quickly spread to other industries in the late 2000s. Such contracts require workers to be available for work (often seven days a week) but with no hours of work guaranteed by the employer and no compensation paid for that availability, creating significant uncertainty for employees. Most contracts also included no sick pay or other employment rights. Following considerable media coverage of zero contracts, the National Government reviewed employment standards but largely supported employers' arguments that their profitability relies on paying employees only for the hours they are needed. It did outlaw penalties for losses incurred during an employee's shift, while stipulating that employers needed to give 'reasonable notice' of cancelling shifts or 'reasonable compensation' for costs already incurred travelling to work (Woodhouse 2015). But it refused to define what was meant by 'reasonable', essentially leaving those with the greater level of power (employers) to decide. Zero-hour contracts were subsequently repealed in New Zealand via the Employment Standards Legislation Bill that passed through Parliament in March 2016.

Overall, the New Zealand Council of Trade Unions (2013) estimates that at least 30 per cent but possibly up to 50 per cent of New Zealanders are in forms of insecure work, including 'middle-class' occupations such as teaching and nursing, where there is uncertainty about ongoing employment or hours and little employee bargaining power regarding wages and conditions. This is in stark contrast to the high levels of security offered to both workers and employers during the Keynesian era when unions, employers and the government agreed to nationwide award wages and conditions across different industries.

Insecure work often leads to 'churning' back and forth between casual or temporary work and an unemployment benefit. Yet access to such assistance has been restricted since 2010 by a series of significant reforms aiming 'to ensure a fairer system of social assistance with an unrelenting focus on work' (New Zealand Government 2010, 1). Unemployment benefit recipients must reapply every twelve months, while teenagers receiving a benefit are subject to income management controls that limit how they spend their money. National also reduced seven main benefits to three in 2013, effectively treating most benefit recipients with caring responsibilities or health issues as if they were like all other unemployed people. National further employed an 'active investment approach' which tailors support and obligations for varied groups based on statistical predictions of their likely long-term dependence on social security (National Party 2014a).

The impact of this latest phase of neoliberalism is still emerging but its policy settings ensured that wealthy New Zealanders were least affected by the GFC (Rashbrooke 2013a). The level of income inequality in 2013 was similar to that of the mid-1990s and remained above the average of similar countries, but income gaps had grown between working-age citizens heavily reliant on government benefits and those in paid work. Child poverty declined from the mid-1990s, especially after Working for Families was introduced, but this decrease was temporarily reversed by the GFC, and far more New Zealanders lived in poverty in the late 2000s than before neoliberal reforms began in the mid-1980s (Ministry of Social Development 2014). Internationally, young workers replaced the elderly as those most at risk of income poverty (Organisation for Economic Co-operation and Development [OECD] 2014).

## Conclusion

Neoliberalism has fundamentally reoriented the ideas that shaped New Zealand governments and society prior to the 1980s. Although recent years have seen important modifications, notions of individual responsibility and individual self-interest now dominate government policy, where once this was motivated by a collective responsibility to protect citizen rights and the 'common good'. Alongside privatisation and marketisation, this focus has transformed New Zealand from the 'land of milk and honey' to one prioritising 'me and money'. While such shifts addressed some of the key economic problems facing New Zealand and other countries in the 1970s, neoliberalism is increasingly associated with growing income inequality and poverty. So why do New Zealanders keep electing governments who implement neoliberal policies?

Some scholars believe neoliberalism's multiple and sometimes contradictory theoretical ideas have allowed it to 'make sense' to, and gain support from, differing (often opposing) groups in society, strengthening its ideological dominance as the leading form of global political–economic governance (Harvey 2005; Larner 2000). There is certainly some evidence that the New Zealand public has endorsed – or at least come to tolerate – neoliberal values in some areas of policy (most notably social security). But survey data shows such values have not been adopted across the board (Humpage 2015) and the Occupy movement and New Zealand protests against privatisation in the early 2010s further indicate that public acquiescence to neoliberalism remains incomplete.

Indeed, neoliberalism's inconsistent implementation across time and varied policy areas highlight how interest groups and electorates have resisted neoliberalism, at times mediating or even blocking its expression in policy. Even the most regressive reforms of the 1980s and 1990s failed to completely dismantle all Keynesian economic and social institutions or permanently cut government spending: in fact, overall social spending has continued to increase since that time (OECD 2015). Third Way policies also appear to have (re)built expectations around government responsibilities in areas such as health and education, making them too electorally problematic for any political party to ignore (Humpage 2015; Roper 2005). Although the GFC's relatively weak impact on New Zealand allowed the government to argue we should pursue 'business-as-usual', it also provoked some New Zealanders to question neoliberalism. Policy continuities under Labour and National Governments since the 1980s suggest there is no real democratic alternative to neoliberalism but some of our smaller political parties endorse Keynesian ideas, while activist groups promote more radical options that reject capitalism altogether. History also shows us that radical political change is possible – if the public demand it.

CHAPTER 10

# Rich and Poor

## Class Division in Aotearoa New Zealand

## Bruce Curtis and Marko Galic

> Actually, there's been class warfare going on for the last 20 years, and my class has won.
>
> —Warren Buffett, quoted in Sargent (2011)

### Where Are We Today?

In 2015, the international charity group Oxfam reported that half of all global wealth is owned by the richest 1 per cent of people (Hardoon 2015). The richest 1 per cent has more wealth than the other 99 per cent of the world's population. Wealth is even more concentrated than this split suggests. In 2013, the 85 richest people on the planet owned more than the poorest 3.5 billion people, or half of the global population (Hardoon 2015). In 2014, that number dropped to 66 people (Oxfam New Zealand 2014). Clearly, the process of the concentration of wealth and the diffusion of poverty is an ongoing one. The figures for New Zealand tell pretty much the same story:

According to the most recent data, taken from the 2013 Credit Suisse Global Wealth Databook, 44,000 Kiwis . . . hold more wealth than three million New Zealanders. Put differently, this lists the share of wealth owned by the top one per cent of Kiwis as 25.1 per cent, meaning they control more than the bottom 70 per cent of the population. . . . New Zealand's wealthiest individual, Graeme Hart, is ranked number 200 on the Forbes list of the world's billionaires, with US$7 billion. That makes his net worth more than the bottom 30 per cent of New Zealanders, or 1.3 million people. (Oxfam New Zealand 2014)

Social inequality is accelerating globally and locally. One of the most concerning facts that characterise this country is that Aotearoa New Zealand is one of the most unequal societies in the so-called developed world (Wilkinson and Pickett 2009). But for many decades of the twentieth century New Zealand entertained a popular myth: the egalitarian myth. For example, John Key was a working-class kid, raised in a state-owned house in the 1960s and 1970s, but that did not stop him from becoming Prime Minister. The myth was that we lived in an equal society, a paradise for workers and their kids, a country proud of its social and economic developments, and of its good relations between waves of settlers and indigenous peoples. Austin Mitchell (1972) humorously celebrated this notion of New Zealand as heaven on earth (as 'Godzone') in his book *The Half Gallon Quarter Acre Pavlova Paradise*. Clearly the myth was not true even way back then, as David Bedggood (1980) described in his ground-breaking book *Rich and Poor in New Zealand*. It is a complete nonsense today. For some people this 'egalitarian myth' (Nolan 2007) might still feel true, but clearly not for the majority of people – and no longer even for Austin Mitchell (2002).

The increasing gap between the rich and poor has been greatly accelerated by neoliberal policies introduced by the Fourth Labour Government in 1984 and pursued by every government since. Neoliberalism is a way of organising the capitalist economy that involves a focus on improving profitability (Harvey 2005). In a relatively short time, neoliberal policies transformed social life in New Zealand. Many of the social relations that were seen as the basis for a democratic and open society were commodified (turned into commodities) through the sale of state-owned assets to big business or by introducing 'user-pays' for services still owned by the government (Harvey 2005; for more on neoliberalism in New Zealand, see Humpage in this volume). Let us return to John Key for a moment; he was brought up in a state-owned house with subsidised rents and his mother received a state benefit. He also received a free primary, secondary and tertiary education. Almost all of the Labour and National politicians who have pushed through neoliberalism also got free university education; this hasn't stopped them commodifiying education by making today's students pay for theirs. You might say that the people who most want us to believe in New Zealand's egalitarianism (neoliberal politicians and policy-makers) have done the most to make it a myth (Kelsey 1995, 2015; Pusey 1993; Rashbrooke 2013c; Rata 2000; Richards 2003; Roper 1991, 1996).

This chapter starts with a quote from Warren Buffett, the third-richest man in the world in 2015. Buffett has made his fortune from stripping the assets of unprofitable companies and has probably made more American workers unemployed than any other person. This is a win–win for Warren, as he is now one of the major players in the burgeoning trailer park sector in the United States, where unemployed people end up, if they are lucky (Neate 2015). With great wealth comes great power and, for a smug showman like Buffett, this is an unmissable opportunity to show off. But in 'telling it like it is' Buffett does mention class, and this is a concept we want to explore as a genuine source of explanation. In doing so, we are following in the footsteps of David Bedggood, whose 1980 book was for many decades the best-selling sociological text in New Zealand. The full title of that book is *Rich and Poor in New Zealand: A Critique of Class, Politics and Ideology*.

## Two Great Classes: The Capitalist Class and the Working Class

To understand the increasing gaps between rich (including the mega-wealthy) and poor (including the 800 million people around the globe who go to bed hungry each night) we have to critically examine the system we live in. The results of capitalism may be easy enough to see – the preposterous concentration of more and more wealth and power in the hands of fewer and fewer people; the spread of absolute, grinding poverty and its softer forms for the unemployed and working poor; boring and underpaid 'McJobs' (Mohsin and Lengler 2015); unaffordability of housing; retrenchment of social welfare; and the end of hope – but its mechanisms are obscured or made to look normal and eternal. At the core of capitalism, what can be thought of as the essence of the system, is conflict between two antagonistic classes.

The simplest definition of class is *people sharing a relationship to the means of production* (Marx 1847). Two things emerge from this definition: (1) the importance of the means of production; and (2) classes are multiple; we are talking about several classes. The means of production are precisely that – everything a modern society needs to make production possible. Production involves human effort or *labour*, combined with the output of earlier human efforts: extracted raw materials, machinery, instruments, factories, designs and plans, and even intellectual property. We can call all these previous outputs of production *capital*. The mobile or liquid form of capital is money.

The most important relationship to the means of production is ownership or non-ownership. One group of people in society owns the means of production, and we call them *capitalists* (or the *bourgeoisie*); another group of people does not own the means of production, and we call them *workers* or the working class (or the *proletariat*). Most people in Aotearoa New Zealand, as in the rest of the world, are workers. Not just a majority of people are workers, an *overwhelming* majority of people are (see Haddon 2015). Depending on how you measure class, an estimate that 1 per cent of the population are capitalists may well be an overestimate. Without doubt, almost all the people you will meet in your life are likely to be members of the working class, even the well-dressed, affluent-looking ones and those who consider themselves members of the middle class.

Class is a measure of who owns and does not own the means of production. Capitalists are the owners of capital, and because of this they own the output of the production process, meaning all the commodities in all their forms of goods and services. This is important because having ownership of the means of production and of the commodities produced, is the mechanism by which capitalists make profits and go on to accumulate more capital. The accumulation of capital – through profits made from the ownership of the means of production – is the driver of the capitalist system. Capitalist production exists to make profits. Profits exist to become capital. Capital is the basis of production. This is the endless, cyclical imperative of capitalism and for capitalist accumulation.

Capitalists make profits only when they receive more from the sale of the commodities they own at the end of each production cycle than it cost them to produce those commodities. If the costs of production exceed sales receipts for long enough then capitalists go bankrupt. They cease to be the owners of the means of production. However, the potential for profits is generated in the production process rather than at the point of sale. This potential is simple; workers are paid wages that are less than the value of the commodities they produce. The difference between the value created from labour and the wages paid to the labourers (workers) is called *the rate of exploitation*. Capitalist profits are the direct result of exploitation. The higher the rate of exploitation the greater the profits (Mandel 1971).

Exploitation is the fundamental antagonism and injustice of the capitalist system. It expresses the inequities of a system in which the great majority of people, the working class, use their minds and bodies and even emotions to produce all the goods and services in the world; but, in return, receive only a portion of the value of their labour as wages. This raises the question: Why do workers work? The answer lies in their relationship to the means of production. They do not own them and as a result they are forced to sell one thing they do own, their labour power (their ability to work). Workers are therefore absolutely, tightly, bound to capitalism. While the system exists, there is no escape. A worker who does not work or cannot find work is unemployed, and relies on the charity of other workers, who pay for benefits and pensions from income taxes on wages and salaries.

## The Petite Bourgeoisie and 'the Middle Class'

Class is a measure of who owns or does not own the means of production. Karl Marx argued that the logic of capitalism would mean that increasingly all people would belong to one of the two great classes (the capitalist class or the working class) and that numbers in the working class would grow. But, between the two great classes, there is a third class which combines features of the others. This is the *petite bourgeoisie* (small capitalists). These small capitalists own some capital, some of the means of production, but not enough to allow them to rely solely on the paid labour of workers. As a result, the petite bourgeoisie are forced to work: to work for themselves. The petite bourgeoisie are often called 'owner-operators'. They can include people who have start-up businesses, some professionals/tradespeople, shop owners, taxi drivers and, historically in New Zealand, family-based farmers.

Where to draw the line between petite bourgeoisie and bourgeoisie, between small capitalists and capitalists is tricky. Bill Gates, the world's richest man, works for himself. He famously works very hard, but he no longer has to, to guarantee the survival of Microsoft. For the petite bourgeoisie, in contrast, 'working for themselves' is essential for the survival of their business. Small capital requires both the exploitation of workers and this sort of self-exploitation. Actually such 'self-exploitation' often involves the unpaid labour of family members. Marx predicted that the petite bourgeoisie would be constantly ruined under capitalism, bankrupted and thrown into the ranks of the working class or even the 'lumpen-proletariat' – the unemployable of society. This has proven the case as far as we can see. For example, the vast number of petit-bourgeois businesses have great difficulty staying profitable, mainly because their lack of capital makes staying efficient and productive very challenging. Additionally, the structure of capitalism that privileges big businesses/corporations creates conditions favourable to monopolies, where petit bourgeois businesses find it hard to survive. Think of an owner-operator health food shop: it can easily be put out of business by the local supermarket chain adding some food supplements to its shelves for a few months.

So far, we have analysed three classes in relation to the ownership and control of the means of production: capitalists (those who own and control the means of production), petite bourgeoisie (people who own small businesses) and workers (those who do not own the means of production and have to work for wages or salaries in order to survive). What the breakdown of the population is, in terms of these three classes, is hard to say. You might call it capitalism's best-kept secret. Certainly, governments that support capitalism while claiming to champion democracy, egalitarianism and so on have no interest in collecting statistics on this sort of thing.

But 'capitalists', 'working class' and 'petite bourgeoisie' are not terms we use in everyday life to talk about social structure (Haddon 2015). Instead, most people talk of the middle class. This is either because they feel they are members of the middle class or because they aspire to be. The category of middle class has a very different reality to the three classes we discussed above. The capitalist, working and petit bourgeois classes have an objective reality. An individual belongs to one class or another because of their relationship to the means of production. Their thoughts and ideas about where they belong do not determine their class position. This is an objective measure of class. The notion of the middle class is not really objective; it is subjective, and subjectivity belongs to the realm of ideas or ideology. The greatest success of capitalism – many would say the reason for its continued survival – is ideological. Capitalism as a system has managed to convince most workers that they are (or can be) members of something called 'the middle class'. The capitalist class not only owns the means of production but they also own and control the media, together with the majority of the products produced by the information and entertainment industry, which we 'consume' on our smartphones, laptops and TV screens. One of these products is glamorous images of enjoyable, middle-class lifestyles (Debord 1994). These have nothing to do with reality as such. Instead the images promise us wealth and fame, and provide us with aspirations that capitalism simply cannot deliver on.

Insofar as the middle class exists in an objective sense, it is made up of well-paid workers who are often ideological collaborators with the capitalist class (they receive enough privileges to support and help reproduce the current system). Most of these relatively well-paid workers are paid a premium because the labour they sell to capitalists is used to control the actions of other workers, or to create strategies for capitalists so that they can maintain their own privileges and become even wealthier. Think supervisors, managers, analysts, salespeople, scientists, public servants, and teachers and lecturers as well. Controlling the actions of other workers is what these middle-class, relatively well-paid workers do in the private and public sectors – either through direct supervision/management or indirectly through the formulation and delivery of guidelines, benchmarks, policies, curricula and even new technologies of surveillance and accountability.

## Hegemony and 'Divide and Rule'

We answered the question 'why do workers work?' with 'because they have little or no choice'. Similarly, wanting to be paid well rather than poorly seems a reasonable desire. But why do workers buy into the ideology of the middle class? Sometimes, at least from the outside, this seems ludicrous – many Americans who live in trailer parks consider themselves to be middle class because they own their own trailer. This is the power of ideas, ideology and hegemony.

When the capitalist system and the injustices it creates are accepted and internalised by the working class and 'middle class', we can talk about the role of hegemony. Marxist intellectual Antonio Gramsci (1971) described hegemony as the political, cultural and economic domination of the capitalist class over other classes. Hegemonic domination is legitimised (made to look normal/natural) with ideas and ideology rather than with coercive tools (the police and army). The egalitarian myth we discussed at the start of this chapter is an example of such an idea. Hegemony can be identified in many aspects of our everyday life: from imposed representations of consumerist lifestyles and social processes that do not disturb the interests of the capitalist class to the censorship of collective memories that are based on solidarity and resistance towards injustices. The presentation of the hundredth anniversary of World War I is a prime example of this manipulation. We are encouraged to forget that the war was a global struggle between capitalists (imperialists) over land and resources, and are supposed to believe that all those slaughtered young men were forging New Zealand.

Moreover, class is almost totally obscured in capitalist society. Almost every aspect of the education system, the media and even the entertainment industry presents explanations other than class-based ones for the increasingly grim realities of our world. War, poverty, environmental degradation, intolerance, social and economic exclusion, racism and many other injustices tend to be explained mainly by the stupidity of (working) people or as the result of 'inherent' differences like ethnicity, nationality, gender, sexuality, religion, etc. Obscuring the centrality of class, the relationship about who owns the means of production, is capitalism defending itself as a system, and capitalists and their agents protecting themselves.

In order to maintain its position of privilege, the capitalist class uses what Louis Althusser (1971) called 'the repressive and ideological apparatuses of the state'. The repressive apparatus includes the police, the army, the criminal justice system, state social agencies and other authoritarian forces. The ideological apparatus consists of the mass media, schools and universities, religious institutions and most forms of consumer culture. In the case of New Zealand, the working class is mainly the subject of the *repressive* apparatus (e.g., mass incarceration and over-representation of Māori in the criminal justice system, constant police surveillance of working-class communities such as those in South Auckland, destruction of the trade union movement and so on.). The aspirant middle class, on the other hand, is mostly subjected to the *ideological* apparatus which portrays a successful country, where class division and, consequently, social inequality are not significant issues. This ideological apparatus not only hides antagonistic class relations and 'forgets' the colonial history that allowed for this supposed land of milk and honey to buttress the privileges of the settler society; it also continually instructs New Zealanders to accept capitalism as the only game in town. Most obviously, to minimise united political action against the capitalist class, the mass media highlights and reproduces conflicts *within* the working class also on the basis of ethnicity. This 'divide and rule' strategy is central to the maintenance of power by the capitalist class.

## You Want to Be Middle Class? Welcome to the Precariat

We discussed the problematic reality of the middle class above. It is perhaps better to think of the middle class as a stratum or layer of well-paid workers, rather than as a class in the objective sense used by Marxists. A new stratum of workers has developed both in New Zealand and internationally in the last couple of decades: the precariat. The precariat is a social stratum that is characterised by systematic conditions of precariousness (uncertainty and insecurity) in work and life. They are people who are trapped in a cycle of underemployment and unemployment. The New Zealand Council of Trade Unions (2013, 3) claims that 635,000 people, at least 30 per cent of New Zealand's labour force, are in precarious work, which it defines as

> any job that denies workers the stability they need for a good life and reduces their ability to control their own work situation, with damaging consequences for them, their families and their communities. It is work where the variable and changing nature of a job suits the employer but not the worker. It is work where the burden of adjustment falls on the worker, and the inequality of power in the employment or contractual relationship disadvantages the person doing the work.

One result of precariousness is the minimisation of workers' solidarity and collective help. Because of the imposed competitiveness in the 'flexible labour market', where the rules of the game are made solely by the capitalist class, it is difficult to maintain collective solidarity. This applies to precarious workers (those with temporary, part-time or casual jobs) and increasingly all workers, including those wanting well-paid jobs. The common logic used to maintain these conditions is the constant direct or indirect threat of dismissal ('I have ten other workers who are waiting for your position').

Many of you who are reading this text are at university to achieve educational goals that you hope will lead to a decent and fulfilling life. We could say that the aim is to fulfil your talents and not to be trapped in the precariat and its conditions of uncertainty: to gain a degree, find a well-paid job, make a career and, therefore, to reach or stay in what some believe is the middle class. The analysis of contemporary class relations, however, shows that it is not only the working class that is becoming precarious but also the so-called middle class (Standing 2011).

## Conclusion: Beyond Hegemony

The capitalist system that Marx critically analysed more than 150 years ago has become in many ways even more parasitical since then. Driven by a constant desire and aspiration to gain the maximum amount of profit, the capitalist class did not increase the price of products but they reduced the cost of labour. First, they moved traditional industry into so-called Third World countries where workers work for lower wages and without workers' protection or any kind of labour security. Second, they changed employment relations in their own states to allow them to accumulate capital continuously – and to the great extent, this is still the case. Workers both at home and around the world who have to sweat to prop up the hedonistic life of the upper classes (capitalists) and the ignorant 'middle class' (workers with high salaries who are part of the system and who ignore what is happening around them) are victims of the capitalist system with a neoliberal face. At the same time, the dominant media discourse represents workers as a cost or expense and not as a fundamental part of the economy.

In Aotearoa New Zealand, the capitalist system has been inseparable from the experience of colonialism in the nineteenth century and neo-colonialism since the twentieth century. Our colonial history has often been obscured by myths about equality and reinventing the past. But colonisation created inequalities that are structural and enduring. New Zealand's capitalism, together with the privileges of its ruling elite (the capitalist class), was established on and remains based on the appropriation/seizure of Māori land; the transformation of tangata whenua into working-class labourers or even members of an underclass; the systematic destruction of tikanga Māori (Māori customs and practices); and the ongoing capitalist mode of production in these 'new' lands (Poata-Smith 2013).

With the development of white settler society, its social institutions and capitalist political economy, the land became a component of the ongoing exploitation of the labour force, of Māori, Pākehā, Pasifika and more recent migrants alike. Today, New Zealand is a class-based society within a global capitalist system that not only allows for but hastens poverty, and supports exploitation, opportunism and greed.

However, the oppressive class relation can always be challenged, changed or destroyed by raising the class consciousness of the oppressed people. Historically, resistance towards social injustices, together with changes that brought about better conditions for people, grew either within state institutions (including trade unions and political parties who recognised people's sufferings) or completely outside of the system (via socio-political movements and other radical movements that sought solutions outside of capitalism). One of the main characteristics of the hegemony is that it is under constant threat. To put it differently, the main fear of the ruling elites is that the workers will unite (no matter what ethnicity they are) and will cause, in one way or another, an end to the prevailing system of privileges and disadvantages. As critical thinkers we have the ability to think outside of the frames and boundaries that were made by those in power and to commit to our communities for the well-being of our people. Are alternatives to the existing system then really so impossible?

CHAPTER 11

# Poverty in a Land of Plenty

*The Poor Will Always Be with Us?*

## Kellie McNeill

On returning to live in the neighbourhood of my childhood after an absence of over two decades, I answered a knock on my door one Sunday afternoon to be greeted by a young man seeking food. I didn't ask about his circumstances, but quickly gathered some things from my kitchen which the unknown visitor was happy to receive. I ate my own meal that night wondering what had happened in my old stomping ground to mean that people were now reliant on the charity of strangers to address their hunger. What did it feel like not to have access to the necessities of life in a land of plenty? So began my sociological journey into understanding expressions of poverty in Aotearoa New Zealand, and how we respond to these individually, socially and politically.

That poverty exists in a nation with ample resources to meet the material needs of all its citizens is an emotive and contested assertion. This chapter considers contemporary poverty, its historical and structural underpinnings, and who amongst New Zealanders is most likely to be affected. The reticence to accept poverty as a real and unnecessary feature in the 'land of milk and honey' is also examined as an explanation for its persistence.

## Differentiating Extreme Poverty, Relative Poverty and Deprivation

In the popular mind, the term *poverty* is often associated with subsistence concepts developed at the turn of the twentieth century (e.g., Booth 1889; Rowntree 1901). Within such approaches, poverty is understood as an absolute or extreme condition 'characterized by severe deprivation of basic human needs, including food, safe drinking water, sanitation facilities, health, shelter, education and information. It depends not only on income but also on access to services' (United Nations 1995, 41). While most of us are familiar with the depictions of emaciated children that attract regular media coverage, such portrayals reinforce the view of many New Zealanders that poverty is something that only happens in the poorest of nations. Those who cry poor closer to home are often painted as less deserving of compassion or assistance because they are better positioned to 'help themselves' by virtue of living in a wealthy country.

While poverty in its extreme form is clearly not the situation faced by most poor New Zealanders, the phenomenon of *relative poverty* is widely acknowledged to exist within rich nations. Within this framing, the poor are defined as individuals whose income is too far below that of the other members of the society in which they live. Such a situation results in 'a lack of access to sufficient economic and social resources that would allow a minimum adequate standard of living in that society' (Waldegrave, Stephens and King 2003, 198). Three notable features of relative poverty arise here. First, while some people will always be poorer than others, the key point about relative poverty is that it is defined against the standard of living in the society concerned. What is relative poverty in one society may not be in another. Second, relative poverty is often experienced invisibly in our society because of the judgements and social stigma attached to it in New Zealand. In my work on food poverty, for example, people frequently talked about the lengths they took to hide their foodlessness:

> You just don't want to be seen as not coping, and you don't want to feel like you're not coping. You just work at keeping things looking good from the outside looking in. . . . When you're doing your best and still not cutting it, then you don't really want other people rubbing your nose in it. ('Faye' quoted in McNeill 2011, 197)

The third feature of relative approaches to poverty is that they encompass not only the material resources people require to meet their basic needs, but also capture the social dimensions of being able to participate as a full member of society with the same rights, opportunities and expressions of citizenship and membership as other people. The covert social marginalisation that can occur due to food poverty was described by a participant in my research:

> I don't go out that often. If it's an activity that's around food, like a pot luck dinner or something, then that's not a form of socialising that's open to me anymore. If I can't be seen to be contributing, if I can't give something back, then I won't go. That's changed my social life dramatically. And that bites, because I need those people and I want to be able to contribute to keeping those relationships alive. ('Christina' quoted in McNeill 2011, 203)

There are further important distinctions to be made between relative poverty and *deprivation*. While relative poverty reflects an individual's objective and material access to resources in a quantitative sense, deprivation is associated more with subjective experience (Lister 2004; Tomlinson and Walker 2009; Townsend 1993). Determinations about deprivation will vary according to the social context and the subjective norms that a society uses to characterise 'adequacy'. *Material deprivation* refers to inadequacies in goods, services, resources, amenities and the physical environment. In contrast, *social deprivation* refers to a person's inability to take up the roles, relationships, functions, customs, rights and responsibilities usually implied by membership in a society, including those in one's own community, family and household. The term *socio-economic deprivation* refers to the simultaneous occurrence of multiple forms of deprivation across different domains where people's capacity is impeded by 'the social and economic factors that influence what position(s) individuals and groups hold within the structure of society' (Lynch and Kaplan 2000, 20). In short, then, deprivation can be summarised as a state of experiencing a sense of disadvantage relative to the society in which an individual, family or group lives. As such, this is distinct from measures of poverty themselves. While poverty often contributes to social and material deprivation, the *experience* of deprivation can also occur for reasons that don't relate to a person's economic circumstances.

## Poor Accounting: Measuring Poverty

The subjective aspects of relative poverty and deprivation mean that these concepts remain open to contestation, and even broad agreement on definitions is usually followed by debate about how they should be measured and what constitutes an 'adequate' income, standard of living or degree of social inclusion. 'Adequacy' has the potential to be manipulated according to various agendas. Unlike many other wealthy countries, 'New Zealand has no official measures of poverty or material hardship in the sense of measures to which a government has given formal legitimacy' (Ministry of Social Development 2014, 3), although a number of different methods of estimating the prevalence of relative poverty and deprivation are commonly used by government organisations, academics and social-sector advocates. Each of these produces slightly different end figures because of the different variables used – a matter which confuses debate on the subject.

As we moved into the second decade of this century, the Ministry of Social Development (2010) reported that 15 per cent of New Zealanders fell below an informal national 'poverty line' set at a threshold of 60 per cent of the median income after housing costs. Those whose incomes fall below this are deemed to be relatively poor. If we are to be sociologically inquisitive about the nature of poverty it is important that we seek to understand not only the structural conditions that contribute to it, but also why certain groups in our society are more frequently represented than others in these poverty statistics.

## Who's Living under the Poverty Line?

New Zealand has a lamentable record of child poverty, with one of the highest rates of prevalence amongst wealthy countries (UNICEF 2013). The impacts of child poverty play out across a person's life, in the form of poorer health outcomes, lower levels of educational attainment that affect people's opportunities in the labour market, higher levels of interaction with criminality and increased chances of early mortality (Every Child Counts 2015). All of these carry significant social and economic costs, for society at large as well as the individual.

In 2014, 24 per cent of all New Zealand children – or one in four – lived in relative poverty, with 60 per cent of these likely to spend at least seven of their formative years in this state (Simpson et al. 2014). Child poverty remains an emotive social issue because of children's dependence on adults to meet their material needs. While blaming parental negligence is politically expedient, it does not address the structural factors that undermine caregivers' abilities to provide adequately, and it acts to frame children's poverty as the result of 'poor choices', stigmatising poor parents as irresponsible and feckless in the process. My own experience of working with families in food poverty is that parents – particularly mothers – often go without in order to provide for their children, and that tension between family members around the management of food is common.

> I make a conscious decision and say to myself, 'Right. This is where we're at. I'm going to fast', and I'll just take fluids for the day. . . . When I'm fasting I'm preserving food to meet my son's needs. I will avoid doing the food because I know that there will be enough for him if I go without. ('Sandy' quoted in McNeill 2011, 161)

> In our house, food is the thing that causes the most arguments between us, between us and our kids, and between the kids as well. We're constantly having to play referee and making sure the rules we have about food for the kids are followed. Everybody has to do their bit, and if one gets something

the other hasn't got you know there's going to be trouble. ('Liz' quoted in McNeill 2011, 192)

Statistically, Māori and Pasifika people are more likely to experience relative poverty than other ethnic groups in New Zealand. This can be attributed to both historical and structural factors. Like many other indigenous peoples globally, Māori have not fared well in terms of being able to exercise uninterrupted control over the means of production upon which they traditionally relied (see Wynyard in this volume). The colonial appropriation of land and other resources has left a long legacy of disruption to the Māori economy, from which it has only recently begun to recover (although the present mix of neoliberal economics and Treaty settlements is creating polarised effects for Māori). However, it is erroneous to equate being Māori with being poor, or to assume that the statistical representations of Māori poverty are intractable. Over the last decade, the asset base of the Māori economy has grown at a phenomenal rate (Ministry of Business, Innovation and Employment 2015) and it is now a key component of New Zealand's economic development. While there is some cause for optimism that its returns will assist in reversing Māori poverty and progress the larger project of decolonisation, there are also critiques recognising that the adoption of neoliberal economic management has placed control over the benefits of Māori assets in the hands of an elite class (Poata-Smith 2004).

The migration to New Zealand of Pacific peoples was driven by the post-war expansion of manufacturing and the demand for unskilled labour to fill newly created jobs, particularly in the 1960s and 1970s (Anae 2014). Globalisation, free trade agreements and the concern for New Zealand to remain competitive in the international marketplace have caused dramatic changes to this sector though the widespread adoption of outsourcing. Intensive manufacturing has relocated to countries where labour can be secured at a lower cost – particularly in Asia – scaling down local industries in which Pasifika people were historically employed (Statistics New Zealand 2002b). While contemporary growth in service industries has absorbed many workers of Pasifika ethnicity, the sector is notoriously low paid and highly casualised, a situation that contributes to income insecurity (New Zealand Council of Trade Unions [NZCTU] 2013). In addition, Pasifika people are often expected to financially support local church organisations and to return remittances to their village of origin. Increasing numbers of New Zealand-born Pasifika people are accessing higher-level training and tertiary study, but the development of new skills capacity is likely to take several generations to lift entire communities out of poverty (Statistics New Zealand 2002b).

Certain family forms are also more susceptible to low income, with families headed by sole parents amongst the most vulnerable to poverty (Statistics New Zealand 2012b). Sole parents face a range of barriers to labour market participation and the ability to take up opportunities that enable social mobility and improvements to the household economy. These are attributable to a combination of factors, including social discrimination and the gendered nature of childcare. In 2009, 43 per cent of sole parent families were raising their children in relative poverty regardless of whether their income came from welfare payments or employment (Families Commission 2010).

The working poor are a relatively recent phenomenon in New Zealand. My research with foodbanks and community meal providers found growing numbers of working people in need of these services. Similar observations have been made by budget advisory services witnessing a new cohort of clients unable to make ends meet due to inadequate income underpinned by low wages and insecure hours of work (Kirk 2015). Although current policy approaches aim to move people into prosperity through attachment to the labour market rather than through social security, being in paid employment no longer insures New Zealanders against poverty, and 'even the best budgeting in the world can't solve the problem of not having enough money' (New Zealand Network against Food Poverty 2000, 11).

## What Drives Poverty?

In recent decades, a number of factors have altered the distribution of economic resources in New Zealand, resulting in higher levels of income inequality and fewer guarantees against poverty over time. It is worthwhile considering these shifts as they interact with the view of most sociologists that poverty is the result of powerful structural forces rather than individual deficiencies. The dominance of particular ideological narratives has also contributed to growing acceptance of inequality amongst New Zealanders.

*Driver 1: Changes to the Political and Economic Landscape*
The observable gap between the 'have lots' and the 'have nots' in New Zealand today sits in stark contrast to the political intolerance for inequality expressed in the middle of last century. Following World War II, New Zealand was regarded as one of the most equal societies in the world. This achievement had been fashioned by the policies of both the Liberal Government which held power between 1890 and 1912 and, to a larger extent, by the First Labour Government which came to power in 1935. While the former set about breaking up large land holdings, implementing a programme of income taxation, legislating minimum levels of remuneration for workers and introducing the world's first state pension scheme, it is the initiatives of the latter that are most often credited with entrenching the idea of New Zealand as an egalitarian society – at least in policy terms. In 1938, the Labour Government successfully passed the Social Security Act as a guarantee against the poverty experienced during the Great Depression. Securing its place in history with the world's first entrenched welfare state, the state promised its citizens 'cradle-to-grave' care that included universalised old-age pensions and family benefits; free healthcare and education; social security against unemployment and other conditions where a living wage could not reasonably be secured; and a widespread programme of state-owned public housing (Rashbrooke 2013a). Of course, all of this came at a price which meant that, as well as nationalising some industries, the Government funded redistributions through high levels of taxation. This programme tracked along quite nicely for several decades, measurably reducing inequality by delivering full employment and a generous standard of living for all. But by the 1970s the tide of favourable conditions upon which New Zealand's export economy relied began to turn, as key trading partners tightened their belts, and by the early 1980s the end of the golden weather for New Zealand's economy had well and

truly arrived. The costs of servicing heavy government debt combined with those of universal welfare and social support delivered a combination that was framed as unsustainable. A snap election in 1984 resulted in a Labour Government which, upon inheriting this unenviable legacy from its National predecessors, began an urgent programme of restructuring and reform dominated by a focus on economic rather than social objectives (Cheyne, O'Brien and Belgrave 2008). This programme was presented as a rational strategy to mitigate the nation's impending economic doom, which would eventually lead to money and social benefits 'trickling down' from rich to poor. Yet the mid-1980s marked a critical pivot point in New Zealand's history, the consequences of which underpin the prevalence of poverty and material inequality today.

### Driver 2: Neoliberalism and the Rise of Income Inequality

The ethos adopted by successive New Zealand governments since the 1980s has been that it is the market rather than the state that should act as the main redistributive mechanism for the resources in society (for more details, see Humpage in this volume). Without the mediating role previously played by the state, however, the distribution of resources becomes increasingly uneven as some are better positioned to exploit the conditions of the marketplace than others. From the mid-1980s to the mid-2000s, the gap between those who had and those who had not grew faster in New Zealand than in any other affluent Western nation. The top 10 per cent of New Zealand households now receive incomes which are on average more than nine times those of households in the bottom 10 per cent, and the wealthiest 1 per cent of New Zealanders have accumulated 16 per cent of the country's total wealth (Rashbrooke 2013b, 1–2). Amongst countries in the Organisation for Economic Co-operation and Development (OECD), New Zealand distinguishes itself by displaying one of most significant increases in its Gini coefficient – a standardised measure of income inequality that can be used to make comparisons between different nations – from the mid-1980s onwards (OECD 2011, 24). This widening of the income gap is notable for both its rapidity and its extreme nature, even by international standards, and can be viewed as a direct outcome of the successive neoliberal policy reforms that have taken place over the last three decades.

*Driver 3: Policy Shifts in Work, Welfare and Housing*

Policy approaches which leave the distribution of resources and income to the market have had a number of sinister social results. One of the most widely observed has been changes to the nature of work. Full employment, job security and liveable wages are no longer policy aspirations, and paid work has become increasingly casualised and insecure as employers exploit competition amongst workers for fewer jobs (NZCTU 2013). Although New Zealand was the first country in the world to legislate a 40-hour working week and a family wage, on average New Zealanders now undertake longer hours of paid work than workers in almost all other OECD nations ('Govt Ignores UN Recommendation of Work-hour Limit' 2013). Incremental changes to benefit policies since the early 1990s mean that people can no longer look to the state to ensure that their standard of living is maintained while they move between precarious jobs. The universalism which characterised transfer payments in earlier eras is also long gone, and entitlements – such as those delivered by the Working for Families policy package – are now more strongly linked to participation in the labour market than to citizenship. The combination of a low-wage economy and the retraction of the state's role in the provision of public housing has also meant an increased proportion of people's income is absorbed by housing costs, with many who would previously have been housed by the state now at the mercy of private landlords. While these changes have demonstrably advantaged the owners of capital – particularly businesses and rental housing – they also go some way towards offering a structural explanation for the growth in income inequality and the material divide that has become a feature of New Zealand society (for more on the impact of the neoliberal reforms on social mobility, see Cotterell in this volume).

## Why Do Relative Poverty and Socio-economic Deprivation Matter?

The existence of poverty and socio-economic deprivation matter because they impact in varying ways on people's well-being. Poverty erodes people's abilities to exploit opportunities for social mobility that could improve their circumstances. Families living in poverty are faced with 'poor choices' because these are the options that are economically rational. Children growing up in poverty generate long-term costs to society through losses to productivity, crime and ill health (Boston and Chapple 2014). Older people in poverty are at risk of not receiving the medical care they need, becoming socially isolated, or skimping on food or heating costs.

Richard Wilkinson and Kate Pickett (2009) are well known for their 'Spirit Level' thesis, which asserts that inequality impacts on everyone in a society, not just those on the losing end. New Zealanders who are not directly subjected to poverty are still affected by it through the tax burden associated with providing higher levels of secondary healthcare and funding the provision of social security and services for those unable to move out of the poverty trap over time. Less obvious costs to society include losses to productivity and economic development as well as the social contribution that those in conditions of relative impoverishment might otherwise have been able to make. Deprivation also creates ripe conditions for social unrest, distrust and crime, when those who feel excluded from access to resources or power seek to correct their status in ways that negate social cohesion. Poverty and socio-economic deprivation matter because they carry real human, economic and social costs. These costs of inequality are borne not just by those who are poor, but by all New Zealanders.

## The Poor Will Always Be with Us?

As we have seen, neither the state nor the market now provides any guarantees against New Zealanders falling into poverty. What is perhaps even more concerning for sociologists is that public attitudes on the whole appear to be increasingly accepting of the existence of poverty and inequality, and people even believe that these are necessary. An analysis of public opinion data undertaken by Humpage (2015) confirms that New Zealanders in general now favour tax cuts over redistribution, and there is a clear preference for delivering targeted assistance to the 'deserving poor' – the elderly, the sick and those with disabilities – as opposed to more universal forms of assistance that would provide for low-income families and sole parents, as well as the unemployed. Similarly, Philip Morrison (2015, 61) has observed that 'despite growing evidence of the negative effects of inequality on [New Zealand] society as a whole, fewer than half of us believe incomes should be made more equal or that government has a responsibility to do more to reduce income differences between people with high and low incomes'. Unless New Zealanders are prepared to revise current ideological constructions of poverty in light of structural realities, the broad consequences that accompany inequality will remain a feature of New Zealand's political, economic and social landscape. There is much that sociology can teach us about the real causes of poverty, and about the gains that come with gracing the tables of all New Zealanders with milk and honey.

CHAPTER 12

# Social Mobility in Aotearoa New Zealand in the Neoliberal Era

*Increasing or Decreasing?*

# Gerry Cotterell

New Zealand is seen by many people to be an egalitarian society. The story of the New Zealand Prime Minister John Key, who grew up in a state house and went on to become a foreign currency trader in a major foreign corporation and then became Prime Minister, is seen as providing evidence for this egalitarianism. For others, however, the idea that New Zealand is an egalitarian society, one in which upward social mobility is accessible to those who work hard, is a myth (Nolan 2007).

    This chapter seeks to understand the concept of social mobility in the New Zealand context, with a particular focus on the post-World War II period. To do this I first discuss the meaning of social mobility, its importance in the current context, and how it is defined and measured. I then sketch the different ways in which social mobility has been experienced in New Zealand over the past 70 or so years. I argue that upward social mobility has been made more difficult by the neoliberal reforms of the past 30 years.

## What Is Social Mobility?

Social mobility, broadly defined, refers to the ability of individuals or groups of people to change their social class, in other words, their social and economic position in society. Measures of socio-economic status include occupation, wealth and income, and can be used to demonstrate that those being measured have either improved their position in society (been upwardly mobile) or seen it worsen (been downwardly mobile). Because social mobility has a number of different meanings, it is important to specify the parameters of social mobility to which we are referring. For example, it can mean movements of individuals or social groupings between classes or occupations; mobility in an upward or downward direction; or the state of sons' or daughters' fortunes compared to their parents, over varying time scales (Payne 2012).

## Why Is Social Mobility Important in the Current Context?

Social mobility is important because it is a measure of a society's 'openness to talent'; that is, the way a society provides opportunities for individuals or groups of people, whatever their ethnic background or social class, to 'get ahead', to improve their socio-economic position and to better themselves. If a society has a high rate of social mobility, then sociologists argue that this is evidence that there are few barriers to each person's abilities to get ahead provided they work hard. Van Leeuwen (2009, 399) argues that '[s]ocieties open to "talent" are better geared for innovation and economic growth, and we are likely to think of them as fairer than societies that block the social ascent of their talented members in favour of inherited positions'. New Zealand is viewed as a society 'open to talent', a view exemplified in John Key's story, which is important in sustaining the country's alleged egalitarianism. In contrast, societies with low levels of social mobility are seen as hierarchical, typically structured around predetermined social positions and providing little opportunity for those with talent from so-called lower social classes or ethnic groupings or genders to get ahead.

In order to understand the role social mobility plays it is necessary to understand whether there is equality of outcome or equality of opportunity in the society under examination. Equality of outcome refers to the level of dispersal of rewards in a society. If there is a high level of equality of outcomes, that is, only a small gap between the highest and lowest incomes, then the level of social mobility is not so important. This is because even if you were not able to move up some social scale, such as moving into a more highly skilled occupation, you would still be as well off, or nearly as well off in terms of income, as those who had moved up this scale. Equality of opportunities refers to a context where most people in a society have an opportunity to get ahead and are not denied this because of their gender, ethnicity or class. A society can have equality of opportunity without having equality of outcomes.

The concept of equality of opportunity is important in this discussion because it underpins the view of social justice incorporated in the neoliberal policy paradigm currently dominant in New Zealand. Under the previous Keynesian policy framework, which existed in New Zealand from the end of World War II until the early 1980s, the concept of social justice underpinning social democracy was equality of outcome (see also Humpage in this volume). Thus, government policies were generally aimed at limiting differences in income through progressive taxation, to ensure that inequality remained low. The goal was a more or less equal distribution of economic outcomes (e.g., income, consumption and material well-being) across society.

Under the neoliberal model, however, the conception of social justice as equality of outcome was abandoned in favour of equality of opportunity. Equality of opportunity requires that a society ensures that all its members have equal access to opportunities, such as access to funding to participate in tertiary education, regardless of their circumstances. In an equality-of-opportunity context, individuals are seen as having a personal responsibility to work hard to ensure that they get ahead through their own efforts. In this paradigm, the role of the state is to remove impediments that hinder individuals from personally benefiting from their hard work, such as lowering rates of income tax so that individuals can retain more of their earnings, and opening up access to tertiary education.

Social mobility is therefore important in the current policy environment because neoliberals argue that high levels of inequality in a society are not a problem provided there are corresponding high levels of social mobility. That is, as long as people are able to get ahead through their endeavours and not have their earnings heavily taxed, for example, then high levels of inequality can be tolerated as people will not stay in a disadvantaged position for long when there are incentives to 'move up the social ladder' and opportunities to do so if they work hard.

## Measuring Social Mobility

The most common types of social mobility identified by sociologists are *intragenerational mobility* and *intergenerational mobility* (Nunn et al. 2007). Intragenerational mobility refers to the extent of social mobility within a single generation and reflects the ability or lack thereof of a specific individual to move up or down some measure of socio-economic status within their lifetime. Thus, if a person begins their working life as a supermarket checkout operator and ends it as the manager of a chain of supermarkets they are considered to have been upwardly socially mobile. Similarly if they start their working lives as an accountant and end up as a street cleaner they would be considered to be downwardly socially mobile in terms of intragenerational mobility. Changes in intragenerational mobility are typically measured by changes in occupation.

Intergenerational mobility refers to the existence of social mobility between multiple generations and to the differences of socio-economic status of different generations of family members over time. So if the daughter of a woman who worked as a nurse became a medical specialist, then the family would be seen to have experienced upward intergenerational mobility. Intergenerational mobility is measured by the relationship between parents' and adult children's socio-economic status. Socio-economic status is portrayed by different measures with the most frequent being occupational status, social class, and individual or family income.

Sociologists make use of two kinds of measures of both intragenerational and intergenerational mobility – absolute and relative. *Absolute intergenerational mobility* refers to whether people are higher up or lower down in the class hierarchy than their parents. This involves a comparison between a person's current social-class position or some other measure of socio-economic status and that of their parents. A woman who became a surgeon while her father was a truck driver is an example of absolute social mobility for the daughter. Changes in absolute social mobility are typically measured in terms of class position or income – the results can be difficult to assess because the relationship between class and income can vary over time. *Relative intergenerational mobility*, in contrast, assesses whether a person's situation relative to that of other people of their generation is better than or inferior to their parents. If a person's income puts him in the top 10th percentile of income distribution and his parents were at the 40th percentile at a comparable point in their lives, he has experienced upward relative intergenerational mobility.

*Absolute intragenerational mobility* refers to the extent to which individuals have higher or lower levels of income compared to the income they started with. If a person began their career with an income of $35,000 and ten years later they were earning $50,000, they have experienced upward absolute intragenerational mobility. *Relative intragenerational mobility* refers to the extent to which individuals move up or down compared to others in their cohort. For example, if a person's income increases from $35,000 at the start of his working career to $40,000 a decade later, but most people who began their work life around the same time experience a larger increase to, say, on average $50,000, then that person has experienced downward relative mobility but upward absolute mobility.

It is important to note that relative mobility is what is called a zero-sum game. That is, if a person moves up some scale in relative terms, then by definition, another person must have moved down. However, this is not the case where absolute mobility exists.

The measurement of social mobility is complicated and requires good-quality data over a long period of time. Such information is not often available to researchers in the social sciences. For example, if social mobility is measured by assessing the occupation of a child in comparison to one of their parents then the obvious comparison point requires data on both the parent's and the child's highest status positions in occupational terms. This assessment would potentially require data over a time span of 40 years or more, and it would also need to take into account changes in occupational structure in a society over that time. Such data are not readily available, nor are they easily analysed.

## What Factors Impact on Social Mobility?

A number of factors impact on the extent of social mobility or social immobility in a given society. These factors include the pre-existing socio-economic positions of families and individuals; the overall level of inequality in a society; the structure of the labour market; and the state of the economy, that is, whether it is growing or in recession. Each of these is discussed in turn below.

The existing socio-economic positions of families have a significant impact on the ability of their members to be socially mobile. For example, children living in low-income households have a reduced chance of obtaining the high-quality education received as a matter of course by children born to wealthy parents. Research in the United Kingdom notes that '[c]hildren with parents on lower incomes appear to be less likely to do well at school, whereas children from parents with higher incomes achieve higher educational outcomes' (Blanden and Macmillan 2011, 201). This finding points to the existence of a vicious circle: without quality education good outcomes are less likely, and without good outcomes social mobility is less likely. In addition, low-income families are unlikely to have access to the social networks that are available to those further up the socio-economic scale. As McNamee and Miller (2009, 16) note, 'the most important factor for determining where people end up economically is where they started in the first place'.

For those born into high-income households, opportunities to aspire, backed by inherited wealth and position, are much greater than for those born into low-income households. As Collini (2010, 30) suggests, calls to people to aspire to be upwardly social mobile are 'intended to deflect attention from the basic fact that the most important determinants of who ends up in which category are not the miraculously independent qualities of "ability" or "effort" on the part of the individual, but the pre-existing distribution of wealth and power in society'.

The existing level of inequality in a society impacts on social mobility such that countries with higher levels of income inequality are inclined to have lower social mobility (Crawford et al. 2011). In a recent report, the Organisation for Economic Co-operation and Development (OECD 2010) noted that increasing income inequality serves to restrain upward social mobility, making it harder for talented and hard-working people to get the rewards they would receive in a more equal society. These findings pose significant challenges to the neoliberal claim that high levels of inequality are of little importance as long as there is upward social mobility.

The state of the economy in a society – whether it is growing, undergoing restructuring or in recession – also has important implications for levels of social mobility. During an economic recession, for example, many jobs are often lost and so opportunities for upward social mobility are lost, possibly for considerable periods of time if the downturn is long. The changing job structure in an economy also plays an important role. The post-World War II period in many Western countries saw an increase in absolute mobility due to the expansion of jobs in professional occupations and a decline in traditional working-class occupations. These changes in the overall structure of opportunities ('more room at the top') are usually referred to as absolute *social* mobility, in contrast to absolute *intergenerational* mobility. Of course, movements in absolute mobility can also occur downwards.

## Social Mobility in New Zealand during the Post-war Long Boom: 1945–1980

The first two or so decades following World War II in New Zealand were characterised by a period of extended prosperity. Unemployment was exceptionally low and strong economic growth underpinned a steady growth in wages while inflation also remained low. The sustained rise in prosperity over much of this time saw standards of living in New Zealand rise considerably. During the 1950s and 1960s, gross domestic product per head of population in New Zealand was estimated to be the fifth highest amongst OECD countries (Easton 1997). During this long post-war boom in New Zealand upward social mobility was largely taken for granted and even those people in low-skilled paid employment were able to experience a rising standard of living as wages for the low-skilled were relatively high. People therefore expected that over time their position and that of their families would improve. Parents expected their children, with the aid of education, to find better work than they did. In other words, this was a period characterised by absolute upward mobility overall, and relative and absolute intergenerational mobility.

Much of the increase in absolute social mobility in New Zealand during this period was due to changes in the occupational structure. These changes included growth in professional occupations such as teaching and public service and declines in traditional manual work such as mining and farm labouring. The proportion of men in white-collar jobs increased from 25 per cent to 33 per cent of the workforce between 1951 and 1971, while the proportion employed in agriculture, forestry and fishing declined from 23 per cent to just over 14 per cent. Over the same period, the proportion of women in white-collar work increased from 54 per cent to 62 per cent (Dunstall 1981, 407–8).

While most groups in New Zealand experienced some form of upward social mobility, the experience was different for different groups. During this period many Māori migrated from rural to urban areas, with the proportion living in urban areas rising from 35 per cent in 1956 to 62 per cent by 1966 (Meredith 2009). In many cases, despite not having high skill levels, they were able to earn relatively high wages in industries such as agricultural processing (e.g., at the freezing works). This period also saw a slow expansion in the proportion of women participating in the paid workforce. Gilson (1969, 190) notes that the percentage of Pākehā married women in paid employment rose from 8 per cent in 1945 to 20 per cent in 1966. Furthermore, married women were increasingly permitted to obtain employment that had formerly been closed to them after marriage, in order to fill the shortage of teachers, nurses and public servants (Carlyon and Morrow 2013, 40), providing another path for intragenerational social mobility.

Over this period the number of migrants coming to New Zealand from the Pacific also increased to fill labour market shortages. These migrants were attracted by the opportunity for a higher standard of living for themselves and their families, which provided them with a form of social mobility (for further discussion on Pacific peoples, see Mila in this volume).

## The Neoliberal Reforms of the 1980s and Their Aftermath

The election of the Fourth Labour Government to power in mid-1984 is typically seen as heralding the arrival of the neoliberal project in New Zealand (Kelsey 1999). Following its election, the Labour Government implemented a programme of extensive economic reforms which sought to 'roll back' the post-war Keynesian policy framework (Peck and Tickell 2002). These 'roll-back' policies included dismantling forms of social support; extending the role of the market; privatising publicly owned assets; and reducing the progressivity of the tax system, the influence of trade unions, and the scope and generosity of welfare provision (Peck, Theodore and Brenner 2012). The National Government elected to office in 1990 extended these reforms of the economy into parts of the labour market, the health sector, public pensions and social policy. Measures included significant cuts to welfare entitlements; a wholesale deregulation of the labour market with the introduction of the Employment Contracts Act (1991); extension of a user-pays policy in the health and tertiary education sectors; reduction in the generosity of, and eligibility for, superannuation; introduction of market-based rentals in the public housing sector; and further privatisation of public assets. While some aspects of these reforms have been modified under subsequent governments, the underlying neoliberal policy framework remains in place (for further discussion of neoliberalism, see Humpage in this volume).

Among the outcomes of the reforms was a large rise in unemployment, with overall unemployment rising from around 4 per cent in 1984 to a peak of 11.2 per cent in 1991 (Statistics New Zealand 2008). The impact was worse for specific groups in the population. Māori unemployment peaked at over

24 per cent in 1991 and Pacific unemployment peaked at around 30 per cent at the same time (de Raad and Walton 2007). In addition the levels of inequality rose significantly with the Gini coefficient rising steadily from .28 in 1984 to a high of .39 in 2014 (Ministry of Social Development 2015b, 75).[1]

The reforms of the neoliberal era (1984 to the present) have impacted on social mobility in a number of ways. Many forms of support provided by the state under the Keynesian policy framework have been removed under the neoliberal regime. Two particular examples are worth bearing in mind. As mentioned earlier, Prime Minister John Key was brought up in a state house. Thus, he and his family benefited considerably from government-provided and -subsidised housing. Under his Government, however, people's ability to access state housing has been significantly undermined with sections of the state housing stock being sold off. Another example relates to the previous Minister for Social Development, Paula Bennett, who as a single parent received a Tertiary Incentive Allowance to allow her to undertake tertiary study. As Minister, however, she oversaw a decision in 2009 to remove this allowance so that people in her former circumstances wanting to study were left without this crucial financial support. If single parents cannot obtain funds for expensive tertiary training then the chances of them being upwardly mobile are likely to be greatly reduced. In both cases, forms of state support previously available were removed, in effect lessening chances for social mobility. What this means is that the 'ladder of support' available to people such as Key and Bennett has been pulled up for the generations that follow.

In response to the lower standard of living and depressed economic conditions experienced in New Zealand in the early to mid-1990s, many people chose to emigrate. Both Māori and Pākehā, for instance, moved to Australia to live and work, attracted by higher wages and a better standard of living. In 2011 there were an estimated 128,430 individuals who identified as Māori by ancestry in Australia, a figure likely to underestimate the real number, which is expected to be between 140,000 and 160,000 (Kukutai and Pawar 2013, 17). As of 30 June 2012, an estimated 647,863 New Zealand citizens lived in Australia (Spinks and Klapdor 2014).

Being part of this diaspora has been a source of social mobility for some. Many gained significant additional income by working in the Australian mining industry, for example. For others, migration to regions such as North America, the Middle East and Europe has led to employment opportunities in occupational fields which are not common in New Zealand, enabling upward occupational mobility not available in New Zealand (Larner 2007).

For those choosing to remain in New Zealand the prospects have been mixed. Many well-paid working-class jobs, such as those in the freezing works, disappeared under the reforms of the 1980s and 1990s. The intentional weakening of the trade union movement, which occurred as a consequence of the 1991 Employment Contracts Act, resulted in a lessening of workers' ability to obtain decent wage increases. Evidence for this is seen in the decline in the returns-to-workers share (wages) of the total national income, which dropped by 8.5 percentage points from 1978 to 2010. This decline confirmed that income going to business owners (profits) over this period had grown much more quickly than labour income (Conway, Meehan and Parham 2015, 6). Alongside this downward pressure on wages, there was a rise in service industry work – much of which is low paid – such as the care of old people and fast food hospitality.

As noted earlier, obtaining higher levels of educational qualifications is seen as a primary route to improved social mobility. In recent decades, however, the cost of higher education has risen considerably. Average annual tertiary student fees increased from $3,624 in 2000 to $5,076 in 2010 (Ministry of Education 2011, 20), and over the same period the total amount owing on student loans nearly doubled from just over $781 million to $1,551 million (Ministry of Education 2014, 24). In addition, workers now often pay for training that was previously paid for by their employer.

For another group, however, New Zealand is still seen as a place in which they can get ahead and be socially mobile. This group comprises migrants from a number of countries who move to New Zealand for a broad range of reasons. For many, the move is successful as they are able to use their skills to advance their own and their families' position. For some migrants, however, the form of mobility they experience may be downward. The news media regularly produces anecdotes about highly skilled immigrants working as taxi drivers and about doctors unable to work as medical professionals because their qualifications or English-language abilities do not meet local requirements (Mentjox 2006).

## Conclusion

The pattern of social mobility in New Zealand has varied in recent decades. New Zealand was once seen as a place where talent and hard work enabled you to get ahead, regardless of your background. This outcome was attainable for many during the long post-war boom as economic growth and changes in the occupational structure of the economy provided space for an increase in absolute social mobility for a broad range of groups and individuals. However, the neoliberal reforms implemented in the 1980s and thereafter have made attaining such outcomes more difficult for many people. This difficulty exists despite the architects of the reforms arguing they were needed to free up a heavily regulated economy in order to allow people to prosper (New Zealand Treasury 1987; Richardson 1995). For many groups in New Zealand, the opportunity for upward social mobility has been lessened or removed altogether as high levels of unemployment, increased levels of inequality, the higher cost of education and housing, and lower growth in incomes limited people's ability to improve their lot. In addition, the removal of many forms of support enjoyed by the previous generation – such as assistance for tertiary study and access to state housing – have undermined the conditions needed to assist people to improve their lives. While many people in New Zealand still believe in the possibility of getting ahead, the prevailing economic circumstances in which they seek to do so will severely limit their ability to achieve this aim.

### Note

1   The Gini coefficient measures the extent to which the distribution of income among individuals or households in an economy deviates from a perfectly equal distribution. A coefficient of 0 represents perfect equality and 1 represents perfect inequality. This measure is widely used to compare inequality between countries.

**PART IV**

# Genders and Sexualities

CHAPTER 13

# We Still Need Feminism in Aotearoa

*The Achievements and Unfinished Tasks
of the Women's Movement*

## Julia Schuster

On 13 January 2012, the *New Zealand Herald* republished a commentary by Harriet Walker (2012), a British journalist, who proclaimed: 'Of course we still need feminism'. Walker was responding to public pronouncements of a post-feminist era in which women allegedly enjoy full gender equality and feminism is said to be redundant. It is true: women in Aotearoa New Zealand have the same legal rights as men. They have the right to vote, to attend school, to get a university degree. They have the right to be paid as much as their male colleagues for the same kind of work, and they may retain that income. They can marry the spouse of their choice and choose to get divorced. From today's point of view, it would be absurd to suggest that the law should treat women differently from men. This was not always the case. None of the above rights were served to women on a silver platter – women had to fight for them.

But although contemporary New Zealand women enjoy the same legal rights as men, the feminist struggle is not over. Legal equality is only one building block of gender justice and several other blocks are still missing. For instance, women's lower average income and higher responsibility for housework suggest that the achievement of gender justice remains a work in progress (see Elizabeth on gender in this volume). Using two examples of ongoing feminist battles – increasing women's political empowerment and fighting violence against women – this chapter discusses the history of New Zealand's women's movement, including its achievements and challenges, and examines its unfinished tasks. Additionally, it briefly reviews whether the women's movement is for women only.

Before I delve into this discussion, two terms need to be clarified: 'feminism' and 'the women's movement'. Feminism is a worldview that demands gender justice, which – depending on one's perspective – can entail the pursuit of gender equality, striving for gender equity or the wish to abolish patriarchy. The term patriarchy refers to 'the structuring of social life – labor, state and consciousness – such that more social resources and value accrue to men as a group at the expense of women as a group' (Hennessy 2000, 23). Many scholars and/or members of the women's movement disagree about the specifics of feminist values and therefore several branches of feminism exist (Gray and Boddy 2010). Liberal, radical, socialist, anarchist, transnational and post-colonial feminisms represent various positions on the feminist spectrum. Additionally, feminist ideas can be fundamentally shaped by cultural values, creating distinctions between Māori, Pacific, Pākehā and Asian versions of feminism, for example. Black feminism, womanism and Third World feminism further illustrate that feminism encompasses different perspectives across cultural and global contexts (Hill Collins 1996; McNicholas 2004). Generations of feminists have also developed their respective interpretations of feminism, responding to their particular historic, political and economic contexts (e.g., First, Second and Third Wave feminism[1]). Thus, while feminism informs the aims of women's movements, its plurality indicates that such movements can differ in their goals and practices.

Women's movements are social movements, similar to gay liberation movements, anti-racist movements, environmental movements and anti-capitalist movements (e.g., Occupy). While some of these movements focus on identity politics (e.g., the gay liberation movement aims to improve rights for people identifying as gay; see Schmidt in this volume), other movements challenge social conditions, such as capitalism or environmental destruction. The women's movement can be understood as a challenge to patriarchy. It is also often portrayed as an identity-based movement because it makes claims on behalf of *women*. Addressing women as a collective group with shared political aims can help generate a large group of supporters for feminist demands. However, this chapter will illustrate that the notion of a 'united sisterhood' has to be treated with caution. Not all women are exposed to the same kinds of discrimination or enjoy the same access to social resources (e.g., education, the labour market, political representation). Thus, political interests among women vary and can even contradict each other. Consequently, women's movements have the difficult task of defending the interests of a diverse group of people.

## Women's Political Empowerment

Only about 30 per cent of New Zealand's Members of Parliament (MPs) are female. Women's representation on local government bodies is roughly at the same low level (Statistics New Zealand 2014c). This illustrates the general under-representation of women on political bodies, which worries feminists for at least two reasons: first, because this means that women are missing out on the opportunity to become MPs simply because they're women; and second, because past feminist successes have relied on a strong voice for women in the political process (Gilling and Grey 2010). Women need positions of political leadership to influence political discourse and to shape public opinion. Raising awareness of feminist issues requires activists and lobbyists to get involved; petitions need to be signed by as many supporters as possible; and legislation can only be changed with the support of policy-makers. While there is no doubt that men can (and often do) support feminist causes, increasing *women's* political representation is vital for achieving and securing gender justice. It is also important to remember that even today's imperfect representation of women in politics is the result of a long history of feminist struggle.

Internationally, First Wave women's movements of the mid-nineteenth to early twentieth century are renowned for achieving women's suffrage. In New Zealand, this was an especially monumental success since New Zealand was the first country in the world to grant women the right to vote in national elections in 1893 (see Shaw in this volume). Using petitions, suffragists like Kate Sheppard and Kate Edger sought support for their cause among New Zealanders and subsequently introduced Women's Suffrage Bills to Parliament. From today's perspective, this does not seem to be a particularly radical approach to social change, but the involvement of women in formal politics was unusual at the time (Grimshaw 1987; Hutching 2010).

Although Māori women shared the demand to be enfranchised with European women, the suffragist movement was dominated by Pākehā. Meri Te Tai Mangakāhia (Te Rarawa) was one of the few Māori women in the leadership of this movement who is named in the literature. Additionally, a number of Māori women signed the franchise petitions of 1892 and 1893. The relative lack of Māori involvement can be explained by the opposition of European suffragists to many Māori traditions (e.g., tā moko) and their requirement that members of their organisations complied with European standards. However, parallel to the mainstream suffrage movement but less often recorded in the history books, Māori women fought for their right to vote and stand for Te Kōtahitanga, the Māori Parliament (operating between 1892 and 1902), which they achieved in 1897 (Rei 1993).

Enfranchisement ensured that women were directly able to participate in the democratic process rather than be 'represented' by the votes of their fathers and husbands. Subsequently, women in the nineteenth century who exercised their newly gained right made an important statement against the dominant public discourse of the time that portrayed women as politically incapable. The suffragists' critics claimed that, once enfranchised, no good mother would leave a sick child at home on Election Day, and that all sensible women would stay at home while only 'the worst examples of their sex, the harsh, unsexed, "advanced" women' would exercise such a right (Grimshaw 1987, 77). Proving those opponents wrong, women's turnout in their first election, 1893, was even higher than men's, at 85 per cent compared to 70 per cent (New Zealand Parliament 2013).

Once women started to mobilise for suffrage, they quickly became interested in the enhancement of women's rights on a broad scale. The Women's Christian Temperance Union (WCTU), an organisation important to the suffragists, actively encouraged women to engage with feminist ideas and expanded its agenda to support female prisoners, provide education on nutrition and organise preschool childcare services. The WCTU was also involved in lobbying for the alteration of the prostitution law and the pursuit of equal divorce rights for men and women. In 1884, before women gained suffrage but due, in part, to women's lobbying, Parliament granted the right for married women to own property and to retain their income, and by the end of the 1880s a woman's right to sit on a committee was extended from schools to liquor-licensing committees and charitable boards. In 1919, women achieved the right to stand for Parliament, something that is widely viewed as the mark of full citizenship (Grimshaw 1987).

Many years later, the late 1960s and early 1970s became known for political uprisings and student protests across the West and in parts of the Communist bloc. New Zealand women, who were politically active during that time in anti-war and anti-racist movements, became increasingly frustrated with the dominance of male activists in those movements. Inspired by North American and European women's groups, New Zealand women organised their own meetings to debate issues that were of concern to them (e.g., reproductive and abortion rights, equal pay, violence against women). The emergence of feminist collectives marked the beginning of the Second Wave movement, showing once again that women could and would claim a place in politics (Dann 1985).

By establishing the Ministry of Women's Affairs (MWA) in 1985, the Fourth Labour Government institutionalised mechanisms to ensure that issues of concern to women were considered in the policy process. The MWA's role was to advise on the gender impact of policies and legislation drafted by other government departments. Despite the explicitly feminist ideals of its first CEO, Mary O'Regan, and her team, the MWA had to retreat steadily from a broad approach of enhancing gender justice to a more narrow focus on supporting women's leadership and improving the situation of women in the labour market (Curtin and Teghtsoonian 2010). While this approach neglects many issues that are of importance to women, including those that confront less privileged women (e.g., unemployment), the MWA has to juggle the interests of New Zealand's women with the interests of the government of the day. Given the neoliberal direction of successive governments, which puts more emphasis on economic growth than on pursuing gender justice, the labour-market-oriented programme of the MWA reflects the policy objectives of early twenty-first-century governments.

In 1993, New Zealand's electoral system changed from First Past the Post (FPP) to Mixed Member Proportional (MMP). Women still require parties to offer them prominent listings but, compared to FPP, MMP improves the chance of women winning a seat in Parliament. The new system provides smaller parties with an incentive to participate and these have tended to present diverse lists of candidates, increasing the chances that women might be elected to Parliament. In the 1996 election, for example, the percentage of female MPs increased from 21 to 29 per cent. Consequently, from a feminist perspective, it was a relief that the 2011 referendum – asking whether FPP should be re-introduced – was unsuccessful, because women's representation in Parliament would have been likely to decrease under FPP (Gilling and Grey 2010).

Under the Fifth Labour Government it appeared as if women were 'taking over' the political sphere: Helen Clark became Prime Minister (1999–2008), seven women held ministerial positions, and the roles of Speaker of the House (Margaret Wilson, 2005–2008), Chief Justice (Sian Elias, 1999–present) and the Governor-General (Dame Silvia Cartwright, 2001–2006) were filled by women. The continued neoliberal agenda of the Government, however, restricted the feminist potential of these women. Political strategies influenced by neoliberal thought aim to support individual agency and the personal responsibility of citizens, but are less interested in interest group lobbying on behalf of women as a group, for example.[2] Consequently, having women in important positions is not sufficient when the overall political climate is unsupportive of gender justice (Curtin and Teghtsoonian 2010).

Today, young women show less interest in traditional forms of politics (e.g., party memberships) than their male peers (Coffé and Bolzendahl 2010). This is not surprising when female politicians (such as Helen Clark and Julia Gillard) face public criticism about their appearance and femininity. It has also been suggested that young women avoid traditional forms of political engagement because they know that their voice is not taken seriously within male-dominated politics. Instead, they have developed their own platforms (e.g., blogs and zines) to communicate their political interests (Maddison and Sawer 2013). The 'Ponytail Incident' in 2015 illustrated this dynamic quite pointedly: Prime Minister John Key continued to pull the hair of a 26-year-old waitress despite her clear and repeated disapproval. Thus, he demonstrated that he did not take her statements seriously. She chose to go public by writing a blog post about it, which caused Key to apologise (see Bradbury 2014). However, it remains a feminist concern that a political leader feels entitled to invade a young woman's personal space in such a manner.

## Fighting Violence against Women

New Zealand has the highest rate of reported intimate partner violence in the developed world and more than a quarter of all women will experience domestic and/or sexual violence in their lifetimes (Ministry of Justice 2014; UN Women 2011). Not surprisingly, this important issue has been on the agenda of the women's movement from its early days.

At the time of the suffragists, domestic violence was a widespread experience for New Zealand women (Hutching 2010). It was recognised that the consumption of large quantities of alcohol by many men contributed to turning many homes into unsafe places. Worsening the situation, the law at the time made it almost impossible for women to successfully file for divorce. The suffragists hoped that achieving the right to vote would enable women to participate in referendums on prohibition, leading to the outlawing of alcohol consumption and eventually reducing violence against women. For this reason, the suffrage movement collaborated closely with the temperance movement (Grimshaw 1987; Hutching 2010).

Even though violence against women remained a serious problem, it did not become a prominent concern of policy-makers. When New Zealand's Second Wave movement emerged (in the 1970s), authorities viewed domestic violence as a private matter that neither required nor justified state intervention by the police or legislation (Dann 1985). In response, Second Wave feminists provided grassroots support 'for women by women', rather than relying on a patriarchal government to intervene. They established the first women's refuge in Christchurch in 1973, began rape crisis support services, and took their issues to the streets (Vanderpyl 2004). The 'Take Back the Night' marches – which still continue – became annual public reminders that women are not safe from violence (Coney 1993; Julie 2015).

Differences between ethnic groups mattered with regard to feminist strategies for addressing violence against women in the 1970s. Contrary to the collectivist Māori approach that connected women's empowerment with issues of Māori sovereignty and the broader Māori community (including Māori men), Pākehā understandings of feminism tended to view women as individual agents whose personal interests needed to be taken seriously (Simpkin 1994). Thus, Pākehā feminist strategies for protecting victims of violence focused on supporting individuals, while the Māori approach addressed the needs of the whānau/families and communities in which violence occurred. This strategic mismatch often impeded collaborations (Vanderpyl 2004), and feminist frictions (also between lesbian and straight feminists or between socialist and liberal feminists) gradually grew. They peaked at the 1978 Women's Liberation Conference in Piha, significantly damaging the grassroots base of the Second Wave movement (Coney 1993).

Nevertheless, important feminist achievements for victims of violence were made during the following years, mainly in the form of changes to the law. For instance, the Domestic Protection Act 1982 required the police to interfere in domestic disputes and the amended Crimes Act 1985 recognised rape within marriage as a punishable crime.[3] The Domestic

Violence Act 1995 was another important success that instituted protection orders; broadened the legal definition of domestic violence to include psychological, sexual and physical violence; and acknowledged that anyone (including flatmates and caregivers) could be a perpetrator. This focus on legislation was the result of a change in direction for the women's movement, from grassroots to formalised politics. Many feminists joined the newly established MWA, while others moved into local government, unions and civil society organisations, putting women into positions to lobby for policy changes.

The shift in a neoliberal direction in the 1980s also affected feminist strategies. Organisations working to reduce violence against women – a focus that was not a neoliberal priority – found it increasingly difficult to secure funding. In order to remain eligible at least for some funding programmes, many women's organisations abandoned informal ways of organising and directed more energy into providing services – like refuges or legal advice – that might gain government contracts (Vanderpyl 2004). In the early 1990s, women's refuges organised themselves into the National Collective of Independent Women's Refuges. However, the network's capacity to provide help for women and children in need was, and remains, severely constrained by its (lack of) financial means. Even so, the National Collective has maintained refuges across the country (including separate refuges for Māori and Pacific women) and continues to lobby on behalf of women and children suffering from violence.[4]

In the 1990s and early 2000s a number of high-profile cases of reports of sexual assaults by members of the police force, most prominently the Louise Nicholas case, sparked public debate about the difficulties that survivors of sexual violence face when seeking help from authorities (Taylor 2013). This coincided with and helped to fuel the rise of Third Wave feminism. Subcultures, such as Riot Grrrl or Girl Power, propelled the Third Wave in the United States and in the United Kingdom. Initially, the Third Wave reflected mainly young women's desire to create their own version of feminism independent of their mothers' generation. While many of the political concerns of this new wave remained similar to Second Wave demands (such as combating sexual violence and ending male dominance in political leadership), their approaches to such issues differed. Third

Wave feminism is informed by post-structuralist feminist theory, which sees gender identities in terms of a fluid spectrum rather than distinct, binary categories (e.g., Butler 2004). The Third Wave understanding of patriarchy that follows from this theory implies that not only do women lack social power and resources, but so too do queer, transgender, intersex and all gender non-conforming people (Mann and Huffman 2005). Thus, Third Wave events and political claims rarely address women exclusively.

New Zealand's Third Wave took longer to take off than in some other countries (Coney 1993), but when it did, from the late 1990s on, violence against women remained a core feminist issue. Third Wave feminists have, for instance, a strong focus on 'rape culture'. The term refers to a society that trivialises, excuses and condones sexual violence and tends to blame the victims rather than the perpetrators.[5] 'She was asking for it' is, for example, a common statement growing out of and fuelling rape culture. To protest this issue, feminists of all genders participated in the SlutWalk movement from 2011 to 2013 in several New Zealand cities.[6] The 'Roast Busters' case,[7] which triggered another series of marches and online-based activism in 2013, illustrated the persistence of rape culture depressingly well, as the police and political authorities again failed to take young women's reports of sexual violence seriously (Independent Police Conduct Authority 2015).

However, some Third Wave events, like SlutWalk, have been criticised within feminist communities for ignoring ethnic differences in the experience of rape culture (O'Keefe 2014). Because different racial stereotypes and cultural expectations of gendered behaviour shape their environments, Māori and Pacific survivors of violence face different obstacles in getting recognition of their victimisation and gaining assistance with their recovery than Pākehā survivors. The same is true for Asian survivors, as has been discussed by the activist blog *Mellow Yellow* (see Dumpling 2014). Thus, the youngest generation of feminists continue to struggle with the challenges of women's diversity as did the generations before them. To tackle this challenge in the context of the women's movement, contemporary feminists often draw on intersectionality theory, a feminist theory arguing that different forms of discrimination (such as sexism, racism and homophobia) cannot be thought of as separate dynamics because they interact with each other in context-specific ways (Crenshaw 1991).

## Is Feminism Just for Women?

For the suffragists it was vital to have male allies such as Robert Stout, John Hall and Julius Vogel, because women were not eligible to introduce Bills to Parliament (Hutching 2010). This openness to men was less evident in the 1970s, when female feminists purposefully created 'women-only' spaces to provide small but much needed enclaves that were not dominated by men within a patriarchal society. For many women with experiences of violence, the exclusion of men increased their sense of safety, and in some cases entire, often lesbian, separatist communities emerged, such as Piccadilly Street in Christchurch (Dominy 1986; Vanderpyl 2004).

Yet one does not need to be a woman to support the demands for gender injustice or to oppose violence against women. In 2004 the White Ribbon project, an international campaign initiated by a group of Canadian men in 1991 to end violence against women, was introduced to New Zealand (White Ribbon 2016). This campaign argues that as men are the main perpetrators of interpersonal violence it is mainly men who need to stop this behaviour, and it is also the case that men are more likely to listen to and take advice from other men. Moreover, while their number is not as high as for women, many men are victims too, particularly of sexual violence but also of domestic violence. Thus, today some feminist organisations working in the area of violence employ and work with men (e.g., Rape Prevention Education). Women-only spaces still exist, but they are not as common as they used to be in the 1970s.

In accordance with the aforementioned Third Wave understanding of gender identities, many contemporary feminist events and organisations are open to all genders. There has also been a shift in recent years to change the criteria governing who can enter women-only spaces. The initial biological distinction between men and women was criticised by

Third Wave feminists for discriminating against transwomen who experience particularly high rates of violence (Couch et al. 2007). Thus, some women-only spaces, like the Auckland Women's Centre (AWC), reworded their policies to welcome anyone *identifying* as a woman (AWC 2011).

## Conclusion

The New Zealand women's movement has achieved a great deal for women over the course of three waves of feminism. However, women are still under-represented in Parliament, young women tend to stay away from formal politics and the MWA is constantly challenged to prove its relevance to neoliberal governments. In addition, the number of women who are victims of male violence remains distressingly high, refuges are chronically underfunded and authorities repeatedly fail to support victims of violence appropriately. Women might not be overtly discriminated against in laws and legislation any more, but more subtle ways of disadvantaging women persist – not only concerning violence and political participation. For instance, New Zealand women do not have full control over their bodies (e.g., women do not have a legal right to safe and legal abortions); they face glass ceilings in the labour market; and they do most of the unpaid care work for children and the elderly. Given women's diversity, feminist struggles will probably always be bedevilled by internal frictions. Yet these should and must not distract from the fact that gender justice has not yet been achieved; we still need feminism in Aotearoa New Zealand.

### Notes

1 The history of the women's movement is commonly narrated in 'waves' representing phases of intense feminist activity. However, feminist activism continues before and between those waves.
2 Some authors see feminist potential in neoliberal empowerment of individual women who, for instance, pursue successful professional careers. However, this perspective is contested among feminists because it focuses on a few, relatively privileged women (Rottenberg 2014).
3 Prior to this amendment, there was no legal recognition of marital rape; wives could not file complaints of rape against husbands.

4   The Women's Refuge (2015) website provides submissions on various government documents including the Family Court Review 2011 and the Inquiry into the Determinants of Well-being of Māori Children 2012.
5   It is interesting to reflect on how John Key's 'Ponytail Incident' is situated within this context. Feminists suggest that rape culture encourages men to believe that a woman's body can be used by them for their entertainment without her consent.
6   SlutWalk is an international series of protests that began in Toronto in 2011 in response to a police officer advising female students to 'not dress as sluts' if they wanted to avoid sexual harassment (Maddison and Sawer 2013, 132–47).
7   The Roast Busters were a group of young men who boasted on Facebook about their sexual encounters with underage girls, many of whom reported that they had been raped.

CHAPTER 14

# Homosexuality in Aotearoa New Zealand

*Regulation and Resistance*

## Johanna Schmidt

In the everyday talk that surrounds us, particular forms of sexuality are presented as 'natural' or 'normal'. Connecting sexuality with nature is relatively straightforward because sexuality is linked to bodily actions and biological processes, and is an (almost) necessary part of reproduction. The resulting assumption that reproduction forms the bedrock of sexuality works to legitimate some sexual behaviours and identities while marginalising others. The following quote, from a letter to the editor of the *Otago Daily Times* first published in the weeks leading up to the passing of the Civil Union Act 2004 in Aotearoa New Zealand, exemplifies this linking of reproduction, sexuality and nature: 'When we look at our common humanity and what constitutes the special relationship of marriage, it is obvious from the bonding of a man and woman that their love-giving is life-giving. A same-sex relationship cannot be such, so is contradictory by its very nature' (quoted in Goodwin, Lyons and Stephens 2014, 825).

Sexuality is one of the human constants; people in every society and every historical period engage in sexual activities. These activities also consistently have cultural meanings and explanations attached to them. However, the fact that these meanings and explanations differ between cultures and change throughout history indicates that sexuality is not simply natural but is fundamentally social (Weeks 2007). One of the core components of sexuality as a social phenomenon is its regulation, something that reflects the working of power. This regulation may be manifested in the laws of the state or the edicts of religion, but it is also achieved in everyday talk or discourse.

In this chapter, I focus on the social and state regulation of homosexuality in New Zealand as a way of showing how sexual identities and behaviours are constrained and regulated. This discussion starts with the concept of 'heteronormativity': the 'set of ideas, norms and practices that sustain heterosexuality and gender differentiation and hierarchy, including romantic love, monogamy, and reproductive sexuality' (Hopkins, Sorensen and Taylor 2013, 98). From there, I go on to outline how homosexuality has been constructed historically, examining the regulation (legal, medical and cultural) of homosexuality in New Zealand, and resistance to this regulation. In this chapter I focus on same-sex sexual relations and identities related to Pākehā men. The ways in which the non-heteronormative identities expressed by women, Māori and Pacific peoples in Aotearoa have been both marginalised and accommodated in dominant discourses are different stories that are addressed elsewhere.[1]

## Heteronormativity

In brief, 'heteronormativity' positions heterosexual relations as superior to all others, constructing these as the 'norm' and all other sexual practices as 'deviant'. At the pinnacle of the hierarchy of sexuality is reproductive heterosex (heterosexual sex) which occurs in the context of monogamous marital relationships (Rubin [1984] 1999). The privileging of heterosexuality is based on the notion that sexuality is and should be intrinsically linked to the biological imperatives of reproduction, and that all non-reproductive forms of sexual relations are 'unnatural' and hence 'wrong' (Warner 1991).[2] Although this argument is most commonly applied to homosexuality, it has also been applied to bondage and discipline, sadomasochism (BDSM), pornography and masturbation (Rubin [1984] 1999). Heteronormativity provides the socio-cultural context in which homophobia exists: if heterosexuality is understood to be 'normal', the possibility that some people will fear and hate those who fail to conform to heteronormative standards becomes comprehensible (Renzetti and Edleson 2008).

It is generally accepted that the term 'heteronormativity' was first used by Michael Warner in the 1991 special edition of *Social Text* on queer theory. However, the concept (if not the specific name) was utilised earlier than this, notably in 1980 when Adrienne Rich (1980) argued against 'compulsory heterosexuality'. Heteronormativity is linked to the understanding that we have 'evolved' to enjoy particular forms of sex so as to perpetuate the species (Warner 1991). There are, however, a number of problems with this approach to sexuality, three of which I will outline here. First, the notion that 'natural' equates to 'morally right' is not observed in most areas of life: numerous aspects of social life that are 'unnatural' are not constructed as 'wrong', and in many instances are actually seen as appropriate behaviours – for example, wearing clothes. Second, the vast majority of heterosexual acts are not themselves reproductive: most obviously, using contraception ensures that heterosexual intercourse limits the potential for reproduction, while 'natural' occurrences such as infertility and ageing also result in non-reproductive heterosex. There are also many specific acts (such as oral sex or anal penetration) which can be part of both heteronormative and non-heteronormative sex that have no reproductive potential. This relates to my third point: in contemporary Western contexts, motivations for having sex – even heterosex – are seldom linked to reproduction. For example, American college students provided one group of researchers with 237 reasons for having sex without once mentioning reproduction (Rutter and Schwartz 2012). Of course, this group is younger than the general population and hence not representative, but the research nevertheless suggests that sex is seldom about reproduction. In spite of this, understandings that anything other than heterosex is somehow 'unnatural' continue to prevail.

Embedding sexuality in a bedrock of 'nature' and framing it as an evolutionary necessity also affects how the act of sex itself is understood. Sexologists such as Masters and Johnson have demonstrated that the range of sexual behaviours is extremely wide (see Rutter and Schwartz 2012). In spite of this, it is routinely assumed 'that the most natural form of heterosexuality is coitus i.e. penetration of the vagina by the penis. All other kinds of sexual activity are regarded as either preliminary (as indicated by the term "foreplay"), or optional extras, or substitutes when the "real thing" is for some reason not available' (Jackson 1984, 44).

The 'coital imperative' (Jackson 1984) can be detrimental to women's sexual pleasure; while many women enjoy intercourse, for others it may not be the optimum means of achieving orgasm (if orgasm is the desired outcome) and, for a smaller proportion of women, intercourse may result in no pleasure at all, and may even be painful (Gavey 2006). The positioning of coitus as 'real sex' thus works to privilege a sexual activity that is not always beneficial for women.

The naturalisation of discourses which construct and maintain particular power relations is defined by Antonio Gramsci (1971) as 'hegemony' (for more on hegemony, see Pringle in this volume). Hegemony is a process through which a particular set of ideals becomes accepted as 'right' and 'natural', allowing particular groups to maintain their dominance through consensus, rather than with coercion or force. The naturalisation of heterosexuality, and of specific forms of gendered heterosex, works to favour heterosexual men, shoring up their privileged position in contemporary Western societies. One of the most powerful ways in which this occurs is through the repudiation of homosexuality, which becomes heterosexuality's marginalised 'other'.

## The Construction of Homosexuality

The intrinsic link between hetero- and homosexuality is evident in their nearly simultaneous emergence as concepts in the late nineteenth century (Wilkinson and Kitzinger 1994). Sanctions against particular sexual acts had historically existed in all Christian denominations and, in the 1530s, religious edicts against 'buggery' became legal prohibitions in the United Kingdom (Weeks 2007). However, the law 'made little distinction between buggery between man and woman, man and beast and man and man' (Weeks 2007, 123), indicating that while the act was seen as sinful, it was not considered to demarcate a particular kind of person. The concept of 'homosexuality' as a sexual *orientation* was first developed in 1868, with the notion of 'heterosexuality' emerging just over a decade later (Wilkinson and Kitzinger 1994). Through the 1880s and 1890s psychological publications sought to explain homosexuality as a 'condition' (Foucault 1981; Weeks 2007), and the legal focus shifted from particular sexual acts to the people engaged in those acts. In 1885 all sexual activities between men (but not between women) were outlawed in the United Kingdom (Weeks 2007).

It is possible to trace a similar shift from the regulation of sexual actions to a concern with sexual identities in the history of New Zealand. Although there does not appear to be a definitive term for 'homosexual' (either as an act or an identity) within 'traditional' te reo (Murray 2003), there is evidence of sex occurring between men in pre-contact Māori culture (Aspin and Hutchings 2007). However, colonialism and the introduction of Christianity into Aotearoa heralded a new cultural, moral and legal order that regulated sexual relations between men. The English laws adopted by colonial New Zealand made sexual assault and sodomy illegal, although not oral sex and mutual masturbation between men, a situation that continued with the passing of the local Offence Against the Person Act in 1867 (Brickell 2008). In 1893 the Criminal Code Act redefined sexual assault as *any* act perpetrated by a man on another man, whether consensual or not, and this legal definition was replicated in the Crimes Act of 1908 (Brickell 2008).

## Homosexuality in New Zealand Society

As elsewhere, the emergence of a homosexual 'identity' at the outset of the twentieth century resulted in the eventual development of a culture around that identity, and the 'queer world' that had previously occupied private spaces or darkened areas moved more into the public realm of coffee shops, bars and clubs (Brickell 2008). Increasing visibility and politicisation were inevitably accompanied by escalations in police attention (Brickell 2008). Convictions for homosexual activity increased through the 1950s and peaked in the 1960s and 1970s, echoing a wider public interest in sexual 'misconduct' in general (Brickell 2008), which fed into increasing amounts of sensationalist press coverage. Although overwhelmingly negative, media reports of homosexual activities confirmed the existence of others like themselves for some readers, especially those in small towns, many of whom became part of the trend towards urban migration, further solidifying the communities that developed in the larger centres (Brickell 2008).

At this time, the civil rights movement and Second Wave feminism spearheaded a range of other social movements around the world. The gay liberation movement was one of the more significant of these, with its genesis in the 1969 gay, lesbian, drag queen and transgender riots after the police raid of the Stonewall bar in New York (Brickell 2008; Johnston 2007). The movement expanded over time to include an increased range of queer identities, indicated in the acronym GLBTI.[3] Activism and visibility achieved the desired effect of changing opinions, and research conducted in the 1970s demonstrated that not only were public attitudes towards homosexuality relatively favourable, but also that positive attitudes were more prevalent among younger New Zealanders, indicating a generational shift in perspective (Bowman 1979).

The increasing visibility and social acceptance of homosexuality illustrates another aspect of the hegemonic process, in that social and cultural power is not something the dominant group 'wins' and then holds forever; but is something that must be constantly maintained and defended (Gramsci 1971). This involves periodic renegotiation of power dynamics and hierarchies, and often some degree of accommodation of the perspectives of those at the margins. The activism of the 1960s and 1970s represented the voices of various disenfranchised groups, whose protests were able to gain enough traction to represent a potential threat to dominant forces. As with the demands of various other social movements of the time (Storey [1988] 2009), the demands of those fighting for GLBTI rights and social inclusion were eventually incorporated into mainstream discourses.

## Shifts in Official Discourses

In New Zealand, as in most Western contexts towards the end of the twentieth century, cultural shifts to recognise and accommodate homosexuality were mirrored within more 'official' discourses such as medicine and the law. Up until the mid-twentieth century it was fairly well accepted that homosexuality was 'rightly' considered both illegal and considered pathological. However, in the 1950s two reports were published that had a significant impact on how Western societies understood homosexuality. The American Kinsey Report provided scientific evidence that there was a broad spectrum of sexual experiences and preferences among the whole population, undermining the positioning of homosexuality as 'unnatural' (Pritchard 2005, 85). The British Wolfenden Report argued that homosexuality was a private issue, and therefore should not be subject to legal sanctions (Pritchard 2005; Rishworth 2007). These reports were the genesis of early campaigns for the decriminalisation of consensual sex between adult men. In Aotearoa, such campaigns began with the formation of the New Zealand Homosexual Law Reform Society (NZHLRS) in 1966 (Brickell 2008; Rishworth 2007). The NZHLRS was not particularly 'pro' homosexuality; following the Wolfenden Report, their approach was very much one of liberalism, arguing that what consenting adults did in private was not a matter for public concern nor legal constraints (Pritchard 2005).

Although homosexuality ceased to be an official psychological diagnosis in 1973, when it was removed from the US Diagnostic and Statistical Manual of Mental Disorders, medical constructions of homosexuality still held sway in the popular imagination. Possibly as a result, the pro-reform movement was somewhat fractured by disagreement over the proposed age of consent, with some suggesting that it should be higher than sixteen, which was the age that applied to heterosex (Rishworth 2007), reflecting beliefs that even if homosexuality between consenting adults was a private matter, it was somehow less 'appropriate' than heterosexuality. When the first private member's Bill for the decriminalisation of homosexuality was introduced in 1975, the proposed age of consent was 21 (Rishworth 2007). However, in spite of a swing towards greater tolerance in the general population, the Bill was still defeated in Parliament (Rishworth 2007).

As gay activism took hold through the 1970s, and homosexuality began to be understood not as a 'condition' but rather as an orientation for which a cure was neither likely nor desired, the liberal conservative approach of the NZHLRS was gradually replaced by a more militant and strident voice (Pritchard 2005), which 'adopted the motifs of equality and liberation that by then were associated with race and gender' (Rishworth 2007, 88). This more 'aggressive' campaigning typified the discussions around the Homosexual Law Reform Bill in the mid-1980s. Those supporting the Bill came from a more politically charged position than their predecessors, but the proposed legislation also met with significant opposition. Submissions to the Select Committee were replete with the common tropes of heteronormativity and homophobia, including assertions that anal sex is unnatural (ignoring the fact that this is not limited to same-sex couples), that same-sex sex is not procreative (even though most heterosex is not either) and that homosexual men are paedophiles (McCreanor 1996). The timing of the legislation meant that there was also a particular (and often explicitly homophobic) focus on linking homosexuality with HIV/AIDS (McCreanor 1996). In spite of this, the Bill was passed in 1985, decriminalising sexual activities between males aged sixteen and over. Although the second part of the Bill, which prohibited discrimination on the basis of sexual orientation, was not successful, the groundwork was firmly laid for the eventual inclusion of sexual orientation in the Human Rights Act of 1993 (Rishworth 2007).

Anti-discrimination legislation opened up the debate around marriage, and in 1997 two lesbian women took a case to court arguing that the fact that marriage was only available to heterosexual couples was discriminatory (Rishworth 2007). Although this case was unsuccessful, it is notable that one of the Appeal Court judges 'concluded that the essence of marriage was not procreation but commitment, intimacy, and financial interdependence' (Rishworth 2007, 96), indicating a cultural shift away from understanding sexuality and marriage as fundamentally based in reproductive imperatives. The first years of the twenty-first century saw these cultural shifts enshrined in legislation, initially with the Civil Union Bill in 2004, which allowed couples of any gender to enter into a civil union that had fundamentally the same legal status as marriage (Rishworth 2007). This was followed by the Marriage (Definition of Marriage) Amendment Act in 2013, which explicitly (re)defined marriage as being 'between two people regardless of their sex, sexual orientation, or gender identity'. Opposition to both these Acts utilised the familiar tropes of heteronormativity, including assertions that children are disadvantaged by having same-sex parents, even though this is almost solely because of the homophobia of others (Goodwin, Lyons and Stephens 2014; Seuffert 2006).

While both these pieces of legislation have been presented as significant victories for gay rights activism, this understanding is not universal. The focus of GLBTI activism on civil unions and marriage privileges a certain *kind* of same-sex relationship: those that are 'caring and committed' (Goodwin, Lyons and Stephens 2014, 823) and, as such, largely similar to the heteronormative ideals of what relationships 'should' be like. Many queer theorists are concerned that

> marriage will produce a new 'homonormativity' (Duggan 2002, 188) that will sound the death knell of a distinctively 'queer' LGBT identity and culture by marking the final assimilation of LGBT people into mainstream culture and its most conservative and patriarchal of institutions, marriage, resulting in the containment and control of queer sexuality within monogamous, state-sanctioned relationships. (Hopkins, Sorensen and Taylor 2013, 104–5)

The potential privileging of relationships that follow the heteronormative model – based around commitment, monogamy, and particular legal and economic rights and responsibilities (Hopkins, Sorensen and Taylor 2013) – creates a risk that people in same-sex marriages will be seen as 'respectable', while GLBTI people who do not have legally recognised relationships will be marginalised (Madill 2008). The 2013 Marriage (Definition of Marriage) Amendment Act can thus be understood as both an important step in the advancement of rights for a marginalised group in society, and a possible capitulation to social norms. The simultaneous success of marriage reform agitation, in the form of the legalisation of same-sex marriage, together with the failure to really challenge contemporary heteronormativity, illustrates yet another aspect of the workings of hegemonic power. Accommodations of this kind seldom involve substantive alterations to the dominant norms, and the incorporation of dissenting voices usually results in a 'watering down' of more radical potentials (Gramsci 1971). Hence, hegemonic power is maintained.

## Conclusion

Sexual activity is generally defined as an inherently private matter. However, as I have outlined, the fact that specific sexual behaviours and identities are often the subject of legal regulation at state level, and/or of cultural norms, demonstrates that sex also has a very 'public' aspect. Heteronormativity, and its grounding in an apparently biological imperative, has shaped cultural, legal and medical regulation of sexuality. Although the relative conformity of the culture of twentieth-century Aotearoa New Zealand meant that social, legal and medical shifts were somewhat slow and cautious (Bennett 2009), our ethic of egalitarianism and tolerance has also had a significant impact on how local discourses have shifted, something that was particularly evident in the recent same-sex marriage debates (Goodwin, Lyons and Stephens 2014; Seuffert 2006). The broadening of the scope of marriage to include same-sex couples seems to indicate that the voice of gay activism has been loud enough to result in change at both social and legal levels. These changes, however, ultimately do little to challenge heteronormative models of sexuality. In order to really problematise the constraints of heteronormativity, we need to be attentive to the myriad forms that sexuality takes. Recognition of non-heteronormative sexualities has the potential for opening up challenges to the normative ideal of the monogamous, dyadic, lifelong and reproductive marriage, an ideal that is seldom a complete reality even for heteronormative relationships (Jagose 2013). For example, non-heteronormative populations may approach family from a 'queer' perspective by forming 'families of choice' based on considerations other than biological or legal ties, or become parents by diverse means that challenge the primacy of biological reproduction. Existing outside the confines of heteronormativity also increases the potential to query monogamy as an ideal (Hopkins, Sorensen and Taylor 2013). It has been suggested that the shift in the focus of GLBTI activism from these potentials to state-sanctioned marriage is indicative of a 'post-gay politics', which aligns 'the desires of gays and lesbians with those of a heterosexual middle class' (Johnston 2007, 30) and which has a tendency to 'emphasize perceived similarities to the majority, muting differences and supressing what is distinctive about gay identity' (Hopkins, Sorensen and Taylor 2013).

As I finished the first draft of this chapter, the film *Fifty Shades of Grey* was released. At first glance this story, with its BDSM theme, seems to challenge conservative models of sexuality. However, at its core the narrative replicates many of the fundamentals of heteronormativity, valorising a gendered power dynamic that stretches from the sexual to the emotional, the physical and the economic, and perpetuating the notion of the 'chase' as a model for heteronormative relationships (Jackson 1984). At whatever point in time you are reading this chapter, I would encourage you to think of current texts that replicate the tropes of heteronormativity – even while seeming to be 'resistant' – but also of texts that genuinely challenge these norms.

## Acknowledgements

I would like to thank Bonnie Scarth and Scott Brandon for commenting on various versions of this chapter, the editors of this volume for their feedback and patience, and, as always, my little family.

### Notes

1   A fuller analysis of lesbian behaviours and identities in the context of Aotearoa New Zealand can be found in the collection edited by Alison Laurie (2001). The specificity of the Māori cultural context – the intersections of culture and sexuality, and the relatively recent development of takatāpui as a sexuality (Murray 2003) – are discussed by Clive Aspin and Jessica

Hutchings (2007). Likewise, significant levels of Pacific migration have led to a cross-pollination of cultural understandings, with the identities of Samoan faʻafāfine and other Pacific transgendered identities having a strong influence in Aotearoa New Zealand (especially, but not only, in Māori cultural contexts), but Western notions of 'gay' are also inflecting how Pacific men understand their own sexual behaviour and identities, issues which I have discussed elsewhere (Schmidt 2010).

2   Religion is the other main influence on the construction of sexual hierarchies. There is not enough space in this chapter to adequately discuss the role of religion in regulating sexuality, but this is outlined by Michael Stevens's (2013) contribution to *Being Sociological*.

3   Gay, lesbian, bisexual, trans and intersex. This acronym can also, at various points, include Q ('queer') and A ('asexual'), and is likely to include other non-heteronormative sexual and gender identities in the future.

CHAPTER 15

# Man-Up?

## A Socio-historical Examination of Pākehā and Māori Masculinities

## Richard Pringle

In a recent lecture I asked students to make a list of the most respected and/or greatest New Zealanders. In the subsequent discussion, many names were mentioned including Ernest Rutherford, Peter Blake, Edmund Hillary, Richie McCaw, David Lange, Helen Clark, Jonah Lomu, Colin Meads, Michael Joseph Savage, Peter Jackson, Tim Finn and Charles Upham. The students were quick to identify that Pākehā men were overwhelmingly represented within their list. With further discussion, additional names such as Apirana Ngata, Hone Heke and Kate Sheppard were added.

The class was then challenged to see if they could select the one most respected or greatest New Zealander. This proved a difficult task, but discussion eventually centred on three individuals: Edmund Hillary, Peter Blake and Richie McCaw. In attempting to defend these selections, students discussed their respective achievements and underpinning qualities and values. Stories were told of how they were leaders: brave, hardworking, pragmatic, skilled, successful, determined, strong, down-to-earth, able to rise above adversity and, most importantly, humble. The class broadly decided that aside from their achievements, these men were the most respected because the qualities they exhibit(ed) resonate with the (dominant) ideals and values of Aotearoa New Zealand.

With respect to this last point, I quoted a number of descriptors for Hillary, Blake and McCaw. I mentioned that Hillary was declared 'the epitome of New Zealand manhood' ('Editorial' 2008) and that McCaw has been described as embodying 'the ideal national character' in the 'manner of the New Zealand hero' (Hastings 2013). Helen Clark (2001) in her eulogy about Blake described him as a 'national hero' and talked of his courage, stamina, tenacity and humility, and his simply 'being a decent human being'. I used these quotes – and use them again here – to argue that New Zealanders typically respect these men because they are regarded as nationalistic exemplars of a socio-culturally dominant form of masculinity.

This dominant form of masculinity, I suggest, is connected to inequitable relationships between males and females, and between males from different ethnic groups and sexual identities. This form of masculinity is therefore a prime reason why so few women, Māori or (other) ethnic minorities were named within the students' list of the greatest or most respected. In other words, this idealised form of masculinity is linked to the workings of power that provides a social advantage to white males.

In this chapter, I explore this proposition by examining the historical formation of masculinities in Aotearoa New Zealand in order to understand how particular representations and forms of masculinity have become dominant and how they influence contemporary social relations, particularly gender/ethnic relations and performances of masculinities. I begin by detailing how masculinities have been examined and theorised. I then discuss the historical formation of masculinities with respect to Pākehā and Māori men.

## Theorising and Examining Masculinities

The issue of how to theorise and examine masculinities has generated considerable debate. Although 'masculinity' is a contested term, most researchers accept that understandings of masculinity change over time, are performed differently in various cultures and contexts, and can be considered as multiple, socio-historical constructions (Connell 1995). Females can and do perform 'masculinity', yet the term is typically defined as 'the socially constructed gender attributed to the male sex' (Paris, Worth and Allen 2002, 11). In this respect, masculinity has been described as the manner in which men perform what they believe to be their manhood, or as that complex range of meanings attached to males (Kimmel and Messner 1998). The performance of masculinities is primarily enacted in ways to differentiate males from females: through wearing recognised styles of dress, practices of bodily comportment (e.g., sitting with legs apart) or display of certain attitudes or values, like toughness.

Interest in researching males and masculinities developed from formative feminist studies literature from the 1970s and early 1980s. Researchers, accordingly, began examining masculinities in relation to the detrimental impact of sexism and heteronormativity on women and non-heterosexuals in particular (Kimmel and Messner 1998). Concerns were also raised about the relationships between masculinities and men's health/well-being. Within Aotearoa New Zealand, for example, evidence suggests that men are three times more likely than women to die from intentional injury and suicide; are the victims and perpetrators of the majority of interpersonal violence; have the largest alcohol and drug problems; constitute the majority of pathological gamblers; and typically have a life expectancy six years shorter than that of women (Ministry of Health 2014). This recognition of 'masculine' problems encouraged numerous sociologists to examine the gendering processes associated with 'the transformation of biological males into socially interacting men' (Kimmel and Messner 1998, xv).

The most influential theoretical lens for examining masculinities revolves around the concept of 'hegemonic masculinity'. This concept was popularised by Robert W. Connell (1995) and colleagues. For example, Carrigan, Connell and Lee (1987, 178) recognised that there are multiple ways of performing masculinity but claimed that the 'crucial division is between hegemonic masculinity and various subordinated masculinities'.

The hegemonic form of masculinity is the one that is dominant and gains the greatest respect in a particular context.

Connell took the concept of hegemony from Antonio Gramsci (1971), who used it to explain how a ruling group or class establishes and maintains cultural dominance over subordinate groups through ideological practices and beliefs. Gramsci describes how ideology, as an interrelated set of ideas, stems from the ruling classes and derives power or social influence primarily via means of consent rather than by force. Connell (1995) subsequently argues that hegemonic masculinity, as an ideology, ensures that dominant ways of performing masculinity seem natural and normal and, therefore, people broadly consent to them. However, the process of maintaining hegemony, or socio-cultural dominance, is complex and involves processes of negotiation. In this respect, understandings of masculinity are subject to change over time.

Hegemonic masculinity within Aotearoa New Zealand historically framed the ideal man as pragmatic, strong, resilient, skilled, unemotional, intelligent and knowledgeable (Phillips 1996). This ideology of masculinity normalises the idea that men should be social leaders, and offers an explanation for why males have dominated in politics, business, education, religion and sport, through assumptions that link masculinity with the kinds of skills and qualities thought necessary for success in these fields. Conversely, the operation of hegemonic masculinity makes it difficult for women to gain leadership positions in such fields and, at times, women have been (and, in some sites, remain) actively discriminated against or even forbidden entry (e.g., from religious and, historically, military leadership, and from various sporting codes). For this reason, Connell (1995) defines hegemonic masculinity as the culturally exalted form of masculinity that ensures the legitimacy of patriarchy. For Connell, 'patriarchy' refers to a system of gender relations within which men in general gain from the subordination of women, gains that Connell (1995, 41) refers to as the 'patriarchal dividend'. The idea that men gain from patriarchal gender relations does not mean, of course, that there are no costs associated with this structure for men (e.g., higher levels of risk-taking behaviours among young men that result in premature death for some and serious injuries for others).

The hegemonic form of masculinity not only produces divisions between males and females, it also structures a hierarchy between males. Connell (1995) argues, for example, that males who are regarded as 'feminine' risk marginalisation within the gender order, and that homosexual masculinity is subordinated to heterosexual forms. Within this context it is perhaps not surprising that the process of 'coming out' as gay has been typically fraught.

Although the concept of hegemonic masculinity is widely recognised as a useful theoretical tool, it has also been subject to a number of critiques. Howson (2009), for example, takes issue with the apparent gap between the concept of hegemonic masculinity and the 'material practices' of masculinity, suggesting that many powerful men, across the globe and within New Zealand (e.g., John Key), do not exemplify the markers of hegemonic masculinity. Other critics have suggested that the tenets of hegemonic masculinity were identified at the time of the Second Wave of feminism and that these ideas no longer reflect the complex dynamics associated with contemporary gender relations and the increasingly diverse range of sexualities, ethnicities and 'fluid' identities in the twenty-first century (Seidler 2006).

Given these critiques, a number of gender scholars have reformulated hegemonic masculinity and/or turned to intersectional approaches. An intersectional approach recognises that ethnicity, sexuality, economic status, age, dis/ability and social context, amongst other factors, are important in shaping different types of masculinity and the associated relations of power. An intersectional approach, therefore, recognises that a Māori man's sense of identity includes his understanding of what it means to be both Māori and a man, and that the complexities of the interlinkages between class, sexuality and gender mean that a medical doctor who identifies as gay might be able to craft a more privileged form of masculinity than an unemployed straight man.

Taking heed of the concept of hegemonic masculinity and the ethos of an intersectional approach, I provide in the following section a sociohistorical account of the development of Pākehā and Māori masculinities.

## A Socio-historical Examination of Pākehā Masculinities

The stereotypical image of the Pākehā man is associated with mateship, social independence, a do-it-yourself mentality, hard work, and rugged or risky leisure pursuits such as rugby, hunting, gambling and binge drinking. Although this image is under threat in the face of increased urbanisation, feminism and changing demographics, this caricature of masculinity still holds social influence.

Early colonists developed narratives of national identity linked to a 'model of tough, rural, "pioneering" white masculinity whose presence is naturalized by association with the landscape and . . . pragmatic physical industry' (Bannister 2005, 2). Such narratives were built on the colonisation of Aotearoa New Zealand but in ways that did not typically reveal the destructive effects of colonisation. For example, the pioneering romanticism associated with 'breaking in the land' does not reveal Māori responses to stolen land or the problematic environmental effects of this particular practice.

Jock Phillips (1996), in his ground-breaking text *A Man's Country?*, contends that influential understandings of the Pākehā male stem from two seemingly contradictory traditions of manhood that came to the fore at different moments in New Zealand's history: a primary tradition that celebrates the hard-working, rural, resourceful, itinerant, heavy-drinking bloke – the pioneer man; and a secondary tradition that acknowledges the self-restrained, temperate, family man that first emerged in the 1920s alongside the increasing urbanisation of New Zealand. Although Phillips stresses that his socio-history of masculinities is one focused on images, myths and stereotypes, his explanation for the stereotype of the pioneer man rests on what he calls 'truth by numbers' (4), which relates to the imbalance of males to females throughout the nineteenth century. In 1861, for example, for every 1000 white males there were only 622 white females and, as late as 1874, there were more 'never married' men than 'married' men. In this socio-historical context, many men did not have family responsibilities and they turned to other men 'for support and comfort' (9).

For this reason, Phillips argues that mateship was central to the everyday lives of Pākehā men during the 1800s and early 1900s. Reliance on mateship typically occurred wherever 'footloose' men could find work, which was predominantly in rural areas. The type of work these men did involved strenuous physical labour – mining, whaling, farming, shearing, clearing land, gum digging, forestry – and this exhausting work typically took place in damp, rugged and potentially dangerous environments. Phillips suggests that, in these settings, strength, physical prowess, pain tolerance and coping with adversity were valorised because they were useful.

Mateship was forged not just by working hard but also by playing hard: 'drinking was without doubt the most important and defining ritual of the male community' (Phillips 1996, 35). Alcohol, however, was not consumed via regular, moderate or solitary processes but was characterised by binging and drunkenness in a way that allegedly forged communal bonds amongst men. Within drinking establishments, prostitution was reported to be relatively common and women were perceived as legitimate 'objects' for male consumption. In contrast, 'respectable' women, who might entice men into marriage, were perceived as a feminising threat to the priority men gave to their bonds with each other and to the exclusivity of masculine culture (36).

Consequently, Phillips argues that homosociality (socialising only with one's own gender), mateship and male isolation from – and contempt of – feminising influences were formative in the development of the ideology of Pākehā masculinity. This ideology, in a context of a surplus of independent men, acted to roughen or masculinise the emerging culture, and to masculinise the men themselves. Thus, Aotearoa New Zealand became a 'man's country'. Or did it? Phillips's very title questions whether New Zealand was really a man's country. On this issue Macdonald (1999, 18) raises the possibility that the 'scarcity of women, especially those of young adult years, provided women with a fulcrum from which they were able to extract some advantage in economic power, legal rights, political status and social position – both individually and collectively'. It was an advantage that enabled New Zealand's suffragists, many of whom were also members of the temperance movement, to pursue and achieve enfranchisement, not simply as a way to realise an important liberty for women, but also as a mechanism to exercise some collective control over men (Phillips 1996).

Attempts in the late 1800s and early 1900s to reframe the rugged 'Kiwi bloke' within newly defined 'boundaries of acceptable male behaviour' (Phillips 1996, 275) show that hegemonic forms of masculinity are susceptible to challenge. The kind of tensions between the 'boozer and the decent bloke', the itinerant pioneer versus the civilised urbanite, and the hard man versus the family man, which Phillips argues shaped the Pākehā male stereotype, have continued to inform ongoing negotiations over Pākehā masculinity throughout the twentieth and into the twenty-first century.

Although the Pākehā male stereotype, as described by Phillips, is not the most common form of contemporary masculinity in Aotearoa New Zealand, it still holds cultural relevance (Pringle and Markula 2005). Indeed, this image of Pākehā masculinity has been indirectly promoted (and simultaneously problematised) in numerous movies and forms of literature, such as the movies *Sleeping Dogs* (1977), *Smash Palace* (1981), *The World's Fastest Indian* (2005) and *Everest* (2015); and literature such as Barry Crump's *A Good Keen Man* (1960), Murray Ball's *Footrot Flats* comic strip (1976–94), John Mulgan's *Man Alone* (1949), the satirical 'rural' humour of John Clarke (aka Fred Dagg) and the poetry of Sam Hunt. Yet the contemporary cultural relevance of this form of masculinity is perhaps best reflected in the commercial connections between masculinity-sport-beer, or what Gee and Jackson (2010) refer to as the 'holy trinity', in New Zealand. Steinlager, as an example, sponsors the All Blacks (the national rugby team) and until 2020 holds the naming rights for forthcoming international tours. Beer advertisements, more broadly, often draw on nostalgic images (e.g., Speight's and the Southern Man) and a formula of (typically Pākehā) men bonding over hard work and then enjoying a beer with other males. When women are present in beer or sporting commercials they are often 'accessories', in traditional roles or sexualised. In this manner, masculinity is defined through a disassociation from femininity and in relation to traditional notions of manliness. Such representations draw on nostalgic and national representations in a way that reproduces old myths and stereotypes but blends these with contemporary ways of performing masculinity. The series of DB Export Dry advertisements known as the 'great wine depression' (2012), as an example, illustrates that although contemporary urban men may socialise in a variety of trendy cafés and restaurants, they can still perform masculinity by refusing to drink wine (which is portrayed as feminine) and by drinking beer. These adverts work via 'lifestyle branding'. In other words, the adverts hail men via the creation of images that offer a plausible and desirable masculine lifestyle and through illustration of how this lifestyle can be obtained through beer consumption.

Brendan Hokowhitu (2007, 65) argues that this culturally dominant version of masculinity is also predominantly a working-class phenomenon. He further argues that although working-class masculinities – including the 'skewed population of Māori men' – have remained more closely linked to the traditional traits of rugby, racing and beer, 'middle- and upper-class New Zealand men are transforming'. Indeed, Auckland's demographics reveal a population of vast socio-cultural diversity and the stereotypical form of Pākehā masculinity has been recognised by some as anachronistic and even an identity to increasingly parody (Pringle and Markula 2005).

As with any influential research, Phillips's arguments about the image of Pākehā masculinity have been subject to critique (see Macdonald 1999). A prime critique suggests that Phillips underestimates how Māori and Pākehā have shaped each other in the process of forming gendered identities and associated relations of power (Macdonald 1999). Accordingly, in the following section, I examine the socio-historical formation of Māori masculinities to understand how 'contemporary indigenous forms of identity have been constructed in relation to colonialism' (Aspin 2002, 92).

## Māori Masculinities in Neocolonial Times

As a Pākehā sociologist (from a broader family/whānau that includes Māori members) I have reservations about writing about Māori masculinities. Social theorist Michel Foucault argued that the human sciences act as a form of power, given their ability to construct knowledge that subsequently categorises, disciplines and shapes social relations. Many Māori are also aware of how scientific knowledge can act as a form of power. Linda Tuhiwai Smith (1999, 1) argues that the word 'research' 'is one of the dirtiest words in the indigenous world's vocabulary' as 'it is implicated in the worst excesses of colonialism'. She stresses how scientific knowledge acted to produce Māori as a dark-skinned 'other', an uncivilised savage, and how this knowledge justified colonial rule. Furthermore, Donna Matahaere-Atariki (1999, 111) asserts that the 'context in which native masculinities are articulated can be seen to be saturated with contemporary anxieties about New Zealand's colonial past'. In order to navigate this terrain, I draw from researchers who identify as critical indigenous scholars, particularly Brendan Hokowhitu (2003, 2007).

Māori masculinities, similar to Pākehā masculinities, can be understood as pluralistic socio-historical constructions. Hokowhitu (2007), however, argues that through processes of colonisation, Māori masculinities have been defined in relation to Pākehā masculinities. Pākehā men, Hokowhitu (2007, 64) argues, 'have maintained power by defining what they are not . . . through the constructions of "Others" such as Māori and women'. He explains, for example, that constructions of 'Māori savagery inherently define Pākehā as civilised' (64). Through the material and symbolic violence of colonisation, Māori masculinities have been adversely impacted so that dominant representations of Māori men have focused on the harmful and undesirable with a disproportionate emphasis on 'physicality and passions' (94). Jake the Muss, the lead character from *Once Were Warriors*, is a representation of this negative image, given his portrayal as a violent, sexist, alcoholic and dysfunctional father/husband.

Hokowhitu (2007, 68) argues that underpinning 'this performative dysfunction is the colonial construction of Māori men as "physical beings"'. It is important to understand that Māori masculinities were different prior to colonisation. Hokowhitu argues this point, in part, with reference to a photograph, taken in the late nineteenth or early twentieth century, illustrating Māori men reclining with their arms around each other and their children, in overt displays of relaxed friendship and caring. The contrast between this image and the problematic and hyper-masculine form depicted in *Once Were Warriors* is marked (for discussion of the relationship between masculinity and violence, see Elizabeth on domestic violence in this volume).

In pre-European times, Māori identified themselves in relation to one of many hapū (sub-tribe) and iwi (tribe) (for more detail, see Walker as well as Kukutai and Webber in this volume). This close form of kinship was governed by a code of practice commonly referred to as tikanga (obligatory ways of knowing, doing and being) that aimed to protect and sustain the whānau (family) (Mead 2003; Patterson 1992). The reciprocity of human relations is, accordingly, a key factor for understanding Māori gender relations. Male identities were constructed, for example, in a communal and reciprocal fashion so that it would have been considered self-centred or disrespectful for a man to act in relation to his own desires or needs (Pringle and Whitinui 2009). Over the years, however, various Pākehā researchers have attempted to define Māori pre-colonial society as patriarchal. Yet Hirini Mead (2003) argues that patriarchy is a Eurocentric concept and suggests that Māori understood gender relations through a different conceptual lens, a lens that did not consider gender roles in a hierarchical manner. Although Māori males and females had distinct roles, they were judged as equally important and contributing to the unified aim to nurture the well-being of their whānau (Mead 2003).

In order to understand how the negative representation of Māori men developed and has gained dominance, Hokowhitu (2003) undertook a socio-historical examination. He identified that colonisation took place under the guise of Social Darwinism and belief in the survival of the fittest. Māori mythology and tikanga were subsequently framed as heathen, unscientific and uncivilised. Within this context, Māori were depicted as 'inherently inferior' and as a 'hindrance to the social and economic development of the new colony' (195). This perspective silenced the legitimacy of a Māori worldview, demanded an eradication of Māori ways of being and justified European dominance. An early parliamentarian, quoted by Hokowhitu, reflected this problematic sentiment in 1867 by claiming:

> The 'Haka' is an exposé of the evil which really lies at the root of their [i.e., Māori] present prostrate condition, an exhibition of the substratum of utter immorality, depravity, and obscenity, which forms the ground work of their race; and in spite of the veneering with which we clumsily cover the rough wood, we shall do nothing until we alter their entire character, by taking in hand the education, per force, of the young growing saplings. (199)

State education, correspondingly, became a tool to suppress Māori tikanga and te reo for the alleged benefit of the colony (i.e., for the benefit of Pākehā). Yet it also became a means to perpetuate the stereotype of Māori men as physical beings. From the 1880s to the 1940s, educational policies reinforced a restricted and damaging view of Māori academic capability. To illustrate this argument, Hokowhitu (2003, 201) quotes the headmaster of a Māori boarding school, the Reverend Butterfield. In 1910, Butterfield claimed that

> [a]bout 999 out of 1000 could not bear the strain of higher education. In commerce Maori could not hope to compete with the Pakeha. In the trades the Maoris were splendid copyists, but not originators. As carpenters they would cope under a capable supervisor but not otherwise. Agriculture was the one calling suitable for Maoris. . . . It was therefore necessary to teach them the 'nobility of labour'.

Māori boys subsequently received an education that emphasised manual and agricultural skills and were prevented from gaining academic qualifications that could lead to white-collar employment. The legacy of this biased education is reflected in the fact that by 1965 the overwhelming majority of Māori men were employed as labourers and transport operators (Hokowhitu 2007). As 'physical beings', however, Māori men were allowed 'level-playing field' entry into the Pākehā domains of war and rugby. Hokowhitu (2003, 210) asserts that Māori gained access not simply because 'they were "damned goods" but, more importantly, because representations of Māori athletes or Māori warriors did not conflict with stereotypes of Māori as a physical and savage people'. Māori success in sport and war inadvertently perpetuated the view of Māori men as physical beings but also allowed them opportunities to assimilate into the 'Kiwi bloke' culture, with its emphasis on aggression, pain tolerance, violence and competitiveness.

Hokowhitu (2007, 73) argues that the stereotype of Māori men as physical beings has obscured the 'creative, constructive and feminine voice of Māori men'. Yet he also acknowledges that, given this stereotype is socially produced, it can be disassembled. Hokowhitu asserts, however, that this process must be Māori-led, as the Western neoliberal view of the world 'does not encapsulate the complexity of Māori culture' (73). He correspondingly points to a range of Māori men who have successfully transcended the damaging stereotypes of Māori masculinity to inhabit alternative and more respected ways of being. He cites, for example, academics such as Ranginui Walker, Mason Durie and Graham Smith, and artists and writers such as Hone Tuwhare, Witi Ihimaera and Ralph Hotere. In this respect he offers hope for future change. Indeed, contemporary names that could be added to this list include comedian Jemaine Clement, film directors Taika Waititi and Lee Tamahori, songwriter/ musician Jason Kerrison, and politicians such as Pita Sharples and Kelvin Davis.

## Conclusion

In this chapter, I have introduced and drawn on the concepts of hegemonic masculinity and intersectionality to understand how culturally dominant representations of Pākehā and Māori masculinities have developed, and to consider their contemporary impact on ethnic relations in particular. This examination illustrated how Pākehā men inhabited positions of influence in the colonisation of Aotearoa New Zealand and how the associated promotion of an ideology of Pākehā masculinity developed to broadly advantage Pākehā men over women, Māori and other minorities. Conversely, Māori masculinities have been stereotyped in a way that has acted to disempower, silence and negatively portray Māori men in contrast to Pākehā men. In linking these generalised conclusions back to the chapter's introduction, we can gain insight into why the students in one of my classes overwhelmingly identified Pākehā men in a list of the most respected and/or greatest New Zealanders. An intersectional approach, however, acknowledges that it is too easy, and problematic, to draw sweeping conclusions about men of diverse backgrounds. As such, the broad conclusions drawn in this chapter should be read with a degree of caution, as there is a need to recognise the great diversity within masculinities (and femininities) and between individual men.

CHAPTER 16

# Gender Inequalities Are a Thing of the Past. Yeah, Right!

## Vivienne Elizabeth

As a young single woman my mother escaped the slums of Glasgow – made worse by the ravages of World War II – through an assisted immigration scheme, arriving in Aotearoa New Zealand during the 1950s. The scheme would bring 77,000 migrants, mostly from the United Kingdom, to New Zealand's shores between 1947 and 1975 (Ministry for Culture and Heritage 2014a). In exchange for the cost of her passage my mother was bonded to work as a general nurse for two years, nursing and teaching being amongst the very few professions open to women at the time. Yet involvement in a professional occupation was not viewed as a career for life; rather, it was a mere interlude before women undertook their real life's purpose as wives and mothers. My mother confronted the reality of this social norm encoded as a condition of employment when she was placed on permanent night shift shortly after marrying my father. Although a talented nurse, my mother soon left nursing and found employment in the retail sector. A few years later she had the first of four children and left regular paid employment behind her to become a full-time housewife and mother.

The general elements of my mother's story – a relatively brief period of paid work before marriage, in one of a narrow range of professions open to women, followed by childbearing and (near) full-time domesticity – were relatively typical for women of her generation, particularly Pākehā women. Her biography was very much the product of that era, and the gendered (and classed and ethnicised) opportunities and constraints that characterised it. These women came into adulthood during the heyday of Keynesianism, a political economy predicated on a gendered division of labour, with women (especially middle-class Pākehā women) working in unpaid care and service work in the home, and men working as family breadwinners in the public domain. While we often associate Keynesianism with cradle-to-grave welfare (see Humpage in this volume), it was also a period of relatively rigid gender differentiation and pronounced gendered inequalities at home and at work. These inequalities were grounded in law; the formal rules of key social institutions, like education and the labour market; and social norms.

In this chapter I explore, in necessarily limited terms, how gender as a social division impacts on women living in the early part of the twenty-first century in Aotearoa New Zealand. We're encouraged to think that the influence of gender in the current era is radically different from its influence during the eras our mothers and grandmothers lived through. But does radical difference – the fact that women of today face far more opportunities and far fewer obvious constraints – add up to gender equality? Have we yet achieved gender justice Down Under?

## Liberation Achieved: From Social Constraint to Free Choice

Stories of New Zealand women who entered adulthood prior to the women's movement of the late 1960s and 1970s illuminate differences between the past and the present. They enable us to draw a contrast between an historical moment where women's choices were highly constrained by socio-cultural norms encoded in legislation and formal institutional rules, and a contemporary moment where legislation and formal institutional rules are gender-neutral in their articulation if not in their application or implications. Young women, since the 1980s, confront a socio-cultural environment that lacks formal barriers to their participation in any field, at any level; they can be hairdressers or plumbers, nurses or doctors, office workers, managers or CEOs, etc. Indeed, McRobbie (2011, 182) argues that today's young women are 'encouraged to achieve in school, at university and in the world of work – and in each of these spheres they [can] rightly expect norms of gender equality to prevail'. This kind of cross-generational comparison has been harnessed by post-feminism to support its claims that gender inequality is a thing of the past.[1] In the post-feminist milieu that dominates Western culture, including the culture of Aotearoa New Zealand, young women are represented as the inheritors of successful liberal feminist campaigns for choice, freedom and individual empowerment. Or to put this slightly differently, post-feminist discourse posits that today's young women are not members of an oppressed category – 'women' – but individuals who have been liberated from the constraining effects of gender as a social division. In this state of liberation, according to post-feminist rhetoric, there can be no legitimate reason for young women to pursue feminist action. The prohibition against feminist politics remains in place even when young women are confronted with evidence (e.g., the Roast Busters scandal[2] or ponytailgate saga[3]) of 'just how intact and unchanged sexual hierarchies' remain (McRobbie 2011, 183; see also Baker 2010; Pomerantz, Raby and Stefanik 2013). Critics have thus argued that post-feminism operates to render oppressive dimensions of the contemporary Western gender order invisible (Gill and Scharff 2011; McRobbie 2011; Pomerantz, Raby and Stefanik 2013, 187).

Post-feminism resonates powerfully with neoliberalism (Gill and Scharff 2011, 7; see also Jacques and Radtke 2012; Pomerantz, Raby and Stefanik 2013). As Gill and Scharff explain (2011, 7), both post-feminism and neoliberalism presuppose a social order characterised by a high degree of individualism. Thus, they assume that individuals are liberated from external 'pressures, constraints or influence' (7). In other words, post-feminism and neoliberalism both conceive of a social world in which the power of gender and other social divisions to structure lives has all but disappeared. This viewpoint gives rise to a closely related idea of individuals as autonomous beings who are rational, self-managing agents pursuing their self-interest. The synergies between post-feminism and neoliberalism lead to an image of today's young women as competitive, can-do individuals, who are self-reliant and entrepreneurial (McRobbie 2011). Consequently, normative ideas about femininity have been resynthesised and now incorporate ambition and assertiveness, qualities that were previously aligned only with masculinity and defined as antithetical to normative femininity (Baker 2010; Pomerantz, Raby and Stefanik 2013).

A similar understanding of individuals as autonomous and socially unconstrained can be found in the work of individualisation theorists Ulrich Beck (2002), Elisabeth Beck-Gernsheim (2002) and Anthony Giddens (1991). These theorists likewise argue that the power of social divisions (like gender, sexuality and ethnicity) and social institutions (like the life course,[4] labour market and families) has dissipated. As a result, people's lives are no longer formulated in terms of standard biographies, following a life course preordained for them by their class, gender and cultural locations (Baker 2010; Beck and Beck-Gernsheim 2002; Brannen and Nilsen 2005). Instead people are tasked with piecing together 'choice' or 'do-it-yourself' biographies (Beck and Beck-Gernsheim 2002; Brannen and Nilsen 2005). A key point of difference between standard and choice biographies is that the latter are 'more internally referential' (Baker 2010, 187) than influenced by gender, class and ethnic structures. The upshot of this, according to Giddens (1991, 68), is that 'we are, not what we are, but what we make of ourselves'.

But is it really the case that the lives of women (and men too) in Aotearoa are the outcome of a process of self-invention unconstrained by the socio-cultural environment in which we/they live? Critics of individualisation theorists, like Brannen and Nilsen (2005), argue that it is the privileged, because they have ready access to valuable social and economic resources, who experience their lives as a field of open choices. In contrast, those who are not as privileged may be more aware of the constraints they face, yet find that the language of choice and agency means that they are blamed and blame themselves for their misfortune (423). Moreover, this same language closes down spaces for speaking about unfairness or ongoing inequalities; young women are 'now told they have it all so they have nothing to complain about' (Pomerantz, Raby and Stefanik 2013, 202; see also Baker 2010).

In the section below I consider whether post-feminist and neoliberal rhetoric matches reality by examining the extent to which gender difference and gender inequality is a characteristic of the contemporary labour market of Aotearoa New Zealand.

## Liberation Achieved? Yeah, Right!

On 30 August 2015 the *Sunday Star Times* ran the headline 'Midwives Drop Bombshell with Court Action over Pay Discrimination' (Mussen and Mathewson 2015). The story appeared in advance of the New Zealand College of Midwives, the organisation representing an almost exclusively female profession, lodging their pay discrimination case in the High Court. In a press release, the College argued that community-based midwives were 'paid the equivalent of someone considered semi-skilled or unqualified' (New Zealand College of Midwives 2015). The actions taken by the College prompted two other organisations representing female-dominated occupations – the New Zealand Nurses Organisation and the New Zealand Education Institute – to indicate that they were planning similar action to advance pay equity claims for their members (New Zealand College of Midwives 2015).

If we accept that 'wages are the most direct expression of economic value and status in any society where workers sell their labour for money' (Gordon and Morton 2001, 1),[5] then contemporary gender pay parity claims raise questions about how far Aotearoa New Zealand has come in addressing a central feature of a patriarchal gender order[6] – the undervaluation of women and things tagged with the feminine (England 2010; Mann 1994). The Gender Pay Gap (GPG) is used internationally as a key measure of the extent of pay inequality between women and men. Typically the GPG is 'expressed as a single percentage measure by which women's pay falls short of that of men' (Hyman 2015, 4). Despite the apparent simplicity of this statement there is a great deal of debate about exactly how the GPG should be determined (Hyman 2015; Statistics New Zealand 2015).

Should it be based on hourly, weekly or even annual wages? Should it include only those men and women in full-time employment? Or should it include part-time workers too? And which measure of central tendency should it compare – median pay or mean pay?

Differences in how the GPG is calculated lead to noteworthy differences in the seeming size of the GPG (Statistics New Zealand 2015). For example, using figures from the June 2015 quarter of the New Zealand Income Survey, the GPG is 14.1 per cent when measured on the basis of comparing the *average hourly* pay for men and women earners, yet the GPG shrinks to 11.8 per cent when it is based on *median hourly* pay. Interestingly, the GPG based on median hourly earnings has been on the rise in New Zealand over recent years (Hyman 2015). In other words, inequality as measured by the GPG has been worsening, albeit by a modest amount. If the GPG is calculated by contrasting the *median weekly* earnings for men and women in *full-time* employment, it is even larger, at 17.0 per cent (or $189/week), and blows out to 26.6 per cent (or $275/week) when it is calculated by comparing the *median weekly* earnings for all men and women in either full-time or part-time employment.

The most common basis for determining the GPG is median hourly rate, either for all those in employment (generally used in New Zealand) or for all those in full-time employment (used by the Organisation for Economic Co-operation and Development [OECD]). The use of the median in preference to the mean is justified by noting that the median is less susceptible to being skewed by unusually high incomes (Ministry of Women's Affairs 2015a). However, given that the vast majority of those with very high incomes are men, the use of the median to determine the GPG obscures the contribution of gendered occupational hierarchies to gendered disparities in pay (Hyman 2015). Similarly, the reliance on comparing hourly rather than weekly earnings hides the opportunity cost women bear by undertaking paid work on a part-time basis more frequently than men in order to undertake unpaid caring work. This opportunity cost is significant: it diminishes women's immediate purchasing power, reduces their capacity to save for their retirement[7] (for more on ageing, see Kerse in this volume) and, for some women, it increases their economic dependence on male partners.

The Ministry of Women's Affairs, on its 'Occupational Segregation' webpage, estimates that 30 per cent of the GPG is attributable to vertical and horizontal segregation. Both vertical segregation (with men being over-represented in higher-level positions in organisational hierarchies) and horizontal segregation (with women and men being clustered in different occupations and industries) continue to be prominent features of the labour market in Aotearoa New Zealand. As result, the labour market is characterised by ongoing gender differences in the kinds of work women and men do, and ongoing gender inequalities in the kinds of recognition and rewards they receive for it. The problem of the persistent undervaluation of female-dominated occupations is not unique to New Zealand, however. Commenting on the situation in the United States, England (2010, 153) argues that the pay gap between female- and male-dominated occupations is the outcome of 'employers [seeing] the worth of predominantly female jobs through biased lenses and, as a result, [setting] pay levels for both men and women in predominantly female jobs lower than they would be if the jobs had a more heavily male sex composition'.

Gender differences and inequalities emerge early in workers' lives. The uptake by young women of apprenticeships in non-traditional trades remains staggeringly low in Aotearoa New Zealand: in 2010 women made up only 0.3 per cent of apprentices in building and construction, 1.2 per cent of apprentices in the engineering sector and 2.5 per cent of motor engineering apprentices (Human Rights Commission 2011). Although women now outnumber men as tertiary education students, there are noticeable gender differences in the fields of study pursued by young people: women are still under-represented in engineering, mathematics, computing, and architecture and building, but over-represented in education, law, social sciences and health (Callister et al. 2006).[8]

Despite women's high rate of participation in tertiary education across diverse fields, they often do not reap the same rewards as men from their studies (Mahoney, 2014). Five years out from graduating with a bachelor's degree, women on average earn only 92 per cent of what their male counterparts earn (Mahoney 2014, 41). This gender disparity is apparent even in areas where women dominate, like education, nursing and law

(Mahoney 2014, 70). The GPG (based on annual median earnings) for female graduates five years after completing their bachelor's degrees in teacher education was 7.6 per cent, in nursing 14.4 per cent and in law 6.1 per cent. Exceptions to the trend of higher financial returns for men were found in the fields of the performing arts, engineering, veterinary studies, rehabilitation therapies, politics and policy studies, where women out-earned men (Mahoney 2014).[9]

## Tradition in an Era of Choice

The gendered inequities in the labour market might be construed as the outcome of women's and men's freely made choices about what subjects to study, what sorts of work opportunities to pursue, whether to become parents and, if so, how to handle the care needs of children. As discussed above, post-feminism and neoliberalism encourage us to see choices about such matters in just this way. However, this viewpoint obscures the way in which life choices are framed by gendered social processes like socialisation and the distribution of financial resources, as well as cultural expectations and beliefs about gender (Risman and Davis 2013). The relevance of these kinds of social processes will become clear in my discussion of two New Zealand-based qualitative studies.

LifeLines was a project undertaken in Aotearoa New Zealand in 2007 with 100 young people – 23 young men and 77 young women – aged 16–18 years who were in their final year of high school (Patterson et al. 2007). The aim of the LifeLines project was to explore how young people imagined their future lives. Participants were asked to take part in a guided writing exercise in which they described their current lives, their imagined lives at aged 80, and what had happened to them at four intervening time periods: ages 18–25, 25–40, 40–55, 55–80. Remarkably, the plot lines of young men and women's stories were very similar: each gender imagined their early adult years as a period of development and self-discovery, followed by partnership and family formation, then a period of consolidation during their middle years and, finally in their later years, a period of enjoying the fruits of their labours.

There were nevertheless stark gender differences in how young men and women imagined the place paid work and family life would occupy in their lives (Patterson and Forbes 2012). Young men often produced detailed and concrete accounts of their anticipated work lives, in which they imagined a continuous relationship with the labour market. Young women, by contrast, typically generated more vague accounts of their work lives that often described them working in female-dominated sectors, which they perceived to be compatible with a disrupted attachment to the labour market that would result from their anticipated childcare responsibilities. When young men did explicitly refer to the care of children – and not all did – this usually took the form of 'stay at home' care provided by mothers.

These findings confirm that of other research showing that many young people remain attracted to stereotypical male or female occupations (Francis 2002; Miller and Haywood 2006); plan for a family life organised in terms of a male breadwinner and female carer-worker (Jacques and Radtke 2012); and generally see their future lives in gender-traditional terms (Jacques and Radtke 2012). The persistence of gender differences in young people's imagined futures, both in Aotearoa New Zealand (Patterson et al. 2007; Patterson and Forbes 2012) and other Western countries (see, e.g., Jacques and Radtke 2012), points to the continued influence of socio-cultural norms in creating and re-creating gendered lives. While contemporary gender norms are not as tightly drawn as they were in the middle of the twentieth century and adherence to them is neither as institutionally enforced nor as socially obligatory, they still lead to widely shared expectations about what women and men should do with their lives. The power of these norms, and the expectations to which they give rise, lies as much if not more in their capacity to shape our desires – who we want to be and what we want to do – as it does in any institutional enforcement. Indeed, as Foucault argued, the operation of power is more effective when it works through our desires and subsequent choices because it faces very little opposition, rather than when it operates in the form of a veto or 'no' (see Sawicki 1991).

It would be a mistake, however, to ignore the role of constraint in shaping people's choices, as shown by Schmidt's (2014) research into the decisions first-time parents make about who will care for their baby. Recent social changes, some mentioned earlier, mean that heterosexual couples who are about to become parents typically discuss who will be primarily responsible for paid work and who for caring for their children; most couples no longer assume that men will be breadwinners and women caregivers. Instead, labour divisions are a site of negotiation and choice. Yet, even so, a modern version of the traditional division of labour is commonplace in New Zealand and the majority of other Western countries to varying degrees (Baker 2014). Schmidt's study (2014) provides some insight into why this social pattern is reproduced, over and over again. In 2008, Schmidt interviewed twelve heterosexual, middle-class couples, who were first-time parents living in Auckland, about who would withdraw from paid work, and for how long, to look after their baby. The reasons these couples gave for their decisions reveal that their choices were strongly influenced by the structural conditions of New Zealand's labour market – in particular men's higher earnings – as well as social norms that still define women as better suited (both biologically and temperamentally) to care for babies, norms which mean that many women have a strong preference for being the stay-at-home parent. Parental choices, rooted in the structural conditions of the labour market and cultural parenting norms, had a number of gendered ramifications for the mothers and fathers in Schmidt's study. Mothers did the majority of 'baby maintenance', including getting up at night, visiting health professionals and doing the associated housework. Fathers became helpers (i.e., assistants as opposed to the parent in charge), with some mothers reporting that they felt obliged to ensure that fathers actually spent time interacting with their babies. Thus, the decisions that parents made, about who would stay home and who would stay working, established the foundations for what is often an enduring gendered distinction between a primary maternal parent and a secondary paternal parent.

## Conclusion

As this chapter shows, what gender means for the lives of women, and by implication for the lives of men, has changed in highly significant ways, largely as a result of the determined actions of those involved in the women's movement of the 1960s and 1970s (see also Schuster in this volume). In particular, young women today face a wider horizon of possibilities, although this is tempered by differences of ethnicity and class. Yet the story of radical changes is only one side of the story about gender that needs to be told in relation to Aotearoa New Zealand. The structuring effects of gender are still manifest in gender differences (e.g., in the kinds of work women and men do) and gender inequalities, for instance in the differing monetary rewards and social recognition they receive. These differences and inequalities are consequential for both women's and men's lives, and of course, the lives of children. Just as importantly, they are also consequential for the kind of country we live in.

## Acknowledgements

I would like to thank Dr Lesley Patterson for her generosity in sharing her ideas about this chapter, including some of the literature that could usefully contribute to a discussion of the structuring effects of gender.

### Notes

1. Post-feminism has been defined in a number of competing ways. Here I am using it to mean, following Gill and Scharff (2011, 4; see also McRobbie 2011), a sensibility that promotes the belief that feminist battles for gender equality have been won, and which consequently rejects both the need for feminist political action in the present and the figure of the feminist.
2. The Roast Busters were a group of young men who allegedly intoxicated young, often underage, girls in order to rape them and then went on to boast about this on Facebook. In a subsequent investigation of the police handling of complaints made by some of the young women involved, police were found to have 'failed to adhere to the basic tenets of any form of criminal investigation' (Papatsoumas 2015).
3. 'Ponytailgate' was the name the news media used to refer to allegations made by a young female waitress in 2015 that Prime Minister John Key repeatedly pulled her hair despite her obvious displeasure, allegations which prompted the Prime Minister to apologise (also see Schuster in this volume).
4. Although seemingly natural and somewhat inevitable, our lives are socially organised according to ages and stages, thereby producing a high degree of regularity to how our lives unfold at any particular point in history – the life course.
5. Aotearoa New Zealand is also characterised by significant pay disparities based on ethnicity. Consequently, the median hourly earnings of Pākehā women are higher than those of Māori and Pacific men.

6 The idea of a patriarchal gender order is derived from the work of Raewyn Connell (2009). It is used to indicate the existence of enduring gender arrangements in societies that are characterised by gender differences and gender inequality/hierarchy.
7 The Ministry of Women's Affairs quotes findings from the 2004 Survey of Family Income and Employment on its 'Retirement Income Prospects' webpages that show the median net worth enjoyed by men in the 45–65 year age bracket is $21,000 more than the net worth of women in the same age bracket.
8 Importantly, the gendered pattern of tertiary study – which is marked by concentration of female students in the humanities, social sciences and business studies – means that the emphasis being placed on funded places in science, technology, engineering and mathematics in the 2010s by the Government is not gender-neutral in its effects even though it is presented as a gender-neutral policy.
9 Women out-earning men was most pronounced in the field of veterinary science, where at the five-year mark women earned over $8,000 or 13 per cent more than men.

**PART V**

# Contemporary Issues and Divides

CHAPTER 17

# Ageing Well?

*Social Support and Inequalities for Older New Zealanders*

## Ngaire Kerse

Our population is getting older. The simplicity of that sentence belies the significant social changes that an ageing society produces. Changes in the demographic make-up of the country have profound implications for social and economic policy and planning. Allocation of resources for healthcare and economic investment, for example, is determined to a significant degree by the way census and other demographic data are assessed and evaluated. Such allocations – who will the money be spent on, and how, when and why? – speak to social, cultural and political power as well as related political and policy agendas. While ageing societies are a dominant feature of contemporary Western countries, the experience of ageing is inflected by questions of class, gender and ethnicity.

    The socio-cultural context of ageing in New Zealand is important to appreciate, and interesting times are ahead for whānau/families, society, health planners and social support providers responding to the major structural demographic changes currently underway. This chapter provides an overview of the current state of health and support for older people in New Zealand.

## Changing Patterns and Expenditure

The demography of New Zealand, like that of all countries in the Organisation for Economic Co-operation and Development (OECD), is changing, with a projected increase in the older age groups. The population of New Zealand is around 4.6 million people. Of that, over 612,000 are 65 years old or older. By 2051 it is estimated that there will be over 1.14 million people in this age bracket. At the moment the 65+ group has a ratio of around one in eight of the total population. However, by 2051 we can expect one in four New Zealanders to be 65 or over (Statistics New Zealand 2012a). Those who are 85 or older are expected to increase seven-fold in the same period, growing from around 35,000 individuals currently to over 250,000 by 2051 (Statistics New Zealand 2012a).

The economic significance of the ageing demographic in New Zealand rests with the projected associated increase in health and social welfare expenditure, which is expected to exceed the tax dollars contributed predominantly by those of working age within the next two decades. This has implications, for example, for the sustainability of New Zealand Superannuation, currently provided for all citizens and permanent residents over the age of 65. In 2012/13 the total costs of residential care, other services and support, and New Zealand Superannuation were around $13 billion (Dale 2014). As the old-age dependency ratio (the ratio of people aged 65 years and older to those aged 15 to 64 expressed as a number out of 100) rises from 18 in 2000 to between 37 and 45 in 2050, these costs will rise exponentially.

Meeting the costs created by this projection will depend on immigration, mortality and changing birth rates (Bell et al. 2010). The dependency ratio depends as much on the birth rate over time as it does on longevity. Birth rates in New Zealand have been falling but remain higher than Australia's, largely due to greater-than-average fertility rates amongst Māori and Pacific people. Deaths have also varied, with a gradual increase from 20,000 to 30,000 per annum over the last century as the population has risen. The importance of the ageing demographic to society is yet to be debated fully and will require the many sectors involved with older people to reflect and respond.

After superannuation, the other main area of government expenditure for older people is healthcare and social support services. Public hospital admission is free for New Zealand citizens and permanent residents. Prescribed medications are subsidised and primary healthcare is partly subsidised according to a formula that provides additional funding to support those over 65 years old, and those with complex health needs and multiple diagnoses. Residential aged care is subsidised according to a means test and a standardised needs assessment. In-home support is provided – such as personal care, housework, and shopping and gardening services – depending on the provision of a standardised needs assessment that is also means tested in different ways in different parts of the country.

As a result of the ageing of the population, older people will become the dominant group consuming health expenditure. In 2012/13, those aged 65+, comprising 14 per cent of the population, fully accounted for 33 per cent of the $14 billion health budget. Continued growth is expected. Currently health expenditure accounts for about one-fifth of all government expenditure and over 70 per cent of all health costs are publicly funded. New Zealand is close to the OECD average for the proportion of gross national product spent on health (Mays, Marney and King 2013). Although population ageing does contribute to increased health expenditure, the age effect is modest as the greatest increases in cost are due to increases in the cost of treatment, growth in volume per capita and technological advances (Mays, Marney and King 2013). The significant rise in the prevalence of chronic disease amongst the general population also leads to far greater (and longer) complexity of care.

Residential aged care will be experienced by up to 40 per cent of all New Zealanders close to the time of their death and it is common for New Zealanders to die in institutional care (Connolly et al. 2014). However, the 'Ageing in Place' part of the Health of Older Peoples Strategy (Ministry of Health 2002, 2006) and other policies has encouraged increased community care. Over the last twenty years age-standardised rates in rest home-level care (low-level dependency care for those assessed as requiring assistance with activities of daily living) reduced from 65 to 33 people per thousand, and in hospital-level care (high-level dependency care for those requiring assistance with basic activities such as getting out of bed and feeding themselves), from 29 to 23 per thousand in the Auckland region (Broad et al. 2011).

Creating social environments that allow a quality of life that the aged and other members of society value is both a challenge and an opportunity. New Zealand, like many other countries, can expect to experience pronounced social effects from an ageing population that will push us to rethink our values and our priorities in the coming decades. The number of organisations that will become involved in providing and delivering services for an ageing population will increase. The balance between government support, community organisations, iwi and hapū engagement, and personal expenditure devoted to caring for older people will be an area for public debate over the next decades.

## Ways of Living in Older Age

LiLACS NZ, a recent cohort study of Māori and non-Māori octogenarians (Dyall et al. 2014; Hayman et al. 2012), showed that for around 40 per cent of Māori and 20 per cent of non-Māori in New Zealand, New Zealand Superannuation was the only source of income, and that Māori were more likely than non-Māori to feel that they 'could just make ends meet' (Kerse and LiLACS NZ 2014a). The amount of resources needed for living depends largely on the situation in which older people live, with distance to amenities, availability of transport and who they live with all being important factors.

With age, more people live alone, particularly women due to increased likelihood of loss of loved ones and an increasing tendency away from intergenerational living (multiple generations of one whānau/family living in the same dwelling) in New Zealand. LiLACS NZ showed that 51 per cent of Māori women aged 80–90 years, and 65 per cent of non-Māori women aged 85+, lived alone. In contrast 26 per cent and 33 per cent of Māori and non-Māori men respectively lived alone (Kerse and LiLACS NZ 2014d). Women in general have lower incomes than men, meaning that women living alone are at an economic disadvantage. More Māori than non-Māori lived intergenerationally (26 per cent and 9 per cent for Māori and non-Māori men, and 30 per cent and 10 per cent for Māori and non-Māori women, respectively). However, most octogenarians lived alone or with their spouse, representing considerable resilience and independence in advanced age.

The informal (unpaid) support received by older participants in LiLACs NZ was mainly received from daughters for those who lived alone (although sons and others did also offer support) and spouses for those who lived with a spouse. Over 80 per cent of octogenarians said they had someone who gave practical and emotional help (Kerse and LiLACS NZ 2014d), and the lack of this support, seen as an unmet need, was associated with lower physical- and mental-health-related quality of life. Māori men living intergenerationally were more likely than either those living with a spouse or those living alone to express an unmet need for emotional support and this was associated with lower mental-health-related quality of life. Most of the support received was from family and whānau; however, a sizeable proportion of non-Māori men living alone named their paid home help as their main support person (Kerse and LiLACS NZ 2014d).

This shows that regardless of the living arrangement, adequate support may not be available. The disability level of a small number of older people living intergenerationally was very high, and thus the greater level of assistance needed could potentially exhaust whānau and families. One size and type of support does not suit all, and an individualised approach to care and support for older people is needed.

## Ethnicity and Ageing

It is in this context of overall structural change in the population of New Zealand, and increasing health and social expenditure, that changes in the ethnic make-up of the older population need to be considered. In 2013,

74 per cent of the total New Zealand population comprised New Zealand Europeans, 15 per cent identified as Māori, 12 per cent Asian, 7 per cent Pacific and remaining ethnic groups made up 3 per cent. These percentages add to more than 100 per cent as more than one ethnic group can be chosen per individual (Statistics New Zealand 2014a). In contrast, 91 per cent of the population aged 65 years and older were New Zealand Europeans. Māori made up 7 per cent, Asian peoples 4 per cent and Pacific peoples 2 per cent.

As can be seen above, while New Zealand as a whole is ageing there are still considerable differences across New Zealand society. Māori and Pacific populations have a relatively youthful structure. Māori currently make up around one-quarter of the country's child population but are under-represented amongst older people with fewer than 1 in 20 Māori aged 65 years or older (Kukutai 2011). As the Māori population ages, it will reflect many of the same characteristics as the non-Māori population. The number of older Māori is projected to double in the next fifteen years with the most rapid growth occurring among the oldest groups: 60–64 years of age, and 65 and over. However, it is important to note that the majority of Māori (56 per cent) will still be under the age of 30 in 2026 (Kukutai 2011). This mix of young and ageing Māori means that policy levers and service delivery must be sensitive to their diverse needs. While this poses challenges there are also considerable demographic dividends to be had from recognising and supporting both the young and the elderly's aspirations to lead lives that contribute to collective Māori well-being, as well as to the future prosperity of the nation, remembering that it is today's young people who will need to support the ageing population in the future.

## Māori

Well-being, for Māori, means more than a sense of health alone. Māori, in qualitative interviews, indicate that they age positively by drawing on the concept of taupenui – realised potential – which, in turn, is made up of several domains including tākoha – contribution; whanaungatanga – connectedness; and tino rangatiratanga – self-determination (Edwards 2010). Community belonging and the right to self-determination are related to the ability to realise their potential while ageing. LiLACS NZ participants emphasised ongoing contribution to whānau, particularly mokupuna (grandchildren), and the practice of cultural activities as being associated with higher health-related quality of life (Dyall et al. 2014). This data confirms the findings of an earlier survey of over 400 older Māori that showed that active participation and cultural affiliation were associated with higher standards of health (Waldon 2004).

Māori experience disparities in incomes throughout the life course and these disparities in income continue in old age (Kerse and LiLACS NZ 2014b). Living standards for Māori are lower than for non-Māori, and older Māori are three to four times more likely to experience disadvantage and hardship than older non-Māori (Cunningham et al. 2002). Amongst the elderly, older single Māori, particularly women, have the least material well-being. Older Māori are more likely than older non-Māori to live in neighbourhoods of high deprivation (Teh et al. 2014), eat fewer vegetables and fruit, and are more likely to be under- or overweight than non-Māori (Ministry of Health 2011). Disability affects 24 per cent of Māori aged 65 and over, while 18 per cent of non-Māori are similarly affected. Despite socio-economic disparities, levels of mental-health-related quality of life indicators were high amongst Māori octogenarians engaged in the LiLACS NZ study (Dyall et al. 2014). Older Māori in the LiLACS NZ study were also important repositories of te reo Māori (Māori language) and cultural knowledge, were likely to spend time with mostly other Māori (Kerse and LiLACS NZ 2014c) and had high levels of social support (Kerse and LiLACS NZ 2014d). While there were some older people with unmet social and support needs (Kerse and LiLACS NZ 2014a), contributions from older Māori to whānau and Māori society were common. Ageing was viewed positively by most.

The projected change in the population age structure differs between Māori and non-Māori. Between 2011 and 2026, the population of Māori aged 65 years and older is predicted to grow by 7.1 per cent, double the growth expected for non-Māori, so that older Māori will make up 9.8 per cent of the total older population. Thus, the New Zealand European dominance in the older age groups will lessen (Ministry of Social Development

2015a). Māori aged 80 years and over have more than tripled from 1400 to over 5000 in two decades. This compares with a mean doubling of the 80 + non-Māori population, from 82,200 to 159,500.

Māori are less likely to be living in residential care. Fewer than a third of care facilities house Māori, while Māori contribute to the paid caring workforce in about 40 per cent of care facilities (Kiata, Kerse and Dixon 2005). Housing solutions for the ageing population will be needed to maximise independence and community engagement. Recent innovations include kaumātua housing located near Māori settlements and marae.

## Pacific Peoples

In the second half of the twentieth century, Pacific peoples migrated to New Zealand in increasing numbers. Most came from Samoa, the Cook Islands, Tonga, Niue, Fiji and Tokelau, with a rapid increase from 1960 onwards. New Zealand citizenship is held by people from the Cook Islands, Niue and Tokelau, and populations in New Zealand now outnumber the home country populations for these Pacific people. Additionally, up to one-third of all Samoans live in New Zealand. The age structure of Pacific populations is similar to that of Māori, and the ageing of Māori and Pacific peoples is much faster than that of non-Māori and non-Pacific people. Pacific families are the usual caregivers for older Pacific people and thus Pacific elders are rarely placed in residential aged care. In 2005 only 15 per cent of aged care facilities housed a Pacific resident. Interestingly, the same study showed that Pacific caregivers worked in at least 43 per cent of aged care facilities, with this characteristic most marked in Auckland (Kiata, Kerse and Dixon 2005). Qualitative interviews showed that Pacific people's attitudes to caregiving are based on respect and a need to fully provide for older people (Kiata and Kerse 2004). Workers often cared for their older family members at home and the differing views of ageing between Pacific and European/Pākehā have sometimes resulted in misunderstandings and tensions within aged care facilities (Kiata and Kerse 2015).

## Asian Peoples

Asian peoples are now the third-most populous group in New Zealand, the population having doubled in size from 2001, with the Indian sub-population increasing the most. Due to both migration into New Zealand and ageing within New Zealand, the median age of the Asian population has risen from 28 to 31 years in the 12 years since the 2001 census. This compares to a median age of 24 for Māori, 22 for Pacific and 41 for European/Pākehā (Statistics New Zealand 2014a). Chinese migrants to New Zealand came in the nineteenth century for the gold rush and have continued to arrive steadily since then, with a more recent influx of younger professionals. Transitions were not always smooth, with 'astronaut' family relationships (members of the same family inhabiting different countries) inhibiting intergenerational caring for some (Ho 2006). However, there is also evidence that some elderly Chinese appreciate the relative independence from family that state support for the elderly gives them (Zhang 2014).

The lives of older Koreans in New Zealand are multi-faceted with at least one study outlining challenges related to the complex situations faced by older immigrants and the intergenerational relationships that can be difficult to sustain across several nations. Hidden isolation and social exclusion also seem to be issues that arise for elders in these communities (Park and Kim 2013). Other international studies report that Asian elders are likely to have holistic views of health and are said to adapt well to change while seeking to maintain their continuity of world view (Torsch and Ma 2000). The increasing Asian population in New Zealand with attendant elders will present challenges to health and social planners in the next decades.

## Disparities and Ageing

Disparities in health and socio-economic status for Māori can be traced to both colonial and neocolonial policies. Research has indicated that poor health outcomes can be attributed in part to a range of policies including discriminatory legislation against Māori language use in schools, Māori rights and land transfer throughout the first half of the twentieth century, and legislation aimed at disrupting cultural practices such as the Tohunga Suppression Act 1907. Documented health disparities for Māori were used to argue that Māori rights were not protected as promised under the Treaty of Waitangi (Te Rōpū Rangahau Hauora a Eru Pōmare 2000). However, since the late nineteenth century, health policy responses to promote participation of Māori in health initiatives in order to achieve better health outcomes for Māori have developed (Ellison-Loschmann and Pearce 2006).

A strengthening of Māori culture and reversal of discriminatory legislature from the 1970s onwards led to recognition of and compensation for land loss through the Treaty of Waitangi Act 1978 and increasing moves towards self-determination. The Māori population had the highest growth rate in New Zealand through the second half of the twentieth century, and Māori language was rekindled. Life expectancy rose, but health disparities in diabetes and cardiovascular disease prevalence and outcomes for Māori continue to exist into the twenty-first century (Blakely, Simmers and Sharpe 2011; Carter, Blakely and Soeberg 2010; Hill et al. 2010; Jatrana and Blakely 2008; Robson and Harris 2007; Rumball-Smith et al. 2013).

*Life* expectancy continues to rise, increasing from 72 years to 83 years between 1951 and 2006 for non-Māori women and from 68 years to 79 years for non-Māori men. The longevity disparity of nearly fifteen years for Māori (compared to non-Māori) in the 1950s reduced to less than ten years, but since 1980 this disparity has not continued to decrease, maintaining a lag of up to seven years (Ministry of Health 2010).

*Health* expectancy is an estimate of the number of years a person will live without requiring assistance with everyday living and reflects independent life expectancy at birth. Updated in 2013, health expectancy for men in 1996 was 64.7 years and increased to 67.4 years by 2006. For women, health expectancy increased from 67.5 years in 1996 to 69.2 years in 2006. Māori lag behind non-Māori by up to five years on this measure (Statistics New Zealand 2013b).

Mortality disparities are also well described (Ministry of Health and University of Otago 2006), and half of the differences observed in the mortality rate of Māori people are due to socio-economic disadvantage, other sources of disadvantage in health that may relate to social structure, epidemiological factors, and access to health services.

Māori collectivist culture may suggest greater intergenerational care and greater contribution to Māori society by older people, and these features may result in resilience to unmet need. The future of ageing in New Zealand will be shaped by a higher birth rate for Māori and the impact on care and support for older Māori. It is still unclear, given these two factors, what the outcome will be.

What *is* clear is that ongoing attempts to address the ethnic disparity in longevity and health outcomes for Māori are needed and are related to the state's Treaty of Waitangi obligations. In addition, a growing Pacific health focus will be needed to address increasing Pacific ageing in New Zealand and in the Pacific Islands.

## Positive Ageing

Creating social environments that allow a quality of life that the aged and other members of society value is both a challenge and an opportunity. New Zealand, like many other countries, can expect to experience pronounced social effects from an ageing population. In recognising the dynamics of population growth, there is a need to be creative and innovative, and to move away from thinking of the elderly as largely a passive population sector that has moved beyond the productive sphere. Just as there is great diversity in other age sectors of the population in terms of abilities and talents, we must appreciate that this also exists amongst our older people. In fact, most older people are active contributors to whānau, families, the community volunteer sector and to society in general.

The traditional working definition of the elderly has been a person over 65 years of age but, as life expectancy extends, such definitions are increasingly tested. Arriving at definitions that capture the experience and aspirations of those who could be classified as 'young-old' through to the 'oldest old' is a unique challenge. Differentiating between the age groups within the elderly population will become ever more necessary to articulate and address the different stages and needs of those within each group.

The fact that the New Zealand Government has a *Positive Ageing Strategy* (Office for Senior Citizens 2001) signals the recognition of the need to promote the value and participation of older people in communities. The strategy acknowledges the skills, knowledge and experience of older people, and their capacity to continue to contribute in varied ways to the broader society. Seeing senior citizens as a resource rather than as a financial drain means that policy development has to envisage extended participation in the labour market, as well as greater participation in civil society. Identifying barriers (social, economic, cultural, physical) to extended participation, as well as working with all sectors to develop initiatives to address these barriers, demands a careful balancing of the needs of the elderly alongside the needs of younger and successive generations (Office for Senior Citizens 2001).

CHAPTER 18

# No Promised Land

*Domestic Violence, Marginalisation and Masculinity*

# Vivienne Elizabeth

Bodily frailty is part of the human condition. This frailty makes all of us vulnerable to violent assaults on our bodies, irrespective of how that violence is inflicted. It is our awareness of this vulnerability that undoubtedly causes most of us to fear violence or threats of violence. Yet the likelihood of being a victim of violence is unevenly distributed across the globe and within nations, and has changed over time. Likewise, while most of us have the capacity – even unaided by knives, guns or drones – to be violent, the perpetration of violence is socially patterned.

This chapter explores how domestic violence (DV), as a specific form of interpersonal violence, is socially patterned in Aotearoa New Zealand. Although not a new pattern of behaviour, some argue that DV has now reached epidemic proportions in New Zealand (Kruger et al. 2004). Such high levels of DV mean that Aotearoa is not a land of milk and honey for many. In the following section, I briefly map New Zealand's pattern of DV perpetration and victimisation, then in subsequent sections discuss the role played by contemporary macroeconomic conditions, mediated through gender and ethnicity, in experiences of DV and interpersonal violence more broadly.

## Domestic Violence: A Case Study in the Social Patterning of Violence

In Aotearoa, 'domestic violence'[1] usually refers to a pattern of gendered behaviour[2] between heterosexual partners that reproduces relations of oppressive male power and inequality.[3] The term draws our attention to the most visible form that power takes – physical or sexual violence, or the threat of physical or sexual violence. However, expressions of male power that cause oppressive relations between intimate partners can take a range of forms, including (but not limited to) any combination of physical assaults and/or threats of assaults; sexual assaults; attacks or threats of attacks on personal property, pets or significant people; stalking and harassment; degrading insults; jealous surveillance; and/or financial restrictions and control (Adams 2012; Anderson 2009; Stark 2007). This kind of exercise of power over female partners typically leads to bodily and psychological injuries, restrictions on movement, weakened social networks, deferential and compliant behaviour, and feelings of fear, anger and shame. It would be a mistake, however, to envisage DV in episodic terms linked to a momentary loss of control, rather than as an overall 'architecture of abuse' (Family Violence Death Review Committee [FVDRC] 2014, 21) that shores up men's power and dominance at the expense of women's agency and autonomy (Adams 2012; Stark 2007). Relations of oppressive male power do not go uncontested: most women fight back, sometimes lashing out with their tongues, sometimes with their fists, and the majority seek help.

From the 1970s onwards, DV has been increasingly recognised as a significant social problem in New Zealand and internationally. The transformation of DV from a private problem to a social issue in the 1970s is largely attributable to the actions of the (anti-)DV movement in Aotearoa and elsewhere, which has played a lead role in establishing and delivering services to women and children wanting to escape violence,[4] as well as a critical role in defining the causes of DV. Drawing on feminist critiques of the heterosexual family, anti-DV advocates and DV scholars view the use, or threat, of violence by male partners who are invested in patriarchal family regimes as an historically condoned mechanism of last resort that reinstates male power when men perceive this to be under threat (Adams 2012; Moore 1994).

Getting a reliable sense of how many families are affected by DV in New Zealand (or any other country for that matter) is a challenging task. One source of data that we have traditionally relied upon is the statistics from agencies like the police or Family Courts.[5] Drawing on police data from New Zealand, the Australian state of Victoria and Scotland, Herbert and Mackenzie (2014) show that New Zealand's rate of successfully prosecuted family violence offences at 929 per 100,000 population is nearly double that of Victoria's at 478, and also significantly higher than Scotland's at 571. These figures suggest that Aotearoa has a much larger problem with family violence than similar Western jurisdictions.

Yet we need to be cautious about adhering too firmly to this conclusion for a number of reasons. First, the police designation of a crime as one of family violence may vary from jurisdiction to jurisdiction, as might the way police prosecute family violence offences. Thus, these figures may not accurately reflect the extent of family violence reported to the police. Second, it is well known that people (victims, perpetrators and witnesses) under-report crimes like DV because the morally inflected nature of these crimes means reporting poses a risk to the identities of victims and perpetrators. Reporting also increases the likelihood that the victims or someone they care about (including pets) might be assaulted or worse; and/or jeopardises the victims' economic security. Third, current estimates suggest that a staggering 80 per cent of DV goes unreported in Aotearoa (Herbert and Mackenzie 2014).

Homicide is one violent crime that is less susceptible to variation in reporting behaviours. International figures show that the proportion of female homicide victims who die because of the violent actions of an intimate partner or other family member is relatively high in New Zealand and Australia, where approximately 76 per cent of all female homicides are family-related compared with 68 per cent in the United Kingdom,

60 per cent in Canada, and 52 per cent in the United States (United Nations Office on Drugs and Crime 2013). Since 2008, family-violence-related homicides in New Zealand have been referred to the FVDRC. Between 2009 and 2012, there were 63 intimate partner homicides, with women comprising 73 per cent of the victims (or 46 deaths), having been killed by their male partners in 96 per cent of these cases (FVDRC 2014). In comparison, male victims made up 23 per cent of intimate partner homicides (or 17 deaths), with 76 per cent of these male victims being killed by their female partners. Further examination of available records by the FVDRC shows that in homicide cases involving women as the perpetrators, a significant proportion had previously been the primary victim of DV. In contrast, in all bar one case involving male perpetrators and female victims, records show that the men had also been the predominant aggressor of DV. Significantly, 50 per cent of all intimate partner homicides occurred at the point of separation or planned separation.

Given the under-reporting of DV, more reliable estimates of the prevalence of DV are obtained through the use of survey data, though this can be fraught with methodological problems (Contesse and Fenrich 2008; Jansen 2012). Of the fourteen Organisation for Economic Co-operation and Development member countries for which data are available on DV, New Zealand women experience the highest rate of lifetime exposure to physical violence at 30 per cent, compared to Australia at 25 per cent, Germany at 23 per cent, the United States at 22 per cent and the United Kingdom at 19 per cent (UN Women 2011, 134).

Further, these figures do not reveal the impact of ethnicity on DV victimisation. Yet DV victimisation is not only higher among indigenous women in settler societies like New Zealand, Australia, Canada and the United States, but the DV they experience is also more frequent and severe (Cooper 2012; Kuokkanen 2015; Poupart 2003). In Aotearoa, Fanslow et al.'s (2010) analysis of data collected through the Violence Against Women Study shows a lifetime prevalence rate for physical DV of over 50 per cent for Māori women, compared to 31 per cent for Pacific women, 30 per cent for European/Other and 10 per cent for Asian women.[6] These findings indicate that the exposure of Māori and Pacific women to DV is disproportionate to their share of the population, and particularly so for Māori.

Māori are also shown to be over-represented in New Zealand's intimate partner homicides by the FVDRC (2014, 125), making up 32 per cent of the victims and 29 per cent of the perpetrators (roughly twice the proportion of Māori in the population overall, which is approximately 14.5 per cent). Importantly, the fourth FVDRC (2014) report points to strong connections between intimate partner homicides and economic marginalisation, with the majority of these deaths occurring in Aotearoa's most deprived areas, where Māori and Pacific peoples are over-represented.[7] This finding, along with those showing strong links between masculinity, ethnicity and violence perpetration, deserve consideration at more length.

## The Macroeconomic Conditions of Violence

The social patterning of DV and other forms of interpersonal violence is strongly linked to economic conditions. Richard Wilkinson and Kate Pickett (2009, 135) demonstrate a relationship between overall homicide levels and income inequality across the Western world, such that countries with higher levels of income inequality also tend to have higher rates of homicide. Drawing on research findings from the United States and Sweden, Currie (2007) shows that exposure to interpersonal violence among the poor has increased in the last 40 years, a fact obscured by plateauing or even declining rates of interpersonal violence overall. True (2012) similarly observed a rise in DV in Ireland, the United Kingdom and the United States following the 2008 Global Financial Crisis. In all three countries, DV service providers reported a significant increase in demand for their services between 2007 and 2010, which they struggled to meet because their budgets were cut as part of austerity programmes. Lastly, although the overall crime rate has fallen in Aotearoa over the last twenty years (Workman and McIntosh 2013), convictions for family violence offences rose until the late 2000s, falling again slightly from 2010 to 2013 (Family Violence Clearinghouse 2014).

These findings suggest that worsening macroeconomic conditions increase rates of interpersonal violence, including DV. A number of authors argue that the global rise in neoliberal economies has led to increases in violent perpetration in general (Currie 1997; Wilkinson and Pickett 2009; Young 2003) and against women in particular (True 2012; Weissman 2007). As Currie (1997, 147) says of the United States, '"market societies" – those in which the pursuit of private gain becomes the dominant organizing principle of social and economic life – are especially likely to breed high levels of violent crime'. What is it about the 'market society' of the United States and, by extrapolation, the neoliberal economy of Aotearoa that produces this effect?

New Zealand underwent a rapid transformation into a market or neoliberal society following the 1984 election of the Fourth Labour Government (see both Humpage and Cotterell in this volume). This process of transformation led to rising levels of unemployment, underemployment and precarious employment. The erosion of conditions of work and rewards from working occurred in tandem with other changes that negatively impacted on people's economic and social well-being, especially for the poorest. Such changes included a scaling back of the welfare state, a weakening of the redistributive function of the state through changes to the tax structure, and the downsizing of public sector employment and government investment in employment.

These changes are implicated in the incredible rise in economic inequality that has taken place in New Zealand and other Western countries (Rashbrooke 2013a). Paradoxically, the growth in inequality has been matched by the rise of a materialist culture that incessantly demands that we consume (Currie 1997; Wilkinson and Pickett 2009; Young 2003). The contradiction between the injunction to consume, which applies to us all, and the striking differences in the capacity of people to do so, leads to vast differences in individual capacities to secure a widely recognised marker of social status. Or to put this another way: those who are marginalised by being work-poor, or working poor, are also marginalised by being unable to consume. Consequently, they are more likely to be marked by their 'unfashionable' (because old or inexpensive) clothing, housing, car, food and pastimes. This group – and it is a group that is racially identified in New Zealand discourse – face the stigma and shame that arises from this double marginalisation (in terms of both income source and consumption) and double loss of status.

According to Richard Wilkinson (2004; also Wilkinson and Pickett 2009; Young 2003), experiences of marginalisation and powerlessness, when combined with socio-culturally created expectations of power and agency, generate a potent cocktail of emotions – frustration, anger and fury, resentment and shame. In turn these emotions, in particular, fury and shame, are well recognised as providing the wellspring for violence (Gilligan 2003; Scheff 2003; Websdale 2010a, 2010b). For Gilligan (2003, 1154), violent behaviours are motivated by a 'wish to ward off or eliminate the feeling of shame and humiliation – a feeling that is painful and can even be intolerable and overwhelming – [and to] replace it with its opposite, the feeling of pride'.[8]

But while shame plays a significant role in the perpetration of violence against intimates and strangers, it would be a mistake to locate the source of DV in the experience of shame and rage alone. As Workman and McIntosh (2013) argue in relation to crime in general, prohibited behaviours like DV and other forms of family violence have multiple and often complex causes. And while Gilligan (2003) sees shame as a necessary precondition for violence, he too agrees that it is not sufficient. Rather, he argues that for shame to lead to interpersonal violence three other factors are usually present: first, the individual feels that they have no other way of restoring their status and worth; second, they believe their violence is entirely justified and so do not feel guilt or remorse; and third, being male vastly increases the chances that shame will be converted to violence.

Importantly, it is not shame per se that is the source of male violence against their intimate partners, but shame that arises out of thwarted expectations of male agency and power (including its privileges and entitlements) associated with structures of gender and heterosexuality (Moore 1994). By way of elaboration on this final point, Gilligan (2003, 1167) notes that in patriarchal cultures (which create expectations of male power and dominance), violence for men, as one way of enacting power, has often been a source of pride and honour, and 'that is why for men violence can diminish feelings of shame, temporarily if not permanently'.

In sum, the rise of a neoliberal economy in Aotearoa, like the rise of a market economy in the United States, is responsible for the creation of social conditions that increase the likelihood of the perpetuation of violent behaviour at home, in the bar or on the street. Neoliberal economies produce powerful fissures between those who are included and those who are marginalised or excluded. And in New Zealand, as elsewhere, marginalisation is racialised (McIntosh 2005; Mila 2013; Poata-Smith 2013). The experience of marginalisation is typically marked by reduced status and feeling ashamed and inferior. Especially for men who are conditioned to expect to be powerful agents in their work and domestic lives, and who are enculturated into physical domination and violence as a badge of pride and respect, feelings of shame often form the basis of violent behaviour, including DV. As Herbert and Mackenzie (2014, 11) proclaim, 'The single most common factor shared between men who use violence against their partners and children is their belief in rigid gender roles and their position as "head of the household" – that they are the one in charge.'

## Adding Masculinity, Colonialism and Yet More Shame into the Mix

In the preceding section I outlined profound changes to the conditions of employment in Aotearoa over the last 30 plus years as a result of the rise of neoliberalism. These labour market changes have weakened worker rights and protections, turned workers into expendable commodities, and conveyed to those who are cast aside during restructuring processes that they are of limited worth or value. In this section I want to examine in greater depth the links between paid work, masculinity and violence, before touching briefly on the role of a history of colonisation on the social patterning of violence against women in New Zealand (for more on masculinities, see Pringle in this volume).

The process of neoliberal globalisation has not only shaped the general conditions of the contemporary labour market, it has also had a profound effect on men's and women's employment patterns. Although employment has become more contingent (i.e., less taken-for-granted) for everyone, the wave of redundancies that occurred in the earlier phase of neoliberal globalisation in New Zealand in the late 1980s and early 1990s largely affected a masculinised industrial workforce, pushing large swathes of men, especially Māori and Pacific men, into the queues of the unemployed or the underemployed. The loss of manufacturing and industrial jobs was paralleled by the growth in generally lower-paid, feminised service work, a factor that has contributed since the 1970s to a significant rise in female employment levels. These changes to the world of paid work have gender implications, making (some) men marginal to the employment market while simultaneously making (some) women more central.

Inevitably, Weissman (2007) and True (2012) argue, these transformations are brought back home in the form of changes to the economic order of heterosexual nuclear families. As men face unemployment, underemployment, precarious employment and/or stagnant wages, the patriarchal power and privileges they are socialised to expect as breadwinners are increasingly not realised. Instead, as families become progressively more reliant on the economic contributions of both partners or, in some cases, solely reliant on the economic contributions of the woman, men's control over the family economy, and their power and influence over family matters more broadly, wanes.

The failure of individual men to realise cultural expectations associated with patriarchal masculinity is widely recognised as creating a crisis of identity, particularly for those men who remain invested in the patriarchal power that accrues to them as a result of a traditional gender division of labour. When a sense of masculine success is reliant on paid work or consumption but cannot be realised through these means – and/or female partners pursue egalitarian gender roles, achieve financial autonomy or otherwise appear to challenge male power and privilege – violence becomes a mechanism for enacting power that confirms an identity (masculinity) and social structure (gender hierarchy) perceived to be in jeopardy (Adams 2012; Jewkes 2002; Moore 1994; True 2012; Weissman 2007).

The inculcation of patriarchal gender norms into Māori and Pacific societies, by the colonial missionaries and later by the Native Schools, means that gender dynamics similar to those of Pākehā families are also at play in Māori and Pacific family households (Hoeata et al. 2011; Jenkins and Matthews 1998). These norms create an expectation that men will reap patriarchal rewards, like respect and deference, at least at home. However, because Māori and Pacific peoples have been more systematically marginalised and excluded through the economic changes and welfare reforms mentioned above (Mila 2013; Poata-Smith 2013), challenges to the domestic economic order and masculine identities have been proportionately greater. Furthermore, experiences of marginalisation for Māori and Pacific men have occurred in the context of ongoing racism and neoliberal ideologies that encourage us to see economic failure (or success) in individual terms. Thus, economic and cultural marginalisation is personalised; people are told that the problem lies with their own deficiencies, reinforcing feelings of shame and anger. And these feelings, as we have seen, are more likely to be turned by men than women into violence against intimates and/or strangers.[9]

Relatively recent experiences of economic and cultural marginalisation among Māori and Pacific peoples are compounded by a history of colonial relations and systematic racism (Mila 2013; Poata-Smith 2013; see also both Wynyard and Mila in this volume). The processes of colonisation, both here and in other settler societies, have had lasting adverse effects, including the over-representation of indigenous peoples as perpetrators and victims of DV (as evidenced in the beginning of this chapter). The latter is intrinsically connected to the diminished status of Māori in a Pākehā-dominated society. Colonisation is premised on and produces a hierarchical relation between the colonisers and the colonised. Relations of domination and subordination are, as Neckel (1996) argues, frequently experienced as feelings of superiority or inferiority. To be structurally positioned as 'inferior' often generates feelings of shame, which in turn may be masked by rage and violence, especially by men who are invested in patriarchal power as a source of esteem and whose masculinity is defined through dominance and physical toughness. Along with the obvious often-seriously detrimental effects on their families and their relationships, the paradox for Māori and Pacific men who express their protests against shaming experiences through violence is that it not only serves to confirm colonial and racist stereotypes (Hokowhitu 2004), it puts them at risk of further marginalisation through criminalisation (Workman and McIntosh 2013).

## Conclusion

Economic changes under neoliberal globalisation have jeopardised the chances of some men to realise modes of manhood premised on the power derived from breadwinning and the status achieved through consumption. This is particularly the case for Māori and Pacific men whose level of economic and cultural marginalisation far exceeds that experienced by Pākehā men or men of other ethnicities. Aotearoa New Zealand is not a promised land for these men. Those men for whom gender difference and hierarchy are important to secure their sense of masculinity are more likely to use violence against their female partners to try to compensate for the stigma and shame associated with the failure to realise the breadwinning-consuming modes of manhood (Jewkes 2002). The perpetration of DV then is pivotally linked to men's expectations of being able to exercise power and agency in general, and in relation to women in particular, and their shame and rage when these expectations are not realised (Jewkes 2002; Moore 1994). At the same time, this means that dismantling patriarchal norms of masculinity, along with patriarchal family structures and practices, is pivotal to the reduction of DV. This does not mean the neglect of male vulnerabilities generated by the forces of colonialism and/or contemporary capitalism, but it does mean that addressing these sources of male injury alone will not be sufficient. To solely focus on male vulnerabilities would surely lead to the reinstalling of the patriarchal family as norm, and the ongoing subordination of women's interests to those of men's (Kuokkanen 2015). And that is far too high a price to ask victims of DV to pay.

### Notes

1. In North America the same phenomenon is often referred to as 'intimate partner violence' (IPV). Both IPV and DV refer to a toxic and oppressive dynamic between adults. An analysis of the dynamics of other forms of family violence (e.g., child abuse) is beyond the scope of this chapter.
2. Domestic violence is a gender-related and not gender-specific pattern of behaviour. The fact that some women also use violence against their male partners does not obviate the claims that DV is gendered. As Kristin L. Anderson (2009) shows, the socio-cultural conditions in which women seek to exercise power over their male partners through violence and coercive control differ from the socio-cultural conditions that surround men's use of violence and

coercive control. Not only does this mean that female-perpetrated domestic violence is less common and generally less severe, but we also attribute different meanings to it.

3 Domestic violence also occurs in same-sex relationships. In these relationships DV is usually underpinned by struggles over different axes of social power, like race/ethnicity, class, age, education and so on. Space constrictions prevent discussion of this form of interpersonal violence.

4 The first women's refuge in New Zealand was established in the early 1970s in Christchurch. About ten years later the National Collective of Women's Refuges was formed, and remains in operation. The refuge movement is committed to biculturalism and in 1987 opened its first Māori Women's Refuge in Hamilton.

5 Police statistics record instances of violent offences, thereby encouraging us to understand DV in terms of counts of violent incidents. However, DV is better understood as a problem of power; more aptly a relationship of domination and subordination that may entail the use, or threat, of violence, but may also be achieved without recourse to such overt displays of power (Adams 2012; Stark 2007).

6 The Violence Against Women Study was based on a random sample of 2674 ever-partnered women, aged 15–64, who lived in Auckland or northern Waikato. It explored experiences of victimisation and women's attitudes to violence. Although it found high levels of victimisation among Māori, it did not find high levels of acceptance of violence; quite the contrary (Fanslow et al. 2010).

7 Pacific people are also slightly over-represented among the perpetrators of intimate partner homicides, but not as markedly as Māori. Pacific peoples are not over-represented among victims of intimate partner homicides (FVDRC 2014).

8 It is important to recognise that the role played by strong emotions like shame as antecedents of violence does not rule out intentional action. It is quite possible, as Websdale (2010b, 127) makes clear, for perpetrators of violence to engage in its purposeful planning. Indeed, rational calculation is arguably a prerequisite for the existence of a pattern of coercive control.

9 Clearly violence and coercive control is not the sole prerogative of men who are unemployed, marginally employed, Māori or Pasifika. As Herbert and Mackenzie (2014, 11) state, 'In New Zealand there is a strong element of macho in our culture that is deeply embedded and celebrated at all levels of our society. As a result, violence and abuse occurs in all neighbourhoods.'

CHAPTER 19

# Locked Up

*Incarceration in Aotearoa New Zealand*

# Tracey McIntosh and Bartek Goldmann

How should we think about imprisonment in this country? Our incarceration rate is amongst the highest in the Western world. It has been for decades (Schmitt, Warner and Gupta 2010). Does that mean we are amongst the most dangerous countries in the world? Do we have a worse problem with crime than those countries, like Australia, to which we traditionally compare ourselves? Or do we have a punishment problem? That New Zealand has declining crime rates *and* increasing incarceration rates suggests we have a punishment problem rather than a problem with crime. As such, we need to think about the place of prisons in Aotearoa New Zealand. Evidence suggests that New Zealanders have a high tolerance, even an enthusiasm, for elevated rates of imprisonment.

This punitiveness is not new. John Pratt's (2006) work demonstrates a history of excessive punishment since Pākehā settlement. Early last century commentators noted that modest crime rates did not necessarily translate into low imprisonment rates. Pratt quotes a commentator who in 1932 wrote that 'New Zealand has on the whole very little serious crime.

Its prisons, nonetheless, are always full to overflowing and there is daily on average, a prison population more than three times as great, in proportion to the general population, as that of England and Wales' (Laing et al. as cited in Pratt 2006, 542). The willingness to imprison large numbers of our population has continued through to the present, although there has been a significant change in *whom* we imprison. Contemporary imprisonment, Pratt (2006, 542) argues, is shaped by its 'ethnic toxicity'.

In the early days of colonisation, the percentage of Māori who were imprisoned was low, and usually less than 3 per cent of the prison population (Clayworth 2012). By 1936 the Māori prison population was 11 per cent of the total prison population, and by 1945 it was 21 per cent. From 1955 the proportion increased dramatically so that by 1971 40 per cent of the prison population was Māori. Since 1980 Māori have consistently made up over half the prison population (Clayworth 2012, 5). These rises emerge from specific forms of social control. Prison is now often positioned as a 'natural' part of the social environment for particular sectors of society. This chapter explores transformations in public and academic discourses of punishment in neoliberal Aotearoa New Zealand and how these have influenced the Criminal Justice System (CJS), resulting in the increasing criminalisation of the poor and of Māori. We conclude by considering some more recent changes and proposals for alternatives to mass incarceration.

## Penal Populism

Perceptions of crime and punishment are shaped by various factors. Research demonstrates discrepancies between public perception of the frequency of crime, attitudes towards punishment and actual crime rates (Pratt 2008a, 32; Roberts and Hough 2005, 10–15; Weatherburn and Indermaur 2004). The media exerts a strong influence on the public's attitudes towards crime and punishment. By reporting on the most violent and sensational crimes, it confirms the 'common-sense' assumption that crime levels are rising, even when statistics show the opposite is true (Jewkes 2004). This situation is exacerbated by the changed structure and content of news reporting with the privatisation and deregulation of the news media. As newly commercialised media networks began to compete for advertising revenue, the content of current affairs programmes was simplified. Political commentary diminished and the average length of news items reduced (Cook 2002). Simultaneously, crime reporting, particularly of sensational and violent crime, increased, fuelling public anxieties about 'rising' crime. One of the consequences of New Zealand's sensationalised media reporting on crime is an increased stigmatisation of Māori as criminal (Gregory et al. 2011; McIntosh 2007).

Loretta Stalans (2013) suggests that public opinion represents a contradictory 'kaleidoscope of sentencing preferences' ranging from the punitive to the merciful. While there appears to be significant popular support in New Zealand for harsh punishments for violent offenders, some members of the public express much more liberal positions (Pratt 2008a, 32). International research shows that the public's support for incarceration decreases when they are better informed about community alternatives (Doble 2013; Roberts 2013). Demands for tough sentencing partly stem from a lack of knowledge of alternatives and from the difficulty of imagining a society without the prison as the central mode of punishment: 'The appeal of simplified and tough-minded penal policy lies in its ability to resonate with public emotions such as fear and anger. . . . Anyone who wants to improve public debate about crime needs to be attuned to this emotional dimension' (Indermaur and Hough 2013, 210). 'Penal populism' refers to a public climate in which advocates of zero-tolerance approaches to crime and punishment come to wield considerable clout over criminal justice policy-making (Pratt 2008b, 364). Such advocates include law-and-order lobbyists, the tabloid press, talkback radio, and conservative academics and think tanks. Advocates of penal populism often claim to speak on behalf of 'the people' and to represent the public's mood.

Public opinion is often used by politicians to justify harsher sentences or to suggest inadequacies in the CJS and penal system (Pratt 2008a, 31). Penal populism is driven by scandal and particular events that resonate with the public, and these can have significant repercussions 'both at the level of popular consciousness and of political, legislative and system level change' (Sparks 2000, 133).

Penal populism is deeply problematic for policy-making because it can 'allow the electoral advantage of a policy to take precedence over its penal effectiveness' (Roberts and Hough 2005, 16), meaning it wins votes rather than necessarily reducing crime or rehabilitating offenders. The disproportionate influence of (misinformed) public opinion is a considerable impediment to rational penal reform, the aims of which are to reduce re-offending by addressing the drivers of crime, to reduce social harm and to preserve public safety.

## The New 'Penal Expertise'

In 1984, under the Fourth Labour Government, New Zealanders witnessed the beginnings of neoliberal reform as the state sector began to be rapidly deregulated. The Fourth National Government, which came to power following the 1990 election, retained and deepened the extent of these reforms. The welfare state also found itself under attack during the terms of the 1990s National Government. These changes created a climate of generalised anxiety and vulnerability for many New Zealanders which fed anxieties about crime.

During this period, criminal justice policy was characterised by a mix of punitive approaches – marked by the increased use of sentences involving imprisonment, often for longer periods of time – and more liberal policies of rehabilitation and community involvement (Williams 2001). For example, the implementation of the Criminal Justice Act in 1985 allowed for community programmes as alternatives to custodial sentences. However, by the early 1990s the focus on community-based programmes shifted towards punitive punishments.

During this time, the liberal elites (including civil administrators, academics, judges and penal reform groups) became increasingly marginalised from public discourses on crime and punishment and from the policy-making process, and their capacity for containing populist desires for retribution diminished. Meanwhile, the authority and influence of victims' advocate groups, such as the Sensible Sentencing Trust, and other 'anti-crime' social movements increased, coalescing in a new kind of 'penal expertise' grounded in 'common sense' and anecdote rather than fact-based research (Pratt 2008a, 38; Pratt 2007, 3; Pratt and Clark 2005, 315). These new experts positioned themselves as advocates for a fearful public. They claimed to speak on behalf of 'vulnerable victims'. Consequently, the crime and punishment discourse has become increasingly emotionalised and politicised, while policy-making has become driven less by empirical research and more by public opinion based on 'nebulous feelings, intuitions and sentiments' (Pratt 2008a, 31–33). The rise of penal populism might be read as symptomatic of fickle forms of political engagement that are focused on specific crimes and events without reference to the structural conditions that may have caused them.

## Incarceration and the Criminalisation of Poverty

Prisons are institutions that systematically isolate, remove, marginalise and disconnect those convicted from wider society. Incarceration often marks a downwards shift in a life trajectory, and a narrowing of what is already a constricted path, culminating in a further embedding of a marginalised status (McIntosh 2011, 272). Institutionalisation encourages the cultivation of patterns of behaviour which, while useful inside the prison environment, can be maladaptive and detrimental to the prospects of reintegration. Re-entry to society is further inhibited by a prison record which often entrenches an already stigmatised status.

It is important to recognise that individual incarceration is also a collective experience given that the effects of incarceration go well beyond the individual, affecting all types of social relationships. Foster and Hagan (2007) argue that prisons can exacerbate existing ethnic and social-class disparities by excluding, for example, the children of incarcerated parents from central public institutions such as healthcare, housing and political participation. The eviction of Housing New Zealand tenants from houses where they were known to associate with gang members with prison convictions who are deemed to be involved in anti-social behaviour has largely been felt by women (who usually hold the tenancy) and their children. In most cases the people they were 'associating' with were partners and fathers of the tenants. A study on the children of prisoners in New Zealand noted that they experienced poorer health and higher levels of emotional trauma, faced discrimination in education settings and high levels of exclusion from the compulsory education sector, moved houses and schools frequently, lived in conditions of poverty and were on occasion excluded from court settings when they went to support parents (Gordon and MacGibbon 2011). As Phillips and Bloom (1998) note, getting tough on crime has often meant getting tough on children and creating pathways for their own future incarceration. Incarceration is therefore also linked to the intergenerational transmission of inequality and exclusion.

Loïc Wacquant (2001, 401) has argued that neoliberal regimes are characterised by a pattern of 'penalisation of poverty', whereby prisons function as a means for managing the social insecurity produced at the lower end of the class structure by neoliberal policies of social welfare cutbacks and economic deregulation. From this perspective, prisons are increasingly used to manage social problems resulting from mass unemployment and precarious labour markets (Kramer 2015). As such, imprisonment can be seen to be an element of neoliberalism's class project of disciplining the working class, neutralising its most politically disruptive fractions, and 'warehousing' any labour that is surplus to the needs of capital (Wacquant 2001, 405).

Reflecting on who goes to prison gives us some basis to argue that poverty is one of the drivers of crime. Too many prisoners have experienced considerable social harm and have gone on to perpetuate social harm on others (Workman and McIntosh 2013). The vast majority of people who live in conditions of material scarcity make strong contributions to family and community. For most, offending is not a feature of their lives. However, research and statistics suggest that there are links between crime and poverty. Both victimisation and crime rates are more elevated in poorer communities and the poor are more likely to be arrested and convicted. The statistics also tell another story. They demonstrate that poverty is racialised and that Māori and Pasifika experience ongoing, disproportionate levels of poverty (Workman and McIntosh 2013, 123).

## Māori and Mass Imprisonment

Māori, as noted earlier, are particularly over-represented in the prison population with an incarceration rate of 693 per 100,000. This imprisonment rate is seven times that of non-Māori (Salvation Army 2016, 27). This over-representation is even more marked in the remand than in the sentenced population, with Māori being almost twice as likely to be remanded in custody as Pākehā across all types of offences (Salvation Army 2016; Workman 2011, 17–18). While this is partly due to the fact that Māori are over-represented among those charged with offences that are likely to result in remand in custody (such as aggravated robbery and burglary), a Cabinet paper has also suggested this difference is due to the lack of access of Māori to support services such as housing, which makes it difficult for them to meet bail conditions (Ministry of Justice 2006; Workman 2011, 17). Patrick O'Malley (1973, 49–50) noted that bail serves a key function in the administration of justice in that it provides the defendant with the freedom to prepare an adequate defence, and with the support of family and community. However, at the time of his research, Māori were less likely to arrange bail and to obtain legal counsel as a result of limited financial means. Furthermore, those defendants who were not legally represented were more likely to plead guilty. Recent legislation that has further tightened remand conditions has contributed significantly to the current burgeoning prison population and to the resulting incarceration rates of Māori (Salvation Army 2016).

Prisons have become increasingly punitive and concerned with managing and mitigating risk. Official reports are less likely to characterise prisoners as people in need of support, and more likely to refer to them as 'culpable, deserving of punishment' and 'risks to be carefully managed', and therefore best subjected to (over-)restrictive security requirements (Workman and McIntosh 2013, 126). This risk-aversive logic was reflected in the Integrated Offender Management System (IOM) implemented in 2002, which was predicated on the ongoing assessment of each offender's risk of re-offending and involved providing interventions tailored to meet each offender's needs (Quince 2007, 22; Webb 2011). IOM emphasises scientific psychotherapeutic principles focused on responding to the individual needs of each prisoner (Webb 2011). A Criminogenic Needs Inventory was compiled for each inmate, with the aim of identifying risk factors that precipitated their offending behaviour. These included emotions and beliefs that supported offending; drug or alcohol dependence; criminal associates; lifestyle problems involving accommodation, financial and employment status; violent behaviour; and family or relationship problems. However, the programme failed to lower re-offending rates for Māori, largely due to the fact that many Māori were not willing to engage in a treatment model largely administered by non-Māori staff (Webb 2011).

It is important to recognise that the Māori experience of prison is also gendered. To fully understand the intergenerational aspects of prison life in New Zealand it is critical to understand the experiences of imprisoned Māori women (Bentley 2014; Dennehy and Newbold 2001; Goldingay 2007; Kingi 1999; McIntosh 2011; Quince 2008). Following global trends, we have seen the number of women incarcerated in New Zealand increase dramatically. The trend of Māori over-representation in the CJS is particularly pronounced for Māori women who are even more over-represented than Māori men in apprehensions, convictions and imprisonments (Quince 2007, 16). Māori women's overcriminalisation, overincarceration and high rates of victimisation are at least partly a product of their poor socio-economic status. Māori women are also vulnerable to victimisation, and young Māori women in particular are the most likely to be repeat victims of domestic violence and sexual victimisation (Morris and Reilly 2003; see also Elizabeth on domestic violence in this volume). Māori women's risk of victimisation is further multiplied if coexistent with mental illness, physical disability or sexual orientation (McIntosh 2007, 6). Young Māori women in prison are a socially submerged population as they are both marginalised and socially invisible by virtue of their age, gender and incarcerated status (McIntosh and Radojkovic 2012, 40).

The causes of disproportionality within the CJS are complex. Some commentators assert that higher Māori offending is the product of a developmental pathway, proposing that, in their early lives, Māori are particularly vulnerable to adverse family and environmental factors that are closely linked to socio-economic status, marginalisation, and structural and institutional racism that may contribute to subsequent offending behaviour (Department of Corrections 2007; Quince 2007; Webb 2011; Workman and McIntosh 2013). Former Police Commissioner Peter Doone (2000, 10) suggested that factors leading to criminal behaviour include family instability and violence; lack of social ties or anti-social peers; lack of vocational skills or employment prospects; drug and alcohol abuse; poor self-management; aggressiveness; truancy and poor educational outcomes; living in overcrowded housing; and disconnection from cultural institutions such as whānau, hapū and iwi. Many whānau may lack the means to access the support needed to address these risk factors, or to respond to the offending once it occurs.

## Structural Discrimination

At the same time, to better understand the 'statistical gulf' (Quince 2007, 12) that exists between Māori and Pākehā, Māori commentators also insist that it must be interpreted in the broader context of colonisation, dispossession of land, Māori urbanisation, the imposition of the Western system of common law, cultural assimilation, and the undermining of tikanga and traditional forms of Māori social control (Jackson 1988; Quince 2007; Tauri 2013). The Māori experience of colonisation is in many ways paralleled by struggles of indigenous peoples in other settler states who have also been systematically brutalised and marginalised by state policies and practices, and where they too continue to be over-represented in prison populations (Webb 2011, 252).

This broader, colonial context results in various forms of *structural* discrimination against Māori. It is important not to conflate these with individual forms of racism or discrimination. While we need to identify and address interpersonal forms of discrimination and violence, we also need to consider the ways in which social systems and institutions can facilitate, inhibit or protect groups of people from violence and discrimination. Discriminatory institutional policies can entrench existing disadvantage for groups on a much larger scale, often across generations (McIntosh and Radojkovic 2012, 42).

Research demonstrates that structural discrimination is evident across many sites and processes of the CJS. Analysis of those convicted in court in 2006 indicates that Māori were more likely to receive custodial sentences and community work sentences than Pākehā or Pasifika offenders, while being less likely to receive monetary penalties (Morrison, Soboleva and Chong 2008, 104; Webb 2011, 250). Further studies have shown that while they are generally sympathetic to Māori defendants, prosecutors tend to view Māori as anti-police and anti-Crown (Quince 2007, 15–16). Research also found that Crown counsel is twice as likely to challenge Māori being appointed to sit on juries than non-Māori in the High Court, and three times as likely in the District Court (Dunstan, Paulin and Atkinson 1995). The established method of jury selection also produces a monocultural bias (Quince 2007, 15–16). Potential jurors must be over eighteen years of age, registered on the electoral roll, live within 30 kilometres of the court and have no disqualifying criminal convictions. These criteria systemically exclude Māori from juries given that the Māori population tends to be younger on average and that Māori are more likely to have previous convictions and more likely to live in rural areas than non-Māori. That Māori are under-represented on juries means that juries consequently fail to represent Māori defendants' communities or their values. This is compounded further by Māori under-representation within the key professional groups that comprise the CJS: police, judges, legislators and lawyers (Quince 2007, 13).

Processes of structural discrimination and developmental pathways to crime are not mutually exclusive (Workman 2011, 3); they interact. One can amplify the other. Individuals may become more predisposed to certain types of illegal behaviour due to early-life environmental, family and socio-economic factors, thus increasing the risk of their entanglement with the CJS. Further, due to formal and informal profiling by police, other state agencies and members of the public, the likelihood that these individuals will be apprehended and become more entangled with the system is amplified. Overcriminalisation of Māori not only stems from poor socio-economic status, but from the complex interplay of policing practices, legislative change, media practices, stigma, shifts in public attitudes, and the ongoing adverse effects of colonisation, resulting in multi-layered and entrenched forms of disadvantage. A focus on social harm so as to better understand the causes of high levels of violence and drug and alcohol dependency 'at the collective, social and structural levels with special attention to systematic deprivation and entrenched disadvantage moves us away from looking for deficit at the individual level' (McIntosh 2011, 269). This may allow us to move away from simple (but deceptive) crime/punishment binaries and imagine other ways to ensure the safety of the community and its flourishing.

## Unlocking the Prison?

Prisons are part of our social landscape but they should not be seen as a natural part of our environment. Our penal history has largely been about locking up people but there are signs that this position is shifting. Given that Ministers of the 2014–17 National-led Government have noted the fiscal and moral failure of prisons, there may be a greater appetite to look at ways that we can unlock people (Workman and McIntosh 2013, 120). An increased focus on reintegration, rehabilitation and social justice linked with progressive policy may pave the way to rethinking crime and punishment.

There have been reforms to the CJS that have benefited Māori and that have reflected concepts in tikanga Māori (Quince 2007). For instance, family group conferences were implemented in 1989 in order to include different cultural family dynamics and to emphasise collective decision-making. Likewise, the development of marae justice initiatives has provided offenders with the opportunity to have their legal proceedings diverted to a community panel that sits on marae. Many of these initiatives have drawn criticism from individuals who have argued that these types of cultural justice amount to a co-optation of tikanga on the part of the Crown, and are part of a process of colonising the Māori mind (Jackson 1988; Tauri 1998, 2013). Khylee Quince (2007, 20) adds that these amount to a '"browning" of the legal system [that] defuses critique of its colonial form without meeting Māori demands for recognition of Te Tiriti o Waitangi'. However, the development in 2008 of Ngā Kooti

Rangatahi/the Rangatahi Courts – marae-based youth courts for young Māori offenders – has been seen as the 'most significantly and potentially game-changing development in our system in recent years' (Cleland and Quince 2014, 246). The Rangatahi Court is a Māori initiative that is designed and run by Māori. Some of its features align with a Therapeutic Jurisprudence approach.

Therapeutic Jurisprudence recognises the impact of the law on emotional life and psychological well-being and argues that the law can be employed as a therapeutic agent (Winick and Wexler 2003). This approach has resulted in the development of the specialist courts such as the Family Violence Court, the Homelessness Court and, to some degree, the Rangatahi Courts. These are largely seen as problem-solving courts that seek to address the offending by looking at the broader context, and identifying and delivering support services to address the drivers of offending. These systems operate on a sanctions-and-rewards model, working with an individual in a holistic manner. Currently, the effectiveness of these courts is being assessed through evaluations and other forms of research (Ministry of Justice 2012). The findings, particularly in the Rangatahi Courts, are promising. Critical success factors include the recognition that holding the courts on marae has engendered respect from both rangatahi and whānau and has impacted favourably on the way they respond to and engage with the court. Further, the presence of kaumātua has a positive impact on rangatahi behaviour, as has the use of lay advocates for the rangatahi. These courts have also produced a wraparound effect in that they encourage the collective commitment of participating agencies to the process (Ministry of Justice 2012, 60).

Further possibilities for reform are suggested by a Justice Reinvestment approach (Allen and Stern 2007), which can directly address inequalities in the system. This model identifies the amount of financial and non-financial resources consumed by the CJS and seeks to demonstrate what could be done if these funds were distributed differently in order to provide a greater level of social well-being. Presently well over $700 million is being spent each year in New Zealand to keep people in prison. How could this level of funding be used in communities to effect positive social change and reduce the structural sources of much crime?

To reduce our prison population we will need to face up to the inequalities that exist both inside and outside of our current CJS. A commitment to reducing inequalities and social harms (poverty, sexism, racism, violence, lack of opportunity) could be aligned with a renewed justice sector. Our prison rates are not an intractable problem. They are amenable to positive change. Reducing offending *and* reducing our prison population is possible through an awareness of the issues we face as a society, a consciousness of the drivers of crime, sufficient resourcing and the political will to create transformative change.

CHAPTER 20

# The Urban(e) and the Metro-rural in Aotearoa

## Peter J. Howland

In many ways our understandings of life in the city and in the country are defined by their opposition to one another. Indeed, the cultural theorist Raymond Williams (1973, 289) argues that the 'city and country are changing historical realities, both in themselves and in their interrelations', and that through their comparison we may become conscious 'of the crises of our society'. Williams documents the urban–rural interplay in Europe since the rise of capitalism and industrialisation. This interplay oscillates between the idealisation of the city as site of civilization, economic and political power, high culture and cosmopolitanism, with the country viewed as a rural backwater, and the reverse image of the city as corrupt, alienating, polluted and overcrowded, while the country is seen as the site of honest toil, authentic traditions, unified communities and natural beauty. In this chapter, I explore some of the changing urban–rural dynamics within Aotearoa, from the rural influence on early European settlement to contemporary urbanisation and gentrification. I also examine Auckland, Tāmaki Makaurau, as a super-diverse city within a global setting, and, lastly, the evolution of a local rural idyll and how this plays an enduring moral role in the generation of a more recent metro-rural idyll.

## Settling Aotearoa

Early European settlers coming to Aotearoa were part of a nineteenth-century European diaspora in which 50 million people migrated around the globe. Many were escaping terrible circumstances, such as Ireland's potato famine (1846–48), chaotic population growth (e.g., Britain's population grew from 16 million in 1801 to 26 million in 1841), economic deprivations, rural land closures and/or civil disorder throughout an industrialising Europe. These immigrants were pursuing economic and social advantage in which settlement was frequently a calculated 'business proposition' (McAloon 2002, 52). For example, Edward Gibbon Wakefield and his New Zealand Company – which established settlements at Wellington, Nelson, Whanganui and Dunedin – promoted New Zealand as an investors' paradise founded on the free-enterprise, meritocratic ideals of capitalism. Similarly, James Belich (1996) argues settlers were motivated to establish a 'Better Britain' that would signal a return to a mythical Golden Age of Arcadian pastoralism and a 'Greater Britain' that championed utopian, innovative technologies alongside progressive corporate and government management. Many settlers possessed attitudes that affirmed an essential 'malleability of the world' (Grey 1994, 16), which meant that the alienation of the supposedly uncultivated wilderness of Aotearoa – including alienating Māori from their lands and culture – was a moral right and obligation (see Wynyard in this volume). This perspective clashed with that of Māori, who through hunting, burning and cultivating had converted large tracts of forest into grassland and, despite using many farming techniques that resonated with European methods (e.g., terraced gardens), had an economy that was primarily subsistence-based, often seasonal, and founded upon ancestral and kin-based values of stewardship, so that even land that looked unoccupied was important economically and culturally:

> To the incoming British settlers such [Māori] land appeared empty and unused and therefore available for a 'superior use'. In their minds they had every justification for purchasing or otherwise appropriating land. Ironically it was not the 'unused' land they often sought first but

land already plainly occupied and cultivated by Māori people. (Grey 1994, 20)

From the outset, colonial townships were closely linked with rural concerns, including the provision of general stores, blacksmiths, accommodation, stables and hotels for growing farming populations and associated travellers. Many were situated near river crossings, staging posts, road junctions and extractive industries such as timber mills and goldmining. Moreover, town newspapers routinely addressed farming concerns and townsfolk provided seasonal rural labour. Settlements were closely spaced, proximity being determined by the distance a farmer could travel to and from market in one day, and by bush-clad, hilly, swampy and river-strewn topography. Towns that survived were those that established hegemony over a rural region, ensured the profitable development of farming, and/or were important transport nodes, especially sea and river ports (Aotearoa's largest seven cities – Auckland, Wellington, Christchurch, Hamilton, Napier-Hastings, Tauranga and Dunedin – fulfil this criterion).

## Urban Aotearoa

For all the rural focus of colonial settlement, and the continuing importance of the rural economy to national gross domestic product (GDP), over time Aotearoa has become increasingly urban. In 1881, Aotearoa was firmly a rural society with 60 per cent of the population living in the countryside, but by 1906–7 just over 50 per cent were living in urban areas of more than 1000 people. By 2001 this proportion had increased to 85.7 per cent—approximately 3.3 million of the total national population of 3.9 million (Statistics New Zealand 2004). Most of these urbanites – approximately 2.8 million people or 71 per cent of the national population – lived in main urban areas,[1] with Auckland ranked as the largest city with 1.16 million people or 30 per cent of the national population (Statistics New Zealand 2002a). The trend of increasing urbanisation is predicted to continue and by 2031 it is projected that 5 million or 91 per cent of the national population will be urbanites, with 2 million (40 per cent) residing in Auckland. These transformations are part of a global trend and in 2007, for the first time, the majority of the world's population lived in urban areas. This majority is also predicted to increase – to 66 per cent by 2050 (Demographia 2015).

During this same time period, Aotearoa has also become increasingly enmeshed in globalised networks of investment, people, products and communications (Castells 1996). Notably, in the 1990s the local economy underwent a distinct shift, becoming more focused on services, discretionary consumption and cultural commodities as a way of benefiting from the profits and the tourists, investors and labour migrants that now routinely bounce around the cities of the world. For example, Sir Peter Jackson's Wingnut Films and Richard Taylor's Weta Digital (producers of *Lord of the Rings* and *Hobbit* films) developed a creative film industry in Wellington (Wellywood) enabled by globalised communication and labour networks. With approximately 1400 staff drawn from around the world, Weta Digital is one of the largest digital effects companies globally (for an example of an issue arising from such globalisation in the New Zealand film industry, see Bell in this volume).

Globalising flows of urbanity also spurred Auckland's emergence as a super-diverse city. As a primate city (i.e., being at least twice as populous as the second-largest city), Auckland dominates Aotearoa's population and economic dynamics. Cities such as Auckland are magnets for international migrants – well-resourced, aspirational, landless or disenfranchised alike – as they offer more investment, occupational and social opportunities than less populous areas. Just over 39 per cent of Aucklanders are immigrants and, if their New Zealand-born children are included, these families make up 56 per cent of the city's population (Social and Economic Research Team [SERT] 2014, 13). High proportions of this immigrant population are Asian – Chinese and Indian in particular – and some Auckland urban spaces are transforming into ethnic precincts, so that the cityscape increasingly resembles a mosaic of distinct cultural locations (see Spoonley in this volume).

The future of humanity – which is ever more riven by economic, social and political disparity[2] – will increasingly play out in such densely urbanised areas, although what that future will look like is uncertain. Geographer David Harvey (1996, 38) argues that, for many, 'to talk of the city of the twenty-first century is to conjure up a dystopian nightmare in which all that is judged worst in the fatally flawed character of humanity collects together in some hell-hole of despair'. Cities may become evermore concentrated sites of proprietorial power, privilege and inequity, police-state (and corporate) surveillance and control, chronic disease, crumbling or stressed infrastructures, pollution, congestion and violence. Already, in Auckland, housing inaffordability – exacerbated by undersupply leading to lack of choice – and unhealthy and overcrowded houses are significantly more pronounced than elsewhere in Aotearoa. In 2013, Auckland homeowners spent 15.2 per cent of their income on housing on average, compared with 12.0 and 10.6 per cent in Wellington and Canterbury respectively,[3] while 49.4 per cent of the nation's overcrowded households were in Auckland, an increase from 35.7 per cent in 1991 (Goodyear and Fabian 2014). And just as Auckland's most expensive domestic residence – a $35-million, 1730-square-metre, five-bedroom, nine-bathroom, eight-car-garage house in Clifton Road, Takapuna – went up for sale, the city was experiencing record rates of homelessness (Beaton et al. 2015).

Yet cities are also sites of resistance and social change that offer hope for other possible futures. Recent examples include the 'free pass' public transport protests in Rio de Janeiro, anti-development Gezi Park protests in Turkey, anti-austerity protests in Greece and Spain, and the Occupy protests in more than 900 cities worldwide. These movements, although weakly cross-class (being predominantly made up of educated middle-class members) and weakly interethnic, were nevertheless triggered by 'urban disaffection and alienation' and expressed 'universal outrage at rising social inequalities, escalating costs of living, and gratuitously violent police repressions' (Harvey 2014, 3).

In this context of ever-increasing urbanisation and inequality, it is interesting to take stock of the state of urban and rural Aotearoa and what that can tell us about the present 'crises of our society'.

## Urbanism and Gentrification

Forces of urban-based privilege and exclusion similar to those that have driven the resistance campaigns mentioned above are at work also in Aotearoa and are particularly obvious in (though not exclusive to) Auckland. For many of Auckland's critics, the gentrification of its urban areas is of particular concern. Gentrification is the process whereby property developers, purchasers, renters, retailers and governmental administrators, policies and regulations recognise an area as undercapitalised, and effectively collude to profitably upgrade it to middle-class, urbane standards. Such transformations often result in the social exclusion and relative deprivation of working classes, urban Māori and Pasifika, and young people.

A notable example of 'first-wave' gentrification is the transformation of Ponsonby in Auckland's inner suburbs. After World War II, large numbers of relatively prosperous trades people and professionals deserted Ponsonby for Auckland's expanding suburbs, and by the 1970s it was occupied by many working-class Māori migrating to the city, and first-generation Pasifika migrants 'substantially poorer than those that had left' (Latham 2003, 1704). This exodus was termed 'white flight' and Ponsonby became a by-word for 'urban decay and blight' (Latham 2003, 1704). Then, attracted by lowering rents, cheaper house prices and the socio-cultural diversity, young, liberal and tertiary-educated Pākehā moved in and set about renovating housing, retail and community spaces in an exploration of new ways of living – self-expressive, communal, counter-cultural and cosmopolitan. These residents introduced a 'new form of urban public culture' (Latham 2003, 1706) that rejected the masculine-dominated, beer-swilling, opaque-windowed public bar culture in favour of chic cafés and specialty food, clothing and knick-knack stores. In 1976 there were only four cafés, restaurants and bars in Ponsonby. By 2002 there were more than 90 (including gay- and female-friendly establishments, and some with pavement seating). As an unintended consequence, house prices began to skyrocket (between 1991 and 1998 the average Ponsonby house price increased from approximately $165,000 to $415,000). Already by the 1980s significant residential displacement had occurred, with many Māori and Pasifika Ponsonby residents forced to seek more affordable accommodation in areas of South Auckland such as Māngere, Manurewa and Ōtara (Friesen 2009; Latham 2003).

This interplay of inclusion and exclusion, privilege and inequity – which are routine structural dynamics of capitalism – is also evident in the more recent, neoliberal waves of gentrification. What might be termed the 'second-wave' gentrification of inner-city apartment developments occurred in the 1990s as the state withdrew from old-style regional policies, ushering in an era of urban transformation that emphasised individual gentrifiers and real estate developers; the free flow of capital, labour and markets; and consumer sovereignty. Key pieces of neoliberalising legislation were the Local Government Act 1989, Resource Management Act 1991 and the Building Act 1991. Although interpretation varied across regional authorities, Auckland City embraced a *laissez-faire*, free market, attitude that resulted in three distinct investor markets: the owner/investor (75 per cent of units – includes general rentals), student accommodation (9 per cent of units) and serviced apartments (15 per cent of units) (Murphy 2008, 2581).

Moreover, it was not until 2007 that formal design protocols and minimum apartment-size regulations were introduced: 'By then, apartment development in Auckland had developed a reputation for poor design with the smallest apartments measuring only 16 square metres' (Murphy 2008, 2525). Overall, the deregulation of the building industry has left Auckland a legacy of poorly designed inner-city apartments and 'leaky buildings'.

Between 1991 and 2007, approximately 16,000 apartments were developed in the Auckland Central Business District (CBD) and the numbers of apartment dwellers more than quadrupled (from 2805 to 13,311 between 1996 and 2006). Similar developments were experienced in Wellington, where the numbers of inner-city dwellers rose from 1410 to 4743 between 1996 and 2006 (Goodyear and Fabian 2014). Furthermore, population density in the Auckland CBD more than doubled every five years between 1991 and 2006, and is predicted to increase from 4600 people per square kilometre in 2006 to more than 13,300 by 2031. By comparison, the average urban density for Aotearoa was 522 people per square kilometre in 2006 (Statistics New Zealand 2006b).

The subsequent, 'third wave, new-build' gentrification (Murphy 2008, 2521) of Auckland's Viaduct Harbour was underpinned by neoliberal (roll-out) collaborations between corporate investors and government. As part of greater Ponsonby, the Viaduct Harbour was also notorious for poor housing conditions in the 1930s. However, Auckland hosting the America's Cup regatta in 2000 and 2003 provided a spur for central and local government to invest in hosting the super-yachts of the super-rich. The Auckland City Council contributed $40 million to the development of public squares, walkways and sea walls, while the Auckland Regional Services Trust contributed $70 million, and central government $10 million, on reclamation projects in anticipation of immediate and long-term benefits from hosting a global, yet transient, sporting event. Viaduct Harbour's gentrification – including the development of architecturally designed apartments (e.g., Latitude 37 and The Point), upmarket restaurants and stylish public spaces patrolled by 24-hour private security, and bans on public alcohol consumption – resulted in an area 'centred on issues of quality, exclusivity and global urbanity' (Murphy 2008, 2535). Significantly, the median household incomes of 'Harbourside' (a CBD census meshblock that includes the Viaduct) exceeds the Auckland City median by 29 per cent and other CBD median household incomes by 150 per cent. This new-build gentrification has produced yet another urban-based, 'polarised social space' in which 'Harbourside represents an élite enclave and the rest of the CBD houses a low-income, student-dominated population' (Murphy 2008, 2532–3).

## Metro-Rural Aotearoa

Despite the intensification of urbanisation in Aotearoa, the rural, as ideal and practice, has enduring significance. In some respects, the urban areas of Aotearoa, and especially the surfeit of small towns, can be viewed as islands of settlement dotted amidst oceans of green pasture populated by sheep, cattle and crops in the millions. Agriculture accounts for 43 per cent or 14.3 million hectares of total land use and forestry for 7 per cent (2.3 million hectares), whereas urban use accounts for only 3 per cent or 1 million hectares. Indeed there are only seventeen main urban areas (of 30,000 or more inhabitants), but literally hundreds of towns with only a few thousand, or a few hundred, souls.

For some, rural Aotearoa is in a state of near-perpetual crisis, especially when compared with the growth and vibrancy of urban Aotearoa, particularly Auckland. Undoubtedly the countryside has suffered a marked 'rural decline', especially since the removal of government farming subsidies in the 1980s and the more recent neoliberal roll-back and removal of infrastructural services such as banking, postal services and schooling. Agricultural employment has fallen by 20 per cent since the mid-1980s, and only about one-third of rural dwellers work in agriculture, fishing or forestry, with non-agricultural income (including off-farm) occurring on 30–50 per cent of farms. Moreover, the rural areas of Northland, Gisborne and Bay of Plenty all have lower median incomes, higher rates of unemployment and higher deprivation scores than the national average. Rural Aotearoa has also experienced the demise of the family farm (80,000 in 1986 to 65,000 just 20 years later) and the correlated rise of large-scale, corporate-run, ecologically suspect (land- and river-polluting) dairy farms – approximately 3 million dairy cattle in total in 1982, increasing to 5.26 million in 2007. The average dairy farm increased from 151 cows on 65 hectares in 1988 to 322 cows on 118 hectares in 2006 (Organisation for Economic Co-operation and Development [OECD] 2009; Statistics New Zealand 2004).

Yet others argue that rural Aotearoa is as vital as ever. Evidence pointing in this direction includes agriculture's reasonably stable share of total GDP (5–6 per cent since the 1980s); median household incomes that frequently mirror, sometimes surpass, urban rates; increasingly diverse rural populations (including 'ethnic' migrants and seasonal workers); and – as well as the well-known industries of dairy, sheep and everyday produce – varied economies, including vineyards; olive groves; tea plantations; lifestyle blocks; iwi and Waitangi Treaty Settlement investments; ostrich, bison and llama farms; and rural tourism accommodation which more than doubled in the 1980s (OECD 2009; Statistics New Zealand 2004).

Romanticised, idealised notions of rural life, transported here originally by European settlers eager to return to a mythical Golden Age of Arcadia, have played a key role in framing the rural in mainstream culture – particularly for Aotearoa's urbanites. The national imagining of the rural idyll celebrates a productionist ethos of hard work (or 'hard yakka') and maximum yield parading as moral virtues (Egoz, Bowring and Perkins 2001) alongside close-knit rural communities and farming families, an innovative 'Number 8 wire' ethic, slow-paced lifestyles, and the natural aesthetics and tranquility of green-pastured farms (Bell 1996). Indeed, this rural idyll ethos was carried into the quarter-acre sections of towns and cities in Aotearoa, which copied the suburban sprawl of Australia and the United States instead of 'unsuitable' European city features, like narrow streets, high population density and terrace housing (save for novelties such as Dundas Street, Dunedin). The enduring adulation of rurality within mainstream, urban culture is also evident in the popularity of the documentary television show *Country Calendar*, the nation's longest-running television series (50 years in 2016), which regularly attracts weekly audiences of 500,000.

Yet perhaps we are experiencing a generational tipping point where the homage historically paid to an idealised rurality is being replaced by misty-eyed corporate branding of New Zealand Inc., in which IT creatives and hipster entrepreneurs are increasingly dominant, and where the adulation once reserved for rugged farmer All Blacks such as Sir Colin Meads, who purportedly trained by tucking a sheep under each arm and running around the home paddock, is substituted by 'Brand All Blacks' and quixotic visions of a fully professional square-jawed Richie McCaw, flying his glider over the Southern Alps.

The relationship between the urban and the rural is certainly changing, as evidenced by the growth of a number of rural areas with high urban influence; that is, rural areas in which a significant proportion of residents are employed in a nearby main urban area. Populations of these areas are collectively predicted to grow to 203,700 or approximately 3.7

per cent of the national population by 2031. Here, former urbanites are among those who reside on an estimated 175,000 rural lifestyle blocks, also popular and 'profitable' with urban tourists, vacationers and retirees. These areas include Matakana, promoted as 'just forty minutes from Auckland' and home to 30 'boutique' vineyards, olive groves, restaurants and the 'famous' Saturday Farmers' Market (Matakana Village 2016); and the 'charming', 'quirky', former gold-rush village Arrowtown, nestled aside the 'sparkling' Arrow River in Central Otago, where 'history meets nature', meets urbane shopping, meets gourmet dining (Arrowtown.com 2016).

Another such site is Martinborough, a small boutique 'wine village', approximately one hour's drive from Wellington, and where I have conducted fieldwork for a number of years. Founded in 1879 by John Martin, an illiterate nineteen-year-old Irish migrant who rose to prominence in Wellington as a property developer and politician, Martinborough was a private subdivision (593 town sections up to 1 acre and 334 small farm blocks ranging from 4.5 to 1100 acres) developed to offset Martin's national-record costs (£50,000) of purchasing the 33,000-acre Huangarua Station. Martinborough also fulfilled Martin's country squire aspirations and he laid the town out in the shape of the Union Jack, naming its central streets after places he had visited on his European 'Grand Tour' – New York, Cologne, Venice.

The wine industry in Martinborough developed in the 1980s as part of the diversification and land sell-off that followed the removal of government farming subsidies, and today the town is a popular holiday destination for Wellington's affluent, tertiary-educated and urbane middle classes. Renowned for its pinot noir, Martinborough hosts some 40, mostly boutique, vineyards (producing less than 200,000 litres) and numerous tourist accommodations – ranging from the five-star Martinborough Hotel to about a hundred homestays and bed and breakfasts.

Easily the biggest population in Martinborough are tourists. The resident population of about 1400 people is dwarfed by the 30,000 who attend the Martinborough Fairs in February and March, the 20,000 who attend the Toast Martinborough wine festival in November, and by many more who visit on day trips or for weekend retreats. Most are drawn by the prospects of an *in situ* vineyard experience, tasting local wines, and meeting personally with a winemaker. Many desire a relaxing break from city life (Martinborough has frequently been promoted as a 'Capital Country Escape'), to spend 'quality leisure time' with friends and lovers, and to consume other cosmopolitan offerings (e.g., luxury accommodation, handmade chocolates and cheeses) in a rural setting. Many thus seek out the rural idyll discussed above, although a key difference is that their experience is intentionally sporadic, transient, and focused on urbane leisure and consumption activities that reflect their middle-class, metropolitan sophistications.

Martinborough's wine tourists, who are predominantly tertiary-educated, white-collar bureaucrats, professionals and business owners, Pākehā-European and earn significantly more that the national average, reproduce romanticised rural ideals (often unconsciously) in ways that emphasise certain moralities, which are then used to affirm their contrasting metropolitan-derived pursuits. As such they construct a 'metro-rural idyll' (Howland 2014, 228) that firstly frames rural places, people and products as consumable attractions for urban visitors and, secondly, uses the ideals of the rural idyll to morally validate the pursuit of their own urbane endeavours in the countryside. For example, many tourists who celebrate idyllic notions of intimate family farms nevertheless leave their own dependent children at home in favour of spending holiday time with friends and lovers. As such they evoke, and then transfer, the idealised sociality of farming families to validate their enjoyment of their adult holiday companions. Tourists also frequently walk around Martinborough waving and saying hello to complete strangers in the belief they are replicating the authentic neighbourliness of rural communities – although anyone who has lived in a rural place will know that neighbourly relations typically range from the friendly to the hostile. At the same time, while tourists frequently adulate the urbane vision and artisanal products of winemakers and others as representing the highly valued ideals of autonomy and self-realisation, they 'glaze over' with disinterest whenever the same artisans talk about the hard work and economic difficulties of small family farms and rural businesses. Finally, tourist admiration of pristine, symmetrical and bucolic vineyards is sometimes matched only by their complaints about the smell, filth and noisiness of sheep and cattle farms – thereby demonstrating a valuing of urbane, yet rural, commodity production over primary agriculture.

In effect, a rural-based holiday, lifestyle block or retirement abode is often not a withdrawal from urbanity or a fulsome embrace of rurality. Rather, it is a leisured retreat towards various metropolitan ideals and practices underpinned by the moralities of the metro-rural idyll and ideally experienced in a sun-drenched, aesthetically agreeable, pastoral setting.

## Conclusion

Raymond Williams challenges us to compare life in city and rural settings as a way of understanding their entangled dynamics and to identify 'crises of our society'. We have explored the rural influence on early European settlements in Aotearoa, a legacy that continues in the contemporary sprawl of urban settlements, in the multitude of small towns and in an enduring romanticisation of country life. In addition, we explored urbanisation – local, networked, global – and how this results in increases in urban populations and densities; in concentrations of wealth, privilege and culture flows; and in Auckland's super-diversity. We also looked at how globalised capitalism, urbanity and gentrification have resulted in crises of inequity, social exclusion, housing inaffordability, overcrowding and homelessness, crises which in turn provoke urban protest.

Rural Aotearoa, which has in part experienced a marked decline, has nevertheless long functioned as an idealised touchstone that provides urbanites with moral images of harmonious families and communities; clean, green environments; self-directed hard work; and productive reward. Yet, as we have witnessed, the vernacular idyllic rural is being pressed into serving, and morally validating, the urbane aspirations of city-dwellers who ascribe to a metro-rural idyll. In this we observed an urban and generational shift away from indentured homage to the rural and towards an ethos in which rural spaces and lives (especially those adjacent to areas of urbanity) are increasingly being bent to a metropolitan, urbane will.

Clearly, in the contemporary interplay of city and rural life in Aotearoa, we can conclude that the spread and influence of the urban(e) is on the rise.

## Notes

1. Areas with more than 30,000 residents (Statistics New Zealand 2002b).
2. As described in Curtis and Galic in this volume, the wealthiest 1 per cent globally now own more than the half the world's wealth (Hardoon 2015), and the richest 66 people own more than the poorest half of the world's population (Oxfam New Zealand 2014).
3. Data are from the Household Economic Survey. The homeowners figure includes households that have already paid off their mortgage. The average housing spend for Auckland renters is 25 per cent of their income.

CHAPTER 21

# Clean, Green Aotearoa New Zealand?

## Corrina Tucker

'Clean and green' was a slogan used to describe Aotearoa New Zealand that emerged in public discourse during the early to mid-1980s in relation to the overwhelming desire of New Zealanders for a nuclear-free nation. It has since become 'an essential part of our identity' (Hansard 2007, 9723). Since this time, 'clean and green' has also come to be used as a branding and promotion tool, and in 2005 it was reported to be worth $20.17 billion per year (Stewart 2012).

Yet numerous claims are made in both scientific literature and the mass media that this identity and branding tool is fallacious (see, for example, Joy 2011). As a branding tool for tourism it works superbly, with tourism contributing $10.6 billion to the gross domestic product for the year ending March 2015 (Tourism Industry Association New Zealand 2015). In addition, its broad association with New Zealand identity has persisted, including through capture by the genetic engineering (GE) resistance movement prominent in this country from the late 1990s to early 2000s. That movement used the phrase in an effort to align itself with the earlier anti-nuclear movement, promoting a GE and nuclear free 'clean and green' New Zealand (Tucker 2011a, 2011b). But this identity starts to unravel when discourse based on wider environmental indicators is considered.

This nation certainly has a clean and green appearance with its range of geographical features, from glaciers to native forest, and the relatively sparse population. But are appearances deceiving?

The construction of 'clean and green' Aotearoa New Zealand was initially politically motivated and designed to draw New Zealanders into an idyllic and idealised framing, or imagining, of the country that would make people feel proud. It has since been used by some of the same people – in an ironic way – to draw attention to the perceived threats of new biotechnology and, more recently, to the dire condition of fresh waterways (Profitt 2010; Tucker 2011b). In this sense, 'clean and green' has been referred to as something to be maintained, and as something that is threatened. Yet at the same time there is speculation regarding whether 'clean, green New Zealand' is a valid claim to make in the first place. In this vein, the catchphrase can be understood as a national place myth. It is embedded with symbolic meaning that impels a particular mood or identity with reference to a given locale – but it may not be wholly grounded in reality (Coyle and Fairweather 2005). The following discussion probes these ideas a little further by considering some key environmental issues relating to Aotearoa New Zealand.

This chapter begins by looking at how environmental well-being can be measured through ecological footprinting, which considers available biocapacity (or biological capacity) – that is, 'the ecosystem's capacity to produce biological materials used by people and to absorb waste material generated by humans, under current management schemes and extraction technologies' (Global Footprint Network 2015, para. 4). Following on from this is an exploration of two interrelated environmental challenges facing New Zealand – agricultural production and climate change – and a discussion of rates of meat consumption as a problematic part of human dietary consumption. The conclusion draws these areas together to reconsider the question initially posed: How clean and green is Aotearoa New Zealand?

## New Zealand and Ecological Footprint

Ecological footprint is one of several ways to measure a nation's environmental resourcefulness and self-sufficiency. This involves looking at how much 'biologically productive land and water [is] required to produce the resources consumed and to assimilate the wastes generated' by a given number of humans (Harper 2012, 175). As at 2014, the total biocapacity of Earth was estimated at 1.7 global hectares (gha) per capita, which means the maximum amount of land available per capita is 1.7 hectares for sustainable resource extraction, consumption and waste assimilation. But the global ecological footprint per capita reached 2.6 gha at this time (Econation 2015). In short, collectively we are exceeding the planet's biocapacity to a level that would need 1.53 planet Earths to sustain. Ecological footprint varies considerably between different nations given the mass inequalities in resource consumption and availability. Accordingly, it is wealthier individuals who are most responsible for contributing to the global ecological footprint (Alcott 2008).

New Zealand's ecological footprint as at 2012 was an estimated 4.31 gha – more than double the Earth's biocapacity (Econation 2015). Yet given New Zealand's relatively small population compared to productive land available, the estimated biocapacity of this country was 10.19 gha at 2012. This means there is significant reserve capacity – in other words, we have land to spare (Econation 2015). This excess capacity is not due then to New Zealanders being careful about consumption and lifestyle practices; rather, how we live our lives is on average exceedingly unsustainable in an environmental sense. The excess capacity is, instead, the result of our relatively low population. Having land available is a great thing, but it could also mean that it is easier to be complacent and to ignore those practices we engage in, such as the disposal of human, farm and industrial waste into waterways, that in the long term cannot be sustained.

The New Zealand Footprint Project found that over half of this country's ecological footprint (56 per cent) is related to food: its production, processing, waste, refrigeration, transportation and so on (Lawton 2013). Most likely to be disproportionately contributing to this statistic are older, white, wealthier males, as they are less likely to be food insecure and tend to consume foods higher on the food chain that are less sustainable (Carter et al. 2009; Tucker 2014). Two key actions that would reduce the food-related footprint substantially are 1) eliminating meat and fish from diets (for a reduction of 25 per cent from the total footprint); and 2) growing half of our food ourselves (28 per cent reduction of the total footprint) (Lawton 2013). With such high stakes existing around food and environmental sustainability, it is surprising how little political and wider public acknowledgement (and indeed action) there is of the relationship between environmental well-being and the food we eat.

Food production is critical to the New Zealand economy and integral to the cultural and social identity of many. While not usually held up as an environmental problem area unless concerning 'dirty dairying' or methane-producing (farting, belching) cows (Basset-Mens, Ledgard and Boyes 2009; Jay 2007), the relationship between what is produced and eaten and environmental well-being is significant. With around 40 per cent of land in New Zealand used for agricultural purposes (McDowell et al. 2011), most of which is intensive and high-input, the implications for resource use are extensive.

Climate change and fresh potable water availability are arguably the two biggest global environmental threats facing this planet. Climate change due to rapidly increasing amounts of greenhouse gases (GHGs), particularly carbon dioxide and methane, being emitted into the atmosphere has led to a slowly warming planet (global warming) and more frequent, extreme weather events (Ministry for the Environment [MfE] 2010). Challenges around freshwater supply are closely related to climatic change: as climate change impacts intensify, so too will freshwater-related issues, though these will not be equally distributed across the planet (Grantham Institute, Imperial College London 2012).

According to the National Institute of Water and Atmospheric Research (NIWA 2013), freshwater supply in New Zealand is generally plentiful, though droughts do occur regularly and will increase in frequency and duration over the years to come. Most impacted by droughts – or climate change more generally – is agricultural production, which in turn can significantly affect the national economy (NIWA 2013). The interrelationship, then, between climate change, freshwater supply, agricultural production and food consumption is a messy one where each element feeds into the others.

## Agricultural Production

Meat and other animal-derived products are the most resource-intensive foods to produce, making agricultural production one of the most critical and escalating environmental issues facing the planet (Chemnitz and Becheva 2014; Science News 2010). Meat and meat product exports constitute New Zealand's second-largest export next to dairy products (New Zealand Treasury 2012). And, while climate change and water availability affect agricultural production, agricultural production is itself a key sector for the production of GHGs, land degradation, and waterway pollution from fertilisers and run-off from manure and urine (MfE 2007; New Zealand Agricultural Greenhouse Gas Research Centre [NZAGRC] 2010; Tucker 2013).

Globally, agriculture is the second-largest emitter of GHGs (approximately 13 per cent of global emissions in 2011),[1] and emissions are expected to continue increasing (Russell 2014). In New Zealand, this sector is responsible for the largest amount of GHG production, contributing 48 per cent of total national emissions (MfE 2015). In keeping with two international treaties, the United Nations Framework for the Convention on Climate Change (1992) and the Kyoto Protocol (1997) – ratified by New Zealand in 2002 – New Zealand has agreed to reduce its GHG emissions. When the nation ratified the Kyoto Protocol, it agreed to attempt 'reducing its overall emissions of such [greenhouse] gases by at least 5 per cent below 1990 levels in the commitment period 2008 to 2012' (United Nations 1998, 3). While New Zealand's emission targets were met for this period, this was not due to 'absolute reductions in gross domestic emissions', which have instead risen significantly, but is rather 'largely due to forestry offsets . . . and units acquired under the Kyoto flexibility mechanisms' (Richter and Chambers 2014, 62). The challenge of reducing our GHGs then has still not been faced.

Attempts to address the level of GHG emissions from agriculture were first brought into the public spotlight in 2003 when the Fifth Labour Government attempted to introduce a levy payable by farmers to be used towards research on emissions. This proposal was nicknamed the 'fart tax', even though burps or belches are actually more problematic (Fowler 2014). However, Federated Farmers (farmer advocates) organised protests against the move. One protest in particular created quite a spectacle: on 4 September 2003, a protest in Wellington involving around twenty tractors and other utility vehicles drove through the city to Parliament grounds with a petition signed by 64,000 individuals who were opposed to the legislation. Once on Parliament grounds, National Member of Parliament (MP) Shane Ardern drove a tractor up the steps of Parliament, while at another point two cows were led up Parliament steps by National MP Lockwood Smith (Taylor 2003). The legislation never went through.

The next major move to address agricultural emissions in New Zealand occurred in 2010, with the opening of the New Zealand Agricultural Greenhouse Gas Research Centre. The Centre's mission is to 'provide knowledge, technologies and practices which grow agriculture's ability to create wealth for New Zealand in a carbon-constrained world' (NZAGRC 2015). In the meantime, those in the agricultural sector must report biological emissions produced on their farms, but are not required to account for these under the New Zealand Emissions Trading Scheme (NZ ETS) (MfE 2013). Such a move would only occur if it were deemed financially viable for farmers, if technologies were available to assist in emissions reduction, and if our trading partners also progress with addressing their emissions (MfE 2013). Overall, research has found that there is not much confidence in the NZ ETS, and there is some speculation that it is unlikely to be in place beyond 2020 – though what will be in its place is also uncertain (Richter and Chambers 2014).

While the relationship between agricultural production and climate change is important – with significant environmental, social, political and economic implications – there is little reason for confidence that there will be progress on this issue in the near future. That said, the issue will surely become impossible to ignore over time. I propose that the same can also be said of our dietary consumption practices, particularly for produce that is high on the food chain such as meat.

## Food Production Footprint and Meat Consumption

Meat, especially beef, comprises the most resource-intensive food that humans can consume, described by Vinnari and Tapio (2012, 46) as 'the most environmentally harmful foodstuff to produce'. Similar to many wealthy nations, New Zealanders consume far more meat than required for a balanced diet, consistently ranking in the top ten nations for average per capita consumption (Organisation for Economic Co-operation and Development/Food and Agriculture Organization [OECD/FAO] 2015; Tucker 2014). However, meat consumption is not equally distributed. For example, males in Western cultures tend to eat more meat than females (Rozin et al. 2012). Moreover, meat consumption is expected to continue increasing, driven mainly by increasing populations, wealth and urbanisation in rapidly developing nations (Fiala 2008; OECD-FAO 2015), making it increasingly economically attractive for New Zealand farmers to produce meat for export.

Three key areas that together explain why meat is so intensive to produce are water, land and GHGs, especially carbon dioxide and methane. These are all measured to find a food's 'overall footprint', which is the resource intensiveness of a food. Measuring water usage through 'water footprinting' is one way to determine food production requirements. There are three water footprint types: green, blue and grey, each referring to water use at a different stage of food production (Mekonnen and Hoekstra 2010). In simple terms, each footprint type can be defined as follows: green water is the amount of rainwater used during food production; blue water is the amount of ground and surface water (e.g., water from aquifers) used during food production through incorporation into the product or by evaporation; and grey water is the amount of water needed to assimilate pollutants so that water quality remains acceptable (Water Footprint Network 2015). Table 1 takes the total water footprint (green, blue and

**Table 1:** Water footprint of selected food products (by weight) (Mekonnen and Hoekstra 2010).

| Food | Water footprint per ton (m³/ton) | Calorie (calories per kg) | Protein (g per kg) |
|---|---|---|---|
| Vegetables | 322 | 240 | 12 |
| Cereals | 1644 | 3208 | 80 |
| Milk | 1020 | 560 | 33 |
| Eggs | 3265 | 1425 | 111 |
| Chicken | 4325 | 1440 | 127 |
| Pork | 5988 | 2786 | 105 |
| Sheep | 8763 | 2059 | 139 |
| Beef | 15415 | 1513 | 138 |

grey) of selected food products, and compares these with the calories gained and the amount of protein available for each,

It is clear that cereals (e.g., maize) consume a relatively small quantity of water relative to calorific value, and are a greater source of protein than milk. Sheep, and particularly beef, demand an extraordinarily large amount of water comparative to calorific value, with a protein value that does not compare favourably to cereal when the water resource required is considered. In short, the production of red meat for human consumption is particularly water-intensive, and is therefore not necessarily the best way to gain energy and protein nutrition.

Land is a second critical resource that contributes to a food's overall footprint. One way that this can be analysed is by considering the number of people who could have their energy (calorie) needs met by using the same amount of land, dependent on what food is produced on it. A range of food types and the number of people who could have their caloric needs met from 2.5 acres of land is shown in Figure 1.

According to Figure 1, beef and eggs provide enough energy per 2.5 acres to feed only one individual, while chicken and milk provide for two. However, 22 individuals could be sustained by calories from potatoes and 23 from cabbages on the same amount of land. While in practice it is highly unlikely that an individual would exist on cabbages alone (or beef!),

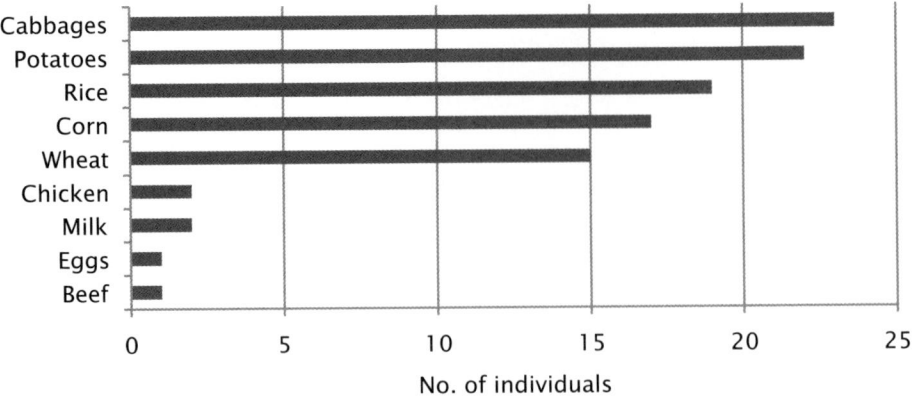

**Figure 1:** Number of individuals who could have their caloric needs met per 2.5 acres of land by food type produced (Robbins 2001).

a pattern similar to that demonstrated in Table 1 in relation to water use emerges: meat and dairy are substantially more resource-intensive.

The question of beef production does warrant some further attention. In New Zealand, beef is mainly grass-fed; there may be some grain added to silage used to feed cattle in winter, and there is grain-finished beef production too (Wakanui 2015), but cattle are not raised on grain alone. On a global scale, however, around 35 per cent of the global grain harvest is fed directly to animals rather than humans, requiring additional pesticides and land to feed the cattle itself (Worldwatch Institute 2013). Perhaps grass-fed beef, for example, is therefore better environmentally? Certainly beef marketing both domestically and internationally suggests grass-fed product is preferable to grain-fed. For example, the Beef+Lamb New Zealand (2015) website markets New Zealand beef to Japan based on the grass-fed 'point of difference' and, in Korea, grass-fed meat is described as using 'natural systems'. Meanwhile, AngusPure's (2015) website markets its beef as 100 per cent New Zealand-grown, 'grass fed' beef. But as Robbins (2001) has pointed out, while feeding grain to cattle requires more land (pesticides and water) to grow the grain, using grass feed tends to mean that more land is required where the animal actually resides (per meat unit). In other words, grass-fed meat production results in less meat per hectare than grain-fed production, and both have

**Table 2:** Carbon footprint of selected food types showing comparison in emissions by equivalent distance travelled by car (Ritchie 2014).

| Food | Carbon dioxide produced per kg of food | Equivalent distance equivalent travelled in average car per 110 g of food |
| --- | --- | --- |
| Sheep | 39.2 | 11 km |
| Beef | 27 | 10.5 km |
| Pork | 12.5 | 4.9 km |
| Chicken | 6.9 | 2.8 km |
| Eggs | 4.8 | 1.5 km |
| Potatoes | 2.9 | 1.2 km |
| Broccoli | 2 | 0.9 km |
| Lentils | 0.9 | 0.1 km |

high food production footprints. In short, either way, beef production is problematic.

A final key area to consider relating to the resources used in the production of given foods is the GHG value (or how much a food contributes to climate change). Table 2 shows the amount of carbon dioxide produced by the production of selected foods and, to help demonstrate the amount of carbon produced, the distance an average-sized car would need to travel to produce the same amount of carbon is provided as a comparison.

Again, red meats feature as the worst products in relation to their carbon dioxide contributions, while lentils and vegetables are more benign. When it comes to anthropogenic (human-induced) climate change, carbon dioxide is the main culprit, with human-induced carbon dioxide production occurring primarily through burning fossil fuels (Environmental Protection Agency 2015). Methane – the second most common GHG – is produced in large quantity, however, by livestock, and given that cattle, sheep and, to a lesser extent, goats are common livestock in New Zealand, it becomes clearer why GHG emissions are a big problem in this country. Table 3 shows how much methane is produced by different species, clearly showing how Western cattle – dairy cows as well as beef cattle – are mass producers of the GHG methane.

**Table 3:** Methane emissions by different species per year (Bell 2009).

| Species | Methane emissions per individual animal per year |
|---|---|
| Western cattle | 120 kg |
| Non-western cattle | 60 kg |
| Sheep | 8 kg |
| Pig | 1.5 kg |
| Human | 0.12 kg |

In sum, the more meat each of us consumes, the more we are contributing to overall environmental harm, in large part because of the volume of resources required in meat production and the GHGs emitted as a result. There's one more factor that is also worthy of consideration here, and that is animal-derived food waste.

Food waste in itself is a growing issue internationally and in New Zealand, where in 2009 organic waste (green and food waste) was the largest (28 per cent) proportion of total waste going to landfill (MfE 2009). Although food waste can occur at any point on the food supply chain, waste resulting from consumer behaviours – 'post-consumer losses', in this case throwing away edible food – is associated with resource-intensive food products such as meat and with developed nations like New Zealand (Parfitt, Barthel and Macnaughton 2010). Around 40 per cent of food is wasted post-consumer in New Zealand households, which in monetary terms equates to around $458 per household, per annum (Broatch 2009; WasteMINZ 2013). Contributing to these figures are variations in what people deem edible, and hence avoidable as food waste. Such variability is associated with a number of factors, notably with cultural norms and the socio-economic status of a household. For example, wealthier people eat higher on the food chain and are also more likely to produce food waste (Tucker and Farrelly 2015). The crucial point here is that a lot of the food going to landfill does not need to make that trip. UK research has found that, when looking at the top five foods disposed of by weight, meat or fish meals are fourth while, by cost, meat and fish meals are at the top (WRAP 2008). So not only do people in developed countries like New Zealand overconsume resource-intensive food, they also throw a lot of it away. As long as consumers continue eating high on the food chain, then agricultural production will likely continue intensifying with the assistance of new technologies, increasing its already significant contribution to environmental degradation and risk (Vinnari and Tapio 2012).

## Clean, Green Aotearoa Revisited

The ecological footprint measure reveals that New Zealand has excess biocapacity, but how we consume and how we use a vast proportion of land in this country is not environmentally sustainable. New Zealand faces big challenges such as attempting to reduce GHGs while ensuring continued freshwater supplies as the climate changes and farming is intensified. The answers to the question of whether New Zealand is clean and green depends on how you look at it. On the one hand, citing excess biocapacity, the country's nuclear-free status and/or the idea that certain other nations are notable for more obvious environmental problems, it could be argued that New Zealand *is* clean and green. On the other hand, if one looks at average per capita meat consumption, a gradually changing climate and the amount of intensive agricultural production occurring, Aotearoa New Zealand is *not* clean and green – and is not set to become so any time soon.

It is important to understand that slogans such as 'clean and green New Zealand' are the result of, and subject to, a broad array of claims-making processes. Such claims-making is related to an individual's or group's values, cultural affiliations, political ideologies and so on. Recognising the range of influences that are involved in upholding or challenging the 'clean, green' Aotearoa identity claim is vital for a more critical understanding not only of this nation, but also of those factors that are both contested and valued about it.

### Note
1   The burning of coal, oil and gas to create electricity was the largest source of emissions.

# References

Adams, Peter J. 2012. *Masculine Empire: How Men Use Violence to Keep Women in Line*. Auckland: Dunmore Press.
Alcott, Blake. 2008. 'The Sufficiency Strategy: Would Rich-World Frugality Lower Environmental Impact?', *Ecological Economics* 64 (4): 770–86.
Allen, Rob, and Vivien Stern, eds. 2007. *Justice Reinvestment: A New Approach to Crime and Justice*. London: International Centre for Prison Studies, King's College.
Althusser, Louis. 1971. *Lenin and Philosophy and Other Essays*. New York: Monthly Review Press.
Anae, Melani. 2014. 'Samoans – History and Migration', *Te Ara – The Encyclopedia of New Zealand*. Updated 8 October 2014. http://www.TeAra.govt.nz/en/samoans/page-1
Anderson, Benedict. 1991. *Imagined Communities: Reflections on the Origin and Spread of Nationalism*. 2nd ed. London: Verso.
Anderson, Kristin L. 2009. 'Gendering Coercive Control', *Violence Against Women* 19 (12): 1444–57.
AngusPure. 2015. 'Our Story'. Accessed 17 November 2015. https://www.anguspure.co.nz/about-anguspure
Armitage, Andrew. 1995. *Comparing the Policy of Aboriginal Assimilation: Australia, Canada, and New Zealand*. Vancouver: UBC Press.
Arrowtown.com. 2016. 'Where History Meets Nature'. Accessed 1 February 2016. http://www.arrowtown.com/
Aspin, Clive. 2002. 'I Didn't Have to Go to a Finishing School to Learn How to Be Gay: Māori Gay Men's Understandings of Cultural and Sexual Identity', in *The Life of Brian: Masculinities, Sexualities and Health in New Zealand*, edited by Heather Worth, Anna Paris and Louisa Allen, 91–103. Dunedin: Otago University Press.
Aspin, Clive, and Jessica Hutchings. 2007. 'Reclaiming the Past to Inform the Future: Contemporary Views of Māori Sexuality', *Culture, Health & Sexuality* 9 (4): 415–27.
Atkinson, Neill. 2003. *Adventures in Democracy: A History of the Vote in New Zealand*. Dunedin: Otago University Press/Electoral Commission.
Auckland Women's Centre. 2011. 'Transgender Women Welcome', *Gossip* (Spring): 3.
Awatere, Donna. 1984. *Māori Sovereignty*. Auckland: Broadsheet.
Baker, Joanne. 2010. 'Claiming Volition and Evading Victimhood: Post-Feminist Obligations for Young Women', *Feminism & Psychology* 20 (2): 186–204.
Baker, Maureen. 2014. *Choices and Constraints in Family Life*. 3rd ed. Don Mills, Ontario: Oxford University Press.
Balibar, Etienne. 1991. 'Racism and Nationalism', in *Race, Nation, Class: Ambiguous Identities*, by Etienne Balibar and Immanuel Wallerstein, translated by Chris Turner, 37–67. London: Verso.
Bannister, Matthew. 2005. 'Kiwi Blokes: Recontextualising White New Zealand Masculinities in a Global Setting', *Genders OnLine*, no. 42. Accessed 21 August 2016. http://researcharchive.wintec.ac.nz/217/1/kiwi_blokes.pdf
Bartley, Allen, and Paul Spoonley. 2005. 'Constructing a Workable Multiculturalism in a Bicultural Society', in *Waitangi Revisited: Perspectives on the Treaty of Waitangi*, edited

# REFERENCES

by Michael Belgrave, Merata Kawharu and David Williams, 136–48. Melbourne: Oxford University Press.

Basset-Mens, Claudine, Stewart Ledgard and Mark Boyes. 2009. 'Eco-Efficiency of Intensification Scenarios for Milk Production in New Zealand', *Ecological Economics* 68 (6): 1615–25.

Bayard, Donn, and Carolyn Young. 2002. 'Ethnic Labelling in the Otago Press, 1860–1995', *New Zealand English Journal* 16: 18–23.

Beaton, Sophia, Trudie Cain, Helen Robinson, Victoria Hearn and ThinkPlace. 2015. *An Insight into the Experience of Rough Sleeping in Central Auckland*. Auckland: Auckland City Mission.

Beck, Ulrich, and Elisabeth Beck-Gernsheim. 2002. *Individualization*. Los Angeles: Sage.

Beck-Gernsheim, Elisabeth. 2002. *Reinventing the Family: In Search of New Lifestyles*, translated by Patrick Camiller. Cambridge: Polity Press.

Bedford, Richard D. 1994. 'Pacific Islanders in New Zealand', *Espace, Populations, Sociétés* 12 (2): 187–200.

——. 2007. 'Pasifika Mobility: Pathways, Circuits and Challenges in the 21st Century'. Paper presented at Thought Leaders Dialogue, Auckland, 30–31 August.

Bedggood, David. 1980. *Rich and Poor in New Zealand: A Critique of Class, Politics and Ideology*. Auckland: Allen & Unwin.

Beef + Lamb New Zealand. 2015. 'Welcome'. Accessed 17 November 2015. http://www.beeflambnz.co.nz/

Belich, James. [1986] 2015. *The New Zealand Wars and the Victorian Interpretation of Racial Conflict*. Auckland: Auckland University Press.

——. 1996. *Making Peoples: A History of the New Zealanders from Polynesian Settlement to the End of the Nineteenth Century*. Auckland: Penguin.

——. 2001. *Paradise Reforged: A History of the New Zealanders: From the 1880s to the Year 2000*. Auckland: Penguin.

Bell, Avril. 2004. 'Relating Māori and Pākehā: The Politics of Indigenous and Settler Identities', PhD, Massey University.

——. 2014. *Relating Indigenous and Settler Identities: Beyond Domination*. Basingstoke: Palgrave Macmillan.

Bell, Claudia. 1996. *Inventing New Zealand: Everyday Myths of Pākehā Identity*. Auckland: Penguin.

Bell, Dan. 2009. 'The Methane Makers', *BBC News Magazine*, 28 October. Accessed 8 September 2015. http://news.bbc.co.uk/2/hi/uk_news/magazine/8329612.stm

Bell, Matthew, Gary Blick, Oscar Parkyn, Paul Rodway and Polly Vowles. 2010. *Challenges and Choices: Modelling New Zealand's Long-Term Fiscal Position*. Working Paper No. 10/01. Accessed 21 August 2016. http://www.treasury.govt.nz/publications/research-policy/wp/2010/10-01/twp10-01.pdf

Bennett, James. 2009. 'Keeping the Wolfenden from the Door? Homosexuality and the "Medical Model" in New Zealand', *Social History of Medicine* 23 (1): 134–52.

Bentley, Hannah. 2014. 'The Cycle of Female Prisoner (Re)Integration: Pathways, Criminal Justice and Imprisonment', MA, Victoria University of Wellington.

Billig, Michael. 1995. *Banal Nationalism*. London: Sage.

Blakely, Tony, Don Simmers and Norman Sharpe. 2011. 'Inequities in Health and the Marmot Symposia: Time for a Stocktake', *New Zealand Medical Journal* 124 (1338): 7–14.

Blanden, Jo, and Lindsey Macmillan. 2011. 'Recent Developments in Intergenerational Mobility', in *The Labour Market in Winter: The State of Working Britain*, edited by Paul Gregg and Jonathan Wadsworth. Oxford: Oxford University Press.

Blunkett, David. 2002. *On a Clear Day*. London: Michael O'Mara Books.
Booth, Charles. 1889. *Life and Labour of the People*. London: Macmillan.
Borrell, Belinda, and Amanda Gregory. 2007. *Politics of Privilege Scoping Project: Final Report*. Palmerston North: Whāriki Research Group, Massey University.
Boston, Jonathan. 1999. 'The Funding of Tertiary Education: Enduring Issues and Dilemmas', in *Redesigning the Welfare State in New Zealand: Problems, Policies, Prospects*, edited by Jonathan Boston, Paul Dalziel and Susan St John, 197–217. Auckland: Oxford University Press.
Boston, Jonathan, and Simon Chapple. 2014. 'Why Child Poverty Should Be Addressed', in *Child Poverty in New Zealand*, by Jonathan Boston and Simon Chapple, 47–58. Wellington: Bridget Williams Books.
Bourdieu, Pierre. 1985. 'The Social Space and the Genesis of Groups', *Theory and Society* 14 (6): 723–44.
Bowman, Richard. 1979. 'Public Attitudes toward Homosexuality in New Zealand', *International Review of Modern Sociology* 9 (2): 229–38.
Bradbury, Martyn. 2014. 'Exclusive: The Prime Minister and the Waitress', *Daily Blog*, 22 April. Accessed 21 August 2016. http://thedailyblog.co.nz/2015/04/22/exclusive-the-prime-minister-and-the-waitress/
Brah, Avtah. 2006. 'Thinking through the Concept of Diaspora', in *The Post Colonial Reader*, edited by Bill Ashcroft, Gareth Griffiths and Helen Tiffin, 443–46. London: Routledge.
Brand, Ulrich, and Nicola Sekler. 2009. 'Postneoliberalism: Catch-All Word or Valuable Analytical and Political Concept? Aims of a Beginning Debate', *Development Dialogue* 51 (January): 5–13.
Brannen, Julia, and Ann Nilsen. 2005. 'Individualisation, Choice and Structure: A Discussion of Current Trends in Sociological Analysis', *Sociological Review* 53 (3): b412–b428.
Brash, Don. 2004. 'Nationhood: Speech to the Orewa Rotary Club', *Scoop*, 27 January. Accessed 15 December 2004. http://www.scoop.co.nz/mason/stories/PA0401/S00220.htm
Brickell, Chris. 2008. *Mates and Lovers: A History of Gay New Zealand*. Auckland: Godwit.
Broad, Joanna B., Michal Boyd, Ngaire Kerse, Noeline Whitehead, Carol Chelimo, Roy Lay-Yee, Martin von Randow, Susan Foster and Martin J. Connolly. 2011. 'Residential Aged Care in Auckland, New Zealand 1988–2008: Do Real Trends over Time Match Predictions?', *Age and Ageing* 40 (4): 487–94.
Broatch, Mark. 2009. 'Welcome to the Wasteland', *Sunday Star Times*, 9 August, pp. C1–C2.
Bromley, Tui. 2014. 'Blogger Puts the Boot In', *Greymouth Star*, 27 January. Accessed 21 August 2016. http://www.greystar.co.nz/content/blogger-puts-boot-0
Brookfield, Jock. 2006. *Waitangi and Indigenous Rights: Revolution, Law and Legitimation*. Rev. ed. Auckland: Auckland University Press.
Brooking, Tom. 1992. '"Busting Up" the Greatest Estate of All: Liberal Māori Land Policy 1891–1911', *New Zealand Journal of History* 26 (1): 78–98.
——. 1996. *Lands for the People? The Highland Clearances and the Colonisation of New Zealand: A Biography of John McKenzie*. Dunedin: Otago University Press.
Brooks, Xan. 2010. 'Hobbit Deal Costs New Zealand Changes in Labour Laws and $25 Million Tax Break', *The Guardian*, 27 October. Accessed 31 October 2016. http://www.theguardian.com/film/2010/oct/27/the-hobbit-deal-new-zealand
Butler, Judith. 2004. *Undoing Gender*. New York: Routledge.
Callister, Paul, James Newell, Martin Perry and David Scott. 2006. 'The Gendered Tertiary Education Transition: When Did It Take Place and What Are Some of the Possible Policy Implications?', *Policy Quarterly* 2 (3): 4–13.

Carlyon, Jenny, and Diana Morrow. 2013. *Changing Times: New Zealand Since 1945*. Auckland: Auckland University Press.

Carrigan, Tim, Robert Connell and John Lee. 1985. 'Toward a New Sociology of Masculinity', *Theory and Society* 14 (5): 551–604.

Carter, Kristie N., Tony Blakely and Matthew Soeberg. 2010. 'Trends in Survival and Life Expectancy by Ethnicity, Income and Smoking in New Zealand: 1980s to 2000s', *New Zealand Medical Journal* 123 (1320): 13–24.

Carter, Kristie N., Michael Hayward, Tony Blakely and Caroline Shaw. 2009. 'How Much and for Whom Does Self-Identified Ethnicity Change over Time in New Zealand? Results from a Longitudinal Study', *Social Policy Journal of New Zealand* 36: 32–45.

Castells, Manuel. 1996. *The Rise of the Network Society*. Cambridge, MA: Blackwell.

Castles, Francis. 1996. 'Needs-Based Strategies of Social Protection in Australia and New Zealand', in *Welfare States in Transition: National Adaptations in Global Economies*, edited by Gosta Esping-Andersen, 88–115. London: Sage.

Chemnitz, Christine, and Stanka Becheva, eds. 2014. *Meat Atlas 2014*. Accessed 21 August 2016. http://www.foeeurope.org/meat-atlas

Cheyne, Christine, Michael O'Brien and Michael Belgrave. 2008. *Social Policy in Aotearoa New Zealand: A Critical Introduction*. 4th ed. Melbourne: Oxford University Press.

Clark, Helen. 2001. 'PM's Euology for Sir Peter Blake', *Beehive.govt.nz*, 6 December. Accessed 21 August 2016. http://www.beehive.govt.nz/node/12645

Clayworth, Peter. 2012. 'Prisons – Māori Imprisonment', *Te Ara – The Encyclopedia of New Zealand*. Updated 13 July 2012. http://www.teara.govt.nz/en/prisons/page-5

Cleland, Alison, and Khylee Quince. 2014. *Youth Justice in Aotearoa New Zealand: Law, Policy and Critique*. Wellington: LexisNexis.

Clifford, James. 1997. *Routes: Travel and Translation in the Late Twentieth Century*. Cambridge, MA: Harvard University Press.

Coffé, Hilde, and Catherine Bolzendahl. 2010. 'Same Game, Different Rules? Gender Differences in Political Participation', *Sex Roles* 62 (5–6): 318–33.

Collini, Stefan. 2010. 'Blahspeak', *London Review of Books* 32 (7): 29–34.

Coney, Sandra. 1993. 'Why the Women's Movement Ran Out of Steam', in *Heading Nowhere in a Navy Blue Suit and Other Tales from the Feminist Revolution*, edited by Sue Kedgley and Mary Varnham, 51–74. Wellington: Daphne Brasell Associates.

Connell, John. 2006. 'Migration, Dependency and Inequality in the Pacific: Old Wine in Bigger Bottles? (Part 1)', in *Globalisation and Governance in the Pacific Islands*, edited by Stewart Firth, 59–80. Canberra: ANU E-Press.

Connell, Raewyn. 2009. *Gender in World Perspective*. 2nd ed. Cambridge: Polity Press.

Connell, Robert W. 1995. *Masculinities*. St Leonards, NSW: Allen & Unwin.

Connolly, Martin J., Joanna B. Broad, Michal Boyd, Ngaire Kerse and Merryn Gott. 2014. 'Residential Aged Care: The De Facto Hospice for New Zealand's Older People', *Australasian Journal on Ageing* 33 (2): 114–20.

Constitutional Advisory Panel/Te Ranga Kaupapa Ture. 2013. *New Zealand's Constitution: A Report on a Conversation*. Accessed 21 August 2016. http://www.ourconstitution.org.nz/store/doc/FR_Full_Report.pdf

Contesse, Jorge, and Jeanmarie Fenrich. 2008. *"It's Not OK": New Zealand's Efforts to Eliminate Violence against Women*. Accessed 21 August 2016. http://www.leitnercenter.org/files/CRNZ08.pdf

Conway, Paul, Lisa Meehan and Dean Parham. 2015. *Who Benefits from Productivity Growth? The Labour Income Share in New Zealand*. Accessed 21 August 2016. https://www.researchgate.net/publication/274711793_Who_benefits_from_productivity_growth_The_labour_income_share_in_New_Zealand

Cook, Daniel. 2002. 'Deregulation and Broadcast News Content: ONE Network News 1984 to 1996', in *New Zealand Television: A Reader*, edited by John Farnsworth and Ian Hutchinson, 139–44. Palmerston North: Dunmore Press.

Cooke, Robin. 1999. 'Unicameralism in New Zealand: Some Lessons', *Canterbury Law Review* 7: 233–45.

Coope, Pat, and Andrea Piesse. 2000. *1991–1996 Intercensal Consistency Study*. Wellington: Statistics New Zealand.

Cooper, Erana. 2012. 'Mokopuna Rising: Intervention in Whānau Violence', PhD, University of Auckland.

Couch, Murray, Marian Pitts, Hunter Mulcare, Samantha Croy, Anne Mitchel and Sunil Patel. 2007. *TranZnation: A Report on the Health and Wellbeing of Transgender People in Australia and New Zealand*. Melbourne: Australian Research Centre in Sex, Health and Society.

Cox, Lindsay. 1993. *Kotahitanga: The Search for Māori Political Unity*. Auckland: Oxford University Press.

Coyle, Fiona, and John Fairweather. 2005. 'Challenging a Place Myth: New Zealand's Clean Green Image Meets the Biotechnology Revolution', *Area* 37 (2): 148–58.

Craig, David, and Douglas Porter. 2006. *Development beyond Neoliberalism? Governance, Poverty Reduction and Political Economy*. New York: Routledge.

Crawford, Claire, Paul Johnson, Steve Machin and Anna Vignoles. 2011. *Social Mobility: A Literature Review*. London: Department for Business, Innovation and Skills.

Crenshaw, Kimberlé. 1991. 'Mapping the Margins: Intersectionality, Identity Politics, and Violence against Women of Color', *Stanford Law Review* 43 (6): 1241–99.

Crick, Bernard. 2002. *Democracy: A Very Short Introduction*. Oxford: Oxford University Press.

Cunningham, Chris, Mason Durie, David Fergusson, Eljon Fitzgerald, Bev Hong, John Horwood, John Jensen, Mike Rochford and Brendan Stevenson. 2002. *Ngā Āhuatanga Noho o te Hunga Pakeke Māori: Living Standards of Older Māori*. Wellington: Ministry of Social Development.

Currie, Elliott. 1997. 'Market, Crime and Community: Toward a Mid-Range Theory of Post-Industrial Violence', *Theoretical Criminology* 1 (2): 147–72.

——. 2007. 'Pulling Apart: Notes on the Widening Gaps in the Risks of Violence', *Criminal Justice Matters* 70 (1): 37–38.

Curtin, Jennifer, and Katharine Teghtsoonian. 2010. 'Analyzing Institutional Persistence: The Case of the Ministry of Women's Affairs in Aotearoa/New Zealand', *Politics & Gender* 6 (4): 545–72.

Dale, M. Claire. 2014. *Turning Silver to Gold: Policies for an Ageing Population*. Auckland: Retirement Policy and Research Centre, University of Auckland.

Dann, Christine. 1985. *Up from Under: Women and Liberation in New Zealand*. Wellington: Allen & Unwin/Port Nicholson Press.

Darity, William, and Jessica Gordon Nembhard. 2000. 'Radical and Ethnic Economic Inequality: The International Record', *American Economic Review* 90 (2): 308–11.

de Raad, Jean-Pierre, and Mark Walton. 2007. 'Pacific People in New Zealand Economy: Understanding Trends and Linkages'. Paper presented at Thought Leaders Dialogue, Auckland, 30–31 August.

Debord, Guy. 1994. *The Society of the Spectacle*. New York: Zone Books.
Delgado, Richard, and Jean Stefancic, eds. 1997. *Critical White Studies: Looking Behind the Mirror*. Philadelphia: Temple University Press.
Demographia. 2015. *World Urban Areas*. 11th annual ed. Accessed 21 August 2016. http://www.demographia.com/db-worldua.pdf
Dennehy, Glennis, and Greg Newbold. 2001. *The Girls in the Gang*. Wellington: Reed.
Department of Corrections. 2007. *Over-Representation of Māori in the Criminal Justice System: An Exploratory Report*. Wellington: Policy, Strategy and Research Group, Department of Corrections.
Didham, Robert, and Paul Callister. 2014. 'Ethnic Intermarriage in New Zealand: A Brief Update'. Research Note. Paekakariki: Callister & Associates.
Doble, John. 2013. 'Attitudes to Punishment in the US: Punitive and Liberal Opinions', in *Changing Attitudes to Punishment: Public Opinion, Crime and Justice*, edited by Julian Roberts and Mike Hough, 148–62. Portland, OR: Willan.
Dominy, Michèle. 1986. 'Lesbian-Feminist Gender Conceptions: Separatism in Christchurch, New Zealand', *Signs* 11 (2): 274–89.
Doone, Peter. 2000. *Reporting on Combating and Preventing Māori Crime*. Wellington: Crime Prevention Unit, Department of the Prime Minister and Cabinet.
Doyle, Jamie Mihoko, and Grace Kao. 2007. 'Are Racial Identities of Multiracials Stable? Changing Self-Identification among Single and Multiple Race Individuals', *Social Psychology Quarterly* 70 (4): 405–23.
Dumpling. 2014. 'Sticks and Stones Are Much Quicker Than Words', *Mellow Yellow* [Blog], 14 October. Accessed 21 August 2016. http://mellowyellow-aotearoa.blogspot.co.at/2014/10/sticks-and-stones-are-much-quicker-than.html
Duncan, Grant. 2007. *Society and Politics: New Zealand Social Policy*. 2nd ed. Auckland: Pearson Prentice Hall.
Dunn, John. 2005. *Setting the People Free: The Story of Democracy*. London: Atlantic.
Dunstall, Graeme. 1981. 'The Social Pattern', in *The Oxford History of New Zealand*, edited by W. H. Oliver, 397–429. Wellington: Oxford University Press.
Dunstan, Stephen, Judy Paulin and Kelly-Ann Atkinson. 1995. *Trial by Peers? The Composition of New Zealand Juries*. Wellington: Policy and Research Division, Department of Justice.
Durie, Mason. 2000. *Ngā Tai Matatū: Tides of Māori Endurance*. Oxford: Oxford University Press.
——. 2001. *Mauri Ora: The Dynamics of Māori Health*. Melbourne: Oxford University Press.
——. 2005. *Nga Tai Matatu: Tides of Māori Endurance*. Melbourne: Oxford University Press.
Dwyer, Peter. 2004. *Understanding Social Citizenship: Themes and Perspectives for Policy and Practice*. Bristol: Policy Press.
Dyall, Lorna, Mere Kepa, Ruth Teh, Rangimārie Mules, Simon A. Moyes, Carol Wham, Karen Hayman et al. 2014. 'Cultural and Social Factors and Quality of Life of Māori in Advanced Age. Te Puawaitanga o Nga Tapuwae Kia Ora Tonu – Life and Living in Advanced Age: A Cohort Study in New Zealand (LiLACS NZ)', *New Zealand Medical Journal* 127 (1393): 62–79.
Eaqub, Shamubeel, and Selena Eaqub. 2015. *Generation Rent: Rethinking New Zealand's Priorities*. Wellington: Bridget Williams Books.
Easton, Brian. 1997. *In Stormy Seas: The Post-War New Zealand Economy*. Dunedin: Otago University Press.

Econation. 2015. 'Ecological Footprint'. Accessed 19 September 2016. http://www.econation.co.nz/ecological-footprint/

'Editorial'. 1883. *New Zealand Herald*, 3. Papers Past. Accessed 10 March 2015. https://paperspast.natlib.govt.nz/newspapers/new-zealand-herald/1883/3/02/4

'Editorial: Antarctic Adventures'. 2008. *Taranaki Daily News*, 12 January, p. 9.

'Editorial: Pakeha, the Name We Can Embrace'. 2001. *New Zealand Herald*, 1 January. Accessed 21 August 2016. http://www.nzherald.co.nz/nz/news/article.cfm?c_id=1&objectid=166995

Edwards, William John Werahiko. 2010. 'Taupaenui: Māori Positive Ageing', PhD, Massey University.

Egoz, Shelley, Jacky Bowring and Harvey C. Perkins. 2001. 'Tastes in Tension: Form, Function, and Meaning in New Zealand's Farmed Landscapes', *Landscape and Urban Planning* 51 (3): 177–96.

Eldred-Grigg, Stevan. 1980. *A Southern Gentry: New Zealanders Who Inherited the Earth*. Wellington: Reed.

Electoral Commission of New Zealand. 2014. '2014 General Election Voter Turnout Statistics'. Accessed 21 August 2016. http://www.elections.org.nz/events/2014-general-election/election-results-and-reporting/2014-general-election-voter-turnout

Ellison-Loschmann, Lis, and Neil Pearce. 2006. 'Improving Access to Health Care among New Zealand's Māori Population', *American Journal of Public Health* 96 (4): 612–17.

England, Paula. 2010. 'The Gender Revolution: Uneven and Stalled', *Gender & Society* 24 (2): 149–66.

Environmental Protection Agency. 2015. 'Carbon Dioxide Emissions'. Accessed 8 September 2015. http://epa.gov/climatechange/ghgemissions/gases/co2.html

Every Child Counts. 2015. 'Child Poverty'. Accessed 1 October 2015. http://www.everychildcounts.org.nz/resources/child-poverty/

Fairbairn-Dunlop, Peggy. 2003. 'Some Markers on the Journey', in *Making Our Place: Growing Up PI in New Zealand*, edited by Peggy Fairbairn-Dunlop and Gabrielle Sisifo Makisi, 19–44. Palmerston North: Dunmore Press.

Families Commission. 2010. *Economic Wellbeing of Sole-Parent Families*. Issues Paper 3. Wellington: Families Commission.

Family Violence Clearinghouse. 2014. *Data Summary: Violence Against Women*. Auckland: Family Violence Clearinghouse.

Family Violence Death Review Committee. 2014. *Fourth Annual Report: January 2013 to December 2013*. Wellington: Family Violence Death Review Committee.

Fanslow, Janet, Elizabeth Robinson, Sue Crengle and Lana Perese. 2010. 'Juxtaposing Beliefs and Reality: Prevalence Rates of Intimate Partner Violence and Attitudes to Violence and Gender', *Violence Against Women* 16 (7): 812–31.

Fiala, Nathan. 2008. 'Meeting the Demand: An Estimation of Potential Future Greenhouse Gas Emissions from Meat Production', *Ecological Economics* 67 (3): 412–19.

Ford, Donna Y., Tarek C. Grantham and James L. Moore III. 2006. 'Essentializing Identity Development in the Education of Students of Color', in *Race, Ethnicity, and Education: Racial Identity in Education*, edited by E. Wayne Ross and Valerie Ooka Pang, 3–18. Westport, CT: Praeger.

Foster, Holly, and John Hagan. 2007. 'Incarceration and Intergenerational Social Exclusion', *Social Problems* 54 (4): 399–433.

Foucault, Michel. 1981. *The History of Sexuality*, vol. 1: *An Introduction*, translated by Robert Hurley. London: Penguin.

Fowler, Nina. 2014. 'Our Problem, Not Our Grandchildren's', *Wireless*, 21 August. Accessed 10 September 2015. http://thewireless.co.nz/themes/impact/changing-the-climate-fighting-the-heat

Francis, Becky. 2002. 'Is the Future Really Female? The Impact and Implications of Gender for 14–16 Year Olds' Career Choices', *Journal of Education and Work* 15 (1): 75–88.

Friedman, Milton. 1962. *Capitalism and Freedom*. Chicago: University of Chicago Press.

Friesen, Warlow. 2009. 'The Demographic Transformation of Inner City Auckland', *New Zealand Population Review* 35 (1): 55–74.

Gavey, Nicola. 2006. 'Viagra and the Coital Imperative', in *Handbook of the New Sexuality Studies*, edited by Steven Seidman, Nancy Fischer and Chet Meeks, 135–41. Abingdon: Routledge.

Gee, Sarah, and Steve J. Jackson. 2010. 'The Southern Man City as Cultural Place and Speight's Space: Locating the Masculinity-Sport-Beer "Holy Trinity" in New Zealand', *Sport in Society* 13 (10): 1516–31.

Gibbons, Peter. 2002. 'Cultural Colonization and National Identity', *New Zealand Journal of History* 36 (1): 5–17.

Giddens, Anthony. 1991. *Modernity and Self-Identity*. Cambridge: Polity Press.

———. 1998. *The Third Way: The Renewal of Social Democracy*. Cambridge: Polity Press.

Gill, Rosalind, and Christina Scharff. 2011. 'Introduction', in *New Femininities: Postfeminism, Neoliberalism and Subjectivity*, edited by Rosalind Gill and Christina Scharff, 1–17. Basingstoke: Palgrave Macmillan.

Gilligan, James. 2003. 'Shame, Guilt and Violence', *Social Research* 70 (4): 1149–80.

Gilling, Ana, and Sandra Grey. 2010. *Representing Women: MMP and Women's Political Representation in New Zealand*. Wellington: Women for MMP.

Gilson, Miriam. 1969. 'Women in Employment', in *Social Process in New Zealand: Readings in Sociology*, edited by John Forster and Joachim Fernau, 183–97. Auckland: Longman Paul.

Global Footprint Network. 2015. 'Glossary'. Accessed 8 September 2015. http://www.footprintnetwork.org/en/index.php/GFN/page/glossary/

Goldingay, Sophie. 2007. 'Jail Mums: The Status of Adult Female Prisoners among Young Female Prisoners in Christchurch Women's Prison', *Social Policy Journal of New Zealand* 31: 56–73.

Goodwin, Ian, Antonia C. Lyons and Christine Stephens. 2014. 'Critiquing the Heteronormativity of the Banal Citizen in New Zealand's Mediated Civil Union Debate', *Gender, Place and Culture* 21 (7): 813–33.

Goodyear, Rosemary, and Angela Fabian. 2014. *Housing in Auckland: Trends in Housing from the Census of Population and Dwellings 1991 to 2013*. Accessed 21 August 2016. http://www.stats.govt.nz/browse_for_stats/people_and_communities/housing/auckland-housing-1991-2013.aspx

Gordon, Liz, and Lesley MacGibbon. 2011. *A Study of the Children of Prisoners: Findings from the Māori Data*. Wellington: Te Puni Kōkiri.

Gordon, Liz, and Missy Morton. 2001. 'Women: Well Educated and Poorly Paid'. Paper presented at the Women's Studies Association Conference, Christchurch, 2 June.

'Govt Ignores UN Recommendation of Work-hour Limit'. 2013. *New Zealand Herald*, 17 January. Accessed 21 August 2016. http://www.nzherald.co.nz/business/news/article.cfm?c_id=3&objectid=10859823

Grace, John T. H. [1959] 1966. *Tuwharetoa: The History of the Maori People of the Taupo District*. Dunedin: A. H. & A. W. Reed.

Gramsci, Antonio. 1971. *Selections from* The Prison Notebooks, edited and translated by Quintin Hoare and Geoffrey Nowell. London: Lawrence & Wishart.

Grantham Institute, Imperial College London. 2012. 'How Will Climate Change Impact on Fresh Water Security?', *Guardian*, 21 December. Accessed 21 August 2016. https://www.theguardian.com/environment/2012/nov/30/climate-change-water

Gray, Mel, and Jennifer Boddy. 2010. 'Making Sense of the Waves: Wipeout or Still Riding High?', *Affilia* 25 (4): 368–89.

Gregory, Amanda, Belinda Borell, Tim McCreanor, Angela Moewaka Barnes, Ray Nairn, Jenny Rankine, Sue Abel et al. 2011. 'Reading News about Māori: Responses from Non-Māori Media Audiences', *AlterNative* 7 (1): 51–64.

Grey, Alan. 1994. *Aotearoa and New Zealand: A Historical Geography*. Canterbury: Canterbury University Press.

Grimshaw, Patricia. 1987. *Women's Suffrage in New Zealand*. 2nd ed. Auckland: Auckland University Press.

Haddon, Edward. 2015. 'Class Identification in New Zealand: An Analysis of the Relationship between Class Position and Subjective Social Location', *Journal of Sociology* 51 (3): 737–54.

Hager, Nicky. 2014. *Dirty Politics: How Attack Politics is Poisoning New Zealand's Political Environment*. Nelson: Craig Potton.

Hansard. 2007. 'Daily Debates. Volume 639, Week 46 – Tuesday, 12 June 2007'. Accessed 21 August 2016. http://www.parliament.nz/en-nz/pb/debates/debates/daily/48HansD_20070612/volume-639-week-46-tuesday-12-june-2007

Hardoon, Deborah. 2015. *Wealth: Having It All and Wanting More*. Oxfam Issue Briefing. Accessed 21 August 2016. http://policy-practice.oxfam.org.uk/publications/wealth-having-it-all-and-wanting-more-338125

Harper, Charles L. 2012. *Environment and Society: Human Perspectives on Environmental Issues*. 5th ed. Upper Saddle River, NJ: Prentice Hall.

Harré, John. 1966. *Maori and Pakeha: A Study of Mixed Marriages in New Zealand*. Wellington: A. H. & A. W. Reed.

Harris, David R., and Jeremiah Joseph Sim. 2002. 'Who Is Multiracial? Assessing the Complexity of Lived Race', *American Sociological Review* 67 (4): 614–27.

Harris, Ricci, Martin Tobias, Mona Jeffreys, Kiri Waldegrave, Saffron Karlsen and James Nazroo. 2006. 'Effects of Self-Reported Racial Discrimination and Deprivation on Māori Health and Inequalities in New Zealand: Cross-Sectional Study', *Lancet* 367 (9527): 2005–9.

Harvey, David. 1996. 'Cities or Urbanization?', *City* 1 (1–2): 38–61.

——. 2005. *A Brief History of Neoliberalism*. Oxford: Oxford University Press.

——. 2014. 'The Crisis of Planetary Urbanization', *Post*, 18 November. Accessed 21 August 2016. http://post.at.moma.org/content_items/520-the-crisis-of-planetary-urbanization

Hastings, David. 2013. 'The 10 Greatest New Zealanders'. *New Zealand Herald*. Accessed 21 August 2016. http://www.nzherald.co.nz/tengreatest/

Hayek, Friedrich. 1944. *The Road to Serfdom*. Oxford: Routledge.

Hayman, Karen, Ngaire Kerse, Lorna Dyall, Mere Kepa, Ruth Teh, Carol Wham, Valerie Wright-St Clair et al. 2012. 'Life and Living in Advanced Age: A Cohort Study in New Zealand – Te Puāwaitanga o Nga Tapuwae Kia Ora Tonu, LiLACS NZ: Study Protocol', *BMC Geriatrics* 12 (33): 1–13.

Hayward, Janine. 2011. 'Mandatory Māori Wards in Local Government: Active Crown Protection of Māori Treaty Rights', *Political Science* 62 (2): 186–204.

Healy, Susan, Ingrid Huygens and Takawai Murphy. 2012. *Ngāpuhi Speaks: He Wakaputanga o te Rangatiratanga o Nu Tireni and Te tiriti o Waitangi Independent Report, Ngāpuhi Nui Tonu Claim*. Whangarei: Te Kawariki and Network Waitangi.

Henderson, Anne. 2013. *Immigrants and Electoral Enrolment: Do the Numbers Add Up?* Working Paper 13-01. Accessed 21 August 2016. http://www.stats.govt.nz/methods/research-papers/working-papers-original/immigrants-electoral-enrolment-13-01.aspx

Henley, John. 2007. 'The Maori Resistance', *Guardian*, 6 November. Accessed 21 August 2016. https://www.theguardian.com/theguardian/2007/nov/06/features11.g2

Hennessy, Rosemary. 2000. *Profit and Pleasure: Sexual Identities in Late Capitalism*. New York: Routledge.

Herbert, Ruth, and Deborah Mackenzie. 2014. *The Way Forward: An Integrated System for Intimate Partner Violence and Child Abuse and Neglect in New Zealand*. Wellington: Impact Collective.

Heywood, Andrew. 2012. *Political Ideologies: An Introduction*. 5th ed. Basingstoke: Macmillan.

Hill Collins, Patricia. 1996. 'What's in a Name? Womanism, Black Feminism, and Beyond', *Black Scholar* 26 (1): 9–17.

Hill, Sarah, Diana Sarfati, Tony Blakely, Bridget Robson, Gordon Purdie, Jarvis Chen, Elizabeth Denett et al. 2010. 'Survival Disparities in Indigenous and Non-Indigenous New Zealanders with Colon Cancer: The Role of Patient Comorbidity, Treatment and Health Service Factors', *Journal of Epidemiology & Community Health* 64 (2): 117–23.

Hilliard, Chris. 1999. 'Stories of Becoming: The Centennial Surveys and the Colonization of New Zealand', *New Zealand Journal of History* 33 (1): 3–19.

Ho, Elsie. 2006. 'Contemporary Migration and Settlement of Chinese Migrants in New Zealand', in *Experiences of Transnational Chinese Migrants in the Asia-Pacific*, edited by David Ip, Raymond Hibbins and Wing Hong Chui, 41–57. New York: Nova Science.

Hoeata, Chloe, Linda Waimarie Nikora, Wendy Li, Amanda Young-Hauser and Neville Robertson. 2011. 'Māori Women and Intimate Partner Violence: Some Sociocultural Influences', *MAI Review*, no. 3: 1–12.

Hokowhitu, Brendan. 2003. '"Physical Beings": Stereotypes, Sport and the "Physical Education" of New Zealand Māori', *Sport in Society* 6 (2–3): 192–218.

———. 2004. 'Tackling Māori Masculinity: A Colonial Genealogy of Savagery and Sport', *Contemporary Pacific* 16 (2): 259–84.

———. 2007. 'The Silencing of Māori Men: Deconstructing a "Space" for Māori Masculinities', *New Zealand Journal of Counselling* 27 (2): 63–76.

———. 2009. 'Māori Rugby and Subversion: Creativity, Domestication, Oppression and Decolonization', *International Journal of the History of Sport* 26 (16): 2314–34.

Hollis, Hinekura. 2013. 'Te Kete Whanaketanga – Rangatahi: A Model of Positive Development for Māori Youth', MA, University of Auckland.

Hopkins, Jason, Anna Sorensen and Verta Taylor. 2013. 'Same-Sex Couples, Families, and Marriage: Embracing and Resisting Heteronormativity', *Sociology Compass* 7 (2): 97–110.

Howard, Sarah, and Robert Allan Didham. 2007. *Ethnic Intermarriage and Ethnic Transference amongst the Māori Population: Implications for the Measurement and Definition of Ethnicity*. Wellington: Statistics New Zealand.

Howland, Peter J. 2014. 'Martinborough: A Tourist Idyll', in *Social, Cultural and Economic Impacts of Wine in New Zealand*, edited by Peter J. Howland, 227–42. Abingdon: Routledge.

Howson, Richard. 2009. 'Theorising Hegemonic Masculinity: Contradiction, Hegemony and Dislocation', in *Migrant Men: Critical Studies of Masculinities and the Migration Experience*, edited by Mike Donaldson, Raymond Hibbins, Richard Howson and Bob Pease, 23–40. London: Routledge.

Human Rights Commission. 2011. *Tracking Equality at Work*. Wellington: Human Rights Commission.

———. 2012. *Report to the United Nations Committee on the Elimination of Racial Discrimination*. Auckland: Human Rights Commission.

Humpage, Louise. 2015. *Policy Change, Public Attitudes and Social Citizenship: Does Neoliberalism Matter?* Bristol: Policy Press.

Hutching, Megan. 2010. *Leading the Way: How New Zealand Women Won the Vote*. Auckland: Harper Collins.

Hyman, Prue. 2015. 'Is Active Intervention Still Needed to Improve the Position of Women in the New Zealand Labour Market? If So, What Can be Done?', *Policy Quarterly* 11 (1): 3–10.

Ifekwunigwe, Jayne O. 1999. *Scattered Belongings: Cultural Paradoxes of 'Race', Nation and Gender*. London: Routledge.

Independent Police Conduct Authority. March 2015. *Report on Police's Handling of the Alleged Offending by 'Roastbusters'*. Wellington: Independent Police Conduct Authority.

Indermauer, David, and Mike Hough. 2013. 'Strategies for Changing Public Attitudes to Punishment', in *Changing Attitudes to Punishment: Public Opinion, Crime and Justice*, edited by Julian V. Roberts and Mike Hough, 198–214. Portland, OR: Willan.

Jackson, Margaret. 1984. 'Sex Research and the Construction of Sexuality: A Tool of Male Supremacy?', *Women's Studies International Forum* 7 (1): 43–51.

Jackson, Moana. 1988. *The Maori and the Criminal Justice System: A New Perspective, He Whaipaanga Hou*. Wellington: Department of Justice.

Jacques, Heather A. K., and Lorraine H. Radtke. 2012. 'Constrained by Choice: Young Women Negotiate the Discourses of Marriage and Motherhood', *Feminism & Psychology* 22 (4): 443–61.

Jagose, Annamarie. 2013. 'The Trouble with Gay Marriage', *Conversation*, 7 November. Accessed 21 August 2016. https://theconversation.com/the-trouble-with-gay-marriage-19196

Jansen, Henrica. 2012. 'Prevalence Surveys on Violence against Women: Challenges around Indicators, Data Collection and Use'. Paper presented at the Expert Group Meeting: Prevention of Violence Against Women and Girls, Bangkok, 17–20 September. Accessed 21 August 2016. http://www.unwomen.org/~/media/Headquarters/Attachments/Sections/CSW/57/EGM/EGM-paper-Henriette-Jansen%20pdf.pdf

Jatrana, Santosh, and Tony Blakely. 2008. 'Ethnic Inequalities in Mortality among the Elderly in New Zealand', *Australian and New Zealand Journal of Public Health* 32 (5): 437–43.

Jay, Mairi. 2007. 'The Political Economy of a Productivist Agriculture: New Zealand Dairy Discourses', *Food Policy* 32 (2): 266–79.

Jenkins, Kuni, and Kay Morris Matthews. 1998. 'Knowing Their Place: The Political Socialisation of Māori Women in New Zealand through Schooling Policy and Practice, 1867–1969', *Women's History Review* 7 (1): 85–105.

Jessop, Bob. 2002. *The Future of the Capitalist State*. Cambridge: Polity Press.

Jewkes, Rachel. 2002. 'Intimate Partner Violence: Causes and Prevention', *Lancet* 359: 1423–29.

Jewkes, Yvonne. 2004. *Media and Crime*. London: Sage.

Johnston, Lynda. 2007. 'Mobilizing Pride/Shame: Lesbians, Tourism and Parades', *Social & Cultural Geography* 8 (1): 29–45.

Jolly, Margaret. 2007. 'Imagining Oceania: Indigenous and Foreign Representations of a Sea of Islands', *Contemporary Pacific* 19 (2): 508–45.

Jones, Pei T. H. 1959. *King Potatau: An Account of the Life of Potatau Te Wherowhero, the First Maori King*. Wellington: Polynesian Society.

Joy, M. 2011. 'The Dying Myth of a Clean, Green Aotearoa', *New Zealand Herald*, April 25. http://www.nzherald.co.nz/business/news/article.cfm?c_id=3&objectid=10721337

Julie. 2015. 'Take Back the Night – AKL – 28th Aug', *Handmirror* [Blog], 18 August. Accessed 21 August 2016. http://thehandmirror.blogspot.co.at/2015/08/take-back-night-akl-28th-aug.html

Kelly, Helen. 2012. 'How the Hobbit Dispute Was Used to Justify Curbs to the Actors' Union', *The Guardian*, November 30. Accessed 31 October 2016. http://www.theguardian.com/commentisfree/2012/nov/30/hobbit-actor-union-dispute

Kelsey, Jane. 1995. *The New Zealand Experiment: A World Model for Structural Adjustment?* Auckland: Auckland University Press.

———. 1999. *The New Zealand Experiment: Success and Failures*. Florence: European University Institute.

———. 2015. *The FIRE Economy: New Zealand's Reckoning*. Wellington: Bridget Williams Books.

Kerse, Ngaire, and LiLACS NZ 2014a. *Extra Help with Daily Activities in Advanced Age: Findings from LiLACS NZ*. Auckland: School of Population Health, University of Auckland.

———. 2014b. *Income in Advanced Age: Findings from LiLACS NZ*. Auckland: School of Population Health, University of Auckland.

———. 2014c. *Participation in Māori Society in Advanced Age: Findings from LiLACS NZ*. Auckland: School of Population Health, University of Auckland.

———. 2014d. *Relationships and Emotional Support in Advanced Age: Findings from LiLACS NZ*. Auckland: School of Population Health, University of Auckland.

Key, John. 2014. Interview with Peter Lucas Jones. *Te Hiku Radio*, 19 November. Kaitaia: Te Reo Irirangi o te Hiku o te Ika.

Keynes, John Maynard. 1936. *The General Theory of Employment, Interest and Money*. New York: Harcourt, Brace & World.

Kiata, Liz, and Ngaire Kerse. 2004. 'Intercultural Residential Care in New Zealand', *Qualitative Health Research* 14 (3): 313–27.

———. 2015. 'Working with the Aged: Lessons from Residential Care', in *Cultural Safety in New Zealand*, edited by Dianne Wepa, 204–19. Port Melbourne: Cambridge University Press.

Kiata, Liz, Ngaire Kerse and Robyn Dixon. 2005. 'Residential Care Workers and Residents: The New Zealand Story', *New Zealand Medical Journal* 118 (1214): 1–11.

Kimmel, Michael and Michael Messner. 1998. 'Introduction', in *Men's Lives*. 4th ed., edited by Michael Kimmel and Michael Messner, xiii–xxii. Needham Heights, MA: Allyn & Bacon.

King, Michael. 1977. *Te Puea: A Biography*. Auckland: Hodder & Stoughton.

———. 1985. *Being Pākehā: An Encounter with New Zealand and the Māori Renaissance*. Auckland: Hodder & Stoughton.

———. 1991. *Pākehā: The Quest for Identity in New Zealand*. Auckland: Penguin.

———. 2003. *The Penguin History of New Zealand*. Auckland: Penguin.

Kingi, Venezia. 1999. 'The Children of Women in Prison', PhD, Victoria University of Wellington.

Kirk, Stacey. 2015. 'More Kiwis with Jobs Needing Financial Assistance, Budgeting Advice', *Stuff*, 6 October. Accessed 21 August 2016. http://www.stuff.co.nz/national/politics/72733827/More-Kiwis-with-jobs-needing-financial-assistance-budgeting-advice

Kramer, Ronald. 2015. 'Neoliberal States and "Flexible Penality": Punitive Practices in District Courts', *New Zealand Sociology* 30 (2): 44–58.

Kruger, Tamati, Mereana Pitman, Di Grennell, Tahuaroa McDonald, Dennis Mariu, Alva Pomare, Teina Mita et al. 2004. *Transforming Whānau Violence: A Conceptual Framework*. Wellington: Te Puni Kōkiri.

Kukutai, Tahu. 2007. 'White Mothers, Brown Children: Ethnic Identification of Māori-European Children in New Zealand', *Journal of Marriage and Family* 69 (5): 1150–61.

——. 2010. 'The Thin Brown Line: Re-Indigenizing Ethnic Inequality in Aotearoa New Zealand', PhD, Stanford University.

——. 2011. 'Contemporary Issues in Māori Demography', in *Māori and Social Issues*, edited by Tracey McIntosh and Malcolm Mulholland, 11–48. Wellington: Huia.

——. 2012. 'Quantum Māori, Māori Quantum: Representations of Māori Identities in the Census, 1857/8–2006', in *Counting Stories, Moving Ethnicities: Studies from Aotearoa New Zealand*, edited by Rosalind McClean, Brad Patterson and David Swain, 27–51. Hamilton: University of Waikato.

Kukutai, Tahu, and Shefali Pawar. 2013. *A Socio-Demographic Profile of Māori in Australia*. National Institute of Demographic and Economic Analysis Working Paper. Hamilton: University of Waikato.

Kukutai, Tahu, and Moana Rarere. 2013. 'Tracking Patterns of Tribal Identification in the New Zealand Census, 1991 to 2006', *New Zealand Population Review* 39: 1–23.

Kuokkanen, Rauna. 2015. 'Gendered Violence and Politics in Indigenous Communities: The Cases of Aboriginal People in Canada and the Sami in Scandinavia', *International Feminist Journal of Politics* 17 (2): 271–88.

Kymlicka, Will. 2007. 'Ethnocultural Diversity in a Liberal State: Making Sense of Canadian Model(s)', in *Belonging? Diversity, Recognition and Shared Citizenship in Canada*, edited by Keith Banting, Thomas Courchene and Leslie Siedle, 39–86. Montreal: Institute for Research on Public Policy.

Larner, Wendy. 2000. 'Neo-Liberalism: Policy, Ideology, Governmentality', *Studies in Political Economy* 63 (Autumn): 5–25.

——. 2007. 'Expatriate Experts and Globalising Governmentalities: The New Zealand Diaspora Strategy', *Transactions of the Institute of British Geographers* 32 (3): 331–45.

Latham, Alan. 2003. 'Urbanity, Lifestyle and Making Sense of the New Urban Cultural Economy: Notes from Auckland, New Zealand', *Urban Studies* 40 (9): 1699–724.

Laurie, Alison J. 2001. *Lesbian Studies in Aotearoa/New Zealand*. New York: Harrington Park Press.

Lawton, Ella. 2013. 'We Can Have Much More Fun Looking After People and the Planet Than We Ever Had Destroying Them'. Accessed 5 September 2015. http://www.sustainable-practice.org/sites/default/files/The%20New%20Zealand%20Footprint%20Web%20File_0.pdf

Lay, Graeme. 1996. *Pacific New Zealand*. Auckland: David Ling.

Leckie, Jacqueline. 1985. 'In Defence of Race and Empire: The White New Zealand League of Pukekohe', *New Zealand Journal of History* 19 (2): 103–29.

Lee, Helen M. 2004. 'All Tongans Are Connected: Tongan Transnationalism', in *Globalization and Culture Change in the Pacific Islands*, edited by Victoria Lockwood, 133–48. Upper Saddle River, NJ: Pearson.

Liava'a, Sharon Alice. 1998. 'Dawn Raids: When Pacific Islanders Were Forced to Go "Home"', MA, University of Auckland.

Lister, Ruth. 2004. 'Introduction', in *Poverty*, by Ruth Lister, 1–11. Cambridge: Polity Press.

Loomis, Terrance. 1990. *Pacific Migrant Labour, Class and Racism in New Zealand: Fresh off the Boat*. Aldershot: Avebury.

Lynch, John, and George Kaplan. 2000. 'Socioeconomic Position', in *Social Epidemiology*, edited by Lisa Berkman and Ichiro Kawachi, 13–35. Oxford: Oxford University Press.

Macdonald, Charlotte. 1999. 'Too Many Men and Too Few Women: Gender's "Fatal Impact" in Nineteenth-Century Colonies', in *The Gendered Kiwi*, edited by Caroline Daley and Deborah Montgomerie, 17–35. Auckland: Auckland University Press.

——. 2009. 'Ways of Belonging: Sporting Spaces in New Zealand History', in *The New Oxford History of New Zealand*, edited by Giselle Byrnes, 269–96. Melbourne: Oxford University Press.

Mackie, Diane M., and Eliot R. Smith. 1998. 'Intergroup Relations: Insights from a Theoretically Integrative Approach', *Psychological Review* 105 (3): 499–529.

Maddison, Sarah, and Marian Sawer, eds. 2013. *The Women's Movement in Protest, Institutions and the Internet: Australia in Transnational Perspective*. Abingdon and New York: Routledge.

Madill, Marg. 2008. 'Civil Unions and the Recognition of Lesbian Relationships: A Reflection on the Context of Aotearoa/New Zealand', *Affilia* 23 (1): 77–86.

Madjar, Irena, Elizabeth McKinley, Marianna Deynzer and Alice van der Merwe. 2010. *Stumbling Blocks or Stepping Stones? Students' Experience of Transition from Low-Mid Decile Schools to University*. Auckland: Starpath Project, University of Auckland.

Mahoney, Paul. 2014. *Men and Women – Moving on Up: What Men and Women Earn after Their Tertiary Education*. Wellington: Ministry of Education.

Mahuta, Robert. 1993. 'Tawhiao, Tukaroto Matutaera Potatau Te Wherowhero, ?–1894', in *The Dictionary of New Zealand Biography, Te Ara – The Encyclopedia of New Zealand*, accessed 22 August 2013, http://teara.govt.nz/en/biographies/2+14/tawhiao-tukaroto-matutaera-potatu-te-wherowhero.

Mandel, Ernest. 1971. *Marxist Economic Theory*, vol. 1. New York: Monthly Review Press.

Mann, Patricia. 1994. *Micro-Politics: Agency in a Postfeminist Era*. Minneapolis: University of Minnesota Press.

Mann, Susan, and Douglas Huffman. 2005. 'The Decentering of Second Wave Feminism and the Rise of the Third Wave', *Science & Society* 69 (1): 56–91.

Marriot, Lisa, and Dalice Sim. 2014. *Indicators of Inequality for Māori and Pacific Peoples*. Public Finance Working Paper 09/2014. Wellington: Business School, Victoria University of Wellington.

Marshall, Thomas H. [1950] 1963. 'Citizenship and Social Class', in *Sociology at the Crossroads*, edited by Thomas Marshall, 67–127. London: Heinemann.

Marx, Karl. 1847. 'Wage Labour and Capital', *Marxist Internet Archive*. Accessed 9 April 2015. https://www.marxists.org/archive/marx/works/1847/wage-labour/ch05.htm

——. [1867] 1976. *Capital: A Critique of Political Economy*, vol. 1. London: Penguin.

Matahaere-Atariki, Donna. 1999. 'A Context for Writing Masculinities', in *Masculinities in Aotearoa/New Zealand*, edited by Robin Law, Hugh Campbell and John Dolan, 104–17. Palmerston North: Dunmore Press.

Matakana Village. 2016. 'Visit Matakana'. Accessed 1 February 2016. http://www.visitmatakana.co.nz/

Mays, Nicholas, John Marney and Erin King. 2013. 'Fiscal Challenges and Changing Patterns of Need for Health and Long-Term Care in New Zealand', *Policy Quarterly* 9 (4): 35–46.

McAllister, Patrick A. 2012. *National Days and the Politics of Indigenous and Local Identities in Australia and New Zealand*. Durham, NC: Carolina Academic Press.

McAloon, James. 2002. *No Idle Rich: The Wealthy in Canterbury and Otago 1840–1914*. Dunedin: Otago University Press.

McClelland, Sarah. 1997. 'Māori Electoral Representation: Challenge to Orthodoxy', *New Zealand Universities Law Review* 17: 272–91.

McCreanor, Timothy. 1996. '"Why Strengthen the City Wall When the Enemy has Poisoned the Well?" An Assay of Anti-Homosexual Discourse in New Zealand', *Journal of Homosexuality* 31 (4): 75–105.

McDowell, Richard W., Ton Snelder, Roger Littlejohn, Matt Hickey, Neil Cox and Doug J. Booker. 2011. 'State and Potential Management to Improve Water Quality in an Agricultural Catchment Relative to a Natural Baseline', *Agriculture, Ecosystems & Environment* 144 (1): 188–200.

McGuinness, Wendy, and Miriam White. 2011. *Nation Dates: Significant Events That Have Shaped the Nation of New Zealand*. Wellington: Sustainable Futures Institute.

McHugh, Paul. 1991. *The Maori Magna Carta: New Zealand Law and the Treaty of Waitangi*. Auckland: Oxford University Press.

McIntosh, Peggy. 1988. *White Privilege and Male Privilege: A Personal Account of Coming to See Correspondences through Work in Women's Studies*. Working Paper No. 189. Wellesley, MA: Wellesley College Center for Research on Women.

McIntosh, Tracey. 2001. 'Hibiscus in the Flax Bush: The Māori-Pacific Interface', in *Tangata O te Moana Nui: The Evolving Identities of Pacific Peoples in Aotearoa/New Zealand*, edited by Cluny Macpherson, Paul Spoonley and Melani Anae, 141–54. Palmerston North: Dunmore Press.

——. 2005. 'Māori Identities: Fixed, Fluid and Forced', in *New Zealand Identities: Departures and Destinations*, edited by James H. Liu, Tim McCreanor, Tracey McIntosh and Teresia Teaiwa. Wellington: Victoria University Press.

——. 2007. 'Power, Powerlessness and Identity'. Paper presented at the TASA Conference: Public Sociologies: Lessons and Trans-Tasman Comparisons, Auckland, 4–7 December. Accessed 21 August 2016. https://www.tasa.org.au/wp-content/uploads/2008/12/241.pdf

——. 2011. 'Marginalisation: A Case Study: Confinement', in *Māori and Social Issues*, edited by Tracey McIntosh and Malcolm Mulholland, 263–82. Wellington: Huia.

McIntosh, Tracey, and Leon Radojkovic. 2012. 'Exploring the Nature of the Intergenerational Transfer of Inequalities Experienced by Young Māori in the Criminal Justice System', in *Indigenising Knowledge for Current and Future Generations*, edited by Deidre Brown, 38–49. Auckland: Ngā Pae o te Māramatanga.

McLeay, Elizabeth. 2011. 'Building the Constitution: Debates; Assumptions; Developments 2000–2010', in *Reconstituting the Constitution*, edited by Caroline Morris, Jonathan Boston and Petra Butler, 3–33. Heidelberg: Springer.

McNamee, Stephen, and Robert Miller. 2009. *The Meritocracy Myth*. 2nd ed. Lanham, MD: Rowman & Littlefield.

McNeill, Kellie. 2011. 'Talking with Their Mouths Half Full: Food Insecurity in the Hamilton Community', PhD, University of Waikato.

McNicholas, Patty. 2004. 'Māori Feminism: A Contribution to Accounting Research and Practice'. Paper presented at the Asia Pacific Interdisciplinary Research in Accounting Conference, Singapore, 4–6 July.

McRobbie, Angela. 2011. 'Beyond Post-Feminism', *Public Policy Research* 18 (3): 179–84.

Mead, Hirini. 2003. *Tikanga Māori: Living by Māori Values*. Wellington: Huia.

Mead, Lawrence. 1997. 'Welfare Employment', in *The New Paternalism: Supervisory Approaches to Poverty*, edited by Lawrence Mead, 39–88. Washington, DC: Brookings Institution Press.

Meissner, Fran, and Steven Vertovec. 2015. 'Comparing Super-diversity', *Ethnic and Racial Studies* 38 (4): 541–55.

Mekonnen, Mesfin, and Arjen Hoekstra. 2010. *The Green, Blue and Grey Water Footprint of Farm Animals and Animal Products*, vol. 1: *Main Report*. Netherlands: UNESCO-IHE Institute for Water Education.

Meleisea, Malama. 1987. *The Making of Modern Samoa: Traditional Authority and Colonial Administration in the History of Western Samoa*. Fiji: Institute of Pacific Studies.

Mentjox, Lauren. 2006. 'Highly-qualified Immigrants Forced into Low-paid Jobs', *New Zealand Herald*, 23 August. Accessed 21 August 2016. http://www.nzherald.co.nz/nz/news/article.cfm?c_id=1&objectid=10397681

Meredith, Paul. 2009. 'Urban Māori – Urbanisation', *Te Ara – The Encyclopedia of New Zealand*. Updated 24 August 2015. http://www.teara.govt.nz/en/urban-Māori

Metge, Joan. 1964. *A New Maori Migration: Rural and Urban Relations in Northern New Zealand*. London: University of London/Athlone Press.

Mila, Karlo. 2005. 'For Sia Figiel', in *Dream Fish Floating* by Karlo Mila, 13. Wellington: Huia.

——. 2013. 'Only One Deck', in *Inequality: A New Zealand Crisis*, edited by Max Rashbrooke, 99–108. Wellington: Bridget Williams Books.

Miles, Robert. 1982. *Racism and Migrant Labour*. London: Routledge.

——. 1984. 'Summoned by Capital: The Political Economy of Labour Migration', in *Tauiwi: Racism and Ethnicity in New Zealand*, edited by Cluny Macpherson, Paul Spoonley, David Pearson and Charles Sedgwick. Palmerston North: Dunmore Press.

Miller, Linda, and Rowena Hayward. 2006. 'New Jobs, Old Occupational Stereotypes: Gender and Jobs in the New Economy', *Journal of Education and Work* 19 (1): 67–93.

Ministry for Culture and Heritage. 2014a. 'Assisted Immigration to New Zealand 1947–1975'. Updated 5 August 2014. http://www.nzhistory.net.nz/culture/assisted-immigration-to-nz-from-the-uk

——. 2014b. 'Read the Treaty Page 2 – Māori Text'. Updated 3 July 2014. http://www.nzhistory.net.nz/politics/treaty/read-the-treaty/maori-text

——. 2016. 'The 1835 Declaration of Independence'. Updated 16 May 2016. http://www.nzhistory.net.nz/media/interactive/the-declaration-of-independence

Ministry for the Environment. 2007. *Environment New Zealand 2007*. Accessed 21 August 2016. http://www.mfe.govt.nz/publications/environmental-reporting/environment-new-zealand-2007

——. 2009. *Solid Waste Composition Environmental Report Card July 2009*. Accessed 21 August 2016. http://www.mfe.govt.nz/environmental-reporting/waste/waste-composition-2009/index.html

——. 2010. 'About Climate Change'. Accessed 15 September 2015. https://www.climatechange.govt.nz/science/what-is-climate-change.html

——. 2013. *Agriculture in the Emissions Trading Scheme*. Accessed 15 September 2015. http://www.climatechange.govt.nz/emissions-trading-scheme/participating/agriculture/

——. 2015. *New Zealand's Greenhouse Gas Inventory 1990–2013*. Accessed 21 August 2016. http://www.mfe.govt.nz/publications/climate-change/new-zealands-greenhouse-gas-inventory-1990-2013

Ministry of Business, Innovation and Employment. 2015. 'The Māori Economy'. Accessed 1 October 2015. http://www.mbie.govt.nz/info-services/infrastructure-growth/maori-economic-development/the-maori-economy

Ministry of Education. 2011. *Student Loan Scheme: Annual Report*. Wellington: Ministry of Education.
——. 2014. *Student Loan Scheme: Annual Report 2013/14*. Wellington: Ministry of Education.
Ministry of Health. 2002. *Health of Older People Strategy: Health Sector Action to 2010 to Support Positive Ageing*. Wellington: Ministry of Health.
——. 2006. *Health of Older People Information Strategic Plan: Directions to 2010 and Beyond*. Wellington: Ministry of Health.
——. 2010. *Tatau Kahukura: Māori Health Chart Book 2010*. Wellington: Ministry of Health.
——. 2011. *Tatau Kura Tangata: Health of Older Māori Chart Book 2011*. Wellington: Ministry of Health.
——. 2014. *New Zealand Health Statistics*. Wellington: Ministry of Health.
Ministry of Health and University of Otago. 2006. *Decades of Disparity III: Ethnic and Socioeconomic Inequalities in Mortality, New Zealand 1981–1999*. Wellington: Ministry of Health.
Ministry of Justice. 2006. *Effective Interventions: Cabinet Paper 4: Remand in Custody*. Wellington: Ministry of Justice.
——. 2012. *Evaluation of the Early Outcomes of Ngā Kooti Rangatahi*. Wellington: Ministry of Justice.
——. 2014. *New Zealand Crime and Safety Survey: Main Findings*. Wellington: Ministry of Justice.
Ministry of Social Development. 2009. *Non-Income Measures of Material Wellbeing and Hardship: First Results from the 2008 New Zealand Living Standards Survey, with International Comparisons*. Wellington: Ministry of Social Development.
——. 2010. *The Social Report 2010*. Accessed 20 October 2014. http://socialreport.msd.govt.nz/index.html
——. 2014. *Household Incomes in New Zealand: Trends in Indicators of Inequality and Hardship 1982 to 2013*. Wellington: Ministry of Social Development.
——. 2015a. *An Ageing Population*. https://www.msd.govt.nz/what-we-can-do/seniorcitizens/positive-ageing/trends/ageing-population.html
——. 2015b. *Household Incomes in New Zealand: Trends and Indicators of Inequality and Hardship 1982 to 2014*. Accessed 1 October 2015. http://www.msd.govt.nz/about-msd-and-our-work/publications-resources/monitoring/household-incomes/index.html
Ministry of Women's Affairs. 2015a. 'Gender Pay Gap'. Accessed 9 October 2015. http://women.govt.nz/our-work/utilising-womens-skills/income/gender-pay-gap
——. 2015b. 'Occupational Segregation'. Accessed 9 October 2015. http://women.govt.nz/our-work/utilising-womens-skills/paid-and-unpaid-work/occupational-segregation
——. 2015c. 'Retirement Income Prospects'. Accessed 9 October 2015. http://women.govt.nz/our-work/utilising-womens-skills/income/retirement-income-prospects
Mitchell, Austin. 1972. *The Half-Gallon Quarter-Acre Pavlova Paradise*. Christchurch: Whitcombe & Tombs.
——. 2002. *Pavlova Paradise Revisited: A Guide to the Strange but Endearing Land Where Kiwis Live*. Wellington: Penguin.
Mohsin, Asad, and Jorge Lengler. 2015. 'Exploring the Antecedents of Staff Turnover within the Fast-Food Industry: The Case of Hamilton, New Zealand', *Journal of Human Resources in Hospitality & Tourism* 14 (1): 1–24.
Moore, Henrietta. 1994. 'The Problem of Explaining Violence in the Social Sciences', in *Sex and Violence: Issues in Representation and Experience*, edited by Penelope Harvey and Peter Gow, 138–55. London: Routledge.

Morris, Allison, and James Reilly. 2003. *The 2001 New Zealand National Survey of Crime Victims*. Wellington: Ministry of Justice.

Morrison, Bronwyn, Nataliya Soboleva and Jin Chong. 2008. *Conviction and Sentencing of Offenders in New Zealand: 1997 to 2006*. Wellington: Ministry of Justice.

Morrison, Philip. 2015. 'Who Cares About Income Inequality?', *Policy Quarterly* 11 (1): 56–62.

Munro, Doug. 1996. 'Logan, Robert', *Te Ara – The Encyclopedia of New Zealand*. Updated 5 November 2013. http://www.teara.govt.nz/en/biographies/3l12/logan-robert

Murphy, Laurence. 2008. 'Third-Wave Gentrification in New Zealand: The Case of Auckland', *Urban Studies* 45 (12): 2521–40.

Murphy, Nigel. 2003. '*Joe Lum v. The Attorney General*: The Politics of Exclusion', in *Unfolding History, Evolving Identity: The Chinese in New Zealand*, edited by Manying Ip, 48–67. Auckland: Auckland University Press.

Murray, David A. B. 2003. 'Who Is Takatāpui? Māori Language, Sexuality and Identity in Aotearoa/New Zealand', *Anthropologica* 45 (2): 233–44.

Mussen, Deidre, and Nicole Mathewson. 2015. 'Midwives Drop Bombshell with Court Action over Pay Discrimination', *Stuff*, 30 August. Accessed 21 August 2016. http://www.stuff.co.nz/business/better-business/71536143/Midwives-drop-bombshell-with-court-action-over-pay-discrimination

Nana, Ganesh, Fiona Stokes and Wilma Molano. 2011. *The Asset Base, Income, Expenditure, and GDP of the 2010 Māori Economy*. Wellington: Te Puni Kōkiri/BERL Economics.

National Institute of Water and Atmospheric Research. 2013. 'NZ Drought Monitor'. Accessed 15 September 2015. https://www.niwa.co.nz/climate/information-and-resources/drought

National Party. 2014a. 'Welfare Reform', Wellington: National Party. https://www.national.org.nz/docs/default-source/PDF/2014/policy/welfare-reform-policy.pdf

——. 2014b. 'Workplaces', Wellington: National Party. https://www.national.org.nz/docs/default-source/PDF/2014/policy/workplaces-policy.pdf

Neate, Rupert. 2015. 'America's Trailer Parks: The Residents May Be Poor but the Owners Are Getting Rich', *Guardian*, 2 May. Accessed 21 August 2016. https://www.theguardian.com/lifeandstyle/2015/may/03/owning-trailer-parks-mobile-home-university-investment

Neckel, Sighard. 1996. 'Inferiority: From Collective Status to Deficient Individuality', *Sociological Review* 1 (1): 17–34.

New Zealand Agricultural Greenhouse Gas Research Centre. 2010. 'New Zealand Agricultural Greenhouse Gas Research Centre Strategy and Science Plan', http://www.nzagrc.org.nz.

——. 2015. 'Vision & Goals'. Accessed 21 August 2016. http://www.nzagrc.org.nz/mission-vision-goals.html

New Zealand College of Midwives. 2015. 'Midwives Take Legal Action' [Press release], 30 August. Accessed 21 August 2016. https://www.midwife.org.nz/latest-news/midwives-take-legal-action/

New Zealand Council of Trade Unions. 2013. *Under Pressure: A Detailed Report into Insecure Work in New Zealand*. Wellington: New Zealand Council of Trade Unions.

New Zealand Government. 2010. 'Social Assistance (Future Focus) Bill'. *New Zealand Legislation*. Accessed 21 August 2016. http://www.legislation.govt.nz/bill/government/2010/0125/9.0/whole.html

New Zealand Network Against Food Poverty. 2000. *Hidden Hunger: Food and Low Income in New Zealand*. Wellington: Downtown Community Ministry.

New Zealand Parliament. 1867. *Parliamentary Debates 1867*, vol. 2: 336. Wellington: Government Printer.

——. 2013. 'Women, the Vote and the 1893 Election'. Accessed 21 August 2016. http://www.parliament.nz/en-nz/features/00NZPHomeNews201311281/women-the-vote-and-the-1893-election

New Zealand Treasury. 1987. *Government Management: Brief to the Incoming Government*, vol. 1. Wellington: New Zealand Treasury.

——. 2012. 'Composition of Merchandise Exports and Imports'. Accessed 21 August 2016. http://www.treasury.govt.nz/economy/overview/2012/20.htm

Nolan, Melanie. 2007. 'The Reality and Myth of New Zealand Egalitarianism: Explaining the Pattern of a Labour Historiography at the Edge of Empires', *Labour History Review* 72 (2): 113–34.

Nunn, Alex, Steve Johnson, Surya Monro, Tim Bickerstaffe and Sarah Kelsey. 2007. *Factors Influencing Social Mobility: Research Report 450*. Wellington: Department for Work and Pensions.

Oates, Joyce Carol. 1999. 'After Amnesia', in *The Best American Essays 1999*, edited by Edward Hoagland, 188–200. Boston: Houghton Mifflin.

O'Connor, Peter. 1996. 'Pākehā and Proud', *New Zealand Journal of Social Studies* 5 (2): 11–14.

Office for Senior Citizens. 2001. *Positive Ageing Strategy*. Accessed 21 August 2016. http://www.msd.govt.nz/about-msd-and-our-work/publications-resources/planning-strategy/positive-ageing/

O'Keefe, Theresa. 2014. 'My Body Is My Manifesto! SlutWalk, FEMEN and Femmenist Protest', *Feminist Review* 107 (1): 1–19.

Oliver, Steven. 1990. 'Te Wherowhero, Potatau, ?–1860', in *The Dictionary of New Zealand Biography*, vol. 1, edited by W. H. Oliver, 526–8. Wellington: Allen & Unwin/Department of Internal Affairs.

O'Malley, Patrick. 1973. 'The Amplification of Māori Crime: Cultural and Economic Barriers to Equal Justice in New Zealand', *Race & Class* 15 (1): 47–57.

Ongley, Patrick. 1996. 'Immigration, Employment and Ethnic Relations', in *Nga Patai: Racism and Ethnic Relations in Aotearoa/New Zealand*, edited by Cluny Macpherson, David Pearson and Paul Spoonley, 17–36. Palmerston North: Dunmore Press.

——. 2004. 'Ethnicity, Migration and the Labour Market', in *Tangata Tangata: The Changing Ethnic Contours of New Zealand*, edited by Cluny Macpherson, David Pearson and Paul Spoonley, 199–220. Southbank, VIC: Thomson/Dunmore Press.

Orange, Claudia. 1987. *The Treaty of Waitangi*. Wellington: Allen & Unwin.

Organisation for Economic Co-operation and Development. 2009. *The Role of Agriculture and Farm Household Diversification in the Rural Economy of New Zealand*. Accessed 21 August 2016. http://www.oecd.org/agriculture/agricultural-policies/43245582.pdf

——. 2010. 'A Family Affair: Intergenerational Social Mobility across OECD Countries'. Accessed 21 August 2016. https://www.oecd.org/centrodemexico/medios/44582910.pdf

——. 2011. 'An Overview of Growing Income Inequalities in OECD Countries'. Accessed 21 August 2016. https://www.oecd.org/els/soc/49499779.pdf

——. 2014. 'Income Inequality Update – June 2014'. Accessed 21 August 2016. https://www.oecd.org/els/soc/OECD2014-Income-Inequality-Update.pdf

——. 2015. 'Social Expenditure Database'. Accessed 21 August 2016. http://www.oecd.org/social/expenditure.htm

Organisation for Economic Co-operation and Development/Food and Agriculture Organization. 2015. *OECD-FAO Agricultural Outlook 2015–2024*. Accessed 21 August 2016. http://www.fao.org/3/a-i4738e.pdf

O'Sullivan, Dominic. 2007. *Beyond Biculturalism: The Politics of an Indigenous Minority*. Wellington: Huia.

Oxfam New Zealand. 2014. 'Richest 10% of Kiwis Control More Wealth Than Remaining 90%' [Press release]. Accessed 21 August 2015. http://www.oxfam.org.nz/news/richest-10-kiwis-control-more-wealth-remaining-90#sthash.SVRURl2X.dpuf

Page, Dorothy. 1993. *The Suffragists: Women Worked for the Vote: Essays from the Dictionary of New Zealand Biography*. Wellington: Bridget Williams Books/Department of Internal Affairs.

Palmer, Geoffrey. 2013. *Reform: A Memoir*. Wellington: Victoria University Press.

Papatsoumas, Nikki. 2015. 'IPCA: Police "Let Down" Roast Busters' Alleged Victims', *New Zealand Herald*, 19 March. Accessed 21 August 2016. http://www.nzherald.co.nz/nz/news/article.cfm?c_id=1&objectid=11419766

Parfitt, Julian, Mark Barthel and Sarah Macnaughton. 2010. 'Food Waste within Food Supply Chains: Quantification and Potential for Change to 2050', *Philosophical Transactions of the Royal Society of London B: Biological Sciences* 365 (1554): 3065–81.

Paris, Anna, Heather Worth and Louisa Allen. 2002. 'Introduction', in *Life of Brian: Masculinities, Sexualities and Health in New Zealand*, edited by Heather Worth, Anna Paris and Louisa Allen, 11–26. Dunedin: Otago University Press.

Park, Hong-Jae, and Change Gi Kim. 2013. 'Ageing in an Inconvenient Paradise: The Immigrant Experiences of Older Korean People in New Zealand', *Australasian Journal on Ageing* 32 (3): 158–62.

Parker, John. 2005. *Frontier of Dreams: From Treaty to Nationhood, 1830s–1913*. Auckland: Scholastic.

Patterson, Brad. 2012. 'Rhodes, William Barnard', *Te Ara – The Encyclopedia of New Zealand*. Updated 30 October 2012. http://www.teara.govt.nz/en/biographies/1r7/1

Patterson, John. 1992. *Exploring Māori Values*. Palmerston North: Dunmore Press.

Patterson, Lesley, and Katherine Forbes. 2012. '"Doing Gender" in the Imagined Futures of Young New Zealanders', *Young: Nordic Journal of Youth Research* 20 (2): 119–36.

Patterson, Lesley, Robin Peace, Bronwyn Campbell and Christy Parker. 2007. *Lifelines: Young New Zealanders Imagine Family, Friends and Relationships across their Life-Course*. Wellington: Families Commission.

Payne, Geoff. 2012. 'A New Social Mobility? The Political Redefinition of a Sociological Problem', *Contemporary Social Science* 7 (1): 55–71.

Pearson, David. 1989. 'Pākehā Ethnicity: Concept or Conundrum?', *Sites* 18: 61–72.

——. 1990. *A Dream Deferred: The Origins of Ethnic Conflict in New Zealand*. Wellington: Allen & Unwin/Port Nicholson Press.

——. 2001. *The Politics of Ethnicity in Settler Societies: States of Unease*. Basingstoke: Palgrave.

Peck, Jamie, Nik Theodore and Neil Brenner. 2012. 'Neoliberalism Resurgent? Market Rule after the Great Recession', *South Atlantic Quarterly* 111 (2): 265–88.

Peck, Jamie, and Adam Tickell. 2002. 'Neoliberalizing Space', *Antipode* 34 (3): 380–404.

Penetito, Wally. 2011. 'Kaupapa Māori Education: Research as the Exposed Edge', in *Kei Tua o te Pae Hui Proceedings: The Challenges of Kaupapa Māori Research in the 21st Century*, edited by Jessica Hutchings, Helen Potter and Katrina Taupo, 38–43. Wellington: New Zealand Council for Educational Research.

Petrie, Hazel. 2006. *Chiefs of Industry: Māori Tribal Enterprise in Early Colonial New Zealand*. Auckland: Auckland University Press.

Phillips, Jock. 1996. *A Man's Country? The Image of the Pakeha Male: A History*. Auckland: Penguin.

Phillips, Susan, and Barbara Bloom. 1998. 'In Whose Best Interest? The Impact of Changing Public Policy on Relatives Caring for Children with Incarcerated Parents', *Child Welfare* 77 (5): 531–41.

Pickles, Katie. 2009. 'Colonisation, Empire and Gender', in *The New Oxford History of New Zealand*, edited by Giselle Byrnes, 219–41. Melbourne: Oxford University Press.

Poata-Smith, Evan. 2004. 'Ka Tika a Muri, Ka Tika a Mua? Māori Protest Politics and the Waitangi Settlement Process', in *Tangata, Tangata: The Changing Ethnic Contours of New Zealand*, edited by Paul Spoonley, Cluny Macpherson and David Pearson, 59–88. Palmerston North: Dunmore Press.

——. 2013. 'Inequality and Māori', in *Inequality: A New Zealand Crisis*, edited by Max Rashbrooke, 153–62. Wellington: Bridget Williams Books.

Pomerantz, Shauna, Rebecca Raby and Andrea Stefanik. 2013. 'Girls Run the World? Caught between Sexism and Postfeminism in School', *Gender & Society* 27 (2): 185–207.

Poupart, Lisa. 2003. 'The Familiar Face of Genocide', *Hypatia* 18 (2): 86–100.

Pratt, John. 2006. 'The Dark Side of Politics: Explaining New Zealand's History of High Imprisonment', *British Journal of Criminology* 46: 541–60.

——. 2007. *Penal Populism*. New York: Taylor & Francis.

——. 2008a. 'Penal Scandal in New Zealand', in *Penal Populism, Sentencing Councils and Sentencing Policy*, edited by Arie Freiberg and Karen Gelb, 31–44. New York: Routledge.

——. 2008b. 'When Penal Populism Stops: Legitimacy, Scandal and the Power to Punish in New Zealand', *Australian and New Zealand Journal of Criminology* 41 (3): 384–401.

Pratt, John, and Marie Clark. 2005. 'Penal Populism in New Zealand', *Punishment & Society* 7 (3): 303–22.

Pringle, Richard, and Pirkko Markula. 2005. 'No Pain is Sane after All: A Foucauldian Analysis of Masculinities and Men's Experiences in Rugby', *Sociology of Sport Journal* 22 (4): 472–97.

Pringle, Richard, and Paul Whitinui. 2009. 'Navigating Masculinities across the Cultural Ditch: Tales from Māori Men in Australia', in *Migrant Men: Critical Studies of Masculinities and the Migration Experience*, edited by Mike Donaldson, Raymond Hibbins, Richard Howson and Bob Pease, 190–209. New York: Routledge.

Pritchard, Cameron. 2005. 'The Discourses of Homosexual Law Reform', in *Sexuality Down Under: Social and Historical Perspectives*, edited by Alison Kirkman and Pat Moloney, 79–96. Dunedin: Otago University Press.

Profitt, Fiona. 2010. 'How Clean Are Our Rivers?'. Accessed 21 August 2016. https://www.niwa.co.nz/publications/wa/water-atmosphere-1-july-2010/how-clean-are-our-rivers

Pusey, Michael. 1993. 'Reclaiming the Middle Ground: From New Right Economic Rationalism', in *Economic Rationalism: Dead End or Way Forward?*, edited by Stephen King and Peter Lloyd, 12–27. Sydney: Allen & Unwin.

Quince, Khylee. 2007. 'Māori and the Criminal Justice System in New Zealand', in *Criminal Justice in New Zealand*, edited by Julia Tolmie and Warren Brookbanks, 333–58. Wellington: LexisNexis.

——. 2008. 'Māori Women in Prison: Ngā Wahine Ngaro', MA, University of Auckland.

Radio New Zealand. 2013. 'Govt Faced Intense Pressure over Hobbit', *Radio New Zealand*, 26 February. Accessed 21 August 2016. http://www.radionz.co.nz/news/political/129127/govt-faced-intense-pressure-over-hobbit

Rashbrooke, Max. 2013a. 'Inequality and New Zealand', in *Inequality: A New Zealand Crisis*, edited by Max Rashbrooke, 20–34. Wellington: Bridget Williams Books.

——. 2013b. 'Why Inequality Matters', in *Inequality: A New Zealand Crisis*, edited by Max Rashbrooke, 1–19. Wellington: Bridget Williams Books.
——, ed. 2013c. *Inequality: A New Zealand Crisis*. Wellington: Bridget Williams Books.
Rata, Arama. 2012. 'Te Pītau o Te Tuakiri: Affirming Māori Identities and Promoting Wellbeing in State Secondary Schools', PhD, Victoria University of Wellington.
Rata, Elizabeth. 2000. *A Political Economy of Neotribal Capitalism*. Lanham, MD: Lexington.
Rattansi, Ali. 2005. 'The Uses of Racialization: The Time-Spaces and Subject-Objects of the Raced Body', in *Racialisation Studies in Theory and Practice*, edited by Karim Murji and John Solomos, 271–301. Oxford: Oxford University Press.
Rei, Tania. 1993. *Māori Women and the Vote*. Wellington: Huia.
Renan, Ernest. [1882] 1990. 'What Is a Nation?', in *Nation and Narration*, edited by Homi K. Bhabha, 8–22. London: Routledge.
Renzetti, Claire M., and Jeffrey L. Edleson, eds. 2008. *Encyclopedia of Interpersonal Violence*, vol. 1. London: Sage.
Rich, Adrienne. 1980. 'Compulsory Heterosexuality and Lesbian Existence', *Signs* 5 (4): 631–60.
Richards, Len. 2003. 'Class Struggle and Traveling Theory: From the Chile Experience to the New Zealand Experiment', *New Zealand Sociology* 18 (2): 115–34.
Richardson, Ruth. 1995. *Making a Difference*. Christchurch: Shoal Bay Press.
Richmond, James Crowe. 1865. 'Native Commission Bill', in *New Zealand Parliamentary Debates, 1864–66*. Wellington: Government Printer.
Richter, Jessika Luth, and Lizzie Chambers. 2014. 'Reflections and Outlook for the New Zealand ETS. Must Uncertain Times Mean Uncertain Measures?', *Policy Quarterly* 10 (2): 57–66.
Rishworth, Paul. 2007. 'Changing Times, Changing Minds, Changing Laws – Sexual Orientation and the New Zealand Law, 1960 to 2005', *International Journal of Human Rights* 11 (1–2): 85–107.
Risman, Barbara, and Georgiann Davis. 2013. 'From Sex Roles to Gender Structure', *Current Sociology* 61 (5–6): 733–55.
Ritchie, Hannah. 2014. 'Grocery Carbon-Coloured Shelving', *Climate CoLab*. Accessed 7 September 2015. http://climatecolab.org/plans/-/plans/contestId/1300207/planId/1309101
Robbins, John. 2001. *The Food Revolution*. Berkeley, CA: Conari Press.
Roberts, Julian V. 2013. 'Public Opinion and the Nature of Community Penalties: International Findings', in *Changing Attitudes to Punishment: Public Opinion, Crime and Justice*, edited by Julian V. Roberts and Mike Hough, 33–62. Portland, OR: Willan.
Roberts, Julian V., and Mike Hough. 2005. *Understanding Public Attitudes to Criminal Justice*. New York: McGraw-Hill International.
Robson, Bridget, and Ricci Harris. 2007. *Hauora: Māori Standards of Health IV: A Study of the Years 2000–2005*. Wellington: Te Rōpū Rangahao e Eru Pōmare.
Roper, Brian. 1991. 'From Welfare State to the Free Market: Explaining the Transition', *New Zealand Sociology* 6 (1): 38–63.
——. 1996. 'New Zealand's Postwar Economic History', in *The Political Economy of New Zealand*, edited by Chris Rudd and Brian Roper, 3–21. Auckland: Oxford University Press.
——. 2005. *Prosperity for All? Economic, Social and Political Change in New Zealand since 1935*. Melbourne: Cengage Learning.
——. 2011. 'The Fifth (Key) National Government's Neoliberal Policy Agenda: Description, Analysis and Critical Evaluation', *New Zealand Sociology* 26 (1): 12–40.
Rottenberg, Catherine. 2014. 'The Rise of Neoliberal Feminism', *Cultural Studies* 28 (3): 418–37.
Rowntree, Benjamin Seebohm. 1901. *Poverty: A Study of Town Life*. London: Macmillan.

Royal Commission on the Electoral System. 1986. *Report of the Royal Commission on the Electoral System: Towards a Better Democracy*. Wellington: Royal Commission on the Electoral System.

Rozin, Paul, Julia M. Hormes, Myles S. Faith and Brian Wansink. 2012. 'Is Meat Male? A Quantitative Multimethod Framework to Establish Metaphoric Relationships', *Journal of Consumer Research* 39 (3): 629–43.

Rubie-Davies, Christine, John Hattie and Richard Hamilton. 2006. 'Expecting the Best for Students: Teacher Expectations and Academic Outcomes', *British Journal of Educational Psychology* 76 (3): 429–44.

Rubin, Gayle S. [1984] 1999. 'Thinking Sex: Notes for a Radical Theory of the Politics of Sexuality', in *Culture, Society and Sexuality: A Reader*, edited by Richard Parker and Peter Aggleton, 143–78. London: Taylor & Francis.

Rumball-Smith, Juliet, Diana Sarfati, Phil Hider and Tony Blakely. 2013. 'Ethnic Disparities in the Quality of Hospital Care in New Zealand, as Measured by 30-day Rate of Unplanned Readmission/Death', *International Journal for Quality in Health Care* 25 (3): 248–54.

Russell, Stephen. 2014. 'Everything You Need to Know about Agricultural Emissions', *World Resources Institute*, 29 May. Accessed 15 September 2015. http://www.wri.org/blog/2014/05/everything-you-need-know-about-agricultural-emissions

Rutter, Virginia, and Pepper Schwartz. 2012. *The Gender of Sexuality: Exploring Sexual Possibilities*. 2nd ed. Plymouth: Rowman & Littlefield.

Salvation Army. 2016. *Moving Targets: State of the Nation Report 2016*. Auckland: Salvation Army Social Policy and Parliamentary Unit.

Sandel, Michael J. 2012. *What Money Can't Buy: The Moral Limits of Markets*. New York: Farrar, Strauss & Giroux.

Saperstein, Aliya, and Andrew M. Penner. 2014. 'Beyond the Looking Glass: Exploring Fluidity in Racial Self-Identification and Interviewer Classification', *Sociological Perspectives* 57 (2): 186–207.

Sargent, Greg. 2011. 'There's Been Class Warfare for the Last 20 Years, and My Class Has Won', *Washington Post*, 30 September. Accessed 21 August 2015. https://www.washingtonpost.com/blogs/plum-line/post/theres-been-class-warfare-for-the-last-20-years-and-my-class-has-won/2011/03/03/gIQApaFbAL_blog.html

Savage, Patrick. 2010. 'Wai 894: Te Urewera Pre-Publication Part II Released', *Waitangi Tribunal*, 2 August. Accessed 19 March 2015. http://www.justice.govt.nz/tribunals/waitangi-tribunal/news/wai-894-te-urewera-pre-publication-part-ii-released

Sawicki, Jana. 1991. *Disciplining Foucault: Feminism, Power and the Body*. New York: Routledge.

Scheff, Thomas J. 2003. 'Male Emotions/Relationships and Violence: A Case Study', *Human Relations* 56 (6): 727–49.

Schmidt, Johanna. 2010. *Migrating Genders: Westernisation, Migration, and Samoan Fa'afafine*. Farnham: Ashgate.

———. 2014. 'Primary Care Decision Making among First-Time Parents in Aotearoa/New Zealand', *Women's Studies Journal* 28 (1): 18–35.

Schmidtke, Oliver. 2002. 'Transforming the Social Democratic Left: The Challenges to Third Way Politics in the Age of Globalization', in *The Third Way Transformation of Social Democracy: Normative Claims and Policy Initiatives in the 21st Century*, edited by Oliver Schmidtke, 3–27. Aldershot: Ashgate.

Schmitt, John, Kris Warner and Sarika Gupta. 2010. *The High Budgetary Cost of Incarceration*. Washington, DC: Center for Economic and Policy Research.

Science News. 2010. 'Agriculture, Food Production among Worst Environmental Offenders, Report Finds', *Science Daily*, 9 June. Accessed 10 October 2013. https://www.sciencedaily.com/releases/2010/06/100609094353.htm

Seidler, Victor. 2006. *Transforming Masculinities: Men, Cultures, Bodies, Power, Sex and Love*. London: Routledge.

Sennett, Richard. 1977. *The Fall of Public Man*. London: Penguin.

Seuffert, Nan. 2006. 'Sexual Citizenship and the Civil Union Act 2004', *Victoria University of Wellington Law Review* 37 (2): 281–306.

Sheehan, Mark. 2010. 'The Place of "New Zealand" in the New Zealand History Curriculum', *Journal of Curriculum Studies* 42 (5): 671–91.

Sibley, Chris, Carla A. Houkamau and William James Hoverd. 2011. 'Ethnic Group Labels and Intergroup Attitudes in New Zealand: Naming Preferences Predict Distinct Ingroup and Outgroup Biases', *Analyses of Social Issues and Public Policy* 11 (1): 201–20.

Sibley, Chris, and James Liu. 2004. 'Attitudes towards Biculturalism in New Zealand: Social Dominance and Pākehā Attitudes towards the General Principles and Resource-specific Aspects of Bicultural Policy', *New Zealand Journal of Psychology* 33 (2): 88–99.

Sibley, Chris G., James H. Liu and Sammyh S. Khan. 2010. 'Implicit Representations of Ethnicity and Nationhood in New Zealand: A Function of Symbolic or Resource-specific Policy Attitudes?', *Analyses of Social Issues and Public Policy* 10 (1): 23–46.

Simon, Judith. 1992. 'Social Studies: The Cultivation of Social Amnesia?', in *The School Curriculum in New Zealand: History, Theory, Policy and Practice*, edited by Gary McCulloch, 253–71. Palmerston North: Dunmore Press.

Simpkin, Gay. 1994. 'Women for Aotearoa: Feminism and Māori Sovereignty', *Hecate* 20 (2): 226–38.

Simpson, Jean, Glenda Oben, Andrew Wicken, Judith Adams, Anne Reddington and Mavis Duncanson. 2014. *Child Poverty Monitor: 2014 Technical Report*. Dunedin: Child and Youth Epidemiology Service/University of Otago.

Simpson, Tony. 1986. *Te Riri Pākeha = The White Man's Anger*. Auckland: Hodder & Stoughton.

Sinclair, Keith. 1959. *A History of New Zealand*. Harmondsworth: Penguin.

———. 1986. *A Destiny Apart: New Zealand's Search for National Identity*. Wellington: Allen & Unwin/Port Nicholson Press.

Slater, Cameron. 2014. 'Feral Dies in Greymouth, Did World a Favour', *Whaleoil* [Blog], 25 January. Accessed 21 August 2016. http://www.whaleoil.co.nz/2014/01/feral-dies-greymouth-world-favour/

Smith, Anthony D. 1988. *Ethnic Origins of Nations*. Oxford: Blackwell.

Smith, Linda Tuawai. 1999. *Decolonizing Methodologies: Research and Indigenous Peoples*. Dunedin: Otago University Press.

Social and Economic Research Team. 2014. *Auckland Profile: Initial Results from the 2013 Census*. Accessed 21 August 2016. http://www.aucklandcouncil.govt.nz/EN/planspoliciesprojects/reports/Documents/aucklandprofileinitialresults2013census201405.pdf

Somers, Margaret R. 1994. 'The Narrative Constitution of Identity: A Relational and Network Approach', *Theory and Society* 23: 605–49.

Song, Miri. 2003. *Choosing Ethnic Identity*. Cambridge: Polity Press.

Sorrenson, Maurice P. K. 1986. 'A History of Māori Representation in Parliament', in *Report of the Royal Commission on the Electoral System: Towards a Better Democracy*, appendix B. Wellington: Royal Commission on the Electoral System.

Sparks, Richard. 2000. *Perspectives on Risk and Penal Politics*. New York: Routledge.

Spickard, Paul, and W. Jeffrey Burroughs. 2000. 'We Are a People', in *We Are a People: Narrative and Multiplicity in Constructing Ethnic Identity*, edited by Paul Spickard and W. Jeffrey Burroughs, 1–22. Philadelphia: Temple University Press.

Spinks, Harriet, and Michael Klapdor. 2014. *New Zealanders in Australia: A Quick Guide*. Canberra: Parliamentary Library.

Spoonley, Paul. 1991. 'Being Here and Being Pākehā', in *Pakeha: The Quest for Identity in New Zealand*, edited by Michael King, 146–56. Auckland: Penguin.

——. 1996. 'Mahi Awatea? The Racialisation of Work in Aotearoa New Zealand', in *Nga Patai: Racism and Ethic Relations in Aotearoa/New Zealand*, edited by David Pearson, Cluny Macpherson and Paul Spoonley, 35–77. Palmerston North: Dunmore Press.

Spoonley, Paul, and Richard Bedford. 2012. *Welcome to Our World? Immigration and the Reshaping of New Zealand*. Auckland: Dunmore Press.

Spoonley, Paul, Carina Meares and Trudie Cain. 2015. 'Immigrant Economies in Action: Chinese Ethnic Precincts in Auckland', in *Asians and the New Multiculturalism in Aotearoa New Zealand*, edited by Gautam Ghosh and Jacqueline Leckie, 237–64. Dunedin: Otago University Press.

St John, Susan, and Keith Rankin. 2009. *Escaping the Welfare Mess*? Working Paper No. 267. Accessed 21 August 2016. http://www.cpag.org.nz/assets/Backgrounders/Escaping%20 the%20Welfare%20Mess.pdf

Stafford, Jane, and Mark Williams. 2006. *Maoriland: New Zealand Literature 1872–1914*. Wellington: Victoria University Press.

Stalans, Loretta. 2013. 'Measuring Attitudes to Sentencing', in *Changing Attitudes to Punishment: Public Opinion, Crime and Justice*, edited by Julian Roberts and Mike Hough, 15–32. Portland, OR: Willan.

Standing, Guy. 2011. *The Precariat: The New Dangerous Class*. London: Bloomsbury Academic.

Stanford, Jim. 2008. *Economics for Everyone: A Short Guide to the Economics of Capitalism*. London: Pluto Press.

Stark, Evan. 2007. *Coercive Control: How Men Entrap Women in Personal Life*. New York: Oxford University Press.

Statistics New Zealand. 2002a. *New Zealand Official Yearbook 2002*. Wellington: David Bateman.

——. 2002b. *Pacific Progress: A Report of the Economic Status of Pacific Peoples in New Zealand*. Wellington: Statistics New Zealand.

——. 2004. 'Historical Context'. Accessed 21 August 2016. http://www.stats.govt.nz/browse _for_stats/Maps_and_geography/Geographic-areas/urban-rural-profile/historical-context .aspx

——. 2006a. *New Zealand Census 2006*. Wellington: Statistics New Zealand.

——. 2006b. 'Population', table A 1.1. Accessed 21 August 2016. http://web.archive.org/web /20080305185447/http://www.stats.govt.nz/tables/ltds/ltds-population.htm

——. 2008. *Labour Market Statistics 2007*. Wellington: Statistics New Zealand.

——. 2012a. *National Ethnic Population Projections: 2006 (base)–2026*. Wellington: Statistics New Zealand.

——. 2012b. *Vulnerable Children and Families: Some Findings from the New Zealand General Social Survey*. Wellington: Statistics New Zealand.

——. 2013a. '2013 Census Ethnic Group Profiles: Māori'. Accessed 20 October 2014. http:// www.stats.govt.nz/Census/2013-census/profile-and-summary-reports/ethnic-profiles. aspx?request_value=24705&parent_id=24704&tabname=#24705

———. 2013b. *Demographic Trends: 2012*. Accessed 21 August 2016. http://www.stats.govt.nz/browse_for_stats/population/estimates_and_projections/demographic-trends-2012.aspx

———. 2013c. *New Zealand Period Life Tables: 2010–12*. Accessed 20 October 2014. http://www.stats.govt.nz/browse_for_stats/health/life_expectancy/NZLifeTables_HOTP10-12.aspx

———. 2014a. *2013 Census Ethnic Group Profiles*. Accessed 9 November 2014. http://www.stats.govt.nz/Census/2013-census/profile-and-summary-reports/ethnic-profiles.aspx

———. 2014b. *2013 Census QuickStats about Culture and Identity*. Accessed 21 August 2016. http://www.stats.govt.nz/Census/2013-census/profile-and-summary-reports/quickstats-culture-identity.aspx

———. 2014c. 'Female Representation in Parliament and Local Government'. Accessed 21 August 2016. http://www.stats.govt.nz/browse_for_stats/snapshots-of-nz/nz-social-indicators/Home/Trust%20and%20participation%20in%20government/female-rep-parl-local-govt.aspx

———. 2015. 'Measuring the Gender Pay Gap'. Accessed 21 August 2016. http://www.stats.govt.nz/browse_for_stats/income-and-work/Income/gender-pay-gap.aspx

Statistics New Zealand and Ministry of Pacific Island Affairs. 2010. *Education and Pacific Peoples in New Zealand*. Wellington: Statistics New Zealand and Ministry of Pacific Island Affairs.

———. 2011. *Health and Pacific Peoples in New Zealand*. Wellington: Statistics New Zealand and Ministry of Pacific Island Affairs.

Steven, Rob. 1989. 'Land and White Settler Colonialism: The Case of Aotearoa', in *Culture and Identity in New Zealand*, edited by David Novitz and William E. Willmott, 21–43. Wellington: GP Books.

Stevens, Michael. 2013. 'Sexualizing', in *Being Sociological*. 2nd ed., edited by Steve Matthewman, Catherine Lane West-Newman and Bruce Curtis, 139–56. Basingstoke: Palgrave Macmillan.

Stewart, Matt. 2012. '100% Pure Fantasy? Living Up to Our Brand', *Stuff*, 1 December. Accessed 21 August 2016. http://www.stuff.co.nz/environment/8023412/100-Pure-Fantasy-Living-up-to-our-brand

Stoker, Gerry. 2006. *Why Politics Matters*. New York: Palgrave Macmillan.

Stokes, Evelyn. 1990. 'Te Waharoa Wiremu Tamihana Tarapipipi, ?–1866', in *The Dictionary of New Zealand Biography*, vol. 1, edited by W. H. Oliver, 515–18. Wellington: Allen & Unwin/Department of Internal Affairs.

Storey, John. [1988] 2009. 'Rockin' Hegemony: West Coast Rock and Amerika's War in Vietnam', in *Cultural Theory and Popular Culture: A Reader*, edited by John Storey, 88–97. Harlow, Essex: Pearson Education.

Swidler, Ann. 1986. 'Culture in Action: Symbols and Strategies', *American Sociological Review* (April): 273–86.

Tainui Group Holdings. 2014. *Waikato-Tainui Annual Report 2014*. Accessed 21 August 2016. http://tgh.co.nz/admin/documentlibrary/waikato-tainui%20annual%20report%202014.pdf

Tajfel, Henri. 1981. *Human Groups and Social Categories: Studies in Social Psychology*. Cambridge: Cambridge University Press.

Tauri, Juan. 1998. 'Family Group Conferencing: A Case-Study of the Indigenisation of New Zealand's Justice System', *Current Issues in Criminology* 10: 168–82.

———. 2013. 'Indigenous Critique of Authoritarian Criminology', in *Crime, Justice and Social Democracy: International Perspectives*, edited by Kerry Carrington, Matthew J. Ball, Erin O'Brien and Juan Tauri, 217–33. Basingstoke: Palgrave Macmillan.

Taylor, Annabel. 2013. 'Restorative Justice: Issues in Gender-based Violence in Aotearoa New Zealand', *Te Awatea Review* 11 (1): 7–11.

Taylor, Kevin. 2003. 'MP Runs into Strife on Tractor', *New Zealand Herald*, 5 September. Accessed 21 August 2016. http://www.nzherald.co.nz/nz/news/article.cfm?c_id=1&objectid=3521866

Taylor, Stephanie, and Margaret Wetherell. 1995. 'Doing National Construction Work: Discourses of National Identity', *Sites* 30: 69–84.

Te Rōpū Rangahau Hauora A Eru Pōmare. 2000. 'Counting for Nothing: Understanding the Issues in Monitoring Disparites in Health', *Social Policy Journal New Zealand* 14: 1–16.

Teaiwa, Teresia. 2001. 'L(o)osing the Edge', *Contemporary Pacific* 13 (2): 343–57.

Teh, Ruth, Ngaire Kerse, Mere Kepa, Rob N. Doughty, Simon Moyes, Janine Wiles, Carol Wham et al. 2014. 'Self-Rated Health, Health-Related Behaviours and Medical Conditions of Māori and non-Māori in Advanced Age: LiLACS NZ', *New Zealand Medical Journal* 127 (1397): 13–29.

Therborn, Göran. 2009. 'The Killing Fields of Inequality', *Open Democracy*, 6 April. Accessed 21 October 2014. https://www.opendemocracy.net/article/the-killing-fields-of-inequality

Tomlinson, Mark, and Robert Walker. 2009. 'Why Multidimensional Poverty Is Important', in *Coping with Complexity: Child and Adult Poverty*, by Mark Tomlinson and Robert Walker, 15–26. London: Child Poverty Action Group.

Torsch, Vicki L., and Grace Xeuqin Ma. 2000. 'Cross-Cultural Comparison of Health Perceptions, Concerns, and Coping Strategies among Asian and Pacific Islander American Elders', *Qualitative Health Research* 10 (4): 471–89.

Tourism Industry Association New Zealand. 2015. 'Quick Statistics and Figures', http://www.tianz.org.nz/main/key-tourism-statistics/

Townsend, Peter. 1993. *The International Analysis of Poverty*. London: Harvester Wheatsheaf.

Treaty Resource Centre – He Puni Mātauranga o te Tiriti. 2004. 'Examples of Pākehā Privilege'. Accessed 15 October 2014. http://trc.org.nz/examples-p%C4%81keh%C4%81-privilege

Trlin, Andrew D. 1987. 'New Zealand's Admission of Asians and Pacific Islanders', in *Pacific Bridges: The New Migration from Asia and the Pacific Islands*, edited by James Thomas Fawcett and Benjamin V. Carino, 199–227. New York: Center for Migration Studies.

True, Jacqui. 2012. *The Political Economy of Violence against Women*. New York: Oxford University Press.

Tucker, Corrina. 2011a. 'Collective Action Framing Genetic Engineering Resistance in New Zealand', *Journal of Organic Systems* 6 (2): 27–34.

———. 2011b. 'The Social Construction of Clean and Green in the Genetic Engineering Resistance Movement of New Zealand', *New Zealand Sociology* 26 (1): 110–21.

———. 2013. 'Insects, Offal, Feet and Faces: Acquiring New Tastes in New Zealand?', *New Zealand Sociology* 28 (4): 101–22.

———. 2014. 'The Significance of Sensory Appeal for Reduced Meat Consumption', *Appetite* 81: 168–79.

Tucker, Corrina, and Trisia Farrelly. 2015. 'Household Food Waste: The Implications of Consumer Choice in Food from Purchase to Disposal', *Local Environment*, 1–25.

Umaña-Taylor, Adriana J. 2004. 'Ethnic Identity and Self-Esteem: Examining the Role of Social Context', *Journal of Adolescence* 27 (2): 139–46.

UN Women. 2011. *2011–2012 Progress of the World's Women: In Pursuit of Justice*. Accessed 21 August 2016. http://www.unwomen.org/en/digital-library/publications/2011/7/progress-of-the-world-s-women-in-pursuit-of-justice

Underhill-Sem, Yvonne. 2003. 'Marked Bodies in Marginalised Places: Understanding Rationalities in Global Discourses', *Development* 46 (2): 13–17.

UNICEF. 2013. *Child Well-Being in Rich Countries: A Comparative Overview*. Innocenti Report Card 11. Accessed 21 August 2016. https://www.unicef-irc.org/publications/pdf/rc11_eng.pdf

United Nations. 1995. *Report of the World Summit for Social Development*. Accessed 21 August 2016. http://www.un.org/esa/socdev/wssd/text-version/

———. 1998. *Kyoto Protocol to the United Nations Framework Convention on Climate Change*. Accessed 21 August 2016. http://unfccc.int/resource/docs/convkp/kpeng.pdf

United Nations Department of Economic and Social Affairs. 2004. *The Concept of Indigenous Peoples*. Workshop on Data Collection and Disaggregation for Indigenous Peoples. New York: United Nations.

United Nations Office on Drugs and Crime. 2013. 'UNODC Homicide Statistics 2013'. Accessed 21 August 2016. http://www.unodc.org/gsh/en/data.html

Urry, James. 1990. 'The Politics of Anthropology in New Zealand', *Anthropology Today* 6 (6): 20–21.

Van Leeuwen, Marco H. D. 2009. 'Social Inequality and Mobility in History: Introduction', *Continuity and Change* 24 (3): 399–419.

Vanderpyl, Jane. 2004. 'Aspiring for Unity and Equality: Dynamics of Conflict and Change in the "By Women For Women" Feminist Service Groups, Aotearoa/New Zealand (1970–1999)', PhD, University of Auckland.

Veracini, Lorenzo. 2008. 'Settler Collective, Founding Violence and Disavowal: The Settler Colonial Situation', *Journal of Intercultural Studies* 29 (4): 363–79.

Vertovec, Steven. 2007. 'Super-diversity and Its Implications', *Ethnic and Racial Studies* 30 (6): 1024–54.

Vinnari, Markus, and Petri Tapio. 2012. 'Sustainability of Diets: From Concepts to Governance', *Ecological Economics* 74: 46–54.

Wacquant, Loïc. 2001. 'The Penalisation of Poverty and the Rise of Neo-Liberalism', *European Journal on Criminal Policy and Research* 9 (4): 401–12.

Waitangi Tribunal. 2014. *He Whakaputanga me te Tiriti/The Declaration and the Treaty: The Report on Stage 1 of the Te Paparahi o te Raki Inquiry*. WAI 1040. Accessed 21 August 2016. https://forms.justice.govt.nz/search/Documents/WT/wt_DOC_85648980/Te%20RakiW_1.pdf

Wakanui. 2015. 'Wakanui: Grass-fed and Grain-finished Beef'. Accessed 8 September 2015. http://www.wakanuibeef.co.nz/

Waldegrave, Charles, Robert Stephens and Peter King. 2003. 'Assessing the Progress on Poverty Reduction', *Social Policy Journal of New Zealand* (June): 197–222.

Waldon, John. 2004. 'Oranga Kaumatua: Perceptions of Health in Older Māori People', *Social Policy Journal of New Zealand* 23: 167–80.

Walker, Harriet. 'Of Course We Still Need Feminism', *Independent*, 12 January. Accessed 21 August 2016. http://www.independent.co.uk/i/harriet-walker-of-course-we-still-need-feminism-6287944.html

Walker, Ranginui. 1986. *The Meaning of Biculturalism*. Auckland: R. J. Walker.

———. 1995. 'Immigration Policy and the Political Economy of New Zealand', in *Immigration and National Identity in New Zealand*, edited by Stuart Grief, 282–302. Palmerston North: Dunmore Press.

———. 2004. *Ka Whawhai Tonu Matou – Struggle without End*. 2nd ed. Auckland: Penguin.

———. 2007. *Ōpōtiki-Mai-Tawhiti: Capital of Whakatōhea*. Auckland: Penguin.

Ward, Alan. 1973. *A Show of Justice: Racial 'Amalgamation' in Nineteenth Century New Zealand*. Auckland: Auckland University Press.
Warner, Michael. 1991. 'Introduction: Fear of a Queer Planet', *Social Text* 29: 3–17.
WasteMINZ. 2013. *Summary of Existing Information on Domestic Food Waste in New Zealand: Living Document – Version Final 1.1*. Accessed 21 August 2016. http://www.wasteminz.org.nz/wp-content/uploads/Report-on-Food-Waste-in-NZ-2013-Final-1.1.pdf
Water Footprint Network. 2015. 'What Is a Water Footprint?'. Accessed 21 August 2016. http://waterfootprint.org/en/water-footprint/what-is-water-footprint/
Weatherburn, Don, and David Indermaur. 2004. 'Public Perceptions of Crime Trends in New South Wales and Western Australia', *BOSCAR NSW Crime and Justice Bulletin: Contemporary Issues in Crime and Justice*, no. 80: 1–8.
Weaver, John C. 1999. 'Frontiers into Assets: The Social Construction of Property in New Zealand, 1840–65', *Journal of Imperial and Commonwealth History* 27 (3): 17–54.
Webb, Robert. 2011. 'Incarceration', in *Māori and Social Issues*, edited by Tracey McIntosh and Malcolm Mulholland, 249–62. Wellington: Huia.
Webber, Melinda. 2011. 'Identity Matters: Racial-Ethnic Representations among Adolescents Attending Multi-Ethnic High Schools', PhD, University of Auckland.
——. 2012. 'Identity Matters: The Role of Racial-Ethnic Identity for Māori Adolescents in Multiethnic Secondary Schools', *SET Research Information for Teachers* 2: 20–25.
Websdale, Neil. 2010a. 'Of Nuclear Missiles and Love Objects: The Humiliated Fury of Kevin Jones', *Journal of Contemporary Ethnography* 39 (4): 388–420.
——. 2010b. *Familicidal Hearts: The Emotional Styles of 211 Killers*. Oxford: Oxford University Press.
Weeks, Jeffrey. 2007. 'Discourse, Desire and Sexual Deviance: Some Problems in a History of Homosexuality', in *Culture, Society and Sexuality: A Reader*, edited by Richard Parker and Peter Aggleton, 125–49. London: Routledge.
Weissman, Deborah M. 2007. 'The Personal is Political – and Economic: Rethinking Domestic Violence', *Brigham Young University Law Review* 2: 387–440.
Werry, Margaret. 2011. *The Tourist State: Performing Leisure, Liberalism, and Race in New Zealand*. Minneapolis: Minnesota University Press.
White Ribbon. 2016. 'About'. Accessed 21 August 2016. https://whiteribbon.org.nz/about/
Whyte, Jamie. 2014. 'ACT Speech to Waikato Conference: Race Has No Place in Law', *Scoop*, 29 July. Accessed 15 October 2014. http://www.scoop.co.nz/stories/PO1407/S00465/act-speech-to-waikato-conference-race-has-no-place-in-law.htm
Wilkinson, Richard. 2004. 'Why Is Violence More Common Where Inequality Is Greater?', *Annals of the New York Academy of Sciences* 1036 (1): 1–12.
Wilkinson, Richard, and Kate Pickett. 2009. *The Spirit Level: Why More Equal Societies Almost Always Do Better*. London: Penguin.
Wilkinson, Sue, and Celia Kitzinger. 1994. 'The Social Construction of Heterosexuality', *Journal of Gender Studies* 3 (3): 307–16.
Williams, Charlotte. 2001. *The Too-Hard Basket: Maori and Criminal Justice Since 1800*. Wellington: Institute of Policy Studies.
Williams, Raymond. 1973. *The Country and the City*. London: Chatto & Windus.
Wilson, John. 2003. *The Origins of the Māori Seats*. Wellington: Parliamentary Library.
Winick, Bruce J., and David B. Wexler, eds. 2003. *Judging in a Therapeutic Key: Therapeutic Jurisprudence and the Courts*. North Carolina: Carolina Academic Press.
Women's Refuge. 2015. 'Public Policy'. Accessed 11 November 2015. https://womensrefuge.org.nz/what-we-do/public-policy/

Woodhouse, Michael. 2015. 'Addressing Zero-Hour Contracts', *New Zealand Government*. Accessed 21 August 2016. https://www.beehive.govt.nz/release/addressing-zero-hour-contracts

Workman, Kim. 2011. *Māori Over-representation in the Criminal Justice System – Does Structural Discrimination Have Anything to Do With It?* Discussion Paper. Wellington: Rethinking Crime and Punishment.

Workman, Kim, and Tracey McIntosh. 2013. 'Crime, Imprisonment and Poverty', in *Inequality: A New Zealand Crisis*, edited by Max Rashbrooke, 120–33. Wellington: Bridget Williams Books.

Worldwatch Institute. 2013. 'Grain Harvest Sets Record, but Supplies Still Tight'. Accessed 24 September 2015. http://www.worldwatch.org/node/5539

WRAP. 2008. *The Food We Waste: Food Waste Report*. Accessed 21 August 2016. http://www.ifr.ac.uk/waste/Reports/WRAP%20The%20Food%20We%20Waste.pdf

Wynyard, Matthew. 2016. 'The Price of Milk: Primitive Accumulation and the New Zealand Dairy Industry', PhD, University of Auckland.

Young, Audrey. 2014. 'Dirty Politics: SIS Director's Three Apologies', *New Zealand Herald*, 25 November. Accessed 21 August 2016. http://www.nzherald.co.nz/nz/news/article.cfm?c_id=1&objectid=11364052

Young, Jock. 2003. 'Merton with Energy, Katz with Structure: The Sociology of Vindictiveness and the Criminology of Transgression', *Theoretical Criminology* 7 (3): 389–414.

Zhang, Jingjing. 2014. 'Enhancing Quality of Life: The Social Support of Elderly Chinese Migrants in New Zealand', PhD, University of Auckland.

# Contributors

**Avril Bell** is a Pākehā New Zealander and Senior Lecturer in Sociology at the University of Auckland. Her research centres on the legacy of settler colonialism in making sense of Pākehā identities, New Zealand national identity and Māori–Pākehā relations. Her book *Relating Indigenous and Settler Identities: Beyond Domination* (2014, Palgrave Macmillan) extends this focus to make connections between settler colonialism in New Zealand, Australia, Canada and the United States.

**Gerry Cotterell** is a sociologist with wide-ranging research interests including understanding the process, periodisation and impacts of neoliberalisation in New Zealand; the political economy of the welfare state, welfare reform and its consequences; child poverty and inequality; comparative social policy; and the teaching of research methods. His early working life included stints as a freezing worker, mechanic and public servant.

**Bruce Curtis** is an Associate Professor in Sociology at the University of Auckland. His research interests include neoliberalism as neocolonialism, precariousness in working- and middle-class lives, research methodologies, food and farming, and new technologies.

**Vivienne Elizabeth** is a Pākehā New Zealander and Associate Professor in Sociology at the University of Auckland. She brings a gendered lens to thinking about contemporary family life in Aotearoa New Zealand and has mainly researched in two areas: post-separation parenting arrangements and the difficulties mothers in particular face in negotiating these arrangements; and relationship transitions, which led to a co-authored monograph *Marriage in an Age of Cohabitation* (2014, Oxford University Press) (with Maureen Baker).

**Marko Galic** is a PhD candidate at the University of Auckland in the Department of Sociology. His thesis is a class analysis of Aotearoa New Zealand, involving ethnographic research on the everyday struggles of precarious workers.

**Bartek Goldmann** holds an MA in Sociology from the University of Auckland where he is employed as a graduate teaching assistant. He is also the coordinator of *MAI Journal: A New Zealand Journal of Indigenous Scholarship* at Ngā Pae o te Māramatanga, New Zealand's Māori Centre of Research Excellence. His research interests are critical theory, social movements and political economy.

**Peter J. Howland** lectures in Sociology at Massey University and also has a teaching/research background in Anthropology. His main research interests are middle-class identity, consumption, morality and sociality; wine production, consumption and tourism; gifting relations and practices; and Lotto and gambling.

**Louise Humpage** is an Associate Professor in Sociology at the University of Auckland. She has written widely about Māori Affairs policy, social policy and welfare reform and refugee policy and adaptation. She has further research interests in public attitudes to the welfare state, which recently culminated in *Policy Change, Public Attitudes and Social Citizenship: Does Neoliberalism Matter?* (2015, Policy Press).

**Ngaire Kerse** is a Professor and an academic general practitioner at the University of Auckland who has built a programme of research in ageing involving promoting physical activity, preventing falls and encouraging social engagement. She is co-leader of a longitudinal study of Māori and non-Māori New Zealanders entitled 'Life and Living in Advanced Age: A Cohort Study' (LiLACS NZ).

**Tahu Kukutai** (Waikato-Maniapoto, Te Aupōuri) is an Associate Professor at the Institute of Demographic and Economic Analysis at the University of Waikato. Tahu specialises in Māori and indigenous demographic research and has an ongoing interest in how governments around the world count and classify populations by ethnic-racial and citizenship criteria. In a former life she was a journalist.

**Steve Matthewman** is an Associate Professor in Sociology at the University of Auckland and President of the Sociological Association of Aotearoa New Zealand. His teaching and research interests include introductory sociology, social theory, science and technology studies, and the sociology of disasters.

**Tracey McIntosh** (Tūhoe) is an Associate Professor in Sociology and Co-Director of Ngā Pae o te Māramatanga, New Zealand's Māori Centre of Research Excellence. Her teaching and research interests include incarceration, Māori women and prison, indigenous peoples and the criminal justice system.

**Kellie McNeill** is a lecturer in Sociology at the University of Auckland and previously taught Sociology and Social Policy at the University of Waikato. Her research interests are in how people construct well-being – particularly in relation to food and the natural environment – and in participatory democracy and public sociology as mechanisms for achieving social and environmental justice.

**Karlo Mila** is of Tongan and Palangi descent. Her PhD, which she completed at Massey University, explored the culture, identity and health of the New Zealand-born Pasifika population. Her recent research has focused on Pasifika indigenous knowledge. Karlo is a writer, researcher, mother and poet, and the author of two poetry collections, *Dream Fish Floating* (2005, Huia) and *A Well Written Body* (2008, Huia). She lives in Wellington.

**Richard Pringle** is an Associate Professor in the School of Curriculum and Pedagogy at the University of Auckland, with research interests related to socio-cultural studies of sport, exercise and physical education. He is co-author of *Foucault, Sport and Exercise: Power, Knowledge and Transforming the Self and Sport* (2006, Routledge) and *The Social Significance of Pleasure* (2015, Routledge), and co-editor of *Examining Sport Histories: Power, Paradigms and Reflexivity* (2013, FiT).

**Johanna Schmidt** is a lecturer in the School of Social Sciences at the University of Waikato. Her research interests are related to gender and sexuality, with specialisations in the areas of parenting and Pacific transgender studies. She is the author of *Migrating Genders: Westernisation, Migration, and Samoan Fa'afafine* (2010, Ashgate) and co-editor of the Aotearoa-based *Women's Studies Journal*.

**Julia Schuster** received her PhD in Sociology from the University of Auckland in 2014 and currently teaches and researches at the Johannes Kepler University Linz in Austria. Her academic interests include feminist activism, women's movements and discrimination in the labour market.

**Richard Shaw** is a Professor in the Politics Programme at Massey University and the Director BA (External Connections). He teaches New Zealand politics and researches the role of political advisers in executive government. His publications include *Public Policy in New Zealand: Institutions, Processes and Outcomes* (3rd ed., 2011, Pearson) and *Partisan Appointees and Public Servants: An International Analysis of the Role of the Political Adviser* (2010, Edward Elgar) (both with C. Eichbaum).

**Paul Spoonley** is the Pro Vice-Chancellor of the College of Humanities and Social Sciences at Massey University. He is a Fellow of the Royal Society of New Zealand, a Research Fellow at the Max Planck Institute of Religious and Ethnic Diversity, and was a Fulbright Senior Scholar at the University of California, Berkeley. He is lead researcher on the 'Capturing the Diversity Dividend of Aotearoa New Zealand' research programme funded by the Ministry of Business, Innovation and Employment.

**Corrina Tucker** is an environmental sociologist at Massey University. Her work investigates the nexus between the enactment of environmental life(styles) and political in/action. Most recently her research has centred on the topics of waste reduction and the environmental impacts of meat consumption.

Professor Emeritus **Ranginui Walker** (Whakatōhea) was a Māori leader, academic, activist, social commentator and public intellectual who played a major role in shaping the contemporary discussion on Māori and Pākehā relationships. He wrote many books and scholarly articles and his book *Ka Whaiwhai Tonu Matou: Struggle Without End* is essential reading to understand the history of New Zealand. He did not write solely for scholarly audiences and his influence and contribution to national politics was probably greatest through his commentary in magazines such as the *Listener* and *Metro*. After retiring from the University of Auckland in 1998 until his death in 2016 he continued to be a powerful advocate for Māori and expressed optimism for a better future for the nation.

**Melinda Webber** (Ngāti Whakaue, Ngāpuhi) is Senior Lecturer and Associate Dean in the Faculty of Education at the University of Auckland. Melinda's research examines the ways race, ethnicity, culture and identity impact on the lives of young people – particularly Māori students.

**Matt Wynyard** recently completed a PhD in Sociology at the University of Auckland. His research interests include political economy, colonisation, agriculture and the environment, and the sociology of food. He currently lives in Wellington with his family where he works as an historian.

# Index

Ageing: ageing population, 228–230; disparities, 235; ethnicity and, 232–237; intergenerational living, 230–231, 235, 237; positive ageing, 237; women, 230–233. *See also* Health; Life expectancy

Agriculture, 17, 272, 276, 282–284; beef and sheep, 272, 275, 284–288; dairying, 281; employment in, 165; greenhouse gases, 281–283. *See also* Ecological footprint; Primitive accumulation; Water pollution

Anderson, Benedict, 58, 63

Asian: communities, 109, 115; identities, 76, 96, 114, 116; political representation, 62. *See also* Immigration; Super-diversity

Asiatic Restriction Act 1896, 111

Assimilation, 73, 99, 194, 259

Belich, James, 18–22, 66, 265

Biculturalism, 40, 61–62, 66, 88, 109, 116. *See also* Multiculturalism; Super-diversity

Biocapacity, 279–280, 289

Building Act 1991, 270

Capitalism, 14–15, 101–102, 121–124, 133; mode of production, 15, 122, 137. *See also* Colonisation; Marx, Karl; Primitive accumulation

Carroll, James, 23

Census, 72–76, 90, 96, 109, 114, 227, 235, 271

Chinese Immigration Act, the, 1881, 111

Citizenship, 30, 45–48, 52–53, 61. *See also* Voting

Civil Union Act 2004, 7, 186, 194

Class, 122, 137; bourgeoisie, 137, 139; egalitarianism, 61, 135–141 passim, 153, 158–159, 195; inequality, 122; middle class, 127, 129, 137, 139–141, 144, 206, 221, 268–269, 274–275; petite bourgeoisie, 139–140; precariat, 143; working class, 127, 135–144 passim, 164, 168, 206, 256, 269

Climate change, 37, 279, 281–283, 287, 289

Collectivities, 20, 48, 57–58, 80. *See also* Māori

Colonisation, 108–111, 259; consequences of, 116, 203, 207, 260; historical amnesia, 66–67, 142, 144. *See also* Māori land; Primitive accumulation; Racism; Settler societies; Violence

Constitution Act 1986, 39

Consumption, 244, 247, 249, 280; alcohol, 180, 204, 206, 271; consumers, 53–54, 126, 140–141; food, 279, 281, 284–285, 288–289; urbane, 267, 275

Crimes Act 1908, 190

Crimes Act 1985, 180

Criminal Code Act, 1893, 190

Criminal Justice Act 1985, 254

Declaration of Independence 1835, The (Te Wakaputanga o te Rangatira o Nu Tirani), 28–30, 39, 41

Decolonisation, 38–41, 94, 105, 151

Democracy, 43–45, 47, 52, 136; and citizenship, 45–46; democratic system, 44–45, 53; democratic participation, 52; and the public-sector, 52; rights, 46–48

Domestic Protection Act 1982, 180

Domestic violence. *See* Violence

Domestic Violence Act, the, 181

Ecological footprint, 272, 280, 289; methane, 28, 284, 287, 288. *See also* Agriculture; Environmental sustainability; Water pollution

Electoral Act, 48–50

Electoral system. *See* Voting

Employment Contracts Act, 125, 166, 168

Employment Relations Act, 127

Environmental sustainability, 280–281, 289. *See also* Agriculture; Ecological footprint; Water pollution

Equality, 144; equality of opportunity, 93, 160; equality of outcome, 93, 160; gender equality, 173–174, 213–214; and Māori, 98

Ethnicity. *See specific groups*

Family violence. *See* Violence

Feminism, 173–177, 182; and ethnicity, 180; first wave, 176; gender justice, 174–175, 178, 183–184; liberal feminism, 180, 214; Ministry of Women's Affairs, 177, 218;

Feminism (*continued*)
post-feminism, 214–216, 219; second wave, 177, 180–181, 191, 202; third wave, 181–184. *See also* Labour market; Masculinity; Neoliberalism; Patriarchy; Political representation; Sexuality; Violence
Food: food chain, 281–289; food insecurity, 148–150, 152, 156, 281; production, 284–285, 288; waste, 288–289. *See also* Environmental sustainability; Poverty

Gay liberation movement, 175, 191, 193–195; same-sex marriage, 193–195. *See also* Civil Union Act
Gender: differentiation, 187, 213, 220; ethnicity and, 208, 247; gender identities, 182–183, 194–196; gender relations, 201–202; inequality, 173–174, 214–218, 240; norms, 182, 220, 247; transgender, 182, 191. *See also* Feminism; Labour market
Gentrification, 269–271
Globalization. *See* Neoliberalism
Government, 28–29, 35, 40, 45–46, 53–54, 122; Fifth National Government, 65; Fourth Labour Government, 39, 108, 111; Liberal Government, 21–23; and Māori, 85, 99; and migrants, 111; representative government, 46, 61; Third National Government, 100. *See also* Kīngitanga; Settler societies; Voting
Governor Grey, 30, 32–34 passim, 41

Health, 53; and ageing, 227–229; disparities, 99, 235, 256; health expectancy, 90, 236; health outcomes, 97, 150, 156; health problems, 96; health sector, 126, 166; and Māori, 232–233, 235–236; mental health, 24
Hegemony, 60, 141, 144–145, 189, 201, 266; hegemonic domination, 141; and masculinity, 200–205; Pākehā hegemony, 41, 41, 60, 84; and power, 195
Heteronormativity, 187–188, 193–196, 200, 245. *See also* Patriarchy
Housing, 234, 271; affordability, 113, 137, 169, 268; Housing New Zealand, 255; state housing, 153–155, 166–169
Human Rights Act 1993, 193

Identity, 89; collective identities, 57–58, 72, 79; construction of, 60, 73; ethnic, 72, 85, 89; expression of, 78, 82; identity politics, 88, 175; social identity, 72, 287. *See also* National identity; *and specific ethnic groups*

Immigration: Asian migrants, 113–116, 235, 267; policy, 61, 112–113; racism, 109–111; recent migrants and Māori, 74; moral panic, 111–112; Pasifika, 96–101, 151, 269. *See also* Settler societies
Immigration Restriction Amendment Act 1920, 111
Incarceration, 251–256; poverty, 255–256; racialization, 257–259. *See also* Colonisation; Masculinity; Penal populism; Prison; Violence
Indigeneity, 14–15, 26, 71, 73, 88–89, 91, 98, 112, 157; indigenous rights, 114; sovereignty, 98; struggles of, 206, 207, 242, 259. *See also* Māori
Individualism, 53, 128, 214–215, 231; agency, 178, 215, 240, 245; responsibility, 81, 109, 160, 178. *See also* Collectivities; Self-determination
Inequality, 90, 114, 153–157 passim, 160–164, 167, 268; income, 121, 126, 131–132, 152, 154–155, 164, 243–244; and Māori, 15, 24, 76, 89; measurements of, 217; and Pasifika, 104; social inequality, 135, 142; structural causes of, 126, 144–146, 149–150
Insecure work. *See* Labour market; Precarity
Institutional racism. *See* Racism
Intersectionality, 182, 202, 210–211
Iwi, 17, 26, 36–38, 40, 71, 73–75, 78, 208; and government, 40; Ngāpuhi, 31, 38, 42, 66; Ngai Tahu, 17, 41; Ngāti Haua, 31, 32; Ngāti Hine, 27, 42; Ngāti Kahungunu, 28; Ngāti Māhuta, 31; Ngāti Maniapoto, 32; Ngāti Porou, 31; Ngāti Whātua, 41; Tainui, 33, 34, 36, 41; Te Ati Awa, 18

Justice reinvestment, 262

Kawanatanga, 30, 38–41
Key, John, 13, 65, 66, 135, 167, 179
Keynesianism, 121–126, 127, 130, 132, 160, 166–167, 213
Kīngitanga, 27–41. *See also* Iwi; Tino rangatiratanga; United Tribes of New Zealand

Labour market, 128, 143, 150, 152, 166, 218, 221, 246; deregulation, 166; full employment policy, 123, 125, 153, 155; gendered division of labour, 152, 174, 212–213, 217–221, 247; horizontal and vertical segregation, 218; Māori; participation in, 152, 155, 163, 246; and Pasifika, 101–103, 247; pay equity,

216–217, 231; women, 165 178, 213, 216, 218–220; zero hour contracts, 130. *See also* Precarity; Unemployment; Unions
Legislation. *See specific acts*
Liberal Government. *See* Government
Life expectancy, 90, 200, 236–237. *See also* Health
Local Government Act 1989, 270

Māori: culture, 62, 71, 75, 78, 84, 99, 115, 190, 210, 236; mana whenua, 32; Māori identity, 20 71–73, 77–82, 89, 202; Māori privilege, 89–93; resilience, 71, 80–81, 104, 237; resistance, 17, 31, 38, 104; tangata whenua, 20, 26, 39–41, 109, 112; te reo, 75, 80, 190, 209, 235–236. *See also* Kīngitanga; Rangatahi; Tino rangatiratanga; Urbanisation; Voting
Māori land: dispossession, 14–16, 22–23, 151, 259, 265. *See also* Colonisation; Primitive accumulation
Māori Representation Act, 49
Marginalisation, 244, 246; consequences of, 243, 245; and gender, 202; of Māori, 62, 108, 246, 248–249, 258; social marginalisation, 148
Marriage (Definition of Marriage) Amendment Act 2013, 194
Marshall, T. H., 46–48
Marx, Karl, 15–16, 21, 139; capital, 15, 16; capitalism, view on, 144; Marxism, 122, 143. *See also* Capitalism; Primitive accumulation
Masculinity, 199–205, 247–249; alcohol, 206; and class, 206; Māori, 206–210; mateship, 203–204; Pākehā, 203–206; work, 246. *See also* Hegemony; Heteronormativity; Patriarchy; Unemployment; Violence
McCombs, Elizabeth, 49
Migration. *See* Immigration
Multiculturalism, 61, 116. *See also* Biculturalism; Super-diversity

National identity, 57, 59–60, 62, 65, 203, 278, 289; exclusion and inclusion, 60–62, 66, 90, 109, 270; imagined communities, 58, 63, 109; nation-building, 28–30, 84, 92, 108–109; political community, 46; sport and war, 58, 63–64, 84, 205, 210
Native Land Court, 20–21, 23
Native Lands (Violation of Titles) Act 1892, 23
Native Lands Act 1865, 49–50

Neoliberalism, 126–133, 135–136, 154, 166–169, 256; consumer sovereignty, 124, 270; devolution, 40; feminism, 214–215, 219, 246; free market, 53, 270; globalisation, 151, 246, 249, 267; neoliberal reforms, 126–131, 155, 158, 166–169
New Zealand Bill of Rights Act 1990, 39
New Zealand Constitution, 38–40, 50; Constitutional Conversation, 38–42. *See also* New Zealand Constitution Act 1852; Treaty of Waitangi, the
New Zealand Constitution Act 1852, 31, 41, 47, 93
New Zealand Settlements Act, 19
New Zealand Wars, 19–22. *See also* Colonisation

Offence Against the Person Act 1867, 190
Old age pension. *See* Superannuation

Pākehā: and biculturalism, 84; historical amnesia, 66–67; ethnicity, 86–89; and national identity, 60–62; privilege, 83–85, 89–93. *See also* Hegemony; Masculinity; National identity; Settler societies
Parliament. *See* Government
Patriarchy, 180–183, 201, 208, 216, 241, 245–249; patriarchal dividend, 201. *See also* Feminism; Gender; Hegemony; Heteronormativity; Masculinity
Penal populism, 253–255
Political economy, 30, 145, 213
Political representation: ethnicity and, 97, 103; Māori, 31, 49–51, 93, 110; women, 48–49, 174–178. *See also* Voting
Poverty, 132, 137, 146–153, 256; children, 126, 129, 131, 150, 152; crime and, 256; ethnicity and, 151; measurements of, 149; relative poverty, 147–151, 155–156. *See also* Food; Incarceration; Inequality; Labour market; Precarity; Unemployment; Working poor
Precarity, 143–144, 155, 244, 247, 256; insecure work, 130–131, 152–155
Primitive accumulation, 15–24, 138. *See also* Capitalism; Colonisation; Māori land; Marx, Karl
Prison, 251–263; class, 256; deregulation, 256; Māori, 252, 257–259; women and, 258. *See also* Colonisation; Incarceration; Masculinity; Penal populism; Violence
Public housing. *See* Housing
Public-private partnerships, 38

Racism, 63, 79–82, 98–103, 111–112, 142, 248, 259. *See also* Colonisation; Immigration; Incarceration; Structural discrimination
Rangatahi, 78–81, 262; Rangatahi Courts (nga Kooti Rangatahi), 261–262
Rangatiratanga. *See* Tino rangatiratanga
Resource Management Act 1991, 270

Self-determination, 99, 112, 232, 236; Māori agency, 88. *See also* Sovereignty; Tino rangatiratanga
Settler societies, 14, 16, 88, 92, 109–110, 242, 248 259; 'peaceful settlement', 13–15, 17, 18; settlers, 14, 18, 30, 33, 66, 265; settler government, 17–19, 30. *See also* Colonisation; Primitive accumulation
Sexuality, 186–189, 195; ethnicity and, 76; heterosexuality, 187–189, 245; homosexuality, 188–193; regulation of, 187, 195; women and, 189, 193. *See also* Gay liberation movement; Masculinity
Social democracy, 122–128 passim
Social mobility, 152–155, 158–167
Social Security Act 1938, 123, 153
Social Security Amendment Act 2007, 129
Social status, 46, 79, 89–90, 244
Sovereignty, 20, 27–33, 38–42, 53, 66, 98, 180. *See also* Colonisation; Self-determination; Tino rangatiratanga
State housing. *See* Housing
Structural discrimination, 77, 102, 151, 259–260. *See also* Inequality; Racism
Suffrage. *See* Voting
Superannuation, 22, 85, 127, 153 228–230
Super-diversity, 113–116, 276. *See also* Biculturalism; Multiculturalism
Suppression of Rebellion Act, 19

Tangata whenua. *See* Māori
Therapeutic jurisprudence, 262
Third Way, 127–128, 132
Tino rangatiratanga, 26, 36–41, 232; mana, 30, 32, 35. *See also* Self-determination; Sovereignty
Tohunga Suppression Act 1907, 236
Treaty of Waitangi, the (Te Tiriti o Waitangi), 18, 29–32, 38–41, 50, 60, 98–99, 116; constitutional recognition of, 50, 112 116; entrenchment of, 39, 112. *See also* Kawanatanga; New Zealand Constitution; Sovereignty; Tino rangatiratanga; Treaty settlements

Treaty of Waitangi Act, 99, 236
Treaty settlements, 36, 60, 99, 151, 272; Office of Treaty settlements, 36. *See also* Waitangi Tribunal

Unemployment, 100, 126, 143, 166, 244, 272; benefits, 85, 126, 131, 153; Māori, 91, 166, 247; men, 247; Pasifika, 96, 101, 167, 247; youth, 104. *See also* Insecure work; Labour market; Precarity
Unions, 65, 76, 123–130 passim, 181; New Zealand Council Of Trade Unions, 130, 142–143, 152, 166, 168; Woman's Christian Temperance Union, 177
United Tribes of New Zealand, 26–28
Urbanisation, 191, 203, 266–272, 284; Māori, 74, 165, 259, 269; urbane, 269, 274–276; urban-rural, 264, 271, 275–276. *See also* Gentrification

Violence: domestic violence, 174, 181, 239–243, 258; colonisation, 15, 66, 207; family violence, 241, 243, 245; interpersonal, 200, 243–245, 259; and Māori, 85, 182, 243, 258; masculinity, 246–247; Pasifika, 102, 182; sexual, 179, 181–183, 240; shame, 240, 244–248; women against, 174, 179–184, 240–248, 258
Voting, 45–47, 51–52, 54; FPP and MMP, 126–127, 178; Māori, 49–52, 176; migrants, 52; women, 48–49, 176–179, 204–205. *See also* Political representation

Waikato Raupatu Claims Trust Settlements Act 1995, 36
Waitangi Tribunal, 36–38, 42; Tainui report 1983, 36–37; WAI 1040, 66–67
Water Pollution, 147, 279–284. *See also* Agriculture; Ecological footprint
White privilege. *See* Pākehā
Women: discrimination, 201; and ethnicity, 75–76; rights of, 45–48, 173; and unpaid care work, 139, 184, 213, 217, 231; and work, 217–221. *See also* Feminism; Labour market; Political representation; Sexuality; Violence
Women's Parliamentary Rights Act, 48
Work. *See* Labour market
Working poor, 137. *See also* Labour market; Poverty; Precarity; Unemployment

Youth. *See* Rangatahi; Unemployment